Dirty Politics

Dirty Politics

Deception, Distraction, and Democracy

KATHLEEN HALL JAMIESON

OXFORD UNIVERSITY PRESS
New York   Oxford

Oxford University Press

Oxford   New York   Toronto
Delhi   Bombay   Calcutta   Madras   Karachi
Kuala Lumpur   Singapore   Hong Kong   Tokyo
Nairobi   Dar es Salaam   Cape Town
Melbourne   Auckland

and associated companies in
Berlin   Ibadan

First published in 1992 by Oxford University Press, Inc.
198 Madison Avenue, New York, New York 10016-4314

First issued as an Oxford University Press paperback, 1993

Oxford is a registered trademark of Oxford University Press

Library of Congress Cataloging-in-Publication Data
Jamieson, Kathleen Hall.
    Dirty politics: deception, distraction, and democracy /
Kathleen Hall Jamieson.
        p.   cm.
    Includes bibliographical references and index.
    ISBN 0-19-507854-3
    1. Advertising, Political.   2. Advertising, Political—United States.
3. Communication in politics.   4. Communication in politics—United States.
5. Criticism, Personal.   I. Title.
JF2112.A4J36   1992
659.1'932—dc20   92-9386

ISBN 0-19-508553-1 (PBK.)

10 9 8 7 6

Printed in the United States of America

*To Murray Edelman whose insights
about the symbolic action of politics
bridged the disciplines of political science
and communication*

Acknowledgments

In the dozen years that this manuscript has been in progress, it and I have benefited from the generous, patient assistance of more scholars, students, reporters, and consultants than I can possibly list on a single page. These nice folks include, in alphabetical order, Kathy Ardleigh, Ed Blakely, David Broder, Alex Castellanos, Joseph Cappella, Adam Clymer, Bob Donovan, E. J. Dionne, Anita Dunn, Enoh Ebong, Eric Engberg, Tony Fabrizio, Howard Fineman, Susan Forrest, Ellen Goodman, Lloyd Grove, Chris Guarino, Stephen Hess, Ellen Hume, Brooks Jackson, Craig James, Carol Kneeland, Carl Leubsdorf, Carolyn Marvin, Andrea Mitchell, Lisa Myers, Joe Napolitan, Michael Oreskes, George Reedy, Ray Scheer, Tony Schwartz, Craig Shirley, Bob Shogan, Bob Shrum, John Sparks, Bob Squier, Lesley Stahl, John Tierney, Richard Threlkeld, and, out of alphabetical order, Floyd Brown.

Research assistants who contributed include: John Pauley, Lynn Edwards, James Devitt, Cyndy Kater, Kent Goshorn, Steve Luethold, Darin Klein, and Elaine Gebhardt. The Louisana focus groups would not have met were it not for Professors Kathleen Turner, Mary F. Hopkins, and Jim Mackin and for students Rona Buchalter, Sheila Witherington, Andrew Cutler, and James Devitt. The Nielsen data were gotten with the help of Jo LaVerde-Curcio of Nielsen and Kathryn Creech of The Dun & Bradstreet Corporation. And David Hoffman of *The Washington Post* ransacked his basement for a pool report and photo I desperately needed.

On the editorial end of things, David Roll and Laura Brown at Oxford deserve special thanks for shaping the book and simplifying the process of writing it; again Rosemary Wellner undid my Latinate structures and transformed phonetic spellings into English; Beth Macom worked valiantly to catch my many errors before they were immortalized in print.

The work was supported by a grant from the Media Studies Center of the Woodrow Wilson Center where Bruce Knapper and Phil Cook made a summer magical. The MacArthur Foundation underwrote the evaluation of the visual grammar to be used by news to cover advertising. My special thanks to Scott Nielsen. The Annenberg Foundation and its founder Ambassador Walter Annenberg provided a school in which it is a pleasure to research, teach, and learn. Mary Ann Meyers provided intellectual and moral support.

Caryl Knutsen, Lorraine Hannon, and Maxine Beiderman handled the day to day logistics of manuscript care and feeding. Professors David Zarefsky, Herb Simons, Michael Schudson, James David Barber, Tom Patterson, and Roderick P. Hart critiqued ideas in progress. Robert and Patrick did their part by changing the cat box, taking the dog out, chauffeuring their mother around, and foregoing HBO for C-SPAN without complaint. And Bob transformed a Wissahickon stone colonial with a leaking roof into a warm, dry place to bake, write, and sing off-key.

Finally, Murray Edelman, to whom this book is dedicated, served as the kind of role model and mentor I would some day like to be.

Philadelphia   K.H.J.
May 1992

Contents

IV Accountability, Engagement, and Democracy

Dirty Politics

Introduction

Michael Dukakis looked "like Patton on his way to Berlin," observed NBC's Chris Wallace (September 13, 1988). "[A] Massachusetts Rambo on the prowl," noted CBS's Bruce Morton the same evening. Footage of that ride was resurrected by a Bush attack ad that pilloried Dukakis's supposed positions. "Dukakis opposed virtually every weapons system developed," declared the ad in the first of its false statements about the Democrat. The Massachusetts Democrat responded with an ad in which he turned off a set showing the Bush ad. "I'm fed up with it," said Dukakis. "George Bush's negative ads are full of lies and he knows it. I'm on record for the very weapons systems his ad says I'm against."

By the campaign's end, the tank ride had appeared in news, the news footage had appeared in a Bush ad, the Bush ad had appeared in a Dukakis ad, and the Bush and Dukakis ads had appeared in news. The *New Yorker* cartoon showing a man watching a television set had prophesied the endless loops through which the image passed. In the set in front of him, the man sees himself watching the television set. In that set is another image of himself watching the set. Images of images damaged Dukakis's candidacy. One poll indicates that "voters who knew about the ride were much more likely to shift against the Democrat than toward him."[1]

It is difficult to explain to someone unfamiliar with the conventions of our political discourse what facets of presidential character a candidate is featuring by marauding about in an armored vehicle. If past is prophet, the vehicle a president is most likely to drive is a golf cart.

So, why the tank? The answer is simple. Visual, dramatic moments are more likely than talking heads to get news play. Accordingly, Ronald Reagan appropriated the monuments in Washington as the backdrop for his first inaugural and regularly dramatized his State of the Union claims with "heroes" who appeared in the House gallery. Indeed, as CBS's Lesley Stahl reported in 1984, the Reagan presidency pioneered the use of visuals to counter the "facts." If support for nursing homes had just been cut, one could contain the fallout by appearing with seniors in a nursing home according to Reagan logic.

The Reagan presidency accustomed the press to believing that there is no substantive relationship between dramatizing visuals and either performance or policy proposals. So it didn't occur to most reporters to ask whether Dukakis's M-1 tank ride was an attempt to focus the press and public on the fact that, unlike his opponent, he favored a conventional build-up in tanks, antitank weapons, and tank supplies. But that was precisely what Dukakis was trying to do.

The tank ride did get the attention of the press. But the message wasn't the one Dukakis intended. Instead of seeing this as a dramatic incarnation of his substantive policy proposals, the press viewed the event as attempted compensation for his weakness. In short, it was regarded as strategic and silly. After talking with the reporters who covered the tank ride, I am convinced that what evoked this interpretation was something less tangible than Dukakis's goofy grin or Rocky the Squirrel-like helmet. If silliness were the bait, then either of George Bush's two past tank trips or his swing in a fire engine would have garnered comparable news time and tone. But, unlike the visual claim that Bush aspired to be Fireman in Chief, Dukakis's tryout as Tank Commander in Chief tied into the dualistic, poll-driven, strategy-saturated structure through which the press views politics.

Seen from this perspective, the Democrat's martial moment reeked of strategic intent. Here, after all, was a candidate trailing his opponent by a widening margin and perceived in the polls as "weak" on defense. By demonstrating both the Democrat's "attempt" to counter his "weakness" and signalling the incompetence of his failing campaign, the tank ride could do double duty. "The idea," explained CBS's Bruce Morton, "is pictures are symbols which tell the voter important things about the candidate. If your candidate is seen in the polls as weak on defense, put him in a tank."

Bush's appropriation of odd modes of transport went unridiculed because in the context set by the polls they could not be read as acts of desperation or signs of a campaign in disarray. Indeed, the news report that shows him prepared to battle the next Great Chicago Fire confirms that he was "buoyed by his own latest poll showing him leading in Illinois for the first time" (CBS Evening News, October 9, 1988). So nothing was

Figure I-1. To establish that he was "strong on defense," Vice President George Bush took a ride in a tank.

made of the fire truck ride as nothing had been made of his political posturing in a tank of his own at the Illinois State Fair in late August or of an attempt earlier in his vice-presidential term to tie his foreign policy credentials to a picture of himself in a tank.

The tank ride invited reporters to play out the full range of strategic interpretation. Dukakis wants you to believe he is strong on defense, said the reports, but the polls show that the public perceives he is instead weak. Appearance versus reality. Here the reality is not the positions the Democrat has articulated but rather the perception of him in the polls. The story also gave journalists a chance to explain how politics works. Politicians craft visuals to create false impressions. Reporters, by contrast, reveal "what's actually going on."

Once this frame of reference was imposed on the tank ride, its place in the network news lineup was secure. And since the "news hole" is limited, something else had to give up space. The frame also ensured that the news reports would not focus on the actual substance of Dukakis's positions on defense. "Not only was this [Dukakis in the tank] a foolish image but it crowded out any coverage that night on any of the networks of his foreign policy speech," recalls NBC's Andrea Mitchell. "That episode became an emblem of Dukakis's bad campaign."[2]

Figure I-2. George Bush at the 1988 Illinois State Fair.

Now constructed as evidence of Dukakis's weakness on defense, the tank ride could easily be appropriated by the Republican ad team. The resulting ad reduced the complex positions both candidates had taken on new weaponry to simplistic, inaccurate appositions and identifications: Dukakis as the risky commander in chief, Bush as risk free; Dukakis opposed to "virtually every weapons system we've developed," Bush presumably in favor of them all.

The ad suffers from the weaknesses that pervade contemporary campaigning. It tells us what Dukakis is against but not what Bush is for. It assumes but does not argue that the listed weapons systems are vital to our national defense. It suppresses discussion of all the weapons systems the Democrat supports and focuses on those he presumably opposes. And it leaps from specific claims to a broad and unwarranted inference. "America can't afford that risk." Moreover, as reporters finally pointed out in the final weeks of the campaign, three of the claims in the ad are false. The Democrat did not oppose "virtually every defense system we developed." He opposed two not "four missile systems," the MX and the Midgetman. He did not oppose the Stealth bomber but favored using it as a bargaining chip if conditions with the Soviet Union warranted. In short, the ad fails to argue, fails to engage the Democratic and Republican positions, and fails to accept the accountability that comes with making claims.

Lost in press coverage of the tank ride and in the subsequent ad war was the relation between the M-1 and Dukakis's military proposals. The tank ride built upon the speech Dukakis delivered that same day and forecast the speech he would deliver the next morning. On September 14, 1988, the Democrat argued:

> In Central Europe today, the most serious danger we face is the two-to-one Warsaw Pact advantage in modern tanks. Yet the Republicans have already cut our tank production and want to slash it almost in half again

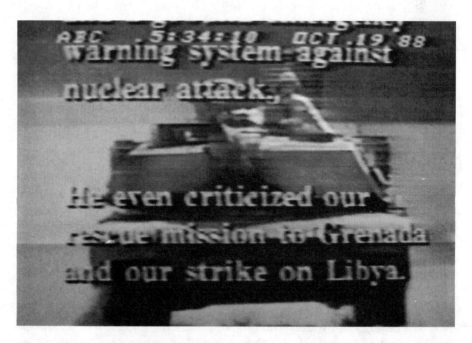

Figure I-3. In 1988, Michael Dukakis took his own tank ride. But where Bush's pseudo-event went unremarked in the press, Dukakis's was roundly ridiculed and became the basis for an anti-Dukakis ad. Ironically, Dukakis favored strengthening such conventional weapons as tanks; Bush did not. Why one pseudo-event failed and the other went unnoticed is discussed in this section.

next year. And after eight years in office, they have still failed to deploy an infantry anti-tank missile that can take out modern Soviet tanks. A recent government report estimated that *up to 85 percent* of the infantry soldiers using today's anti-tank weapons to stop a Soviet tank attack in Europe would be dead after firing a single round! And that round would bounce off the Soviet tank.

By reducing "military issues" to the presupposition that Dukakis was "weak on defense," a claim visually incarnated in the tank ride, reporters obscured a fundamental philosophical difference between the Republican and Democratic contender. Where one favored a nuclear build-up, the other favored a conventional build-up.[3]

Lest reporters miss the relationship between his positions and the tank ride, the Democrat told them, "We'd better do something about our conventional forces instead of spending billions and billions on fantasies in the sky." Dukakis also reminded those assembled at the General Dynamics tank facility in Sterling Heights, Michigan, that in 1987 Bush had lauded the superiority of Soviet tank mechanics. "Mr. Bush," proclaimed the Democrat, "I'd rather have mechanics from Michigan." One of the few print reporters to point out the relationship between the tank ride and Dukakis's defense plan was Carl Leubsdorf of the *Dallas Morning News*. "It was commonsense reporting," he recalls. "He told us why he was doing it. That's what I reported."

Reporters failed to translate the tank ride into coverage of the candidates' policy differences. The Republican ad then locked in the perception that the Democrat was weak on defense. As a result, few now realize how prescient Dukakis's positions were. No nuclear weapons were used in "Desert Storm," the main military action the United States undertook during Bush's first term. Instead the M-1, in which Dukakis had ridden in his much-ridiculed effort to stress his conventional commitments, battled it out with the Soviet T-62 and T-72. Indeed, in February 1991, the M-1 tank backed by the Apache helicopter—two weapons the Reagan-Bush administration had tried to cut—functioned as the military's workhorses. And in Desert Storm, Dukakis's concerns about communication in the field proved well placed. Claiming that the Army may have covered up communication problems between U.S. helicopters and U.S. tanks that contributed to deaths by "friendly fire" in the Gulf War, in November 1991 congressional investigators on the House's Subcommittee on Oversight and Investigations called for a criminal inquiry.

Also ironic is the fact that President Bush abolished two of the weapons systems the tank ad indicted Dukakis for opposing. Republican support documents accurately list the MX and the Midgetman as missile systems Dukakis opposed. On the stump, Bush declared, "I will not do what my opponent has suggested. I will not get rid of the MX, get rid of the Midgetman. . . . I will not make those unilateral cuts in our defense."[4] Yet in October 1991, that is precisely what Bush did. And he did it unilaterally. He then followed up in January by shutting down the last nuclear weapon assembly line still running. That move ended production of the Trident missile warheads that Dukakis had placed in the "negotiable" category.

But the ironies don't end there. Dukakis had argued in September 1987 that he would consider giving up the Stealth if conditions in the Soviet Union were right. Not I, replied candidate Bush. Yet, in November 1991, after learning of "flaws in the radar-evading ability of the Stealth,"[5] Congress denied Bush the funding he requested for more of the planes. The same bill earmarked nearly a billion dollars in Pentagon money for humanitarian aid to our new friend, the Soviet Union. And in his January 1992 State of the Union address, Bush ended production of the Stealth—after completion of only 20 of the original 132 he had sought.

Conventional wisdom says that Dukakis's tank ride in the 1988 general election campaign was an instance of consummate incompetence, a failed attempt to establish that the Democrat was "strong on defense." Instead I would argue that that staged event synopsized an important, far-ranging difference between the Republican and Democratic candidates. At the same time it showed the extent to which the traditional genres of campaign discourse are being reduced to visually evocative ads, with the boundaries between news and ads blurring in the process. Finally, it signals much of what was wrong with the press coverage and advertising of the 1988 campaign.

Dirty Politics asks how we got to this point and where we should go from here. It is divided into four parts. The first examines the uses of attack in political campaigning past and present. The second focuses on the relationship between news and ads. The third addresses news coverage in general. The fourth asks what norms of discourse should govern not just campaign ads and news but speeches, debates, interviews, and press conferences as well.

The book opens by wondering what we can learn from the uses to which William Horton was put in the 1988 campaign. It posits a complex, interactive relationship between voters and campaign messages in which what is shown is not necessarily what is seen and what is said is not always what is heard.

Chapters 2 and 3 catalogue the ways in which attack has changed in the political discourse of the United States and how it has stayed the same. In the past, as in the present, hired hands canonized their own candidate, condemned their opponent, and relentlessly contrasted the two. They conjoined some concepts and disjoined others, identifying their candidate with and opposing the opponent to revered individuals, hallowed words, popular policies, and cherished images. And the identifications and appositions were telegraphed, not argued. Since the founders, sloganeering—not substance—has been the stuff of politics.

But television has granted the manufacturers of campaign discourse some Svengalian powers that print and radio lacked. Specifically, its visual capacity couples with an ability to reconfigure "reality" in ways that heighten the power of the visceral appeal. Its multimodal nature makes analytic processing of rapidly emerging claims all but impossible. And its status as entertaining wallpaper grants television the privilege of surrounding us with claims that education has taught us to reject were they lodged on the printed page. Finally, on both radio and television, the identity of the unseen voice-over announcer is unknown and in that anonymity not accountable in any useful way for the claims he or she insinuates into our consciousness.

Chapter 4 asks whether the propositional can counter primal appeals, examining in the process the ways in which the techniques of television can be used in defense of facticity and fairness.

The process is complicated, however, by the conflation of ads and news. Chapters 5 and 6 argue that the differences between "free time" and "paid time," between news and ads, are blurring. News about electoral contests—"free time"—is becoming increasingly adlike. Indeed in 1988 it was no longer unusual to find segments of ads—adbites—broadcast in news stories in ways that heighten rather than diminish their power. Meanwhile, "paid TV," consisting primarily of thirty-second political spots, is becoming increasingly newslike, and in the process further fuzzing the line between news and ads. And candidate speeches, press conferences, one-on-one interviews, and debate answers are increasingly tailored with a view toward getting adlike news coverage.

The interactive relationship between campaigns and news media coverage of them is the subject of Chapters 7 and 8. How campaigns are reported shapes subsequent campaigning. As the news media allow themselves to be controlled by candidates, they implicitly encourage candidates to do more of the same. The result in 1988 was rhetorical gridlock.

What locked the media into place was reliance on "strategy" as the way of knowing what was important about campaigns. In both its "strategic" and its "substantive" reporting, television news in 1988 allowed itself to be shaped by polls and manipulated by the more artful consultants. In coverage of the issue of crime, the language of the ads became the language of news. In the process of following the agenda set by the "front runner," reporters permitted one campaign to commandeer scarce space with claims that had little relevance to governance. As a result, on election day, the American people could not forecast with much accuracy the first term of the winner and hadn't a clue that a massive savings and loan bailout was in the offing.

A focus on strategy invites viewers and readers to see themselves not as voters but as spectators evaluating the performances of those bent on cynical manipulation. While such schooling would benefit those intent on becoming campaign consultants, it doesn't do much for those intelligently trying to cast a ballot. But, as Chapter 8 argues, there is an alternative. Coverage can as readily ask what are the problems we face, how the candidates propose solving them, and what qualifications they bring to this task.

Chapter 9 argues that the fault lies not in the media but in the uses to which they have been put by those who see no advantage in taking positions on controversial issues or making pledges for which they might later be held accountable. Campaign discourse is failing the body politic in the United States not because it is "negative" or bodied in paid ads but because it has conventionalized genres of candidate and press discourse that minimize argumentative engagement and ignore the responsibility that all parties should shoulder for the claims they make. When all discourse becomes adlike, argument, engagement, and accountability are lost.

Collective handwringing minimizes the likelihood that we will recall that a much better version of how to campaign and cover campaigns was recently with us. Chapter 10 notes that as recently as 1960 and 1980, we have experienced campaigns that accurately forecast the conduct of the winners in office. Yet, as that chapter also notes, the campaigns of 1964, 1972, and 1988 are more noteworthy for what the electorate didn't learn than for what it did. Still, each demonstrates the extent to which the press and the process are governed by strong tendencies to right themselves.

The book argues the case for fair, accurate, contextual, comparative, engaged campaign discourse by candidates ready to take responsibility for the arguments they make and to either defend or repudiate claims made by others on their behalf. It argues as well for news coverage that engages the candidates on matters of public concern while holding them accountable for their past as well as their promises.

For both press and politicians, this is a discourse that argues rather than asserts, seeks the common rather than private good, relates a candidate's past to his or her promises and those to governance, grants the good will of all parties to the dialogue, and engages the issues raised by others while being engaged by them as well. It is a discourse that restores the genres of speeches, debates, press conferences, interviews, and ads to their distinct and distinctly useful roles in the campaign menu.

I

Attack Campaigning

CHAPTER ONE

The Role of Drama and Data
in Political Decisions

Almost three years after George Bush decisively defeated Democrat Michael Dukakis to become the president of the United States, a group of voters* in Pineville, Louisiana, was asked, "Can you tell me what you remember as being important in the 1988 presidential campaign?" The individuals in the group responded.

> Hmm.
> I'm trying to think.
> 1988?
>   Leader: '88.
> That's the last one.
> Dukakis.
> That was Dukakis.
> It's about time for another one isn't it?
> That time again. It was Dukakis wasn't it?
> I just knew I couldn't vote for him.

*Members of my 1988 groups were selected to match the demographic profile of the state's or nation's most recent election. Individuals learn of the existence of the groups by reading recruitment notices in church and community center newsletters and on bulletin boards or by seeing ads in local newspapers. The 1988 groups met weekly from Labor Day through the week of the election. The groups in Louisiana met only once or twice. All members are registered voters. Because they are not drawn randomly from the population as whole, we cannot generalize from focus groups to the larger population. Yet these groups are a useful way of learning how voters process political information.

15

Seems like the Democratic man that ran, he had a lot of problems. His wife and so forth.

A lot of that didn't come out til after the election, though.

That's right.

A lot of us didn't know of her personal problems. They hid . . . that was pretty well hid. She admitted that was . . . I don't know that was a . . .

I think the big thing against him was that, wasn't his criminal . . . I mean not his criminal record, but his . . . the handling of, um . . .

The handling of his state programs.

His state programs. I think that influenced a lot of people, how they voted.

And again, it was still a social aspect of dealing with social issues. And, uh, Bush was more international and people developing things for themselves. Giving them an opportunity to do their own thing and that will support our country. By that I mean build up business and the taxes then, and the income from growth and everything will take care of our country. I saw those as two distinct things.

Focus Group Leader: You had just mentioned how he handled state issues. Can you think of any specific issues?

Well, I think right off the . . . the one I'm thinking about was his . . . his handling of a criminal, um, and I can't right now . . .

What do you mean, a pardon of someone who has . . .

Willie Horton.

Yeah. A pardon.

Pardon.

Yeah. He pardoned that guy that went out and killed someone.

Afterwards. You know, he released this known . . . I guess he was a murderer wasn't he? Originally. And they released him anyway and he went out and killed . . .

Immediately and killed people again.

Right after getting out.

And this was brought out that he was releasing people really without seemingly too much thought. I think that had a lot to do with it.

William Horton and Michael Dukakis are now twinned in our memory. The fact that the memories are factually inaccurate does not diminish their power. Dukakis did not pardon Horton nor did the furloughed convict kill.

Although it does recount the facts of the Horton case, this chapter is not one more rehash of who did what to whom in the 1988 campaign. Instead, it sets a context for the book by examining how voters and reporters came to know what they know of politics. It argues that, in politics as in life, what is known is not necessarily what is believed, what is shown is not necessarily what is seen, and what is said is not necessarily what is heard. It then examines how in the Horton case consultants exploited the psychological quirks that characterize humans.

These quirks include a pack-ratlike tendency to gather up and interrelate information from various places, a disposition to weigh accessible, dramatic data more heavily than abstract statistical information, and a predilection for letting fears shape perception of what constitutes "fact."

At the same time, we have conventionalized journalistic norms that reward messages that are dramatic, personal, concise, visual, and take the form of narrative. In 1988, the psychological dispositions of the public coupled with the news norms to produce an environment in which an atypical but dramatic personification of deep-seated fears would displace other issues and dominate the discourse of the campaign. That dramatic, visual, personalized narrative told the "story" of William Horton.

Voters Are Pack Rats

The role that ads, Bush rhetoric, news, and audience psychology played in transforming William Horton's name for some into a symbol of the terrors of crime and for others of the exploitation of racist fears shows the powerful ways in which messages interact and the varying responses they evoke in individuals. Like pack rats, voters gather bits and pieces of political information and store them in a single place. Lost in the storage is a clear recall of where this or that "fact" came from. Information obtained from news mixes with that from ads, for example.

Although Bush had been telling the tale on the stump since June, in the second week in September 1988, the Horton story broke into prime time in the form of a National Security Political Action Committee (NSPAC) ad. The ad tied Michael Dukakis to a convicted murderer who had jumped furlough and gone on to rape a Maryland woman and assault her fiancé. The convict was black, the couple white.

The ad opens with side-by-side pictures of Dukakis and Bush. Dukakis's hair is unkempt, the photo dark. Bush, by contrast, is smiling and bathed in light. As the pictures appear, an announcer says "Bush and Dukakis on crime." A picture of Bush flashes on the screen. "Bush supports the death penalty for first-degree murderers." A picture of Dukakis. "Dukakis not only opposes the death penalty, he allowed first-degree murderers to have weekend passes from prison." A close-up mug shot of Horton flashes onto the screen. "One was Willie Horton, who murdered a boy in a robbery, stabbing him nineteen times." A blurry black-and-white photo of Horton apparently being arrested appears. "Despite a life sentence, Horton received ten weekend passes from prison." The words "kidnapping," "stabbing," and "raping" appear on the screen with Horton's picture as the announcer adds, "Horton fled, kidnapping a young couple, stabbing the man and repeatedly raping his girlfriend." The final photo again shows Michael Dukakis. The announcer notes "Weekend prison passes. Dukakis on crime."

When the Bush campaign's "revolving door" ad began to air on October 5, viewers read Horton from the PAC ad into the furlough ad. This stark black-and-white Bush ad opened with bleak prison scenes. It

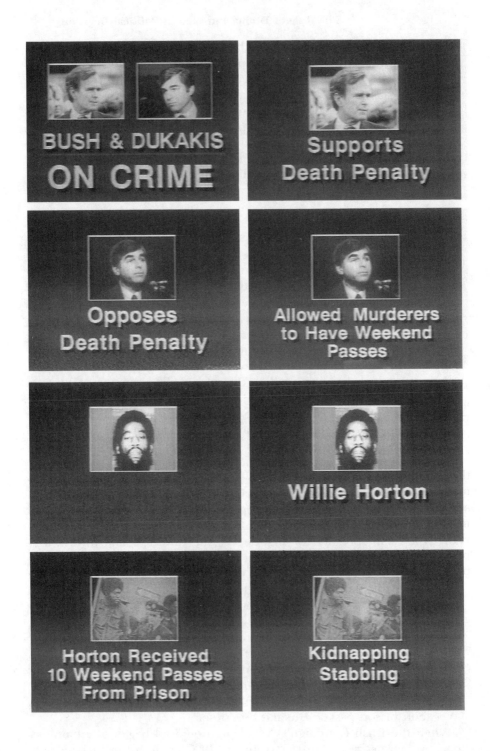

Figure 1-1. This ad by a conservative PAC propelled pictures of William Horton into the news in 1988. Horton was the convicted murderer who committed a rape and assault while on furlough from a Massachusetts prison.

then cut to a procession of convicts circling through a revolving gate and marching toward the nation's living rooms. By carefully juxtaposing words and pictures, the ad invited the false inference that 268 first-degree murderers were furloughed by Dukakis to rape and kidnap. As the bleak visuals appeared, the announcer said that Dukakis had vetoed the death penalty and given furloughs to "first-degree murderers not eligible for parole. While out, many committed other crimes like kidnapping and rape."

The furlough ad contains three false statements and invites one illegitimate inference. The structure of the ad prompts listeners to hear "first-degree murderers not eligible for parole" as the antecedent referent for "many." Many of whom committed crimes? First-degree murderers not eligible for parole. Many of whom went on to commit crimes like kidnapping and rape? First-degree murderers not eligible for parole.

But many unparoleable first-degree murderers did not escape. Of the 268 furloughed convicts who jumped furlough during Dukakis's first two terms, only four had ever been convicted first-degree murderers not eligible for parole. Of those four not "many" but one went on to kidnap and rape. That one was William Horton. By flashing "268 escaped" on

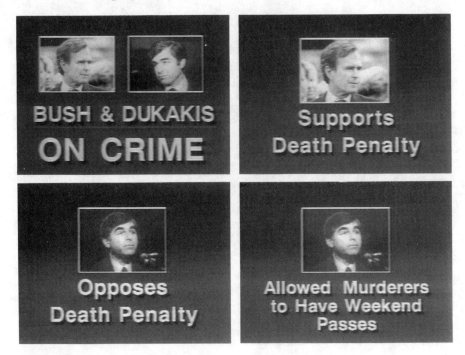

the screen as the announcer speaks of "many first-degree murderers," the ad invites the false inference that 268 murderers jumped furlough to rape and kidnap. Again, the single individual who fits this description is Horton. Finally, the actual number who were more than four hours late in returning from furlough during Dukakis's two and a half terms was not 268 but 275. In Dukakis's first two terms, 268 escapes were made by the 11,497 individuals who were given a total of 67,378 furloughs. In the ten-year period encompassing his two completed terms and the first two years of his third term (1987–88), 275 of 76,455 furloughs resulted in escape.

This figure of 275 in ten years compares with 269 who escaped in the three years in which the program was run by Dukakis's Republican predecessor, who created the furlough program.[1]

Still the battle of drama against data continued. After the Bush campaign's furlough ad had been on the air for two and a half weeks, in the third week of October, PAC ads featuring the victims of Horton began airing. One showed the man whose fiancée had been raped by the furloughed Horton. "Mike Dukakis and Willie Horton changed our lives forever," said Cliff Barnes, speaking in tight close-up. "He was serving a life term, without the possibility of a parole, when Governor Dukakis gave him a few days off. Horton broke into our home. For twelve hours, I was beaten, slashed, and terrorized. My wife, Angie, was brutally raped. When his liberal experiment failed, Dukakis simply looked away. He also

Figure 1-2. NSPAC sent this version of the "Horton" ad to cable stations in early September. It did not show Horton's picture. Once this less controversial ad had been "cleared" to air, the more controversial version was sent by the PAC directly to the network's "traffic" sections. Thus, the PAC avoided legal scrutiny of the ad's controversial and unverifiable claim that Horton had stabbed his victim nineteen times.

vetoed the death penalty bill. Regardless of the election, we are worried people don't know enough about Mike Dukakis."

The second ad was narrated by the sister of the teenager killed by Horton. "Governor Dukakis's liberal furlough experiments failed. We are all victims. First, Dukakis let killers out of prison. He also vetoed the death penalty. Willie Horton stabbed my teenage brother nineteen times. Joey died. Horton was sentenced to life without parole, but Dukakis gave him a furlough. He never returned. Horton went on to rape and torture others. I worry that people here don't know enough about Dukakis's record." The words that recur in the two ads are: "liberal," "experiment," "rape," worry that "people don't know enough about Dukakis," "vetoed the death penalty."

Taken together the ads created a coherent narrative. Dukakis furloughed Horton (PAC ads), just as he had furloughed 267 other escapees (Bush revolving door ad). Horton raped a woman and stabbed her fiancé (crime-quiz and victim PAC ads). Viewers could infer what must have happened to the victims of the other 267 escapees.[2]

The narrative was reinforced by print and radio. The "get out of jail free courtesy of Dukakis" card reappeared in 400,000 fliers mailed by the Bush campaign to Texans. "He let convicted rapists, murderers and drug dealers out of prison on weekend passes," said the flier. "And even after—while out on furlough—they raped and tried to kill again."[3]

ALAMO PAC, a political action committee based in San Antonio, Texas, produced one ad that paralleled the claims of the furlough ad but focused on drugs. While showing a drug dealer at a high school, the ad noted that Dukakis had vetoed mandatory prison terms for convicted drug dealers, had fought the death penalty for drug "murderers," and supported weekend furloughs for drug convicts. A second ALAMO PAC ad showed a burglar, presumably freed under a furlough program, creeping into a darkened bedroom.

Clips from Bush's speeches that appeared in the news reinforced the Horton-Dukakis link. In Xenia, Ohio, in early October, Bush talked in what the *New York Times* described as "vivid detail . . . about the notorious case of Willie Horton." Press accounts vivified the case by supplying details and occasional pictures of Horton. The *New York Times* described Horton as "the murderer who left the Massachusetts prison system on a weekend furlough, only to be caught a year later after he raped a Maryland woman and brutally beat her fiancé."[4] At a rally in Medina, Ohio, Bush referred to the Massachusetts governor as "the furlough king." In Trenton, New Jersey, Bush noted that "the victims of crime are given no furlough from their pain and suffering."[5]

The sister of one of Horton's victims and the man Horton had assaulted while on furlough began holding press conferences just as PAC ads featuring them were beginning to air. In Texas, newspapers devoted front-page space to Donna Fournier Cuomo, whose seventeen-year-old brother Horton supposedly killed, and Cliff Barnes, then the fiancé of the woman the escapee had raped. The press tours were underwritten by a two-million dollar fund raised by the Committee for the Presidency, the pro-Bush Political Action Committee[6] that sponsored the "victim" ads.

In 1988, broadcast news stories allied segments from three ads to create new congeries of images. The ads included clips from the furlough ad, still photos of furloughed convict William Horton, close-ups of the sister of a man Horton "murdered," and the husband of a woman Horton raped. Horton's victims and the murdered teenager's sister recounted their stories. Since Robert McClure and Thomas Patterson's pioneering study of the relationship of ads and news, we have known that viewers import segments of one story into another,[7] a phenomenon McClure and Patterson call "meltdown."

This phenomenon is well explained by former NBC president Robert Mulholland. "I think during the campaign the average viewer starts to

Figure 1-3. This Bush ad invited the false inference that Dukakis had furloughed 268 first-degree murderers who had then raped and kidnapped.

get a little confused. I'm expecting any day now to see Willie Horton endorse a line of jeans. . . . Some of the ads start to look like news stories, they're the same length, 30 seconds. . . . Television is not just separated in the minds of the viewer between this is news, this is commercial, and this is entertainment. Sometimes it all gets fuzzed up because it all comes into the home through the same little piece of glass."[8]

The "melting down" of these images explains the controversy surrounding the Bush campaign's use of William Horton. In late fall 1988 a rising chorus of Democrats condemned George Bush and his Republican handlers for the "Willie Horton" ad. Feigning cherubic innocence, Bush's surrogates pointed out that no picture of the black murderer and rapist Horton had ever appeared in a Bush-sponsored ad.

From Bush strategist Lee Atwater to Bush media advisor Roger Ailes, Bush's aides were telling the literal truth. The scowling convict's mug shot appeared only in the ads of presumably independent political action committees. But the psychological impact was similar. In his stump speeches, Bush routinely raised the case of the furloughed convict without mentioning his race. But once a viewer had seen the PAC ad or a news clip about it, the images of Horton, his victims, and the circling convicts were likely to meld into a coherent narrative reinforced almost daily by Bush's recounting of it in his campaign speeches.

Not All Information Is Created Equal

Democratic nominee Michael Dukakis both opposed the death penalty and favored furloughs. It is no accident that the image chosen by the Republicans to symbolize the Massachusetts furlough system was a black male. By explaining that they used Horton not because he was black but because he "slashed" a Maryland man and raped his fiancée, the Republicans tacitly acknowledged the atypicality of the case. No other furloughed first-degree murderer—white or black—either murdered or raped while out. During the primaries a double murderer did jump furlough but was caught and returned. As one of the authors of the Lawrence, Massachusetts *Eagle-Tribune*'s series notes, the Bush campaign could have selected a white criminal had it wanted. "We did a page 1 story on a white murderer," recalls Sue Forrest. "He was a former cop who was furloughed. My colleagues wrote a story on five furlough cases. Four were white. The fifth was Horton." Former trooper Armand Therrein killed his business partner and a policeman. On December 11, 1987, he jumped work detail. A month later, he was recaptured. The Republicans opted for a street crime involving strangers and a black villain over the story of a white cop-gone-bad who killed a friend for insurance money. Since the Bush campaign relied on the *Eagle-Tribune* for its information on the furlough program, it presumably knew of these cases.

Horton was not a representative instance of the furlough program. Nor were his crimes typical of crime in the United States, where murder, assault, and nearly nine out of ten rapes are intraracial, not interracial.

Yet by late October, Bush was observing that the Horton case had "come to symbolize, and represent—accurately, I believe—the misguided outlook of my opponent when it comes to crime."[9] In my judgment, a single aberrational incident was taken by the Republicans, the press, and the public to be typical of crime, and Dukakis's handling of it seen as symptomatic of the failures of liberalism because dramatic, personalized evidence carries more weight psychologically than do statistics. Moreover, the Horton case played both into the widely held presupposition that Democrats are "soft on crime" and into the conventions of network news.

News Norms Focus on Drama, Strategic Intent, and Effect

The Horton narrative fit the requirements of news. Unlike the "soft" news found in feature stories of the sort pioneered by Charles Kuralt on television, hard news is about an event that treats an issue of ongoing concern. Because violent crime is dramatic, conflict ridden, evokes intense emotions, disrupts the social order, threatens the community, and can be verified by such official sources as police, it is "newsworthy."[10] If one believed Bush's version of the facts, a convicted murderer who should have been executed had been furloughed to rape, torture, and murder again. In newscasts, the villain Horton appeared incarnated in a menacing mug shot. To personalize and dramatize, the news camera showed him in close-up; the less inflammatory visuals in the controversial PAC ad were shot mid-screen. Appearing in tight close-ups both in news and in the ads, the sister of the teenager Horton allegedly killed and the fiancé and now husband of the woman he raped told of their torment and urged a vote against the second villain in the story, Michael Dukakis.

The story structure of news lends itself to reporting that personalizes. A violent crime is committed by one individual against others. A good story has a protagonist and an antagonist, in this case a villain and a victim, the forces of disorder against the force of law. The "typical news story is organized dramatically to identify a problem, to describe it in a narrative of rising action, to locate the protagonists and set them against each other (usually in short interviews), and to create some sort of resolution. This format gives coherence to data, and it makes an item a story in the most literal sense, a story that is likely to gain and hold an audience."[11] The Horton story offered to the news media by the Republicans met these criteria.

The first network story to air on the Horton case (CBS, December 2, 1987) uses interviews to set out the contours of what could have been a prime-time crime show. "The man who murdered my seventeen-year-old brother in 1974 was given a furlough," reports Donna Cuomo. "To think that these people deserve a second chance to get out there and we just have to hope that they're not going to do something to somebody else is—it's crazy." Cuomo is trying to get Massachusetts to ban such furloughs notes the reporter. What prompts her activity? Horton, whom she assumes was her brother's killer, was given a furlough. "He enjoyed, he enjoyed torturing people," says the husband of the woman raped by Horton. "There, there, all the begging and pleading really egged this guy on." Dukakis is quoted saying that after the Horton case, the state tightened its guidelines. But that's not good enough for the woman raped by the furloughed convict. Commenting on the claim that the Massachusetts furlough system has a 99.9 percent success rate, she says, "If 99.9 percent are proven good and there's 1% that's bad, then that tells me the system does not work. I'm a human being and my life has almost been destroyed, and I almost lost my life, not only my husband's life." There is someone who shares her view. "For the Maryland judge who sentenced Horton," says the correspondent, "a furlough or even a return to Massachusetts was unthinkable." "The man should never breathe a breath of free air again," says the circuit court judge. "He is devoid of conscience and he should die in prison."

As the news reports unfold the story, personal details give texture to the identities of the victim while Horton remains a menacing mug shot. "I don't think any of you can understand what it's like to be tied up in a basement and listen to your wife being violated and beaten," says Cliff

Barnes (CBS, July 20, 1988). "He's a big guy," says the rape victim (NBC, January 21, 1988); "He overpowered me and slugged me in the face with a gun and he knocked me to the ground and he tied me behind my back." "It was like a nightmare, you know, seeing this man after what he did to Joey is out on furlough and he is just free to go to a mall or whatever he pleases," says Donna Cuomo. And in the backdrop of the narrative is the law-and-order judge who finally locked Horton up for life. "I just don't know anything about their [Massachusetts'] system. I have no assurance that he won't be on furlough or parole or whatever the devil it is in the matter of two or three years" (NBC, January 21, 1988).

After April when Dukakis signs the bill outlawing furloughs for cases like Horton's, the narrative runs into problems. The victims revive the storyline and hence news interest by asking for an apology from Dukakis. A Republican-sponsored national tour ensures that their request would attract coverage. "My wife and I have never heard from the Dukakis administration," says Barnes. "There's never been even an apology to us for what happened to us." "In Ohio," adds the correspondent, "Bush called on Dukakis to apologize to the victims for a program he called a tragic mistake" (ABC, November 7, 1988). "There has never been even an apology to what happened to us," says Barnes. "Whenever it's been brought up it's been accused of being an aberration or one failure in a successful system, which is a blatant lie." Note that when Barnes asserts without evidence that theirs is not an isolated case, his claim goes unchallenged. Then Bush too joins the chorus faulting Dukakis for not apologizing. "As far as I know the Governor never acknowledged that his furlough program was a tragic mistake" (NBC, October 7, 1988). In the campaign's final weeks, Barnes reappears in news decrying the Dukakis record in a synoptic ad. "For twelve hours I was beaten, slashed, and terrorized, and my wife Angie was brutally raped," he says (NBC, October 28, 1988).

Into this narrative context, Bush fits one soundbite after another. "Willie Horton was in jail, found guilty by a jury of his peers for murdering a seventeen-year-old kid after torturing him." (There is no direct evidence that Horton killed Fournier. Nor was there evidence of torture. But neither of those facts will be brought out in network news.) "What did the Democratic governor of Massachusetts think he was doing when he let convicted first-degree murderers out on weekend passes?" asked Bush. "In no other state would a cold-blooded murderer like Willie Horton have been set free to terrorize innocent people" (CBS, June 26, 1988).

Whenever a soundbite about Horton made its way into news, the requirement that reporters create a context evoked the whole Horton story. As a result, it was told and retold. "Dukakis accused the Bush campaign of exploiting the case of Willie Horton," noted Chris Wallace, adding "the Massachusetts prisoner who brutalized a couple while on furlough" (NBC, October 19, 1988). "The literature," which Dukakis is dismissing as "garbage," says, "quote: 'All the murderers and rapists and drug pushers and child molesters in Massachusetts vote for Michael Dukakis,' " notes ABC's Sam Donaldson (October 19, 1988). "And it refers to Willie Horton, the Massachusetts prisoner who brutalized a Maryland couple while out on furlough. . . ." "The Bush campaign has scored big with TV ads on crime," says CBS's Bruce Morton, "especially on a Massachusetts furlough program under which murderer Willie Horton on furlough committed rape and assault" (October 21, 1988).

The vivid language in which reporters recounted the "Horton story" magnified its recall; by framing his rebuttal in statistics about the effectiveness of the furlough program, Dukakis used abstractions against tangible, visual, personalized threat. Because they prompt visualization and create conceptual hooks on which information can be hung, evocative words are more readily remembered than more abstract ones. The vivid, concrete nature of the words used to capsulize Bush's charges coupled with memories of ads add visual points of reference to reporters' words.

This is the case, for example, when Brokaw says "The Vice President repeatedly has attacked Dukakis on the issue of the Massachusetts prison furlough program, specifically a convicted killer on furlough who brutally attacked a man and a woman. Some new perspective on that issue tonight. A study out today says that more than two hundred thousand furloughs were granted last year to fifty-three thousand prisoners in this country and that there were few problems. The study says that Massachusetts reported a furlough success rate of ninety-nine point nine percent" (NBC, October 12, 1988). Concrete language is more evocative than statistical abstractions. Those exposed to the Horton narrative in the PAC ads and news coverage were now likely to see furlough through the filter provided by Horton.

In news and ads, the Dukakis campaign did as Brokaw had done—responded to evocative narrative with lifeless statistics. "The Dukakis campaign accused Bush of exploiting a tragedy," notes Lisa Myers. "A spokesman claimed the Governor has a tough anti-crime record, with more cops on the beat, five times as many drug offenders behind bars, and overall crime in Massachusetts down 13 percent" (NBC, October 7, 1988).

But the overall thrust of the coverage was uncovering strategic intent and effect. "If Willie Horton is a central issue in October of 1988," comments syndicated columnist Mark Shields, "then Michael Dukakis's chances of a mandate for 1989 are pretty limited" (CBS, July 20, 1988). "What if the big word at the end of October is not Willie Horton but drugs," asks Lesley Stahl of a Democratic consultant. "We win," he responds. "And so," she adds, "the Republicans will keep pushing the Horton line. Bush intends to keep up the pressure, which might even include a campaign commercial starring Willie Horton's victims." The power of the underlying story of violence and victimization is intensified as the piece closes. It is the victim who seems to be summarizing the story.

> *Angela Barnes:* "I'm so mad at this justice. There's none. There's no justice."
> *Lesley Stahl:* "Lesley Stahl. CBS. Atlanta."

In the final weeks of the campaign, Dukakis gained some control over the Horton narrative when his campaign offered reporters a "strategy" peg explaining the Republicans' motivation. On the David Brinkley show, Dukakis's running mate alleged that the Republican use of Horton was racist. But here too the charge elicited recitations of the narrative. "Yesterday on ABC, Dukakis running mate Lloyd Bentsen said he thinks there is an element of racist appeal in Bush's continued citation of Willie Horton, now the star of television ads. Horton, a black man, who raped a white woman while on furlough from a Massachusetts prison" (ABC, October 24, 1988). The Republicans "also denied any racial intent in TV spots about black murder convict Willie Horton, who raped a Maryland woman and stabbed her husband, both white, while on prison furlough from Massachusetts" (ABC, October 25, 1988).

The personal, dramatic, conflict-ridden nature of the Horton case eased it into network news in 1988. The process was abetted by the fact that it spoke to an ongoing news theme—crime—and could be communicated in telegraphic sound and sightbites. As NBC's Ken Bode explained, "Bush's tough talk on crime works because it fits what most Californians see on their news each day" (NBC, October 28, 1988).

Once Horton's case began to resonate with voters, its place in the news lineup was secure. The fact of Horton explained the perception that Bush was tough on crime, reasoned reporters. So, for example, after indicating that "Bush's aides say they would have used the Horton case even if he weren't black," Lisa Myers closes a story late in the campaign by observing, "A key part of Bush's strategy has been to drive up negative opinions of Dukakis, to cast him as a liberal. That strategy clearly has worked and senior Bush aides say that no matter how much Dukakis whines about it they aren't going to change now" (NBC, October 24, 1988).

Narrative and Strategy Sidetracked a Broader Discussion of Crime and Minimized Candidate Engagement

Press coverage in 1988 was driven by explanations of strategy; this focus doesn't lend itself to questions about the candidates' philosophies of justice. When differences on issues were noted by reporters, they were telegraphed not argued, the substance of the disagreement unexplored.

So, for example, Lisa Myers explains the strategic but not substantive rationale for Bush's support for the death penalty. "Bush opposes furloughs for first-degree murderers, rapists, and drug dealers," says Lisa Myers, "and he is trying to make capital punishment a major campaign issue. Bush supports the death penalty for drug kingpins. Dukakis opposes it. The strategy is designed to shore up support for Bush among conservative Republicans and enhance his appeal to blue-collar Democrats who supported Reagan four years ago but now lean toward Dukakis."

Is Bush aware that blacks are more likely to be executed than whites convicted of the same crime? Does Dukakis hold that the death penalty is not a deterrent to other would-be criminals? Would Bush have executed those Dukakis furloughed, as the revolving door ad's juxtaposition of the two claims implies? Would he have executed Horton? That does appear to be the inference invited by such stump statements as "You remember the case of Willie Horton in the *Reader's Digest,* the guy was furloughed, murderer, hadn't served enough time for parole, and goes down to Maryland, and murders again, and Maryland won't even let him out to go back to Massachusetts, because they didn't want him to kill again. I don't believe in that kind of approach to criminals. He opposes the death penalty for every crime" (from speech rebroadcast on the "MacNeil/Lehrer NewsHour," October 31, 1988).

Lost in the focus on strategy is encouragement for candidates to engage each other and the press on the substance of the issue positions they are taking. Had the stories focused on comparative stands on issues, the first question asked of Bush would have been, Where do you stand on furloughs? Or, to personalize the issue, reporters might have asked Bush whether he favored work-release for felons convicted of hit-and-run while drunk. When a reporter finally did ask whether Bush favored any furloughs, his campaign ducked the question. "Campaign officials declined to say whether George Bush favors any furloughs," noted ABC's Jon Martin on October 7. At a broader level, one might ask what exactly a president can do to cope with a problem over which governors and mayors but only rarely presidents have jurisdiction. And if there was some area of federal need, why hadn't the Reagan-Bush administration addressed it? Quietly after the election, the Bush administration did just that. In 1987, the U.S. Bureau of Prisons granted 4,610 furloughs, in 1991 only 3,190.

The belief of reporters that their job is "covering" the news, not "making" it, meant that unless one of the contenders found a visual, dramatic, concise way to refocus the "issue," the debate about Horton would not be transformed into a discussion of the causes and possible responses to crime or of the fairness of the criminal justice system.

At one point in the campaign Bush did try to move from a specific to a more general premise about their differences on crime. Dukakis believes, he said, that "all convicts can be rehabilitated," a view Bush thinks "is not just naive, it is dead wrong" (NBC, June 22, 1988). Had this been 1960 or 1980, reporters would have gone to Dukakis for a response and the issue would have been engaged.

In 1988 the "coverage" metaphor made that unlikely. Not until the network interview with Peter Jennings (ABC, November 4, 1988) in the final week of the campaign did the public hear Dukakis's position. "Of course" there are people who are so dangerous that they should not be furloughed, he responded. The fact that he banned furloughs for first-degree murderers the previous spring indicated that he had come around to that view.

The Democratic corollary of the Republican claim about rehabilitation is equal justice. What is intriguing about the fairness question is its bearing on the way the judicial system treated the creator of the revolving door furlough ad. After being convicted of drunken driving in a hit-and-run accident in 1985, the well-to-do, white admaker served in a work-release program and performed 250 hours of community service. It was the public service ads that Dennis Frankenberry created as part of his community service time that drew his work to the attention of the Republicans.

Police reports indicated that the Milwaukee ad executive hit a motorcycle carrying two young men head on. The accident left one of the cyclists critically injured.[12] Instead of stopping, Frankenberry sped away in his foreign sports car. A witness who pursued him found him hiding behind a house.[13]

The consequences of Frankenberry's actions were serious. One of the cyclists required brain surgery and a lengthy hospitalization after the accident, the other, intensive rehabilitation.[14] While his victims were recovering, Frankenberry checked himself into Hazelton, a private rehabilitation center, for a month.

Frankenberry was charged with intoxicated use of a motor vehicle causing great bodily harm and hit-and-run causing great bodily harm. After pleading no contest, he was convicted of two felonies and sentenced to ninety days in the county jail, which was served on work release, along with 250 hours of community service. He also was required to make restitution to the accident victims. An out-of-court settlement set that figure at $1.2 million.[15]

After the sentencing, the adman's working-class victims raised the issue of equal justice. "If it had been me," said one of them, "I probably would have gotten a longer sentence than he would have had, because we're no bigshots."[16]

If William Horton was shooting himself up with drugs in the getaway car, as one of the participants in the slaying of Joseph Fournier alleged, then one might argue that he was less involved in that killing than Frankenberry was in the hit-and-run. Both were apparently substance abusers. But while Horton received his first furlough after serving ten years in prison, Frankenberry was free to leave the House of Correction twelve hours a day, seven days a week for the ninety days he served.[17] There are, of course, clear and important differences between the two, including a past criminal record for Horton; while outside the correctional institution, Frankenberry committed advertising, not kidnapping and rape.

Still, the contrast in treatment raises serious questions about equal justice under law unexplored in 1988. Had Frankenberry been poor and black or had Horton been well-to-do and white, would the treatment of either have changed? Should it have? That question is particularly germane in a campaign in which one candidate favors and the other opposes capital punishment. Evidence of differential treatment of blacks in sentencing has, after all, spawned much of the controversy over the death penalty.

Dramatic Atypical Instances Displace Other Issues

Reportorial focus on Horton drove coverage of other issues from the agenda. Instead of covering the Democrat's speech on agricultural policy on October 19, ABC's Sam Donaldson picked up the Republican theme of the day—Horton's "endorsement"—magnifying its power as he points out that the Republicans have set it tactically against Dukakis's record.

> *Sam Donaldson:* "This was to have been a day with the Dukakis bus caravan winding through farm country when the candidate spotlighted his farm message. But neutralizing the crime issue is far more important to Dukakis's chances."
> *Donaldson to Dukakis:* "Did you see in the paper that Willie Horton said if he could vote he would vote for you?"
> *Dukakis:* "He can't vote, Sam."
> *Donaldson:* "Willie Horton, because he's a convicted felon may himself not be able to vote, but it's fair to say he's rapidly becoming a symbol of something to voters, Dukakis's record or Bush's campaign tactics, soft on crime or dirty pool."

Lost in the report are Dukakis's proposals. The "symbol" of Horton has waylaid the substance offered by the Democrat that day.

Focus groups reflected the powerful pull of the atypical Horton incident. In early November 1988, nine individuals in a focus group in Dallas were shown statistical evidence from the Massachusetts prison authorities documenting the overall success rate of the furlough program and the atypicality of the Horton case. The group members, who had started out in early September planning 5–4 to vote for Dukakis-Bentsen, were now firmly (7–2) in Bush's corner. The members were told that both the federal government and Reagan's California had furlough programs. Convicts had jumped furlough from both, explained the focus group leader, and had committed violent crimes including rape and murder. "Did any of this make any difference?" they were asked. Their answers resonate with allusions to reference groups, religion, and, sometimes unspoken, raw personal experience.

> *1:* "You can't change my mind with all of that," said a sixty-two-year-old woman. "When you support the death penalty, the really bad ones get killed. That's, er, the liberal, the problem with, about liberals."

2: "They're soft on criminals. Not just blacks. Criminals. . . . It's a fact that Dukakis opposed the death penalty, vetoed it, I think. Wouldn't even use it for his own wife."

1: "The Republicans believe an eye for an eye; the Democrats turn the other cheek."

3: "Dukakis is, says he is a liberal now. On television. Finally. That's what this Horton thing is all about. Do you have any idea how often you are, er, someone is, murdered in Dallas?"

1: "We should ship all our criminals to the college liberals in College Station."

2: "Or Austin. Crime's not statistics, honey."

4: Dukakis supporter (thirty-seven-year-old male): "But Bush's guy killed a pregnant woman, a halfway house, a parole place. That's no different from Dukakis, Massachusetts."

1: "That's not his fault."

5: "If he knew about it, he would have done something."

2: "Look. It comes down to just one thing. If there is a murderer or a rape, the Democrat is going to ask if the bastard has a lawyer to read him his rights, the Republican is going to give 'em the chair."

2: "A permanent furlough" (laughter; unintelligible)

6: "Or the gas chamber" (laughter; unintelligible)

3: "Or the rope."

7: "He'll die of old age first." (laughter)

2: "You know what a conservative is, don't you? A liberal . . ."

7: (completes sentence) who's been mugged."

4: Dukakis supporter: "Suppose the guy is innocent?"

6: "We'll elect him to Congress!" (laughter)

2: "Send him to the ACLU."

8: "The American Commie Lovers Union" (laughter)

1 to 4 (jokingly): "You haven't been living in Dallas very long, have you? (laughter)

4: "All my natural life."

9: "And some of his unnatural life, too."

Throughout the substantive discussion, the second announced Dukakis supporter (no. 9), a twenty-two-year-old female college student, was uncharacteristically silent. In earlier weeks she had spoken enthusiastically about Dukakis's opposition to nuclear power and had brought the group a letter from an environmental group comparing the Democrat's record favorably to the Republican's. It was she who had argued forcefully that claims about Boston Harbor were "just a crock, that's all. Just B.S. from the man who tried to kill the Clean Water Act. He's [Bush's] a real fraud. He really is." On election day, she voted for Bentsen for Senator and an independent candidate for President.

"My family has always supported Lloyd Bentsen," she said the week after the election. "My parents voted for Dukakis and Bentsen and Bentsen again for Senate. I just assumed throughout the election that I'd vote for him for vice president and vote against Bush because of the environment and the recession. My brother lost his job two months ago. Things just don't seem to be getting any better. A lot of empty buildings. . . . But I just couldn't bring myself to vote for Dukakis because of the poor judgment he showed over Willie Horton. I'm a liberal when it comes to the environment but not when it comes to crime. I would have voted for Lloyd Bentsen for president in a minute. But Dukakis? I just couldn't bring myself to do it."

William Horton has outweighed the personal experience of job loss by an immediate family member. Her membership in an environmental group had provided her with information to rebut Bush's claims about Boston Harbor, but she had no comparable source of information about furloughs. The information that was released by the Dukakis campaign took the form of statistical abstractions. A 99+ percent return rate for those furloughed in Massachusetts, said the factsheets. A much lower rate of return to a life of crime after, final release of those furloughed, said the penologists. Horton was the atypical, nonrepresentative instance, said all the available data. In any furlough program in a large state (and most states had such programs) one could find one or two such cases.

But for those with any direct or secondhand experience with crime—a purse snatching, a car broken into, a mugging—Horton was not an aberration. Unspoken in her post-election interview is a fact mentioned in an earlier meeting of the focus group. A year and a half earlier, on her way home from a concert, the respondent had been robbed by an assailant whose race she did not identify to the group. Later, the focus group leader learned that the assailant was white. So crime may have had a special salience to this respondent as it did to respondent number 1 whose house had been burglarized five years before.

Nor was the response of this single all-white group in a Southern state atypical. The "damage" the claims about Horton did the Democrat was capsulized by "MacNeil/Lehrer NewsHour" host Robert MacNeil. "On Friday night on our program, two women voters in Ohio told Judy Woodruff, 'I'm going to vote for George Bush because I can't vote for a man who lets murderers out of jail.' One was a black woman."[18]

Our Fears Shape Our Perception of "The Facts"

Helping propel the false generalizations from the isolated case of Horton to hordes of others who presumably did what he had done were complex and unspoken references to race. " 'Crime' became a shorthand signal," note Thomas and Mary Edsall, "to a crucial group of white voters, for broader issues of social disorder, evoking powerful ideas about authority, status, morality, self-control, and race."[19] "Any reference to capital punishment," argues political scientist Murray Edelman, "is also a reference to the need to restrain blacks and the poor from violence. The liberal argument that poor people and blacks are disproportionately targeted by capital punishment laws doubtless fuels this fear in a part of the public. That the association is subtle makes it all the more potent, for 'capital punishment,' like all condensation symbols, draws its intensity from the associations it represses."[20] Without actually voicing the repressed associations, the image of Horton on the screen as the announcer notes that Dukakis opposes the death penalty serves to raise them. " 'Weekend Passes' [which I have called the Horton ad] is not about Willie Horton," says NSPAC's Floyd Brown. "It's about the death penalty. George Bush stood on the side of the majority. Michael Dukakis stood on the side of the minority. The death penalty is where we win our audience."

The 1990 General Social Survey of Racial Stereotyping among White Americans demonstrates that racial prejudice correlates with support for capital punishment. According to Kinder and Mendelberg, "white Americans who regard blacks as inferior are quite a bit more likely to favor the death penalty for convicted murderers."[21]

In the last week of October 1988, ninety-three members of ten focus groups demonstrated the power of the Horton narrative to elicit racially based fear. "If you saw an ad on prison furloughs with scenes in a prison," these voters were asked, "remember as best you can" the "race or ethnic identity" of the "people you saw in the ad. . . ." Of those who did recall the ad, nearly 60 percent (59.9 percent, 43 individuals) reported that most of the men were black. In fact, only two of the "prisoners" are identifiably black. One of them is the only one in the ad to ever look directly into the camera.

When asked to write out everything "you know about William Horton," all but five of the focus group respondents included the fact that Horton is black in their description. All but twelve wrote that the woman raped was white. One-third of the respondents indicated Horton's race twice in their descriptions. And one focus group respondent referred to Horton throughout his description as "this Black Man." Twenty-eight percent of those in the focus groups indicated that he had committed murder while on furlough.

The power of the narrative is indicated in the extent to which viewers embellished it. After completing their description, focus group members were asked to indicate the source of their information sentence by sentence. They were told to write NS to indicate that they weren't sure where they had heard/read/seen it, to indicate PN for print news, BN for broadcast news, RN for radio news, A for advertising, and H if they had heard it in conversation. Each sentence could be tagged with more than one letter.[22]

A thirty-five-year-old, public-high-school-educated, white, ticket-splitting, self-identified "Independent" Dallas waitress, married with two children (who had twice voted for Reagan but reported leaning toward Dukakis after his selection of Bentsen) wrote:

"Willy Horton is a killer—black—supposed to be gassed or electrocuted when Dukakis was governor (BN/PN). But he [Dukakis] vetoed all death penalties (BN/PN). Willy Horton was a killer and wasn't electrocuted (H/ PN). He and some other criminals were paroled [paroled is then crossed out and replaced by] furloughed on weekends and coming back [sic] he stole a car and went to Maryland (BN). He broke into a home, a married [sic] home—in a small town—Maryland—and then tied up the husband (BN). His wife kept screaming [but?] he couldn't help her (BN). Their children were at school (NS). He [Horton] stayed there for a whole afternoon (BN). He kept raping the wife (BN). He [Horton] was black and the wife [sic] was white. Even when she begged him because she might be [get?] pregnant. Her husband went crazy. He couldn't do anything because Horton had shot him and stabbed him (BN). He [husband] still can't forgive himself. That's why he is against Dukakis (BN). The husband (he was on television) got loose and called the police (BN). But Horton got away before the police came (BN). Her husband says that she is afraid that he will come back (BN/NS). He [Horton] killed a boy in a supermarket in Maryland (H). The police caught him (They must have. He's in jail). He is in solitary confinement (H). I believe in the death penalty for people like that. I saw the boy he killed [sic] mother on television (BN). She wishes she had shot him [Horton]—killed him—before he shot him [her son] (BN). George Bush opposes gun control and favors executing Hortons (Radio—I think it was an ad). I would guess Willy Horton doesn't.

Although this respondent reported that she had learned about Horton's victims on "the news," specifically broadcast news, their stories had not appeared on the station she reported watching. She probably pieced the information together by amalgamating clips from Bush's speeches with the crime quiz and victims ads.

The cues in the available media have triggered a broad chain of associations in this respondent. From them she has constructed her own text. Her text magnifies the culpability of Dukakis. In her construction Horton was reprieved from execution because Dukakis vetoed the death penalty.

She also magnifies the vulnerability of the victims beyond that expressed in the ads or news (e.g., Horton is there all afternoon; the children are at school; presumably if Horton stays longer, the children will come home; Angela Barnes remains afraid that Horton will return). She increases the number of crimes Horton has committed (he shot and stabbed the husband, she says) and shifts the murder of Joseph Fournier to after the furlough. A wish for power is attributed to Fournier's mother (actually his sister). The respondent says that the mother wishes she had shot Horton before he shot her "son" (Fournier was stabbed to death. Whether Horton was wielding the knife is unknown. Three individuals were convicted of being party to the crime.) And all of this connects to the fact that George Bush opposes gun control. (Presumably gun control would make it more difficult for Fournier's mother, and others like her, to kill criminals such as Horton.) Finally Horton favors what Bush opposes. Bush is Horton's enemy. Indeed, he favors "executing Hortons."

Additionally, the Republican use of Horton suggests the power such a story has to trigger more full-blown if inaccurate narratives and to harness them in service of voting behavior. These instances show how visceral and visual readings that do not inhere explicitly can be read implicitly in texts about out-groups.

The power of narrative may account for the claims of George Bush, Lee Atwater, and, more recently, the *New York Times,* that while on furlough, Horton murdered again. The hypothesis comes to mind because it is difficult to believe that a candidate for president would deliberately lie about something so easily checked by reporters and because on February 24, 1992, an article without byline in the decidedly non-conservative *New York Times,* a paper that endorsed the Democratic nominee in 1988, recalled, "The [Horton] advertisement suggested that Mr. Bush's Democratic opponent, Gov. Michael S. Dukakis of Massachusetts was soft on crime because a convicted murderer from the state was given a weekend pass from prison and committed a second murder" (p. A15). The ad made no such claim. Nor did the *Times* in its 1988 coverage of the ad or of the Horton case.

Where one might attribute the Republican statements to calculated deception, I am more inclined to explain them in a context created by the memory reflected in the *New York Times* article. Murderer released to murder breathes irony. It completes in a satisfying manner a narrative that is already cast with a menacing murderer in mug shot; anguished, outraged victims; and an unrepentant, soft-on-crime liberal. In such a narrative construction, the governor will be unmasked for what he is because the murderer will murder again. Horton is incapable of redemption. Prison has accomplished nothing. He deserved the death penalty Bush is touting.

Less satisfying, more troubling, and complex is a story of a young man who may not have committed murder at all but is nonetheless jailed for it for a decade, and after a handful of successful furloughs escapes to assault and rape. In this second story, the initial act is shaded in ambiguity, the final act unparalleled by the first. William Horton, Michael Dukakis, George Bush, Lee Atwater, and *The New York Times* may, in other words, have fallen victim to our natural disposition to construct compelling stories, whether or not they comport with the facts.

An October Harris poll found that 60 percent of those surveyed remembered the furlough ad. From the time that the ad started to the time of the survey, the percent reporting that Dukakis was "soft on crime" rose from 52 to 63 percent.

The fixation of reporters on strategy in 1988 meant that "coverage" would focus on the effectiveness of the charges and countercharges and on their motivation (i.e., were they racist?), not on their accuracy or relevance to the role of president.

In the Horton Case, Reporters Offered Contradictory "Facts"

As Brookings scholar Stephen Hess found, reporters are generalists who use no documents in preparing nearly three-quarters of their stories. When documents are used, they are most often newspaper stories.[23] The documents from which the Republicans drew the Horton narrative were an article in the July 1988 *Reader's Digest* titled "Getting Away with Murder" and a Pulitzer Prize-winning series in the stridently anti-Dukakis Lawrence, Massachusetts *Eagle-Tribune*. The Democrats believe but have been unable to prove that the *Reader's Digest* story was planted by Bush supporters. Behind the scenes, Republican operatives made these accounts available to reporters. The *Eagle-Tribune* embellished the Horton story asserting and then recanting such claims as one that the woman raped by Horton was pregnant at the time and he had cut off the genitals of the man killed in the hold-up that landed him in a Massachusetts prison.

Interviews are the staple of news reports. Reporters who have come to rely on "experts" to arbitrate contentions of fact lack experience in sorting through blizzards of competing claims. The result was Babel. CBS put the number of states with furlough programs as "all" (October 28, 1988), 45 (December 2, 1987), 40 (June 26, 1988), and 32 (July 20, 1988). On NBC, Tom Brokaw (January 21, 1988) indicated that "thirty-two states now permit first-degree murderers to spend short periods out of prison" but five months later his colleague Lisa Myers reports that "few [states] permit furloughs for first-degree murderers" (June 22, 1988). The same week, CBS's Jaqueline Adams claims that "Massachusetts was the only state to furlough first-degree murderers" (CBS, June 26, 1988). Kwame Holman of "MacNeil/Lehrer" puts the number of states furloughing first-degree murderers at 40. Throughout all this, Dukakis insisted that his state was within national norms.

Others using the category "life sentence" set the number of states permitting furloughs at 36 (Tolchin, *New York Times;* Martin, ABC, October 7, 1988), 33 (Cohen, *Washington Post,* July 8, 1988), or 25 (Contact Center, October 13, 1988). Without revealing how many states had the category "first-degree murder not eligible for parole," Cohen of the *Post* announces that Massachusetts alone fell into that category. Not so says the Contact Center (*Atlanta Constitution,* October 13, 1988). South Carolina still does furlough those in that category. Without indicating whether it could do so, the governor of South Carolina announced the next day that his state never had furloughed anyone serving a life sentence without parole (*Hotline,* October 14, 1988).

In the resulting confusion, the public received conflicting answers to the question, was the Massachusetts' program fundamentally similar to those in other states, including Reagan's California, and to the federal

government's or was this a bizarre, unique liberal experiment undertaken by the Democratic nominee? Nor did the public have a clear way
of knowing whether the Massachusetts program was more or less successful than those elsewhere or whether the Horton case was isolated or
representative of justice in Massachusetts under Dukakis.

In the Horton Case Reporters Accepted Assertion as Proof

Under attack for the unfairness of their ads, the Republicans in late
October 1988 held a press conference. Former prosecutor and current
Republican Senator Arlen Specter was given the task of defending the
furlough ad. At the conference, Specter proved anything but an able
defender. He said:

> Now frankly I would focus on the furlough program if there were only
> one or two or three or a few errors, or a few instances where the fur-
> lough program had proved to be disastrous. But the fact is that the Mas-
> sachusetts furlough program makes it a practice to furlough career crim-
> inals identified in their own materials. Convicts who have six or more
> adult incarcerations, convicts who have had four or more parole viola-
> tions, it is a very, very different program.
>
> Secondly, beyond the issue of its being unprincipled, I believe that it is
> a legitimate issue in this campaign because it bears directly on Governor
> Dukakis' judgment. Now, this is not a program, one of many, adminis-
> tered in a large governmental operation like the Commonwealth of Mas-
> sachusetts. This is a program where Governor Dukakis has personally
> had intimate contact, has seen the errors of the system, and then inflexi-
> bly has insisted on keeping the program in operation in the face of those
> demonstrated errors. . . .
>
> *Q:* Senator Specter, in that furlough ad, almost simultaneous with the
> announcer saying that the furlough program furloughed first-degree
> murderers, a graphic comes up that says, "268 escaped." Is it your un-
> derstanding that 268 murderers escaped from furlough in Massachu-
> setts?
>
> *Sen. Specter:* No, it is not my understanding. The total 268 does not
> refer to the number of murderers; it refers to the total number of people
> who have, quote, "escaped" under the characterization of the Massachu-
> setts authorities. That is—that is their term. I might say to you that I
> have been very interested to see the statistics for 1987. When this issue is
> as important as it is to this country, I think we're entitled to have the
> 1987 statistics on furloughs. The 1986 statistics were made available in
> August of 1987, and the 1985 statistics were made available in July of
> 1986. Now we don't have 1987 statistics. I don't think it's a matter for
> Massachusetts, and I don't think the Massachusetts government ought to
> be contorted to suit a campaign. I'd like to know how many more have
> escaped.
>
> *Q:* Well, according to the statistics you know about, how many mur-
> derers did escape while on furlough?

Sen. Specter: I don't know.

Q: What about last—the last—

Sen. Specter: I don't know and—

Q (off mike): Four?

Sen. Specter: Well, if you read the statistics put out by the Massachusetts Department of Corrections, you can't tell a whole lot. Now, I've gone through it personally with a fine-toothed comb to try to identify the number of individuals, for example. They don't tell you how many individuals. They gave you the total number of furloughs. They do tell you how many have been convicted of six or more offenses, or how many have parole violations, but they do not particularize. My personal efforts to get details have been unsuccessful. One of the points made in the Lawrence article was the stonewalling by Governor Dukakis and his officials when those reporters tried to find out the facts. It's very hard to really get the details of that program.

Q: Senator, I experienced stonewalling from the Federal Bureau of Prisons when I asked about furloughs and they withheld totally details on transfer furloughs. Point number 9, here on page 3, says that Angel Medrano [the killer Dukakis is accusing Bush of releasing from the federal system] is not on furlough. Was he not on a transfer furlough, which is one of the furlough programs of the Federal Bureau of Prisons?

Sen. Specter: I don't know.

Q: Was he escorted at the time he escaped?

Sen. Specter: I don't know.

Q: Senator—

Sen. Specter: One, that is not my document. I would respond to you on the specifics, as I have, that I do not know that detail. But I would not cite a case or two cases or five cases as a major indictment of a program. I think a program rises or falls on its underlying philosophical approach in a correctional setting. What do you find to be wrong with it and what you do to correct it.

On the "MacNeil/Lehrer NewsHour" (October 24, 1988) Specter repeated his claim that "I do not criticize the Massachusetts furlough program because of one case. There can be a problem in one instance anywhere." There is only one problem with Specter's answer. Horton was the single instance in Dukakis's first two terms in which a first-degree murderer whose sentence had been downgraded—a process required if he were to be furloughed—had escaped to commit a violent crime. Specter has not responded to three letters and three phone calls asking him what evidence led him to conclude that there were more than five Horton-like cases during Dukakis's governorship.

What is unique about Specter's statement at that press conference is that under questioning from the press he is the only spokesperson for the Bush campaign who admitted that 268 first-degree murderers did not escape. That admission, however, did not filter into print press reports or broadcast news. Instead, the reporters present at the press conference accepted the "form" of proof—thick factsheets, one large chart, and three experts—as proof. "I remember feeling afterward," recalls Tom

Rosensteil who reported on the conference for the *Los Angeles Times,* "that it was a case of how easily manipulated we were. Our reports were not very discriminating. They [the Bush 'experts'] made an awful case. But what appeared in the next day's papers played into the advertiser's hands" (interview, October 4, 1991).

The Psychology of the Bush Use of Horton

Did the Horton case, while atypical and inflammatory, tell a larger psychological truth? Is it possible to lie—by claiming that Horton murdered on furlough when he did not, inviting false inferences about the number of Horton-like instances that had occurred in Massachusetts, and encouraging unwarranted fears about blacks raping and murdering whites— and still tell a psychological truth? No. Had he been a federal prisoner, the death penalty that Bush favored for drug kingpins would not have executed Horton. Under the terms in effect under the Reagan-Bush administration, Horton would have been eligible for furlough.

To reporters who called him in his Maryland prison during the campaign, Horton claimed, as he had at his trial, that he did not stab the youth he and two others were convicted of killing. Indeed, one court official indicated that another of the threesome had confessed to being the killer; the confession was disallowed because the suspect had not been read his Miranda rights. Under Massachusetts' felony rule, the prosecution did not have to ascertain which of the three committed the murder, only that all three were in some way involved. Horton claimed to have been in the getaway car. The prosecutors didn't know if Horton had held the knife; there was "reasonable doubt"; but, by virtue of his presence at the scene, they did know he was an accomplice. As parties to the robbery that occasioned the murder, all would be convicted.

Had a death penalty state handled the evidence on the robbery and murder that led to Horton's conviction in Massachusetts, Horton would not have been executed. The reason is simple. In 1982 in *Enmund v. Florida* [458 U.S. 782, 797 (1982)], the U.S. Supreme Court had invalidated a death sentence in a case that paralleled the one in Massachusetts. Like Horton, the convict in question had been an accessory to a robbery. Under the doctrine that said that a person party to a felony that results in a murder is guilty of the murder even if it cannot be proven that he committed it, Enmund had been convicted of capital murder. Invoking the Eighth Amendment's ban on disproportionate punishment, the Supreme Court set aside the death sentence.

Those who see relevance in the Horton case argue that a liberal Democrat would appoint to the high court justices more disposed to protect the rights of criminals than of the accused. And in that argument resides the final irony of the Horton case. The rollback of the rights of the accused under the conservative Supreme Court could ultimately mean that the original confession obtained from Horton's colleague might have been deemed acceptable. Under the rules of a Bush but not a Dukakis court, Horton might not have been convicted of first-degree murder at all. And hence he would have been on the streets permanently, sooner than he was under the "liberal" court's requirements.

All narrative capitalizes on the human capacity and disposition to construct stories. A compelling narrative such as the Horton saga controls our interpretation of data by offering a plausible, internally coherent story that resonates with the audience while accounting causally for otherwise discordant or fragmentary information.[24]

When news and ads trace the trauma and drama of a kidnapping and rape by a convicted murderer on furlough, the repetition and the story structure give it added power in memory. Visceral, visual identifications and appositions are better able to be retrieved than statistical abstractions.

Repeatedly aired oppositional material carries an additional power. Material aired again and again is more likely to stay fresh in our minds. The same is true for attacks.

Cognitive accessibility is upped by those message traits that characterize the Republicans' use of Horton: the dramatic, the personally relevant, the frequently repeated topic or claim[25]—the menacing mug shot, circling convicts, empathic victims—and a seemingly uncaring perpetrator—the Massachusetts governor.

When it came to William Horton, our quirks as consumers of political information worked for the Republicans and against the Democrats. In our psychic equations, something nasty has greater power and influence than something nice. When evaluating "social stimuli," negative information carries more weight than positive information.[26] Additionally, negative information seems better able than positive to alter existing impressions[27] and is easier to recall.[28] Televised images that elicit negative emotion result in better recall than those that evoke positive ones.[29] As a result, attacks are better remembered than positive reasons for voting for a candidate.[30] And dissatisfied, disapproving voters are more likely to appear at their polling place than their more satisfied neighbors.[31]

Messages that induce fear dampen our disposition to scrutinize them for gaps in logic. When the message is fear arousing, personal involvement and interest in it minimize systematic evaluation.[32] In the language of cognitive psychology, "[L]arge levels of negative affect such as fear may override cognitive processing."[33]

The Horton story magnifies fear of crime, identifies that fear with Dukakis, and offers a surefire way of alleviating the anxiety—vote for Bush. What successful use of fear appeal and narrative share is a capacity to focus audiences on one interpretation of reality while rendering others implausible. When fear is aroused, attention narrows,[34] simple autonomic behaviors are facilitated, complex, effort-filled ones inhibited,[35] and creative thought dampened.[36]

The mood induced by exposure to communication can affect our probability judgments as well. Johnson and Tversky[37] asked college students to read descriptions that were assembled as if they were newspaper stories. After reading the material, the students were asked to estimate how frequently those within a group of 50,000 people would experience specific dangers (e.g., fire, leukemia, traffic accidents) within a one-year period. When the "newspaper" described the violent death of a male undergraduate, the estimates these college students offered increased for all of the risks, including those that were fundamentally dissimilar to the type described in the article. When the story concerned a happy event that occurred to a young man, the frequency estimates decreased.

Here is the answer to the question Peter Jennings put to Michael Dukakis near the end of the campaign. Why, wondered Jennings, for those we talk to across America, is "Willie Horton" so powerful an image (ABC, November 4, 1988)? The answer is that the fear the story inspired minimized the likelihood that it would be evaluated analytically and its atypicality noted; repetition of its riveting details in ads and news invited us to generalize from it. So, when the Bush furlough ad stated "many first-degree murderers" as the phrase "268 escaped" appeared on the screen, the inference that 268 "Willie Hortons" had been released to kidnap and rape was all but inevitable.

The power of the Horton mini-series was magnified as it unfolded soap-opera-like in news and ads; broadcasts that focused on the tale's strategic intent and effect couldn't effectively challenge its typicality. And since statistics don't displace stories nor data, drama, the native language of Dukakis didn't summon persuasive visions of the cops he had put on the street or the murders and rapes that hadn't been committed in a state whose crime rate was down. Abetted by news reports, amplified by Republican ads, assimilated through the cognitive quirks of audiences, William Horton came to incarnate liberalism's failures and voters' fears.

CHAPTER TWO

Tactics of Attack

If Jefferson is elected, proclaimed Yale president Rev. Timothy Dwight, the Bible will be burned, the French "Marseillaise" will be sung in Christian churches, and "We may see our wives and daughters the victims of legal prostitution; soberly dishonored; speciously polluted." [1]

> "The whole object of the coalition is to calumniate me, cart loads of coffin hand-bills, forgeries, and pamphlets of the most base calumnies are circulated by the franking privilege of Members of Congress," wrote Andrew Jackson to a friend in the heat of the election that would put him in the White House. "Mrs. Jackson is not spared, and my pious Mother, nearly fifty years in her tomb, and who, from her cradle to her death, had not a speck upon her character, has been dragged forth by Hammond and held to public scorn as a prostitute who intermarried with a Negro, and [it is alleged that] my eldest brother [was] sold as a slave in California. . . . I am branded with every crime." [2]

To document its claim that Lincoln had been the target of unprecedented mudslinging, in September 1864, *Harper's Weekly* listed some of the terms of endearment applied to the president by his opponents: "Filthy Story-Teller, Despot, Liar, Thief, Braggart, Buffoon, Usurper, Monster, Ignoramus Abe, Old Scoundrel, Perjurer, Robber, Swindler, Tyrant, Fiend, Butcher, Land-Pirate" and "A Long, Lean, Lank, Lantern-Jawed, High Cheek-Boned, Spavined, Rail-Splitting Stallion." [3]

Note the brevity of these charges about Jefferson, Jackson, and Lin-

43

coln, their reliance on assertion not argument, the absence of disclosed evidence, and the strong visceral identification with one candidate or rejection of another that they invite. These are not exercises in reasoned, warranted comparison and contrast but in comparison starved down to identification and contrast simmered down to apposition. Such verbal and visual telegraphy has been a mainstay of U.S. politics. And the telegraphed content has been more often naughty than nice. Those who pine for the pristine campaigns of Jefferson, Jackson, or Lincoln remember a halcyon past that never was.

Rather than assuming the heavy burden of defining and defending the controversial, campaigns generally ally the favored candidate with things uncritically accepted, such as flag and freedom, and tie the opponent to such viscerally noxious things as the murder of innocent men, women, and children. Out of the resulting contrasts between and among candidates are borne the simplistic dualities in which campaigns traffic: friend against enemy, saint against satan, the candidate of the people against the candidate of privilege, the patriot against the traitor.

This chapter synopsizes a history of U.S. political discourse built on simplistic dualities that telegraph messages of exclusion, not inclusion, visceral identification and apposition, not reasoned and warranted comparison and contrast. As critic Kenneth Burke observes, these bodies of identifications "owe their convincingness much more to trivial repetition and dull daily reinforcement than to exceptional rhetorical skill."[4]

Identification

Imagine, if you will, Saddam Hussein. Now conjure up Mother Teresa. It would be decidedly unwise to predicate a campaign on the assumption that the former is a saint or the latter a whore. At any moment in the life of a republic, the public can viscerally distinguish those presumed to be villainous from those presumed to be virtuous. Of such assumptions of virtue and villainy political discourse is made. Countering them is difficult—capitalizing on them simple.

Personal Identification

Like the broadcast commercials they prefigure, nineteenth-century campaign songs paired candidates with revered or reviled predecessors. In the process, they created the sense that Washington had fathered both the country and endless generations of political progeny, some legitimate, some bastards. In 1864 voters sang, "We'll have another Washington—McClellan is the man!" In 1916 they chorused, "I think we've got another Washington and Wilson is his name." In 1920 Democrats assured the country that Cox was like Washington: "The man we have has oft been tried/Like Washington, he's never lied."

Assertions of political bloodline survive today. Every Democratic nominee since FDR has claimed him. And every Republican in the 1988 race hinted in one way or another that he and Reagan were ideological twins separated at birth.

While a party claims the sign of Abel for its own, it works mightily to brand the opponent with the mark of Cain. To the tune of "Yankee Doodle," Jeffersonians chorused their conviction that Adams coveted a crown "like Georgy, great." In 1832, an anti-Jackson handbill characterized his cronies in verse: "And Here are the Trio of Cabinet fame, Amos Kendall and Lewis, and Blair of bad name, the scullions who grovel and revel in shame: Ay—these are the tyrants—the rulers of him, Who, enfeebled by years, is in intellect dim, The dotard of sixty—who 'born to command,' Dishonours himself, and would ruin the land, Ay—these are the minions the People oppose, Apostates, and Tories, and Liberty's foes— The friends of the Traitor, to glory unknown, who would barter his country, and fawn at a throne." And in 1936, Al Smith opposed FDR with the claim that if the "New Deal wanted to don the mask of Lenin and Marx, or even Norman Thomas . . . that was okay 'but what I won't stand for is allowing them to march under the banner of Jefferson, Jackson and Cleveland.' "[5]

Identification with Policies

Some of the strongest rhetoric of recent memory has tied a candidate to failed policies. Richard Nixon entered the U.S. Senate by allying the voting record of his opponent Helen Gahagan Douglas with that of the leftist New York Congressman Vito Marcantonio. Using pink sheets of paper to carry his message, Nixon labeled Douglas the "pink lady." "Hey, Hey, LBJ. How many kids did you kill today?" was chanted outside the White House by antiwar protestors. In 1980, the Republicans allied Jimmy Carter with pictures of blindfolded U.S hostages in Iran.

Accuracy has not characterized policy attacks any more than personal ones. The coffin handbills charged that Andrew Jackson had executed Tennessee militiamen without trial and without cause. In 1960, Kennedy tagged the Republicans with responsibility for a missile gap that he could not find once he assumed office. In 1972 the Republicans succeeded in labeling McGovern a champion of acid, amnesty, and abortion. Despite Carter's claim that Reagan would rend North from South and Jew from Gentile, at the end of Reagan's first term no geographical or religious tears were observable in the social fabric. In 1984, Mondale's ad incorrectly prophesied economic collapse for the country in 1985.

Visual Identification

The visual equivalent of these verbal pairs paints the candidate's likeness into a flag banner's stars while overlaying his slogan on the stripes. Flag banners were popular as early as 1840 and prevalent until 1905 when Congress prohibited compromising portraits or marks on a flag. Eight decades later, the Republicans closed their early fall ads with a photo of incumbent president Ronald Reagan wrapped in a flag.

Then as now candidates were idealized by their supporters and vilified by their opponents. The banners carried for Lincoln in 1860 and 1864 show a more handsome man than the one immortalized in Brady's unpublicized photographs.

Similarly, William Jennings Bryan gazing resolutely from his campaign banners in 1908 lacks the wrinkles and the jowls but sports substantially more hair than the portly, balding, jowly, wrinkled Bryan captured in photographs of the day.

Just as their supporters beautified pictures of them, so too Lincoln's and Bryan's opponents caricatured them. The apelike sketches circulated by Lincoln's enemies seemed to support the Albany *Atlas and Argus*'s claim that he was "the ugliest man in the Union."[6] In his run for the Senate, Lincoln responded to the caricatures with characteristic humor. Parrying Douglas's charge that he was two-faced, Lincoln noted, "I leave it to my audience. If I had another face, do you think I'd wear this one?"

So outraged were California legislators about being pilloried in cartoons that in 1899 they passed an anticartoon law forbidding caricatures that reflected on character. The law was disregarded and unenforced.

The technique survives. No post office wall of wanted posters appeared as menacing as the scowling, unshaven visages of Senators Jenner, McCarthy, and Taft, who, argued a 1952 Stevenson ad, would run the White House if the electorate endorsed Ike. In 1956, the Democrats tried again, this time using the grammar of police file photos to show "the friends Eisenhower would like to forget." This rogues' gallery included such Eisenhower aides as Sherman Adams, who sent political junkies to their dictionaries to determine what manner of beast produced the corrupting vicuna coat that was Adams's undoing. Nearly forty years later, neither Democratic Senator Paul Simon nor his opponent Representative Lynn Martin was easily recognizable in each other's ads. And in California, Pete Wilson's spots showed an opponent who appeared at least a decade older than she did in her own ads.

The invention of photography in the first half of the nineteenth century provided a powerful form of political evidence. "The everyday viewer began to assume the photographic image was the norm for truthfulness of representation," notes a prominent historian of photography.[7]

The assumption that seeing is believing makes us susceptible to visual deception. Awareness of this susceptibility resulted in new forms of attack. To inflame Southern passions in the 1940s and 1950s a campaign needed only to circulate composite photos of a white candidate with blacks.

Placing a candidate's picture next to that of a known Communist was equally effective. In 1950, Maryland Senator Millard Tydings was done in by his Republican opponent John Butler in the dirtiest campaign of that year. The attacks on Tydings as "soft on communism" culminated in mass distribution of a brochure showing him apparently in intimate conversation with Communist leader Earl Browder. Browder had appeared before a Senate Committee that Tydings chaired. A picture of them did exist. But that picture, which showed Tydings looking tough and challenging, didn't suit Butler's needs. The text accompanying the faked photo noted that it was a composite, but, in a lesson to be relearned in future television campaigns, the words did not override the impressions left by the visual images. When, in a televised election eve address, Tydings attacked the brochure as scurrilous and asked Butler to disavow it, Butler replied that Tydings was trying to smear him "by claiming he has been smeared." Tydings lost.[8]

When the trick was next tried, production of a negative foiled the positive impact of the tactic. Unauthorized by the candidate, in 1962 a group in California published a pamphlet showing incumbent governor Pat Brown bowing deferentially to Soviet leader Nikita Khrushchev. The photo was fake. Before the Republicans had tampered with it, the original had shown Brown bowing to a visiting Laotian child. The Democrats produced the photographic negative. Republican state chair Caspar Weinberger repudiated the pamphlet and quashed its distribution through Republican headquarters.[9] Over time, a grammar of the visual image developed.

Apposition

Campaigns try to make their candidate's name a synonym for everything the electorate cherishes and to transform the opponent into an antonym of those treasured values. Decency versus debauchery. Loyalty versus treason. "He cares about the criminals; I care about the victims." Corrupt political insiders against honest citizen outsiders. Tax-and-spend Democrats versus no-new-taxes Republicans. Economic stagnation versus let's get the country moving again.

After associating one's candidate with "good" and the opponent with "evil," all a campaign has left to do is remind voters of the resulting contrasts. From the country's origins, apposition has oiled politics.

Verbal Apposition

Two contrastive moves underlie political attack: contrasting our espoused values and those manifest in the life of the attacked candidate or party, and contrasting the two candidates. In the following litany of claims against Lincoln, for example, we can read the commandments honored by the attackers and their presumed audience. To his enemies the sixteenth president was " 'a man of coarse nature, a self-seeking politician, who craved high office . . . to satisfy his own burning desire for distinction. . . . His real name is Abraham Hanks. . . . He is the illegitimate son by an [*sic*] man named Inlow—from a Negress named Hanna Hanks.' His presumptive parents were immoral, shiftless poor white trash. Unscrupulous as a lawyer, he was unprincipled as a politician. He was a man of low morality, and his 'inordinate love of the lascivious, of smut,' it was whispered, was 'something nearly akin to lunacy.' "[10]

Some of these are the sins catalogued in Sunday School and condemned in *Pilgrim's Progress*. He is Full of Pride ("craved high office . . . self seeking"); Covetous and Lustful ("inordinate love of the lascivious"); and Slothful ("shiftless"). Some are sins against social sensibilities ("coarse by nature," "poor white trash"), others against normalcy ("nearly akin to lunacy"). Hinted throughout is the sin of Hypocrisy; by changing his name and feigning proper parentage, he invites us to believe that he is what he is not.

Contrast also was the modus vivendi of the gauze-like slogan-bearing transparencies held aloft in nineteenth-century parades. Mottoes on the transparencies "were various," noted *Harper's Weekly* on 11 October 1884, "but the majority referred in some way to the admitted honesty of Governor Cleveland and the bad reputation of Mr. Blaine."

Slogans buttressed support for one candidate or blasted his opponent. Implicit in both were contrasts. The claim that Blaine was "The Continental Liar from the State of Maine" makes political sense only if his opponent is presumed honest. And those who chanted "Rum-soaked Romanist" against Al Smith in 1928 presupposed that Herbert Hoover was a temperate Protestant. Some slogans imply that, if in charge, the supported candidate would have acted differently than the incumbent. Why else recall the use of the military to quell the Bonus March with the chant "Billions for Bankers, Bullets for Vets" or "Down with Hoover, Slayer of Veterans" in 1942?

Contrasting a candidate's past and present positions is effective because it raises doubts about what one can believe about the candidate. Accordingly, in 1802 the *Boston Gazette* juxtaposed the views Jefferson had expressed on slavery in his "Notes on Virginia" and in a letter to Benjamin Banneker.[11] In the Lincoln-Douglas debates, the little giant argued that Old Abe was tailoring his views on slavery to his audiences. "Last year. This year. What about next year?" asked an ad attacking McGovern's inconsistencies in 1972.

In 1976, Jimmy Carter invented the misery index, a figure obtained by summing the negative economic indicators. Four years later the misery index had worsened instead of improved. Predictably, Republican ads pointed that out. Where the Republicans focused that year on high inflation and interest rates, Carter concentrated on his successful negotiation of the Camp David Accords.

Simplifying identification and apposition do not invite rebuttal. There is an assumed uncontestability in their absolutism, a sense that the espoused tenets are credal, their identity fixed with unchallengeable cultural certainty. So, for example, after being accused by Fiorello La Guardia of having a "fixed obsession on Anglo-Saxon superiority," Kansas Congressman J. N. Tincher ended the discussion by stating, "I think the issue is fairly well drawn. On the one side is beer, bolshevism, unassimilating settlements and perhaps many flags—on the other side is constitutional government, one flag, stars and stripes; a government of, by and for the people; America our country." [12] The phrases that close Lincoln's conciliatory Gettysburg Address here have been suborned by chauvinism.

Visual Apposition

There is nothing new about the political impulse to visualize. An observer of the campaign of 1840 recalled that "Great processions showed the barrel of cider, the coonskin, and the log cabin with the latchstring hanging out, which typified Harrison's democracy, while in a carriage rode an image of the aristocratic Van Buren, seated on English cushions and holding the golden teaspoons which he had purchased for the White House. . . . Long banners declared that the Whigs would 'teach the palace slave to respect the log cabin.' " [13]

In the contest between Benjamin Harrison and Grover Cleveland, a poster for Harrison portrayed him as a war hero, a champion of workers, and a hard worker. Drawings on the opposite half of the poster showed Cleveland ducking the war, destroying a factory, and wasting time.

Television added the cueing power of sound and the attention-grabbing impulse of movement. Rifle fire is heard. Dead bodies appear in the still photo. "This is what they do," says the announcer. "Death squads in El Salvador. Innocent men, women, and children murdered in cold blood. This is the man accused of directing those death squads. Roberto D'Aubuisson [picture appears]. And [picture of Jesse Helms appears] this is the man whose aides helped Roberto D'Aubuisson set up his political party in El Salvador. This is Roberto D'Aubuisson's best friend in Washington, maybe his only friend. Now Jesse Helms may be a crusader. But that's not what our senator should be crusading for." The ad was aired by Jim Hunt against Jesse Helms in the 1984 North Carolina Senate race.

Televised Identification and Apposition

If the country has survived two centuries of politicking by telegraphic identification and apposition, why worry about them now? The answer is simple. Television has capacities that stump speakers, print barrages, and radio appeals lacked. When skillfully used, television's multiple modes of communication and powerful ability to orient attention can invite strong, unthinking negative responses in low-involvement viewers. And, by overloading our information-processing capacity with rapidly paced information, televised political ads can short circuit the normal defenses that more educated, more highly involved viewers ordinarily marshal against suspect claims.

Broadsides and radio broadcasts each used a single channel or mode of communication; by contrast, television is multimodal. What makes possible the false inference that 268 first-degree murderers escaped while on furlough is the presence of the print claim "268 escaped," the announcer's spoken claim "many first-degree murderers," the visual image of circling convicts, and the music that cues us to respond apprehensively.

Because it is multimodal, television is more easily comprehended than print. We don't think we need to be taught to "read" television. Additionally, because visuals reinforce and contextualize what we hear, making sense of televised news is easier than deciphering the meaning of a newspaper article.[14] By speaking to us in our native language, television eliminates the decoding required to turn C A T into a furry, purring beast.[15]

Some of the audio and visual cues that are part of television's grammar automatically grab our attention. We can't control our subconscious response to television's cuts, edits, lighting changes, camera changes, shifts in the implied distance of the object that we are watching on the screen (e.g., zooms), changing visual images, or introduction of a new voice.[16] These features affect not only attention but recall of messages[17] and can interfere with the performance of some cognitive tasks.[18]

Television's capacity to use both an audio and a visual channel simultaneously can increase the redundancy and hence the memorability of the message.[19] Alternatively, the amount of content available for cognitive processing can be multiplied by putting complementary information in the two channels. Or, as in Nixon's still-montage ads in 1968, the visual channel showing antiwar protesters and the effects of rioting and looting particularized the meaning of an otherwise platitudinous speech.

Over time, the ways in which television's features have been combined has created a grammar of mood. In political ads, for example, a soft focus, long shots, slow motion, color, use of film, the voice of a reassuring announcer, and lyrical or patriotic music are the grammar of the self-promotional biographical spot. In films, tender romantic scenes and nostalgic moments are shot in soft focus. When slow motion is added, we are invited to move into the domain of wistful memory.

Quick cuts, use of black and white, dark colors, shadowed lighting, stark contrasts, videotape, the voice of a seemingly "neutral" announcer, and ominous music are the techniques associated with "oppositional" production spots. The conventional practices of television lead us to associate videotape with news and film with documentary forms.

Established also is music's ability to increase attention, act as a mnemonic aid, cue retrieval of a message, and invite a specific emotional response.[20] Just as McDonald's added "You Deserve a Break Today" to the repertoire of most preschoolers in the United States, so too did the 1976 Ford campaign invite would-be voters to hum along to "I'm feeling good about America, I'm feeling good about me." In 1984, the Reagan campaign took the power of music one step beyond past uses by making a song on the country charts the Republican theme. Lee Greenwood's "I'm Proud to Be an American" bedded the visuals of many of the feel-good ads of the 1984 campaign. It was revived in the 1988 Bush ads and did for the Gulf War what the "Battle Hymn of the Republic" did for the Civil War.

The evocative power of television's visual grammar couples with its use of music to invite strong emotional reactions to what is seen in ads. Because our judgment of information is influenced by the emotional reactions we experience as we process it,[21] these cues can shade and shape our response to a candidate, issues, or both. The Bush furlough ad enwraps us in an alien world of menace, in which isolated individuals move in mechanical rhythm toward our living rooms as the announcer seems to forecast murder and kidnapping as our lot if Dukakis is elected. This is not an informational context eagerly inviting a dispassionate, rational response.

Some wordless images are powerfully telegraphic in their own right. A torn Social Security card functions iconically in Democratic ads against Goldwater in 1964 to make visual the spoken claim, "By making participation in it voluntary, Goldwater would destroy your social security." By tearing a Social Security card to one-eighth its original size, a Dukakis ad in 1988 invited the same inference. Bush, said the image, wanted to cut Social Security substantially. That visually invited inference was false.

Our evolutionary past increases the power of some images. Scholars tell us, for example, that young kittens cower reflexively when a cutout of a hawk appears overhead. Our self-protective instincts are aroused by any large, dark shape that moves toward us. Some images invoke noncognitive emotional states designed to help us recognize and respond to danger.[22] Because processing pictures does not require immediate cognition, visuals can transmit emotionally powerful information quickly.[23] Television's close-ups also provide viewers with a complex range of ver-

Figure 2-1. The ad showing the torn Social Security card was the most aired ad of the Johnson campaign. It telegraphs Johnson's charge that his opponent would destroy Social Security.

bal and nonverbal material that elicit sometimes unexpected emotional responses.[24]

Finally, television has given political discourse and the low-involvement viewer access to each other. When getting political information required the effort of reading or traveling to a place at which the candidate was speaking, those with minimal interest in politics simply opted out of exposure. Those with a high interest sought out political information; in other words, each group engaged in "selective attention."

"Low involvement" viewers of politics do not seek out political information in broadcast or print news; instead they get most of their political information from inadvertent exposure to political ads.[25] The primary indicator of whether a person will be exposed to political ads is simply how often they are aired and how much television the viewer watches. So, for example, the Times Mirror poll on the 1988 campaign found that those under thirty-five who were less informed about politics and less likely than their parents to read newspapers were nonetheless equally able to recall such Republican ad themes as "Willie Horton" and "Boston Harbor." In 1987, of those under thirty 60 percent reported that "they

Figure 2-2. This Dukakis ad invited the false inference that George Bush had voted to substantially cut Social Security.

often did not become aware of candidates until they saw advertisements on television.[26]

By opening low-involvement viewers to the persuasion of ads, television made it possible for political campaigns to address individuals who are more likely than the highly involved to be persuaded by such "peripheral cues" as presumed expertise or attractiveness of the communicator,[27] and are less likely to be persuaded by the quality of the arguments.[28] When individuals are not focused on analyzing the arguments of a message, the number of arguments itself rather than their cogency can serve to persuade.[29]

Indeed, some argue that most of us watch television "passively, without any particular goal." As a result, the information television offers "may be encoded at a relatively low level of abstractness, without thinking about it extensively in relation to previously acquired information. Moreover, the sort of counter-arguing that often occurs when we have a goal of evaluating the candidate and his or her stands on the issues may not be performed."[30]

So, the telegraphic power of television's appositions and identifications is greater than that of print or radio. Moreover, the multimodal capacity of television provides its producers with a greater variety of ways to invite and evoke viewer response. How these features of television have worked and what can be done to counter them when they invite false conclusions are the questions residing at the core of this chapter.

Guilt or Gilt by Association and Apposition

Television can pair previously disconnected images with a speed and seamlessness that defies the scrutiny of the suspicious. Inviting us to impute a causal link to things only associatively tied is such a stock-in-trade of product advertising that over time we have lost our awareness of how strange some of the paired associations are. From 1952 through 1972 this technique was used with increasing sophistication. One of the by-products of Watergate was dispatch of this mode of assertion from political television. In 1984 it was revived and in 1988 was used in one of the presidential campaign's most controversial ads.

The nation's first presidential campaign spot utilized this editing capacity when Eisenhower and citizen questioners were edited together to form the Eisenhower Answers America spots of 1952. Although the viewer had no way of knowing it, the questioners could not actually see Ike, nor he they. His answers had been recorded before their questions had been asked!

The intercutting in a 1960 ad was less benign. From the first Kennedy-Nixon debate, the Democrats lifted moments showing Nixon nodding agreement to the goals he and Kennedy shared. By the wonders of editing, the Democrats injected that scene into a section of the debates in which Kennedy outlined specific controversial proposals.

Had Kennedy proclaimed at the moment before or after the edited insert, "Nixon agrees with me," he would have been lying. Yet there was the Republican Vice President appearing to agree. The false inference prompted by this ad demonstrates the danger harbored by television's ability to reconfigure reality.

But the Democrats weren't through. They also lifted from the debate unflattering reaction shots of Nixon scowling, biting his lip, glancing nervously from side to side, and sweating perceptibly. These too were edited into the Democratic ad. The visual contrasts between Kennedy and Nixon were striking in the debate and strikingly magnified in the ad. This is the first use of negative nonverbal contrast in a televised presidential ad. When, in 1988, the Republicans juxtaposed a darkened picture of the disheveled Democratic nominee with a brightened angelic photo of the Republican nominee, they were employing an amply precedented tactic.

In 1964, the Democrats and Republicans demonstrated that they understood television's power to use visual association to evoke audience inferences. The Democrats juxtaposed a child plucking the petals from a daisy with the explosion of a bomb as Lyndon Johnson extolled the

Figure 2-3. In 1964 the Democrats aired the most famous ad produced in the history of political television. In those disposed to believe that Goldwater was trigger-happy, the ad suggested that as president he might endanger civilization by making use of our nuclear capacity.

value of loving one another. A young girl is picking daisies in a field. "Four, five, six, seven," she says. An announcer's voice (actually the voice used to count down the space launches at Cape Canaveral) begins an ominous count. "Ten, nine, eight . . ." At zero the camera has closed on the child's eye. A nuclear bomb explodes. Lyndon Johnson's voice is heard: "These are the stakes. To make a world in which all of God's children can live. Or to go into the darkness. We must either love each other. Or we must die." Until the tag line appears, that ad has no explicit partisan content. "Vote for President Johnson on November 3. The stakes are too high for you to stay at home."

While the Democrats were bonding children to bombs, the Republicans were associating riots, looting, influence peddlers Bobby Baker and Billie Sol Estes and LBJ. In each case, the visual intercutting prompts inferences more effectively than a verbal argument could.

The 1964 Republican film *Choice* was less successful. The reasons for its failure are instructive. The film contrasts Democrat Lyndon Johnson's "decadent" and Goldwater's "decent, God-fearing, peace-loving" America. Johnson's America featured racial violence, topless and bottomless bathing suits, actors impersonating members of the Kennedy family throwing each other into swimming pools, and a car, supposedly Lyndon Johnson's, racing through a ranch while "Johnson" dispatched beer cans through its opened window.

By contrast, Goldwater's America surfeits with God-fearing, peace-loving pioneers, loyal to the Declaration of Independence, Christianity, and the traditions of the founders. So overdrawn was the contrast that it didn't even seem plausible to some Goldwater supporters. The Democrats actually used a pirated copy to raise funds for Johnson's reelection.

In 1968, argument by visual association reached a new level of complexity and potential duplicity when patterns of images were created and repeated by the Republicans using still photos. As "A Hot Time in the Old Town Tonight" alternated with discordant sounds, still photos of the war in Vietnam, of poverty in Appalachia, and of the rioting outside the Democratic convention were rapidly intercut with pictures of Democratic nominee Hubert Humphrey. No such argument is made on the audio track of the ad. To phrase the argument verbally is to reveal its ridiculousness. Even Humphrey's most rabid opponent was unready to argue that he had caused the war, poverty, and social unrest or that he approved of them or was indifferent to them—the three most plausible readings of the visual juxtaposition. The images move with a speed that allows little or no reflection. When the first airing evoked public protests to Republican headquarters and television stations, the Republican high command withdrew the ad.

Unlike ads from 1964 and 1968, the associative ads of 1976 are for a candidate, not against an opponent. The public revulsion at the disclosures of Watergate transformed the ads of 1976. In its wake, no candidate wanted to whisper the possibility that he or she was another Nixon. The guilt by visual association embedded in the Billie Sol Estes ad against LBJ and the anti-Humphrey ad bespoke a willingness if not to overstep the truth, then at least to lure the electorate into false inferences. After the light at the end of the tunnel in Vietnam had proven to be that of the advancing enemy and after the Watergate cover-up revealed a second president had lied, the candidate who would be president was required to quell the fears raised by these tactics.

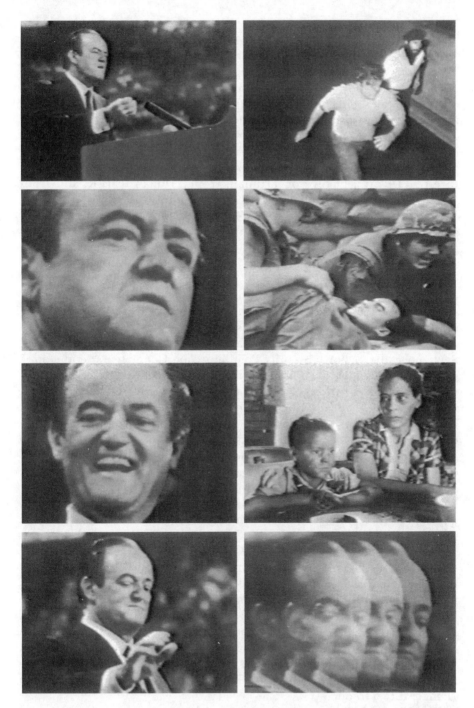

Figure 2-4. In 1968 the Republicans aired an ad linking Humphrey to violence in the streets of Chicago at the Democratic Convention, to poverty in Appalachia, and to the war in Vietnam. No words were spoken during the ad. When the network airing the ad was flooded with calls, the Republicans withdrew it.

Consequently, positive associative ads of the sort that characterized the 1976 Ford and Carter campaigns persevered while ads arguing from negative associations disappeared. By intercutting pictures of the Statue of Liberty, tall sailing ships, and picnics with smiling adults and children, and finally by infusing Ford into the rush of pleasant and patriotic images, the 1976 Republican campaign argued that America was feeling good about itself and about Ford. As E. G. Marshall pointed out that a good man can make a great president, Carter's ad dissolved from a picture of FDR to a picture of Truman, from Truman to JFK, and from JFK to Carter. Notably absent was Lyndon Johnson.

It was the Democrats who in 1984 resurrected attack by visual association. In the closing days of the campaign, predictions of a Reagan landslide created the climate in which the Democrats risked revival of this negative technique. To the tune of "Teach Your Children Well," youngsters were juxtaposed with missiles. Mondale's indictments of Reagan in the ad were as oblique as those Johnson used against Goldwater in 1964. If the prediction of war under Reagan existed in the ad, it was in the inferences invited by the intercut visuals.

By 1988 visual association was back with a vengeance. Beginning in September, the National Security Political Action Committee's "crime quiz" ad allied the Democratic nominee with the mug shot of a black murderer who had jumped furlough in Massachusetts and gone on to terrorize a Maryland couple (as described in Chapter 1). The Democrats tried their hand at linking Bush with damaging pictures as well. Among them were drug-dealing dictator Manuel Noriega and an Hispanic drug dealer who murdered the pregnant mother of two. (Use of unflattering pictures plays on our unrecognized bias toward the physically attractive. In Canada in 1974, the "attractive" candidates for federal office received two and a half times more votes than those deemed "unattractive." Almost three-quarters of those interviewed said that attractiveness had played no part in their vote.)

The Republican ads of 1988 allied Bush with world leaders including Gorbachev and Lech Walesa and situated him in an idyllic world of children and picnics. In a parallel move, the Republican ads placed Dukakis in a world of pollution and waste and menacing criminals.

As controversial was an ad aired in 1991 in Virginia. In fall 1991 a special election was called to replace a retiring Republican in the 7th congressional district. In the resulting race Republican George Allen faced Democrat Kay Slaughter. Allen was a State Delegate, Slaughter a Charlottesville City Councilmember. In the race, the Republican outspent the Democrat two to one.

The National Republican Congressional Committee prepared an ad for Allen showing a rally against the Gulf War held in Washington, D.C. In the scene a protester is holding a sign reading "Victory to Iraq! Defeat US Imperialists." A still photo of Slaughter is then superimposed on the scene. "Kay Slaughter and the liberals in Congress opposed fighting Saddam Hussein," says the narrator as the picture dissolves into a headline reading "City Councilmember Kay Slaughter joined the coalition's December 7 rally . . ." By overlaying a picture of Slaughter on the rally as the announcer describes her opposition to the Gulf War and attendance at a specific rally, the ad invites the false inference that the rally shown was the rally Slaughter attended.

The announcer then states, "Slaughter opposed President Bush and jointed anti-war protesters while our troops were at risk in the Persian Gulf." Troops in the Gulf are shown with a picture of Allen superimposed over them. The ad closes with Allen meeting with Bush in the White House. "George Allen and George Bush. Judgment and leadership we can trust." Slaughter, who had said that she would have voted against movement of U.S. troops against Saddam had she been in Congress at the time of the January 1991 vote, noted, "I am the mother of a National Guardsman, and to imply that I did anything other than give my wholehearted support to our troops is beneath contempt."[31]

Slaughter had attended a peace rally held in Charlottesville, not the rally shown in the ad. The *Charlottesville Daily Progress* editorialized that Allen's ad "is wrong, wrong, wrong. Wrong because it drops the tone of the campaign to a new low. Wrong because it oversimplifies a complicated issue. Wrong because it twists facts and video images to deliberately mislead voters."[32] The ad was aired because the Democrat was closing on the Republican in a traditional Republican stronghold. Some pundits saw it as a forecast of ads to come in 1992. National Republican Congressional Committee Chairman Guy Vander Jagt (R. Mich.) "warned that such ads may await Democrats who opposed the president on the Persian Gulf vote."[33] In what is known as a traditionally Republican district, Republican Allen won with 62 percent of the vote.

In these spots the evidence required to legitimately link the images is absent. It is absent as well in product ads that associate use of the product with beauty, youth, fame, fortune, and friendship. In that they both rely on assertion by visual association, this type of ad sells politicians the way soap is usually peddled.

How Does Association/Apposition Invite False Inferences?

Because we assume that communication is intended to be informative, we don't expect speakers to make claims they believe false or for which they lack evidence.[34] We also bring to communication the belief that those who communicate with us don't offer irrelevant, nonsensical, or implausible information.[35] The underlying presupposition that communication is a cooperative act would be violated if irrelevant information was its stock-in-trade. This premise yields what psychologists call "innuendo effects." A headline reading "Is Kathleen Hall Jamieson a criminal?" followed by an article that answers "No" will nonetheless sway readers toward the conclusion of criminality for the hapless person tagged in the headline.[36]

We don't all respond to any message the same way. Psychologists have gone so far as to differentiate cognitive and behavior styles.[37] But there is emerging evidence to indicate the circumstances, message cues, and attitudinal states that minimize our ability to process messages analytically, to counter-argue against suspect messages, or to process some content at all.[38]

Cognitive psychologists tell us that there are two modes of cognitive processing: central and peripheral. The first is analytic; it tests evidence and frames and evaluates propositions. The second is less conscious and more accepting of the visual cues.

Some believe that visuals are always processed peripherally, on the edges of consciousness, where critical acuity does not come into play. Increasingly, cognitive psychologists are arguing that much of what we absorb from the world around us is peripherally processed. We're influenced by things that don't go through evidence testing. Testing requires time for reflection and demands that we have not been distracted from this process by information overload or alternatively deflected from it by our own fears. To the extent that we have time to deal with visual association, we are able to process it as argument. By giving audiences time to think, *Choice* made a strategic error. Its blatant manipulation and the slow pace of its identifications and appositions invited central processing from its audience. A backlash resulted. It's not an often-made mistake after 1964.

Soon symbols became more subtle. We can be persuaded by communication that we have not carefully evaluated.[39] Indeed, some message characteristics make it *more* difficult to process information systematically. Two of these—rapidly paced information and use of fear appeal—typify many oppositional ads.

The speed with which pictures can now be intercut to identify or contrast two images renders us less able to scrutinize the information coming at us. By flooding us with words, sounds, and images, these stimuli reduce the time that we have to respond and overload our analytic capacity. With that reduction comes a lessened ability to dispute the offered material, a lessened ability to counter-argue. Once these defenses are gone, a persuasive message that might otherwise have been challenged or rejected can slip by.[40] Persuasion without benefit of analytic scrutiny of the message is the result.

The Complicitous Audience

Television's amalgamation of information in different channels and rapid pacing enable the audience to be a partner in its own persuasion. Two campaign examples illustrate how this is done.

In a 1964 Democratic ad, a red phone is ringing on a desk, the hotline from Moscow to Washington. This phone only "rings in a serious crisis," says the announcer. Let's "keep it in the hands of a man who's proven himself responsible." In a campaign in which Goldwater has been portrayed as trigger-happy, the ad encourages the audience to insert the message that the phone should be kept out of his hands, even though there is no mention of Goldwater in the ad.

The technique reappeared in the primaries of 1980. Incumbent Jimmy Carter faced a strong challenge from within his own party. The youngest brother of former president John Kennedy was the challenger whose unremitting attacks on Carter's handling of the economy were laying the groundwork on which the Reagan campaign would build its fall victory. But Edward Kennedy was shadowed by the public's memory of "Chappaquiddick," shorthand for the death of a young woman under unexplained circumstances that implicated Kennedy. The Carter campaign evoked Chappaquiddick without ever mentioning the late night ride across the narrow bridge. "Husband, father, president," said a Carter ad. "He's done these three jobs with distinction."

Another Carter ad invited voters to recall their doubts about Kennedy's explanation of Chappaquiddick. Again there was no direct reference to the fatal accident. The ad simply laid in place the premise that truth telling was important with the expectation that focus would prompt an unfavorable comparison to the Democratic Senator from Massachusetts. "You may not always agree with President Carter," said the announcer. "But you'll never have to wonder whether he's telling the truth. It's hard to think of a more useful quality in a president than telling the simple truth. President Carter—for the truth."

On the face of it, neither of these is an attack ad. If one relies on the content of the ad itself, it is not even clear that the Carter and Johnson ads are oppositional. Unmentioned in both is the name of the opponent or any facet of his record. The audience is free to fill in whatever message it prefers.

In the fourth century B.C. Aristotle wrote that the "enthymeme is the soul of persuasion." This powerful idea explains that persuasion requires audience cooperation. By investing messages with suppressed premises, we become accomplices in our own persuasion. We create enthymemes.

In the classic example, "All men are mortal; therefore Socrates is mortal," the enthymeme suppresses the premise "Socrates is a man." If I assume that Socrates is a gummy bear, I will frustrate the arguer's attempt to forge the enthymeme.

Some of the classics in political advertising function enthymematically. The daisy ad of 1964 shows only a child and an exploding nuclear bomb. Goldwater is nowhere to be found in the ad. But in the context of the 1964 campaign, the ad invited viewers to recall Goldwater's statements on use of nuclear weapons and the attacks his fellow Republicans had made on him for those statements. The audience can supply the premise "Goldwater could lead us into a nuclear war." In fact, viewers asked to recall the ad "remembered" seeing Goldwater's face and hearing the announcer explicitly indict the Republican.

All of this might matter less if we held the notions *implied* in one cognitive warehouse and those *observed* in another. But we don't. Those who study how we comprehend language report that we recode what we hear into a form that doesn't distinguish what was actually said from what was implied.[41]

Enthymematic ads often ask rhetorical questions whose answers have already been revealed to the admakers by the polls. This encourages the audience to reinforce existing predispositions and to act on them in deciding how to vote. A 1968 ad asked, "What has Richard Nixon ever done for you?" It then listed a series of accomplishments attributable to Humphrey and the Democrats. The ad closed by asking viewers to "Think about it." Here the inability of the audience to fill in information about Nixon's accomplishments fueled the anti-Nixon premise. If the audience could list dozens of ways Nixon had helped it, the ad would have failed.

Some ads circumscribe the evidence they offer in such a way that they actively imply a false conclusion. An anti-Johnson ad in 1964 did this by showing pictures of Johnson cronies under investigation (i.e., Billie Sol Estes and Bobby Baker) before asking how Lyndon Johnson managed to build a fortune. The ad is trying to steer the audience to the conclusion that Johnson was on the take. Those who defied the powerful visuals and thought about it realized that there was another possible answer. His wife owned a broadcasting station.

Television has the added power to invite false inferences by amalgamating information in different channels. In the process it allows us to create a whole that is greater than the sum of its parts. The Bush furlough ad of 1988, which I discussed in an earlier chapter, assumes that we will ally material found in one channel (visual: 268 escaped) or within one track of communication with that found in another (audio: many first-degree murderers escaped). The Dukakis ad that says that Bush voted to "cut" Social Security, as it shows a Social Security card being torn down to a small part of its former self, makes the same move. At the end of the ad, only a small part remains. The powerful visual deflects us from questioning what "cut" means. What Bush did was vote to freeze a cost-of-living adjustment. Whether that constitutes a vote to cut is open to debate. What is not debatable is the inference suggested by the shredded Social Security card. If one believes the visual, Bush tried to cut seven-eighths of Social Security. The announcer, of course, never said that. But associating the word "cut" with the rapidly diminishing card invites that inference.

We tend to amalgamate all the information we have available—what we see, what we hear, what we read—into one coherent message. In a rapidly paced ad saturated with evocative fear-inducing claims, the likelihood that we will systematically process the information to ask if we should forge a conclusion is minimized. In short, television has changed the techniques and perhaps the effectiveness, if not the basic tactics, of attack.

CHAPTER THREE

Patriotism and Prejudice: Visceral Responses and Stereotypes That Foil Argument

Identity and enmity are crude but powerful instruments in political campaigning. Among the topics we don't reason together about are our flag and our fears—patriotism and prejudice invite a visceral, not a rational response. This power is magnified by the emergence of short, visual, symbolically powerful televised ads that convey meaning without speaking it. Is warranted engagement possible in such times and on such terms?

Because campaigns thrive on contrasts and more easily reinforce than change attitudes, they naturally traffic in stereotypes. The word stereotype was coined by Walter Lippmann in his influential book *Public Opinion,* published in 1922. We do not react directly to reality but process it through representations or cognitive structures that help us sort information. Stereotypes are "pictures in our heads," said Lippmann. They take features by which we differentiate one group from another (e.g., skin color) and link them to ascribed characteristics that have no necessary relationship.

Social psychologists recently have begun questioning the long-lived assumption that "the most important social knowledge, which influences our perceptions and responses to the current situation, is abstract, propositional, schematic knowledge that we can consciously access and verbally report."[1] In so doing, they are thirty years behind their colleagues in political science. In 1960, Harold Lasswell characterized politics as "the process by which the irrational bases of society are brought out into the open."[2]

We vilify opposing candidates and out-groups in ways that manifest primal needs and invite primitive responses. Maslow's hierarchy could be educed by cataloguing campaigns' themes of threat. The enemy menaces our survival, our identity, and our sense of appropriate sexuality.

In ways that defy conventional logic, issues become enmeshed in the construction of enemies and enemies in the construction of issues. One such interlacing tied Prohibition and Protestantism. As Catholic immigrants competed for scarce urban jobs, the perception that they were both an economic and religious threat increased. Rum and Romanism were linked in campaign discourse. Presumed Catholic immorality threatened America, argued Prohibitionists. This combination of appeals heightened the commitment of rural fundamentalists to Prohibition.[3] At the same time it invited votes against Catholic Al Smith.

Some psychologists hold that we project the dark sides of ourselves onto those we see as menacing. If so, then a group should self-destruct by committing precisely those acts that it has so assiduously condemned in others.

"Do unto others as you fear others will do unto you" is the commandment that helped undo the nativist movement. The anti-Catholicism, anti-immigration claims of the nativists and Know-Nothings included the charge that the pope was about to summon his followers to a slaughter of all Protestants. In the Philadelphia riots of 1844, a Catholic Church was burned and thirteen killed. Not the Catholics but the nativists were responsible.

The result was a setback for nativism. "Particularly alarmed were the sober, church-going citizens who had been attracted to the anti-Catholic cause by the New York school controversy and who now shrank from a continued alliance with such a lawless group as the nativists had demonstrated themselves to be."[4]

Nor is it surprising that the organization known for fabricating tales of rape and murder in order to lynch blacks would be discredited when the head of the Indiana Klan was arrested and convicted "for a particularly repulsive rape murder."[5] Similarly, in recent years evangelists who obsessively decried the sins of the flesh were themselves caught in sex scandals.

One might even suggest that those who see their enemy as a master of deceit are themselves bent on intrigue and duplicity. Perhaps Richard Nixon's sensitivity to the duplicities of Alger Hiss bespoke the inclinations that drew him into either Watergate or its cover-up or both.

One might recall as well that in the 1980 presidential campaign Reagan operatives leaked to Conservative columnists Evans and Novak the false information that Carter had dispatched his legal counsel, Lloyd Cutler, to Geneva to arrange a "deal to exchange American hostages for military equipment vital to the Iranian war effort against Iraq."[6] Midway through Reagan's second term the public would learn that the Republicans themselves had arranged an arms for hostages deal with Iran to free another group of Americans. The "Iran-Contra" affair was, in effect, forecast in 1980 by the Republican projection of Democratic activities.

There are times when we are more inclined to magnify the differences between those we define as "ourselves" and those we define as "other." In the jargon of social science, "the tendency to favor the in-group over the out-group *increases:* when there is an explicit similarity within the in-group; when the out-group is perceived to be capable of controlling the outcomes ('fate') of the in-group; when there is a stronger perception of the in-group as an 'entity'; when a spirit of competition between the groups is fostered; when the in-group experiences distinct success and/or failure; and when there is actual or anticipated interaction with other members of the in-group."[7] So, for example, the lingering recession in Louisiana fed the sorts of voter fears and resentments that translated into votes for Republican gubernatorial candidate David Duke. We also tend to magnify the desirable features of our own group and the undesirable traits of an out-group.[8] And we tend to believe that all groups other than our own are more homogeneous than they are.[9]

Some people are also more intolerant than others. Those with low self-esteem tend to be less tolerant than those whose self-esteem is high, for example.[10] Since they interact with others less than people with high self-esteem, they lack the opportunity to learn that tolerance is a social norm. Those with low self-esteem also are more likely to see the world as a dichotomous struggle between "us" and "them" and are more likely to feel threatened by others.[11] As level of education increases so too does tolerance.[12]

Because political campaigns rely on identification and contrast, they are rife with in- and out-group distinctions. There is political advantage in heightening one's supporters' sense of identity with each other (e.g., "good and patriotic Americans"). Campaigns increase contact among the like-minded. At the same time, there is advantage in magnifying the threat and power of opposing candidates' supporters; votes are gathered by promising to use power to prevent a threatening group from taking control. Unsurprisingly, political discourse routinely reinforces the public belief that one group or another group is menacing. The aliens and the opponent are then married.

Contrasts Between Us and Them

In 1972, in his first Senate campaign, North Carolina's Jesse Helms used as his slogan "He's One of Us." At some level, every political campaign makes that claim about its candidate and in so doing either explicitly or implicitly defines an out-group that "we" are fundamentally unlike and whose designs "our" candidate will thwart. How such appeals have framed Communists, Catholics, blacks, and gays is the focus of this chapter.

Before embarking on it, however, let me note that cataloguing the range of political discrimination in U.S. history could consume shelves of library space and would include most of the immigrant groups that now comfortably sing "America The Beautiful." In the 1850s in Baltimore, for example, street gangs "devised a whole panoply of methods for minimizing opponents' political power. Among them were the Blood Tubs." "Venturesome Irishmen" were dunked in tubs of blood "obtained from local butchers, then chased . . . down the street with knives." "This," notes one historian, "was a most potent deterrent to would-be voters." [13]

Employment was both the symbol and the substance of most conflicts among immigrant groups. "Hostility toward and contempt for Oriental labor, in particular, was an avowed part of the Progressive campaign of 1912, a legacy of its trade union support and the sectional attitudes of the west coast which made an unsympathetic attitude toward Oriental nations a concomitant part of the outlook of many Progressives," notes one commentator on the period. "The *Progressive Bulletin,* the official organ of the party, attacked Wilson in 1912 because he 'prefers Chinese immigrants to white.' " [14]

Loyalty Versus Treason

Whether a candidate is "American enough" to be president has been at issue since the country's founding. But what it means to be "American enough" has changed dramatically. John Quincy Adams, for example, was accused of marrying a British wife; Martin Van Buren was pilloried for riding about in a British coach. And Franklin Pierce was charged with having undemocratic chromosomes—being the direct descendant of "the noble Percy family of medieval England." [15]

Some of our prejudices are institutionalized in the Constitution. Only native-born Americans are eligible for the presidency. By being classed as property, blacks originally were excluded from citizenship entirely. And for much of the country's first century, the word "man" in the founding documents was taken to mean precisely that.

Practically from the beginning of the Republic, candidates for office have wrapped themselves in the flag. If one's biography included military victory, whether fabricated or real, all the better. From "First in War, First in Peace, First in the hearts of his countryman" to "The Man from Abilene," victorious generals have carried the advantage of certifiable patriotism.

From Vincennes to Vietnam, military valor has marshaled votes. Accordingly, candidates are eager to embellish their defense records. Lyndon Johnson's routine inspection tour of foreign bases as a bureaucrat in uniform in World War II was retold as an heroic conquest under fire. "[T]he story of his wartime service bore little resemblance to the reality," wrote biographer Robert Caro, "which was that, exciting though his flight may have been, it was only one flight. He had been in action for a total of thirteen minutes. When, in December of 1942, five months after his return from this action, a reporter asked him, 'Were you actually in combat?,' he replied, 'Yes, I was. I was out there in May, June and part of July.' . . . the details became richer, more vivid. He began saying that because he had been too tall to fit into the parachute provided, he had flown without one; then he added another fillip; only one parachute had been available, and he had given it to a friend. The engine that had malfunctioned on his plane now, in his accounts, had been 'knocked out' by Japanese Zeroes."[16]

Because it shifts the presumption of patriotism, the claim that someone has ducked his country's call can be deadly. So, for example, Jesse Helms assumed that even the insinuation that his Democratic opponent James Hunt hadn't served in the military would damage him. Hence, after arguing that Helms voted against veterans' benefits, in one of their debates Hunt noted:

> "Now I've got every single one of your votes right here, Senator. You can't fool me, and I don't think you're going to fool the people of North Carolina . . ."

How does one counter such a claim? Helms tried with the question, "Which war did you serve in?"

> *Hunt:* "I did not serve in a war."
> *Helms:* "OK."
> *Hunt:* "Senator Helms, now wait just a minute. Since you asked that question. . . ."
> *Helms:* "No, Mr. President. I was. . . ."
> *Hunt:* "I was in college, Mr. Moderator, during the time of the Korean War, and I was too old with two children when Vietnam came along. And I don't like you challenging my patriotism, Senator."
> *Helms:* "I haven't challenged your patriotism."
> *Hunt:* "Yes you have. You know exactly what that question was calculated to do."
> *Helms:* "Well, I just wondered . . ."[17]

At a symbolic level, flag equals country. Accordingly, one can discredit an opponent telegraphically by allying him with flag burners. The Republican claim in 1988 that the Democratic nominee's wife had burned a flag in college was a powerful one. Had proof been produced, the Democrat could have retired to Massachusetts three months early. Calling into play such evocative symbols as the flag short circuits argument.

In 1988 the Republicans charged that Dukakis had vetoed legislation mandating recitation of the Pledge of Allegiance in public school classrooms. What Dukakis mistakenly read as a challenge to the constitutional justification of his action was instead a direct, hard-hitting assault on his patriotism. In a campaign climate characterized by such soundbites as "I

Figure 3-1. This scene of a class reciting the Pledge of Allegiance is from a Goldwater ad that implies that Johnson's conduct in the presidency has corrupted the morals of the country. The ad is referring to scandals caused by influence peddling by a former Johnson aide.

pledge allegiance . . ." and such telegraphic moments as children, hands over hearts, affirming their loyalty to flag and country, a reasoned discussion of whether or not a teacher should lead a class in the Pledge every day was unlikely. It was unlikely even if at stake were the principles of free expression and tolerance of dissimilar religious beliefs.

The question involved was not hypothetical. It had been addressed by the Supreme Court during World War II. On the basis of that precedent and the principle underlying it, Michael Dukakis had opposed a Massachusetts bill to mandate the Pledge in classes. In the earlier case, a state law had required that children recite the Pledge at the beginning of each school day in public schools. A child who was a Jehovah's Witness refused on religious grounds and the child was suspended from school. The Supreme Court overturned the suspension. "If there is any fixed star in our constitutional constellation," wrote Justice Jackson for the majority, "it is that no official, high or petty, can prescribe what shall be orthodox, in politics, nationalism, religion, or other matters of opinion or force citizens to confess word or deed their faith therein." [18]

"Love of country" wears other garb as well. "Soft on defense" has become a code phrase for unpatriotic. Beginning in the late 1940s, linking one's opponent to communism accomplished the same thing. For the next three decades, candidates could mask the fact that they did not stand for a specific foreign policy by affirming that they stood against communism. Simplistic appositions grounded the move. In his January 1949 inaugural, Harry Truman articulated the premises that would be presupposed throughout the cold war.

> [T]he United States and other like-minded nations find themselves directly opposed by a regime with contrary aims and a totally different concept of life. That regime adheres to a false philosophy which purports to offer freedom, security, and greater opportunity to mankind. Misled by this philosophy, many peoples have sacrificed their liberties only to learn to their sorrow that deceit and mockery, poverty, and tyranny, are their reward. That false philosophy is communism.
>
> Communism is based on the belief that man is so weak and inadequate that he is unable to govern himself, and therefore requires the rule of strong masters. Democracy is based on the conviction that man has the moral and intellectual capacity, as well as the inalienable right, to govern himself with reason and justice.
>
> Communism holds that the world is so deeply divided into opposing classes that war is inevitable. Democracy holds that free nations can settle differences justly and maintain lasting peace. These differences between communism and democracy do not concern the United States alone. People everywhere are coming to realize that what is involved is material well-being, human dignity, and the right to believe in and worship God.

In the cold-war frenzy of the fifties, the charge of treason came into currency. With it went calls for loyalty oaths, for banning the Communist Party, and, in the case of one Pennsylvania candidate for the U.S. Senate, for changing the name of the Cincinnati Reds baseball team.[19]

As I noted earlier, Nixon moved from the House to the Senate by identifying Helen Gahagan Douglas as the "pink lady." The link between Douglas and "Representative Vito Marcantonio, an admitted friend of the Communist Party" had been forged in Douglas's own party's primary by the incumbent she defeated, Senator Sheridan Downey. In the general election, Republican Nixon took up the cry.[20] The evidence: 354 instances in which Marcantonio and Douglas's votes were identical. Unmentioned of course was the fact that on many of them, Nixon's ballot was also the same.

But "soft on defense" is benign compared to claims used to question loyalty in earlier decades. In the off-year elections of 1946, a year the Republicans regained control of both houses of Congress, the chairman of the Republican National Committee claimed that "Democratic policy bore 'a made-in-Moscow label,' deplored 'the infiltration of alien-minded radicals' into the government, and assailed the administration's 'brazen public alliance' with the 'radical-dominated' CIO-PACs."

So repulsive were the tactics of one man who dominated the airwaves in the early 1950s that we now memorialize them with the pejorative "McCarthyism." Most of what we now tag as "McCarthyism" is milder than the original. On the evening news on July 25, 1950, the Senator from Wisconsin attacked Maryland Senator Millard Tydings as someone willing to "keep in power those individuals who are in the State Department today, and those who are responsible for American boys lying face down in the Korean mud with their hands behind their backs and their faces shot off. If this fraud is allowed to succeed, it will mean that the trail of blood for which those men are responsible will extend across the sands of Iran right over into the very streets of Berlin." Later that year, Tydings would lose his Senate seat in a campaign tarred by McCarthyism.

In the presidential campaign of 1952, Nixon's attacks on the Democrats paled in comparison to McCarthy's. In a nationally televised speech delivered one week before election day, the Wisconsinite labeled the Democratic foreign policy "suicidal" and "Kremlin-directed." In the speech, McCarthy feigned laughter as he smirkingly referred to the Democratic nominee Adlai Stevenson as "Alger, I mean Adlai." "Alger" was Alger Hiss, a former employee of the State Department sentenced for committing perjury before a congressional committee and widely assumed to be a Communist.

The demise of Joe McCarthy demonstrates that a sustained form of rebuttal is required to dispel an entrenched form of guilt by association. The nationally televised Army-McCarthy Hearings and Edward R. Murrow's exposé of McCarthyism were able to demonstrate to the American people that what McCarthy had in his hand as he waved pages presumably laden with the names of Communists was nothing more than innuendo and smear. McCarthyism taught the American public to recognize the grosser forms of guilt by association. As a result, Republican vice presidential nominee Robert Dole was roundly criticized when, in his debate with Walter Mondale in the 1976 presidential race, he repeatedly referred to past "Democrat wars."

Guilt by association increases in uncertain times—such as during economic hardship—when the populace is fearful. The objects of attack are those of other races, religions, and social classes. Immigrants, notes historian David Bennett, "proved the perfect target for many Americans in . . . troubled times. They could associate their own loss of power or status with the emergence of a subversive group disrupting time-honored relationships. In a social order threatened by catastrophe, polarization between the forces of good and evil satisfied the desire for enemies on whom to pin the blame, whose defeat could restore the stability of the cherished past."[21]

A brief chronicle of attacks on Catholics, blacks, and gays confirms Bennett's observation and also demonstrates that the attack of contemporary politics is a faint echo of far worse that came before.

The God-fearing versus the Worshippers of the False God

Its "immense lore about libertine priests, the confessional as an opportunity for seduction, licentious convents and monasteries," prompted historian Richard Hofstadter to identify anti-Catholicism as "the pornography of the Puritan."[22]

Beginning with the story of Maria Monk and culminating in the election of President John Kennedy, attacks on Catholics and Catholicism worked their way through and finally to marginal status at the fringe of the American political system. John Kennedy's Catholicism called into question his presidential ability, but twenty years later it was not an issue for his brother.

In the 1850s, the "Know-Nothing" party tried to restrict Catholic immigration and rescind the rights of papists who were already on the voter rolls. In the 1890s, the American Protective Association took up the same cry to be followed in the 1920s by the Ku Klux Klan. The Klan's platform called for barring immigrants and saving America from blacks, Catholics, and Jews. In the mid-1920s, the Knights of the Klan gained more than five million adherents.

An historian writing in the 1930s explained the Klan's "feeling that the election of every additional Catholic to public office would hasten the time when our government would be turned over to a foreign Pope."[23] In 1924, the Democratic convention narrowly defeated a platform plank that would have denounced the Klan. That same year, William Allen ascribed his loss of the Kansas governorship to his own condemnation of the Klan. "I was wrong on the Pope," said White.[24]

Inventer of the telegraph Samuel Morse led the mid-nineteenth-century charge against Catholic immigrants. In two widely circulated books, Morse argued that "The evil of immigration brings to these shores illiterate Roman Catholics, the tools of reckless and unprincipled politicians, the obedient instruments of their more knowing priestly leaders."[25]

Morse's claims were fueled by the narrative contained in a small volume first published in 1836 and titled *The Awful Disclosures of Maria Monk as Exhibited in a Narrative of Her Sufferings During a Residence of Five Years as a Novice and Two Years as Black Nun in the Hotel Dieu Nunnery at Montreal*.[26] For a decade this was the best-selling book in the United States, reaching sales of over 30,000. Its actual authorship is uncertain. Monk claimed that after converting from Protestantism to Catholicism, she joined a convent where she was sexually abused by both nuns and priests and bore an illegitimate child. Her mother insisted instead that Monk had been a prostitute who conceived the child while in an asylum. When the Nunnery Committee of Massachusetts investigated the charge that convents were the sites of sadism and sexual abuse, it found no supportive evidence. Nor could the Protestant editor of the New York *Commercial Advertiser* find corroboration.[27]

For much of the country's history, anti-Catholicism has been a political

Figure 3-2. Simplistic apposition and identification have characterized U.S. politics since its beginnings. This cartoon satirizes the posturing of the 1846 campaign. Note the anti-Catholicism in the indictment of "political Jesuitism." (*Library of Congress*)

weapon. Colonial New Englanders pilloried the Roman pontiff on Pope Day, following the British custom of burning the pope (or "Guys") on Guy Fawkes Day, which commemorated the Catholic 1605 Gunpowder Plot against the throne.

At multiple levels, the symbolism of the Colonial celebration affirmed who the colonists were by identifying who they weren't. By appropriating Guy Fawkes Day as the date on which to celebrate, they identified themselves with the British crown and against those who threatened it. By parading with those from either the North or the South of town, they also reinforced social identification with their own kind.

In Boston, Pope Carts were built on the North and South end of the city. Each cart carried a banner proclaiming "North end forever" or "South end forever." An effigy of the pope was mounted on each and the cart strung with lanterns. "Behind the lantern sat the pope in an arm chair, and behind the pope was the devil standing erect with extended arms, one hand holding a small lantern, the other grasping a pitchfork."[28] Residents of the north and south would try to steal each other's cart. Fistfights and rock throwing were common. At the end of the evening, the "popes" were burned.

In the nineteenth century, an anonymous author created a diatribe against the Jesuits. In its first incarnation it was supposed to be an oath taken by priests. At its core was the commitment to war against Protestants in ways reminiscent of the Spanish Inquisition. In the early years of the twentieth century the Ku Klux Klan recast the oath as "The Knights of Columbus Oath."

In 1913, a Committee of the U.S. House of Representatives examined uses of the oath in the campaigns of 1912 and it was denounced as a forgery and publicly repudiated.[29] As part of the investigation the oath appeared in the *Congressional Record*. A decade and a half later its appearance there was used by the Klan to suggest the document's legitimacy! Copies were in circulation as late as the 1960 presidential campaign.

Catholics also were accused of murdering Lincoln, Harding, and FDR and of disabling Woodrow Wilson. To attack Democratic nominee and Catholic Al Smith, news photographs of the Holland Tunnel were identified as a passage to the Vatican. And Blaine was criticized for the Catholicity of his spouse.

As the number of Catholics in a state increased so too did the likelihood that a Catholic would be elected to state-wide office. In 1918 and 1926, Catholic Eugene Bonniwell had run for governor of Pennsylvania and both times was defeated. In the 1958 Pennsylvania gubernatorial race, one candidate ran print ads showing himself going to a Lutheran church. His Catholic opponent, David Lawrence, won nonetheless. By the mid-1970s, Pennsylvania was over 30 percent Catholic.

Short forms of communication such as ads are better able to convey fear than to allay it; the broadcast speech and extended debate are the forms best suited to dispute prejudice. On September 20, 1928, in a speech in Oklahoma City, Democratic nominee Al Smith tried just that. After noting that the constitution bars religious tests for public office, Smith rebutted the claims being circulated against him.

> [N]o decent, right-minded, upstanding American citizen can for a moment countenance the shower of lying statements, with no basis in fact, that have been reduced to printed matter and sent broadcast through the mails of this country. One lie widely circulated, particularly through the southern part of the country, is that during my governorship I appointed practically nobody to office but members of my own church. What are the facts? On investigation I find that in the cabinet of the Governor sit fourteen men. Three of the fourteen are Catholics, ten Protestants, and one of Jewish faith. . . . One of the things, if not the meanest thing, in the campaign is a circular pretending to place someone of my faith in the position of seeking votes for me because of my Catholicism. Like everything of its kind, of course it is unsigned. . . . It was designed on its very face to injure me with members of churches other than my own. I here emphatically declare that I do not wish any member of my faith in any part of the United States to vote for me on religious grounds.[30]

In his confrontation with the Houston Ministers in the 1960 campaign, which combined a Kennedy speech with a tough question-and-answer session, Kennedy took on the religious issue. When his election did not bring a papal entourage to the Lincoln bedroom or a legislative push for aid to parochial schools, religion subsided as a warrant for attack. In 1984, it would be revived in an unexpected way when a Catholic Cardinal criticized vice presidential nominee Geraldine Ferraro for not endorsing her church's stand on abortion.

The Superior versus the Inferior Race

"The elementary determinant in Southern politics," wrote Marion Irish in 1942, "is an intense Negro phobia which has scarcely abated since Reconstruction."[31] "The predominant consideration in the architecture of southern political institutions has been to assure locally a subordination of the Negro population and, externally, to block threatened interferences from the outside with these local arrangements," wrote V. O. Key in *Southern Politics in State and Nation* in 1949.[32]

In the nineteenth century, one could libel an opponent simply by alleging that he had Negro ancestry, supported interracial sex, or considered blacks and whites equal. Jefferson was charged with having a black mistress. A week before the election that would put Harding in the White House, "An Open Letter to the Men and Women of America" was circulated throughout the South.

The letter contained five affidavits swearing that Warren Gamaliel Harding was "not a White man." A genealogical chart traced Harding's parentage to "a West Indian Negro of French stock." The material was

Figure 3-3. Identifying one's political opponent with a despised group has been standard political fare since the early days of the republic. This advertisement appeared during the presidential campaign of 1860. *(Library of Congress)*

the product of a racist professor at Wooster College named Dr. William Estabrook. When he admitted authorship, the trustees of the college concluded that he was "unbalanced" and demanded his resignation.

Meanwhile, the Democratic administration in San Francisco found 250,000 copies of the leaflet and both had them destroyed and banned their further distribution. The Democrats countered this attack by running full-page ads showing Harding's parents. Pictures were responding to words.

Early in the history of U.S. politics, fears of "racial mixing" became campaign fodder. In the Lincoln-Douglas debates, the future president faced an opponent who repeatedly exploited audience fears by tying Negro equality and intermarriage. Responding with one appeal to reason and another to common ground, the person who would issue the Emancipation Proclamation took the charge head on. "I do not understand that because I do not want a negro woman for a slave I must necessarily want her for a wife," said Lincoln to the cheers and applause of the crowd. "My understanding is that I can just let her alone. I am now in my fiftieth year, and I certainly never had a black woman for either a slave or a wife. So it seems to me quite possible for us to get along without making either slaves or wives of negro women."

In 1864 an anonymous pamphlet introduced a new word to politics with its title, *Miscegenation*. Supposedly penned by a Republican abolitionist, it argued that mixed races were not only desirable but were the natural outcome of Republican presuppositions. Indeed, argued the pamphlet, abolitionists should support interracial marriage. The pamphlet, which produced a public outcry, was widely assumed to have Republican origins. In the late 1950s, historians confirmed that the work instead had been authored by two Democratic newspapermen, David Goodman Croly and George Wakeman.[33]

In the decade between 1867 and 1877, secret groups bent on keeping Negroes in their place roamed the South. Of them, the Knights of the White Camellias and the Knights of the Ku Klux Klan were the most powerful. "They used intimidation, force, ostracism in business and society, bribery at the polls, arson, and even murder to accomplish their deeds," note historians John Hope Franklin and Alfred A. Moss, Jr. "Depriving the Negro of political equality became, to them, a holy crusade in which a noble end justified any means. Negroes were run out of communities if they disobeyed orders to desist from voting; and the more resolute and therefore insubordinate blacks were whipped, maimed, and hanged."[34] The Ku Klux Klan was officially dissolved in 1870 but experienced a revival in the 1920s.

To stop black men, and then women, from exercising their right to vote, conservative candidates both threatened and used force. State Senate candidate Democrat James A. Bryan told a fevered crowd in North Carolina in 1898, "When the white man's civilization is at stake we are going to stand together for the white man's government and the white man's rule until the last one of us is put in a box ten feet under. . . . Let the white men go to the polls next Tuesday and run this election. You have got to run it. I tell you, you have got to win it; peaceably if you can, but if you fail that way, win it any way you can."[35]

Political campaigns simply reflected the commonplace rhetoric of the public arena. Academic tracts regularly offered "evidence" that Negroes were the intellectual inferiors of whites. Some argued that unlike whites, Negroes were disposed toward "crime and immorality."[36] As the number of lynchings rose, as they did in 1892, and with them an increased call for federal anti-lynching legislation, writers emerged to justify lynching as a response to alleged murder and rape committed by blacks.

Even though "his own statistics showed conclusively that the victim was not even accused of rape in the overwhelming majority of cases,"[37] in *The Negro: The Southerner's Problem*, Thomas Nelson Page attributed lynching to "the determination to put an end to the ravishing of their women by an inferior race."[38] Calmer voices responded that there was no evidence that the incidence of rape by blacks was higher per capita

Figure 3-4. During and after the Civil War, fears of "miscegenation" were exploited by those opposing the rights of blacks. In 1864, this political message sold for $.25 a copy. (*Library of Congress*)

than that by whites. Indeed some argued that it was less.[39] The need for such rejoinders suggested the pervasiveness of the assumptions being contested.

In 1915, Georgia's demagogic Tom Watson combined racism and anti-Catholicism with the appeal "Think of a Negro priest taking the vow of chastity and then being turned loose among women who have been taught that a priest cannot sin!"[40] Racism and anti-Catholicism were blended as well in an Oxford don's recommendation to a U.S. audience in 1882 that "the best remedy for whatever is amiss in America would be if every Irishman should kill a negro and be hanged for it."[41]

In the backdrop of Southern politics is the fact that freedom for Negroes was won by the victory of the North over the South in the Civil War. For some, the rebel yell is simply an affirmation of regional pride. For others it is a claim to white supremacy. *New York Times* editor Turner Catledge described observing Georgian Senator Walter George in 1938 inflaming a crowd with "anti-Negro, anti-Semitic, anti-Labor, and anti-Yankee" speeches as audiences cheered him on with rebel yells and cries of "Let 'em have it."[42]

"In those days in Arkansas my constituents were not about to be persuaded on civil rights," wrote former U.S. Senator J. William Fulbright in 1989. "I could try to persuade them on subjects they didn't feel directly, immediately, emotionally attached to. But against an emotional fear like miscegenation, I don't think I had a real choice. I mean, what used to really bother them was the prospect of their young daughter marrying a black man. They couldn't tolerate the thought of it. That was what was in their minds, what they talked about. That was the way the fears were manifested throughout the delta region of Arkansas."[43]

From the turn of the century to the early 1960s, support of or willingness to associate with blacks was used as evidence to condemn candidates in the South. In October 1901, Booker T. Washington dined at the White House at the invitation of then president Theodore Roosevelt. The dinner caused an uproar. In the South, TR's opponents circulated campaign buttons showing a black-faced TR seated at a dinner table with Washington.

A ploy used against then Florida Senator Claude Pepper in 1950 pictured him shaking the hand of a black man. Pepper believed that his opponent had paid the man to approach him and had paid a photographer to snap the shot.[44]

In that same year, a North Carolina campaign claimed falsely that a moderate favored integration. Visual support was then constructed to legitimize the claim. Unnamed partisans circulated a fabricated photograph of candidate Frank Graham's wife dancing with a black man. The campaign that gave Willis Smith that Senate seat also included charges that Graham had appointed a black teenager to the U.S. Military Academy, an allegation Graham tried to dismiss by introducing audiences to the actual appointee. In mailboxes appeared anonymous "midnight fliers" alleging that Graham had proposed an end to racial segregation. Graham had led Willis in the Democratic primary but failed to secure the 50 percent needed; he lost to Willis in the run-off. A member of Smith's staff, a young conservative named Jesse Helms, cut his political teeth in this campaign.

In fall 1958 a Southern Republican running for state office in a rural community found in community mailboxes a flier showing a black man and white woman seated side by side on a bed. "This, the leaflet suggests, is to become commonplace, if the candidate, a known integrationist, is elected."[45]

The "Council of White Citizens of Atlanta" sent letters from Atlanta to 6000 black voters in Detroit in the presidential campaign of 1956. The message: Vote Democratic "because the Democratic Party keeps the colored in their place." After the election was over, investigative reporters learned that the Council was a fabrication of a Detroit adman who was doing volunteer work for Michigan Minutemen for Eisenhower.[46]

In 1960, fliers distributed in the South showed Republican presidential candidate Richard Nixon standing next to blacks. And bolstering the argument against him was the noted fact that he was a member of the National Association for the Advancement of Colored People.

Beginning with JFK, presidents began using the rhetorical power of their office to advance racial equality. Although such appeals succeeded in broadening voting rights, they did not stop racist campaign tactics. Unauthorized by Goldwater or his campaign were anonymous fliers disseminated in 1964 saying "If you want a nigger for a neighbor, vote Democratic."[47]

The Civil Rights Act of 1964 and the Voting Rights Act of 1965 were turning points for blacks in the United States. Slowly, political participation began to rise in the South. And with it came a change in political discourse. "Whether or not a particular Democratic politician was strongly preferred by blacks in the Democratic primaries," write political sociologists Earl and Merle Black, "a 'new South' style of campaigning, one in which nominees deliberately refrained from antiblack rhetoric, became standard across the region."[48]

At the national level, 1976 did for black voters what 1960 had done for Catholics. The margin of victory for Georgian Jimmy Carter was provided by blacks who gave the Democrat over 90 percent of their ballots in Ohio, Pennsylvania, New York, Alabama, Texas, and Mississippi. "[W]hen I heard that Mississippi had gone our way," noted Andrew Young of that election, "I knew that the hands that picked cotton had finally picked the president."[49]

By 1982, even the candidate who in the early 1960s had stood in the schoolhouse door to proclaim "Segregation Now, Segregation Tomorrow, Segregation Forever" had begun to court blacks. In that year Governor George Wallace was re-elected governor of Alabama with black support. When former Klansman David Duke sought a place in Congress in 1990 and on the presidential ballot as a Republican in the 1992 primaries, his candidacy was repudiated by the Republican party.

The most dramatic evidence of the political power of blacks emerged in the 1987 fight over the Supreme Court nomination of Robert Bork and the 1991 conflict over the nomination of Clarence Thomas. In 1987, radio ads sponsored by the People for the American Way announced that "The Senate should learn why Mr. Bork criticized a congressional ban on literacy tests used to prevent minorities from voting . . . [why he had written against] equal accommodations for black Americans, and against the principle of one man-one vote."[50] Similar claims appeared in a television ad featuring Gregory Peck. Bork claimed that the ads misrepresented his positions. He was defeated by the votes of Southerners elected with the help of votes by blacks. In 1991, after polls provided them with assurances that most blacks believed Clarence Thomas rather than the woman who had accused him of questionable professional behavior, these same Southern Democrats gave President George Bush the votes needed to confirm Thomas.

Unlike the politics of anti-Catholicism, attacks based on race survive. The Helms-Gantt race of 1990 and the Republican use of William Horton in 1988 pivot on powerful but "deniable" appeals to racial resentment. They were forecast in earlier years in such coded words and phrases such as "the tyranny of the courts," "law and order," "your home is your castle," "neighborhood schools," "forced busing," "individual rights," and "quotas." These implicit appeals are the subject of the next chapter.

The Natural versus the Unnatural/The Normal versus the Abnormal

In difficult-to-understand ways, sexual morality and national survival have been conflated. "I say then," wrote John Adams in 1807, "that national morality never was and never can be preserved without the utmost purity and chastity in women; and without national morality a republican government cannot be maintained."[51] The obverse is evident in identifications of FDR as "a syphilitic, a liar, and a Bolshevik."[52]

"Sexuality is always political," notes political theorist Murray Edelman, "because it establishes bonds, strains, hostilities, and constraints and it generates symbols of the ideal and the repugnant."[53] Accordingly, the favored candidate is portrayed as a "good family man," the opponent as a philanderer. To feared groups, we ascribe forbidden forms of sexuality. "The attribution of a unique measure of eroticism is blatantly political because it defines the group in terms that ignore individual characteristics and potentialities while highlighting a provocation to oppression."[54] In such constructions, Catholic priests and newly emancipated blacks are rapists; Communists and gays, perverts.

It would be difficult today to find a large audience in the United States willing to publicly applaud a direct attack on a candidate for being Catholic or being black. But what would be considered intolerable if referring to religion or race is acceptable when the object is sexual orientation. With rare exceptions (e.g., Rep. Barney Frank and Rep. Gerry Studds in Massachusetts), single male politicians insulate themselves from the assumption that they might prefer those of their own sex. So, for example, aides to bachelor California Governor Jerry Brown made sure that his dates with stars Candice Bergen, Liv Ullmann, and Linda Ronstadt were publicized. During his 1974 campaign, "some campaign strategists considered, mostly in jest, producing a television commercial in which a beautiful Swedish blonde would have gazed into the camera and murmured, 'I don't know a thing about American politics. All I know is, I'm voting for Jerry Brown because he's great in bed.' "[55] Former Miss America Bess Meyerson performed the same function for New York mayoral candidate and then mayor Ed Koch.

The sports and war metaphors that characterize U.S. political discussion are usually associated with heterosexual masculinity and male-identified sports. Reporters, for example, analogize winning a debate to slam dunking the opponent or scoring a knock-out blow. Such references usually don't summon the image of a woman on the court or in the ring. At the same time, odd synonyms applied only to males question whether they are "tough" enough for the office they seek. As George Bush contemplated his 1988 run for the presidency, the press speculated on whether he would be hurt by the "wimp factor." Two years later, Bush's media consultant characterized Democratic Senator Paul Simon as a "weenie." In addition to defining women out of the political domain, this sort of language heightens our sense that the person aspiring to public office should satisfy our expectations of "manliness."

Senator Joseph McCarthy coined the phrase "Communists and perverts." Ridicule of suspect masculinity is at the core of a 1952 Stevenson ad attacking Eisenhower. In a falsetto voice, the male announcer whines "Ike. [Sigh] Bob [Sigh] Oh Ike." Then returning to a natural pitch, the announcer asks if Bob (Taft) and Ike have made a deal that would permit Taft to run an Eisenhower White House. The ad closes with a woman singing to the tune "Rueben." "Rueben, Rueben, I've been thinking. Ike and Bob don't think alike. With the General in the White House, who'll give the orders, Bob or Ike." The tune concludes: "Let's vote for Adlai and John."

Just below the surface of the Army-McCarthy hearings was the whisper that McCarthy had sought to exempt David Schine from military duty because Schine and McCarthy aide Roy Cohn were involved in a homosexual relationship. In the hearings, Senator John McClellan asks Cohn, "[I] will ask you if you have any special interest in Mr. Schine?"

> *Cohn:* "I don't know what you mean by 'special interest.' He is a friend of mine."
> *McClellan:* "I mean in friendship or anything else which would bind you to him closer than to the ordinary friend."
> *Cohn:* "Nothing. He is one of a number of very good friends whom I have. I am fortunate to have a large number."

Two decades later, one of McCarthy's victims, Lillian Hellman, immortalized the hearings and the hints about sexual orientation. McCarthy "and his boys, Roy Cohn and David Schine—the brash but less assured older brothers of Haldeman and Ehrlichman—were indeed a threesome: Schine's little-boy college face, Cohn plump of body, pout of sensual mouth, and McCarthy, a group breaking up before our eyes after years of a wild ride. Bonnie, Bonnie and Clyde, shooting at anything that came to hand on the King's horses that rode to battle in official bulletproof armor."[56]

When LBJ aide Walter Jenkins was arrested during the 1964 campaign for soliciting a male in the men's room of the YMCA, California Republicans created a bumper sticker that read "Johnson is King and Jenkins is Queen." One of Goldwater's TV ads claimed that Jenkins was "Johnson's *closest* friend." Goldwater's own reaction was muted by his own history with Jenkins. As his superior in the Air Force Reserve, Goldwater had written a glowing commendation of Jenkins.

In his race against Jim Hunt and six years later against Harvey Gantt, North Carolina Senator Jesse Helms also would insert "gay rights" into a text that in earlier campaigns would have referred instead to black rights. "Last week wealthy self-proclaimed 'gay-rights' activists co-hosted a posh, Hollywood-style fundraising party at TV producer Norman Lear's Beverly Hills mansion," reported a letter sent by Helms to his supporters in August 1983. Why did the activists meet? To raise money to pump "into a vicious Liberal 'hit squad' to crush my Senate Campaign." Why should you contribute to stop this anti-Helms campaign? "They insist on being considered a 'legitimate minority'—like blacks, Hispanics, and other ethnic groups—so they can collect *millions* of your tax dollars in government benefits. . . . They already have a bundle of your tax dollars! . . . They got $41,000 in CETA tax dollars to stage 'The Leaping Lesbian Follies,' which featured women (only) cavorting in the nude. And your tax money paid fourteen young homosexuals to stage 'Lavender Horizons,' a production of the 'Seattle Gay Youth Summer Theatre.' *Any* conservative who has tried to *get the 'gay-rights' activists' hands out of your wallet* has become their political punching bag."

In the rhetoric of Jesse Helms, we see an alliance between what he presumes to be promiscuous, perverse sexual activity and promiscuous, perverse "liberal" expenditure of tax revenue. There is an association as well between blacks and gays. The assault on "your tax dollars" is being led by a collage of villains—who by implication are now in league with gay rights activists. What they share is the label: liberal. "If it were just Jesse Helms whom the so-called 'gay-rights' crowd, and Jesse Jackson and the big union bosses were after—believe me, I wouldn't be bothering you," writes Helms to his supporters. "But it is not just Jesse Helms the Liberals are after. . . . They are after your tax money—the fruits of a lifetime of your labor."

A Freudian might read symbolic significance into Helms' use of such phrases as "cut off Federal support," "these people are soliciting—and receiving—$1000 contributions," "they spilled out into the streets," "they're pumping it [money] into a vicious Liberal 'hit squad' to crush my Senate campaign," "They are after your tax money—the fruits of a lifetime of your labor," and "keep their hands out of your wallet." The gay rights activists are even depriving Helms of his own homelife. If it weren't that the gay rights crowd is after "your tax money . . . I would be home in Raleigh, with my wife Dot and our four grandchildren, whom I rarely get to see these days because of my 18 hour Senate days."[57] Sociologists have long recognized that "images of 'we' and 'they' are significant in establishing one's own identity, in legitimizing actions and programs, and in providing rationales and models for attaining goals. Invoking the enemy makes it possible to moralize by counter-example."[58]

But even in attacks on this newest out-group there are limits. When a tabloid supporting Helms ran an article titled "Jim Hunt is Sissy, Prissy, Girlish and Effeminate," which claimed that in college Helms' opponent Jim Hunt had "a lover who was a pretty young boy" and as governor kept "a girl friend in his office," Helms canceled all advertising in the tabloid and disclaimed the attack.[59]

Veiled Attack: Harnessing Fears While Retaining Plausible Deniability

Some campaign themes dare not speak their name. They play to whispered fears, prejudices privately held but publicly denied. They are powerful means of channeling hostilities toward one candidate or away from another. A number of recent political campaigns can be understood as carriers of double messages—one acknowledged by the candidate, the other "plausibly denied," one socially acceptable, the other taboo.

As Congress struggled to unravel the Reagan administration's arms for hostages deal known as Iran-Contra, a new exculpatory phrase entered the American political lexicon. Vice Admiral John Poindexter described the concept in his testimony to the congressional committee studying Iran-Contra. "I made a deliberate decision not to ask the President," said Poindexter, "so that I could insulate him from the decision and provide some future deniability for the President if it ever leaked out."[60] When veiled attack succeeds, it accomplishes its end without endangering its creator. It is plausibly deniable.

Masters of persuasion use dual codes either to mystify one audience while seducing another or to convey meanings that for varying reasons could not be made explicit. This analysis will explain how uniquely televisual distortions of the image of black North Carolina Senate candidate Harvey Gantt and his campaign manager Mel Watt served as code-switching cues that invited susceptible North Carolina audiences in 1990 to ventilate their fears of unemployment, immigrant labor, affirmative action programs, preferential hiring for minorities, minority set-aside contracts, a shaky economy, or a future in which their children might not be as well off as their parents would wish. At the same time, the supposition that what was being shown was actual speech by the candidate and his advisor insulated Helms from the charge that this was either ad hominem attack or racist.

Codes and Cues

In *The Advancement of Learning,* Francis Bacon noted that doubled meaning can keep the vulgar from awareness of "the secrets of knowledge, and to reserve them to selected auditors, or wits of such sharpness as can pierce the veil."[61] In contemporary politics, the "vulgar" have become the audience for discourse that contains messages no longer utterable without social penalty before the public at large.

The problem for the critic, of course, resides in the fact that the subtext succeeds only to the extent that its dual meaning is not trumpeted but whispered. Still persuaders often leave clues in the form of otherwise inexplicable details, small lapses in generic propriety, minute blunders— all designed to whisper and gently prompt the sensitive, susceptible audience to divine subtextual meaning. In swayable audiences, these cues invite code switching—a shift from the explicit to the implicit text.

All these issues come to the fore when code words, images, voices, or tones are constructed to telegraph what is otherwise socially unspeakable by a public figure. So, for example, in June 1989, the Republican National Committee distributed a memo titled "Tom Foley: Out of the Liberal Closet." The memo paired Foley's record with that of Rep. Barney Frank (D. Mass.), who had publicly stated that he is gay. The ostensible point of the memo was arguing that Foley was not a moderate but like Frank a liberal. "The headline and use of Frank, who is gay, for comparison purposes was widely interpreted on Capitol Hill as an unsubtle insinuation about Foley's personal life," noted the *Washington Post.*[62] As a chorus of condemnation mounted in the press and on Capitol Hill, the aide who had issued the memo resigned.

Most of us associate the phrase "code words" with the segregationist rhetoric of Southern politicians. In the 1960s, as federal troops implemented orders to desegregate colleges and universities, code words for segregation emerged. These words gained their meaning in contexts where they stood for denial of racial equality. In Alabama, Governor George Wallace did not use any of the words the South had fashioned to label those whose ancestors were transported here in slave ships. "I stand here today as Governor of this sovereign state and refuse to willingly submit to illegal usurpation of power by the central government," said Wallace. "I claim today for all the people of the state of Alabama those rights reserved to them under the Constitution of the United States. Among those powers so reserved in claim is the right of State authority in the operation of the public schools, colleges, and universities."

"States' rights" is a claim that echoed throughout the debates over abolition and Reconstruction in the nineteenth century. In the 1960s the cry was also sounded to bar entry of black students into a Mississippi school. The federal officers at their sides bore witness to the fact that a federal claim to their right to equal education was about to be enforced. In such moments, the meaning that "states' rights" had absorbed in almost a century of struggle was made real for new generations in both North and South, some of whom were unaware that it was the rallying cry of those who defended slavery.

In a contest that almost upset the incumbent, Goldwater conservative James Martin campaigned for the Senate in Alabama in 1962 against Lister Hill by holding forth "earnestly on 'states' rights' and 'constitutional government.' Both expressions had become code words for segregation. The use of federal troops in Oxford to uphold the supreme law of the land was somehow a violation of 'constitutional government.' "[63]

Veiled Verbal Cueing

Public and press interest in veiled discourse has been magnified by the demonstrated vote-getting ability of David Duke, who in three Louisiana races has managed to claim the majority of the ballots cast by white voters. When the former Ku Klux Klan Grand Wizard was elected to a seat in the Louisiana State House of Representatives, his victory speech was different in style and tone from the cartoons included in his former newspapers *The Racialist* and *The Klansman*. These depicted "blacks assaulting whites or blacks as watermelon-eating Uncle Toms unable to function without the direction of the anti-white federal government." One cartoon titled, "Where will it all end?" showed "a white taxpayer, shackled by six blacks clamoring for money from government programs."[64] The cartoons and the victory speech shared an explicit and implicit invitation to attribute the problems of whites to blacks.

> "I can't begin to tell you how much I love you all," declared the victorious candidate. "This isn't a victory for me, it was a victory for those who believe in true equal rights for all, not the racial discrimination of affirmative action and minority set-asides. It was a victory for those who choose to work hard rather than abuse welfare. It was a victory for the poor people who want drug dealers and abusers out of their housing projects and away from their children. It was a victory for the hard-pressed taxpayer and homeowner. . . . It was a victory for the victim rather than the brutal criminal. It was a victory for the young people of Louisiana who demanded the right to attend their own neighborhood schools, to be safe and sound there, and to be educated to the extent of their ability."[65]

Unspoken but read by at least some Duke enthusiasts was the assumption that the hard-pressed taxpayers and homeowners are white and the welfare abusers, criminals, and beneficiaries of busing, black.

Disavowed by the national leaders of his own party in the 1991 gubernatorial race, Republican David Duke had drawn more votes than incumbent Buddy Roemer, and was now facing former governor Edwin Edwards in the run-off. Duke had joined the Ku Klux Klan after college, and in 1975 became a Klan Grand Wizard. In 1980, "amid allegations that he was videotaped trying to sell the organization's secret membership rolls," Duke left the Klan. "That same year, he founded the National Association for the Advancement of White People [NAAWP], which advertises racist and Nazi books."[66] Duke headed the NAAWP until 1989. The organization's early newsletters bore such headlines as "Black Charged With Atlanta Murders—We Told You So." In November 1991, one caption read, "White Woman Brutally Beaten by Gang of Blacks as Crowd Looks On." The current leader of the organization denies that it is a white supremacist group, declaring it a "civil rights organization seeking equality for everyone."[67]

After unsuccessfully seeking the 1988 Democratic nomination for president, Duke accepted the nomination of the fringe Populist Party, an umbrella organization for neo-Nazis, skinheads, and Klansmen. "I can tell you," said Duke in his one regionally aired half-hour TV ad, "the Zionists have long ago bought George Bush and Michael Dukakis." On the ballot in twelve states, he garnered 48,267 votes. In 1989, Duke won a place in the Louisiana State House. A year later, he received 44 percent of the vote for a U.S. Senate seat, losing to Democrat J. Bennett Johnston. It was in the race against Johnston that Duke began publicly calling himself a Christian.

Throughout 1991, the National Association for the Advancement of White People continued to operate from Duke's office. The editors of its newsletter told reporters that "When David is not in session in the Legislature, he's here every day advising us or meeting with his constituents in his legislative office. When in session, he's only a phone call away."[68]

Edwin Edwards served as Louisiana governor from 1972–1980. During that time, five grand juries investigated him for corruption without filing charges. Forbidden by state law to seek a third consecutive term, Edwards did not run again until 1983. That campaign was clouded by an ongoing federal grand jury investigation that ultimately produced an indictment on racketeering charges involving hospital certifications. After a first trial ended with a hung jury, Edwards was acquitted in a second trial. Meanwhile, the state's once booming oil economy had crashed. So too had Edwards's popularity.

If voters took Louisiana gubernatorial candidate David Duke at his word in 1991, they would forecast that as governor he would try to eliminate programs that provide special help to minorities, oppose busing to achieve school integration, encourage welfare recipients to practice birth control, and require that those on welfare work for their checks. He would oppose new taxes while reserving the decision to renew existing, supposedly temporary, sales taxes. He would cut the size of the state workforce through attrition, track children by ability groupings in the schools, provide tax credits for those who enroll their children in private schools, and favor evaluating local teachers using state-drawn guidelines.

Explicitly, Duke said, "I do think the black people of good will, and there are so many in our state, simply want equal rights. That's what most people want. And they're concerned as well about the crime in their communities. They are concerned about what happens to their paychecks. And we do have to work together."[69] Duke also attacked Edwards for encouraging black voter registration,[70] claimed that liberals were "blackmailing" the state,[71] by threatening to take convention business elsewhere if he were elected, and accused Edwards of being a member of the National Association for the Advancement of Colored People. Edwards admitted membership in the NAACP, noting that that put him in the company of such "liberals" as Barry Goldwater and Ronald Reagan.

One of Duke's few slips occurred on October 22 when he said that blacks had been enticed to register with offers of "fried chicken." When pressed, he denied that the remark employed a racial stereotype.[72]

Duke repeatedly renounced his identification with the Klan and with Nazism and affirmed his rebirth as a Christian. "The thing that has really affected me more than anything," Duke told voters, "is my relationship with Christ. I'm a Christian. And I believe that through Christ all of us become more loving and see things in a different way than we saw them before."[73] After making the gubernatorial run-off in October 1991, Duke thanked his supporters and Christ, "who he said has helped him more than any person in his life."[74] The claim to Christian transformation resonated with some voters. Duke supporters brought bibles to rallies for him to sign.[75]

Duke's skill in using the rhetorical forms of both Christianity and television is evident in a sharp exchange he had with a black reporter in a televised debate between the gubernatorial candidates on November 6, 1991. The moment was symbolically powerful, a Rorschach test of an audience member's dispositions. The black questioner held the power of asking whatever he liked; expected to answer was a white man who had in the past questioned the intellectual equality and social value of blacks. The situation is ripe with alternative readings. One might see it as affirmation of equality, a testament to the merits of the U.S. system, and the triumph of the American dream. Alternatively, one might construct it as an illustration of what is wrong with affirmative action. Subtly, Duke did the latter. "Here you see what we have come to," his answers could be read to say. "A qualified white candidate being bullied by an uppity black who got his job not because he was qualified but because he was black."

In the debate's most widely quoted exchange, the New Orleans TV anchor and debate panelist stated, "I've heard you say that Jews deserve to be in the ashbin of history. I've heard you say that horses contributed more to the building of America than blacks did. Given that kind of diabolical, evil, vile mentality, convince me, sir, and other minorities like me, why they should entrust their lives and the lives of their children to you?" Duke responded, "Mr. Robinson, I don't think there's a human being on this earth or in this state who hasn't been at some time intolerant in their life. . . . Now I regret some of the things I've said in my life. . . . But if you want to go back in Louisiana history, there's a lot of Louisiana politicians you respect who were, quote, 'racists' in their younger days. Jesse Jackson. I don't think you'd ask that question to him, but Jesse Jackson admitted spitting in white people's food when he worked in a restaurant as a young man."

Robinson followed up. "When we talk about political and economic genocide, we're not talking about intolerance. We're not talking about spitting on people, sir. But, as a new-found Christian, a born-again, are you now willing to apologize to the people, the minorities of this state whom you have so dastardly insulted?" Duke said he was and did. But he went on to call into question the anchor's fairness in bringing up such past statements. "Mr. Robinson, you're not being fair," noted Duke. "Mr. Duke, you are not being honest," replied the panelist. But Duke got the last word and in it asserted subtly that the reporter had overstepped the reporter's role. "Well, you're doing the debate here, aren't you?" asked Duke. "You're not even asking questions. You're here to put me down and that's your prerogative."

Throughout the exchange, Duke remains calm, his language unemotional. It is Robinson who speaks of genocide and indicts Duke for saying "excoriating and diabolical things," of having a "diabolical, evil, vile mentality," of "directing dastardly" insults toward blacks. Midway through their exchange, Robinson adopts the rhetoric used by the minister in the ceremony of Christian baptism. The minister asks, "Do you renounce Satan?" First the infant's sponsors and later the adult respond, "I do renounce Satan."

Having accused Duke of trafficking in the diabolical, Robinson employs a form of discourse that in its original incarnation signals a commitment to Christianity. "Do you repudiate the Klan?" asks Robinson. "I do repudiate the Klan," answers Duke. "And the neo-Nazis?" continues Robinson. Duke breaks from the pattern to reassert control of the exchange. "Any other racist organization or intolerant organization that exists in this state or this country. I think we've all got to work together. But you don't make up for past discrimination by putting new discrimination on people with these affirmative action programs and policies."

The station carrying the debate, WLPB, was "flooded with phone calls condemning the debate in general and Robinson's remarks in particular."[76] The talk show on WWL-AM was scheduled to devote one hour to discussion of the debate but so intense were the calls and so backed up the switchboard that the show was extended to three hours. Underlying the anti-Robinson calls was the claim that Robinson had asked the questions in a way that overstepped the line between journalism and ideologically driven advocacy. "Reporters have grilled Duke about those subjects before," noted a reporter for the *Times-Picayune.* "But by couching his queries in personal, passionate terms, Robinson rather than Duke became the center of controversy."[77] Incubating in the parenthetical phrases that rushed onto the air was a second claim. Robinson, they believed, had demonstrated that he didn't deserve his job.

Duke's opponents assumed that with or without a white robe, he was a racist whose rhetoric of conservative moderation camouflaged his racism and anti-Semitism. In an effort to demonstrate that his conversion was genuine and his opponents unchristian, Duke asked those without guilt to throw the first stone. After all, he repeatedly told audiences, hadn't Jesse Jackson and Clarence Thomas been Black Panthers in their youths? Hadn't Jesse Jackson admitted to spitting in white people's food? Hadn't Jane Fonda supported our enemy when she visited Hanoi? Why were they forgiven their youthful indiscretions when he was not?

There was much in Duke's past to disclaim. In 1976, Duke had disrupted a state ceremony honoring a black governor from the reconstruction era by entering the state House of Representatives "leading a white companion in blackface on a leash."[78]

At the age of thirty-nine Duke "spoke admiringly of Josef Mengele, the Nazi who conducted experiments on Jewish and other inmates at Auschwitz," wrote one nationally syndicated columnist. "He called Mengele 'a genius.' In the 1980s he formed the National Association for the Advancement of White People and edited its newspaper. In it, he said: 'Rapes resulting from street abduction and break-ins are a plague intrinsically associated with blacks.' He said: 'Jews are not good Americans. They have no understanding of what America is.'" "How," asked the columnist, "could such a person become a serious political force? How could anyone believe his pious assertions that his years of professional hate were 'youthful indiscretions?'"[79]

Duke's past contains ample evidence of anti-Semitism and racism. Unsigned letters in the NAAWP's newsletter condemn Jews for cutting "a wide trail of disgust in history." In a signed article titled "Black Population Bomb," Duke in 1988 wrote, "The choice is clear. You and your actions over the next few decades will decide who will propagate and who will not, who will control and who will be controlled. Is there any sincere white person who really wants their children to live in the nightmare that we are rushing toward?"[80] This rhetoric could readily be mined by those who saw only one plausible answer to Duke's rhetorical insinuation. "You know what's wrong with our schools," said one Duke flier. "You know where the crime problem lies. You know who's carrying the load. You know who's abusing the system."

Liberal columnists provided a translation of Duke's discourse. "If you don't speak white supremacist," noted the *New York Time*'s Anna Quindlen, "here's a handy guide: 'the liberal social welfare system which encourages the rising illegitimate welfare birthrate' means 'poor black people are having babies on your tax dollars.' "[81] Similarly, reporters Bill Walsh and James O'Byrne wrote in the *Times-Picayune* that "When he says 'we,' he means white people. When he speaks of welfare cheats, he means black people. When he speaks of New York interests, he means Jewish people."[82]

The Duke-Edwards campaign demonstrates the extent to which meaning is created by hearers, viewers, and listeners. In the campaign, Duke carefully avoided language that could be identified as "coded" or "racist." Repeatedly, he disclaimed his Klan past, saying that Christianity had taught him tolerance. Yet when the press contacted those from outside Louisiana who were contributing to his campaign, they were told by a Florida supporter, "The man was a KKK member. Big deal. The KKK is not worse than being a Democrat or a Republican." A Texas contributor noted, "Seems like all the other politicians go out and kowtow to any race that has the right to vote."[83]

Letters to the editor revealed the appeal of Duke's message. "Those who help themselves should not have to scrape and scrounge and go to charity hospitals and wonder how to make ends meet from one day to the next while we support those who don't help themselves," wrote a Duke supporter in Colfax.[84]

"Why is it wrong for a person to express his thoughts about the rights of white people while so many politicians are [too] afraid of the blacks to express their honest opinions?" asked one letter writer. "I knew a lot of good men who belonged to the KKK when I was growing up, and there were no murders or making people disabled by these men. It is a good thing your newspaper has no competition."[85]

"Have you ever thought that if our kids could get on these give-away programs that there would be as many white kids playing sports as black?" asked one letter writer. "If they didn't do anything else but play ball they could be as good as the other athletes."[86]

"I've been reading your newspaper for about the last four years and you have made it very clear to me, and to everyone else, that you will go to any extent to promote the advancement of blacks in the face of the white race," wrote one subscriber to the *Times-Picayune*. "The people who voted for Duke know everything about his past. We know what uniform he wore in college, that he was in the Klan and whose birthday he celebrated in the 1980s. We know he didn't care for Negroes, believed in apartheid and had a burning passion to exploit the white race as a superior and well-disciplined machine as the German race was in the late thirties and early forties. What you don't know is that we don't care. What we do care about is the way every city in this country is being reduced to ghettos because of the black race here in this country. Just look at the murder rate in Louisiana this year—who is the majority of it committed by? Blacks. Blacks make up most of the violent crime in the United States, the most inmates on death row, and almost all of the drug crime too. I and many other whites believe that welfare, affirmative action, forced busing, minority set-asides, subsidized housing and redistricting have caused this horrible problem now and for years to come. . . . We know about his past, we know about Louisiana's future, we know he doesn't care for Negroes, we know he won't get along with the Legislature and, just maybe, we like it!" [87]

As the votes were being counted, the owner of a bar in Duke's home district in Metairie told reporters, "I think it's beautiful that the white people stuck together on this one like the niggers did." [88]

"Please help me see the racial undertones in some of the things David Duke is saying," asked one letter writer. "These sound like good, intelligent ideas to me. I respect the man for being honest enough to say what a lot of politicians feel." [89]

Making sense of voters' responses to the campaign's discourse required the constant invocation of a moldy communication maxim: Meaning is in people. When shouted by the mixture of cultures and colors that is the audience for Saints games, the football cheer, created by black fans, isn't interpreted as racist but as a sign of community fellowship. "Who dat say dey gonna beat dem Saints? Who dat? Who dat?" chants the crowd, black and white. But what does a variant of that cheer mean when shouted by an all-white gathering of Duke supporters? "Who dat say dey gonna beat dat Duke? Who dat?" And what was actually being said in the closing days of the campaign, when the Saints' white quarterback Bobby Hebert appeared in a TV ad to declare, "When I step onto the field, the only color I care about is the color of a man's jersey"? Without endorsing Edwards or repudiating Duke, Hebert appealed for a Louisiana where "the black and gold as well as black and white can work together as a winning team."

As allusive were the campaign's visceral visuals. Duke in prayer. Duke in Klan robes. Duke shouldering a hunting rifle. A general in full-dress uniform condemning Duke. A football player preaching tolerance. Pictures of Adolf Hitler juxtaposed with statements by and about Duke. Scenes of burning crosses. Edwards, arms outstretched, palms marked by ketchup asserting visually that he had been crucified by the press.

Voter profiles had concluded that "the most dedicated of Duke's supporters hold virulently racist and anti-Semitic views. Rather than scrambling to explain away Duke's past, as many of his supporters do, these voters embrace it. To them, Duke is the leader of a cause to create a world where white people can live separate from black people, and 'Christian' values can thrive free from 'Jewish guilt.' " [90] But most Duke voters denied that they were racist. "While these voters reject Duke's overtly racist past, they give voice to a racial view of the world: Crime is committed mostly by black people. Good neighborhoods are white. Welfare recipients are black. Middle-class people are white. . . . Many Duke voters share a view that social programs disproportionately benefit black people. And they resent paying for programs they do not view as benefiting them." [91]

Although he carried 55 percent of the white vote and 56 percent of the Republican vote, Duke lost 39 to 61 percent. In his concession speech, he forecast his 1992 run for the presidency by saying, "This campaign was about a lot of issues, and this campaign is not over. It's only just begun. . . . A candidate may have lost but the message goes out loud and clear across Louisiana and across the nation." As Duke positioned himself to run in the 1992 Republican presidential primary in Texas, the *Dallas Morning News* finally smoked his message out. "Republican presidential candidate David Duke says he is 'proud' of his years as a Ku Klux Klan leader and still believes in 'genetic differences' based on race," said the article (January 17, 1992). "Mr. Duke also told the *Dallas Morning News* that blacks and other minorities now have the upper hand in America, and that he sees 'minority problems as a threat' to the white culture he loves." The ostensible tolerance evinced by Duke in the Louisiana race had been a ruse, the rhetoric of conversion a ploy.

Veiled Visual Cueing

As I argued in the last chapter, television has made it possible to show what cannot be said. Visual cueing is enthymematic. What occurred in the 1988 presidential campaign, the 1990 North Carolina Helms-Gantt race, and the 1991 Mabus-Fordice race in Mississippi was not verbal but visual cueing.

In 1987, a Harvard-educated progressive Democrat, Ray Mabus, was elected governor of Mississippi as a reformer. Four years later, Mabus was unseated by Republican Kirk Fordice, a Vicksburg contractor whose anti-establishment campaign attacked liberals, welfare abuse, and racial quotas. His candidacy gained momentum with his call for mandatory hard labor for Parchmount prisoners. Mabus outspent Fordice five to one.

Mabus entered the race in early 1991 with barely 50 percent support. His ambitious plans to improve state education had faltered when he failed to get the program funded. His attempts to secure approval of a lottery to support education also failed. And Mabus's national self-promotion led some Mississippians to conclude that he was more interested in being vice president than in improving his state at a time when the recession was a palpable fact in their lives. In other words, the stage was set for an anti-establishment candidacy that played on feelings of economic insecurity.

Enter Kirk Fordice. Inmates, said Fordice, should be "back in the cotton fields . . . [generating] a cash crop that could compensate victims for their crimes."[92] In the closing days of the campaign, reporters learned that Fordice had responded to a questionnaire by saying he would repeal the Voting Rights Act of 1965. When challenged on that claim, he amended his position to say that he would favor it if it were applied to all states, not simply those, such as Mississippi, with a history of voting rights discrimination. One of Fordice's television ads against the welfare system called for "workfare not welfare" and showed a stark still photo of a black woman holding a baby in her arms. However, the ad also showed a middle-class black woman pushing a shopping cart. Fordice won with less than 5 percent of the black vote and an "overwhelming" majority of the white vote.[93]

The presence of two images of black women in Fordice's ads immunized him from the challenge that he was explicitly inviting audiences to see blacks as the problem. The availability of both images meant, however, that those disposed to focus on one rather than the other—to use one as the dominant interpretive frame—were free to do so.

Democratic consultant Bob Squier had used images in a similar way on behalf of Governor James Blanchard's re-election bid in 1990. In an ad that raised the ire of civil rights activists, Squier showed a boot camp guard, who is white, shouting orders first at a white inmate, then at a black. A white supervisor also is shown surveying the work of young felons, some black, some white, who are scrubbing floors. The interpretive frame invited by the ad is revealed by the markets in which it did and did not air. The time buy placed the ads throughout the state while avoiding the Detroit media market.

In the 1990 Senatorial contest in North Carolina, former Charlotte mayor, Democrat Harvey Gantt faced the conservative Republican incumbent Jesse Helms. Helms won narrowly with 52.5 percent of the vote. At the time of the election, the state listed 2,677,162 North Carolinians as "white" and 635,045 as "black." Gantt, who needed at least 42 percent of the "white" vote to win, received 38 percent or 981,573 votes.[94,95]

In the final ten days, Gantt appeared to be slightly ahead in the polls. By the final weeks of the election, Gantt's advisors thought that the issue of race was dead. Voters now seemed to be dealing with Gantt on the issues he stressed: primarily education and environment. A third of these voters indicated that they were tired of Jesse Helms. Gantt's claim that his opponent didn't really represent North Carolina in the Senate was resonating. But in the last week and a half, something energized Helms's supporters and swung undecided voters behind him.

In early October, ads subtly priming consciousness of Gantt's blackness began to air. Ostensibly the first "race-priming ad" is about an ongoing campaign issue: abortion. Gantt supported *Roe v. Wade*. Helms opposed it. Earlier in the campaign Helms had aired an ad in which a white North Carolina woman in a red dress charges that Gantt favors abortion for sex selection and abortion in the final weeks of pregnancy. The latter claim is untrue.

The ad, whose frames are shown in Figure 3-5, focuses on the accuracy of the allegation about sex selection in that earlier Helms ad. Gantt supports *Roe v. Wade*. Helms opposes it. "Let's set the record straight,"

Figure 3-5. This oppositional ad against Harvey Gantt in the North Carolina Senate race of 1990 employs visual and tonal ad hominem against the Democrat.

says the announcer. "Harvey Gantt denied he would allow abortion for sex selection, when parents want a boy and not a girl. But Harvey Gantt told the press he would *allow* abortions" [the still of Gantt is expanded to full screen and becomes video]. Gantt says: "whether for sex selection or for whatever reason."

In an incredulous voice, as the tape rewinds, the announcer asks, "Did he say even for sex selection?" Gantt is again shown saying: "whether for sex selection or for whatever reason." As the tape rewinds a final time, the announcer instructs us to "Read his lips." The tape is replayed in slow motion, Gantt's voice now slurred to a growling, drawn-out protracted drawl, "Whether for sex selection or for any other reason."

As the screen reads "Harvey Gantt: Extremely Liberal: with the FACTS," the announcer declares, "Harvey Gantt denied he ever said that. Harvey Gantt, extremely liberal with the facts."

As the tape rewinds in each instance, the image of Gantt is transformed from color to black and white. The shadows created by the rapid rewinding image of Gantt's face alternatively lighten and darken his face. The final frames of the image are darker than the first. Moreover, in the rewinding image, Gantt looks out of control, his head bobbing from side to side. First-time viewers who are asked to characterize the sound

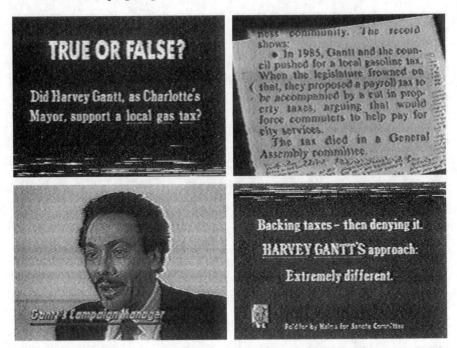

Figure 3-6. In this ad for Senator Jesse Helms (R. North Carolina) and against his Democratic opponent, Harvey Gantt, the voice of Gantt's campaign manager is made to sound odd.

of his slowed voice most often use the words "stupid," "definitely black" (one said, "the kind of really dumb black you used to see in movies"), or "growling."

The switch from color to black and white distances us from Gantt at the same time as it heightens our awareness of race. And it does so in a segment that is calling his credibility into question.

Then ads tying Gantt to gay rights activists began to register a response with high-school-educated white women.[96] One of these spots whispered that Gantt was running a "secret campaign." Why? Gantt "has run ads in gay newspapers . . . fundraising drives in gay bars in San Francisco, New York, and Washington. . . . And Harvey Gantt has promised to back mandatory gay rights laws, including requiring local schools to hire gay teachers. Harvey Gantt is dangerously liberal. Too liberal for North Carolina." On the screen throughout the ad are newspaper clips or print statements supposedly documenting the spoken claims.

A second ad encouraging racial reactions showed Gantt's black campaign manager, Mel Watt, denying Helms's charges as "an out and out distortion of the record." His statement is edited to raise his voice at the end of the claim, a cue that reduces perceived decisiveness and credibility. Additionally, his voice is acoustically reprocessed to give it a "tinny" edge. "I talked with him constantly during the campaign," recalls Gantt's pollster Michael Donlon. "I can tell you, that isn't what he sounds like at all." When asked to describe how Watts looks and sounds, not one person in any focus group offered a single positive adjective or noun.

Helms then released the one ad everyone could have foreseen. The charges in it had figured in Gantt's defeat for re-election as mayor of Charlotte. "How did Harvey Gantt become a millionaire?" asks the announcer. "He used his position as mayor and his minority status to get himself and his friends a free TV station license from the government. Only weeks later, they sold out to a white-owned corporation for three and a half million dollars. The black community felt betrayed, but the deal made the mayor a millionaire. Harvey Gantt made government work for Harvey Gantt."

But that isn't what the newspaper headlines appearing on the screen are actually saying. "Influence Peddling *Charged*." "Gantt, Partners *May* Make Millions Selling Station." "Gantt *Might* Make $3 Million By Selling TV Station." And then a repeat of "Influence Peddling *Charged*" (emphasis added).

The final oppositional ad aired by Helms showed the plaid-shirted arms and white hands of a male, a simple gold wedding ring on the third finger of his left hand, opening, presumably reading and then crumpling a rejection letter as the announcer says, "You needed that job, and you were the best qualified. But they had to give it to a minority because of a racial quota. Is that really fair? Harvey Gantt says it is. Gantt supports Ted Kennedy's racial quota law that makes the color of your skin more important than your qualifications. You'll vote on this issue next Tuesday. For racial quotas: Harvey Gantt. Against racial quotas: Jesse Helms."

When one North Carolina focus group (all members white, all high school graduates) was asked to indicate what they thought they could tell about the man in the ad, they said [each is assigned a number for identification]:

> 1: "He's middle aged." 2: "He had a blue-collar job but he got cut in the recession." 1: "He's been out of work for quite a while." 3: "He has a family to support." 1: "Yeah, a wife and kids." 4: "She can't make enough to support the family." *Focus group leader:* "Anyone else [want to add something]?" 5: "He's white." 1: "Well, of course, we knew that." 2: "He's a hard worker, all he wants is a job." 6: "I think he lives in a more rural part of the state." *Focus group leader:* "How old would you guess his children are?" 2: "They're young." 3: "They're probably in grade school." 6: "No, they could be in college." 1: "Either way he'd be worried about being able to support them." *Focus group leader:* "Would your sense of him be different if he were black?" 5: "Sure, well, the first thing is, eh, that we wouldn't be able to tell how old he is." (Laughter) 6: "It wouldn't

Figure 3-7. The subtle visual cues in this Helms ad are able to be seen clearly and analyzed carefully only when the images are frozen on the screen. Note in frame one that the shadow from the hand of the man in the ad directs your attention to the black mark on the page. The fact that it is an extension of the man's hand may be increasing the likelihood that viewers see it as a "black hand."

make sense. Blacks don't have quotas." 1: "They don't have wedding rings either." (Laughter)

The ability of the group to elaborate the image suggests that the members have a well-developed schema for the concept "unemployed white North Carolina male." The level of elaboration also suggests that the image resonated with the group. Gantt's pollster reports that the quota ad was particularly effective with college-educated white males.

The images in the ad appear in Figure 3-7. Note the black mark that appears on the middle of the "rejection letter" in its left margin. The shadow extending from the hand of the job applicant forms a natural line to the black mark focusing our attention—even if briefly—on it. Note too that in the final frames Gantt is "for racial" and Helms is "against quotas." Here the shot of Gantt is closer—more menacing—than that of Helms. Before this apposition, the hands have exerted control. The fist once clenched in anger is now clenched in action: crushing Teddy Kennedy's head and about to encircle Gantt's! Only one focus group respondent of 77 interviewed in four states including North Carolina reported, without its being pointed out by pausing the frame, that the white hands are poised to crush the photos in the ad's final frames.

Just over one-third of the North Carolina respondents report without prompting that they have seen "some sort of black mark on the letter." Those who report it without prompting are nearly twice as likely to finally report that they would vote for Helms. Of those seeing the black mark, four describe it as "a black hand" or "a black hand holding a black gun." The four people who offered these descriptions cast their final votes in the focus group for Helms.

The admaker contends that the hands clenching the pictures and the black mark carried no special intent. The black mark on the paper "means nothing," says Alex Castellanos, who created the quota ad. "We just grabbed a piece of paper." As for the hands, "It was a natural dissolve to carry the message from one scene to the next. An abrupt cut would have been too jarring."

Paired non-North Carolina groups were exposed to the "broadcast license" and "white hands" ads after seeing four oppositional Helms ads that make no mention of gay rights advocacy and use no direct visual or tonal priming about race. The groups that did not see the "mandated gay teachers," "manager," and "the visual rewind" ads are nearly two and a half times less likely to use pejorative language when referring to race when discussing the "white hands" ad. In other words, those who see the ad featuring the manager, the ad rewinding Gantt's picture, and the ad alleging that Gantt would mandate hiring gay teachers before they see the "broadcast license" and the "white hands" ads are nearly two and a half times more likely to speak in racially pejorative terms about Gantt than those not primed by those earlier ads.

Any conclusions drawn from focus group work must be offered very tentatively. I cannot say with any form of social scientific reliability that the five Helms ads just described are what swayed undecided voters, but data from two focus groups of eighteen white blue-collar and rural undecided voters suggests that that is what occurred with them. In addition, the ads were shown to fifty-two other blue-collar Southerners in six groups in the deep South and one Southwestern state and to a group of seven white highly educated voters in a Midwestern state with a small black population and little racial tension. What appears to be operating here is cueing or priming that licenses focus group members to speak to strangers with a tape recorder in ways such as these:

> "There isn't any Nigra who doesn't think he's owed a living. Every one of 'em is at the trough with his hand out." "We ought to put every one of them in trucks and send them C.O.D. to Jesse Jackson." "All I can think of is his [Harvey Gantt's] big black lips and that ugly guy's face. I was willing to think that Harvey Gantt was good, a good black. But after this. No. (pause) No." "You just have to resent it when those people who aren't qualified take away our jobs." *Focus group moderator:* "Who do you think is taking jobs?" *[Response]:* "You know, like that guy *[motions to TV*

screen which is blank] with Gantt. He's the kind Gantt would give, er, put in charge. Someone who hasn't even gone to school. Can't even, oh, I don't know. They're just taking over, that's all." "I know that it sounds prejudiced but I've worked with 'em and they know they can't be fired so their attitude is 'kiss my black ass.'" *Focus group moderator:* "So, you are saying that you've worked with blacks and" *[interrupted]* "Not by my choice. I've had trouble. You may as well say I've worked for 'em. That they won't work is a fact, a fact. Go out there and look for yourself. There's a big difference between being prejudiced and being fed up."

Survey data provide some explanations. Highly emotional, racially based resentment occasions opposition to some forms of racial equality.[97] At the same time, an increase in the number and prominence of racial appeals increases the political power of prejudice.[98]

By tying Gantt to "quotas," Helms plays on existing anti-black dispositions. Political scientists Kinder and Mendelberg note in their analysis of 1990 survey data that "each of these episodes—the uproar over school busing, the cry for more generous welfare benefits, the danger lurking in city streets and parks, the contentious and continuing debate over affirmative action and reverse discrimination—has been interpreted by many white Americans as an affront to individualism, as a sign of bad behavior and flawed character on the part of blacks."[99]

Data from the General Social Survey in 1990 reveal a pervasive theme: "the failure of blacks, in whites' eyes, to measure up to the standard of individualism. Almost one half of the whites (44.6 percent) thought that blacks tended to be lazy; more than one half (56.3 percent) believed that blacks preferred to live off welfare rather than be self-supporting; a decisive majority (60.1 percent) said that blacks have lousy jobs and crummy housing because they lack the will to pull themselves up out of poverty. Many whites also regarded blacks as dangerous. Fewer whites questioned blacks' patriotism or their inherent intelligence."[100] The groups among which prejudice is more pronounced include the elderly, Southerners, and those with less schooling.[101]

Conclusion

The content of the comparisons and contrasts that populate campaigns mirrors social dispositions. Campaigns simply reinforce themes resonating in the country in noncampaign times. This is true for several reasons. First, it would be difficult to engender new attitudes in the short span of a campaign. By contrast, it is simple and effective to reinforce existing ones. Second, a campaign is loathe to try the untested.

By attributing social ills to an identifiable enemy, campaigns invite the electorate to downplay the importance of external events and magnify the role of human design in both our own successes and failures and in those of others. Accordingly, blacks are seen as economically disadvantaged because they do not work hard enough; governmental intervention is not the solution to their problems.[102] Those who "continue to attribute combinations of events to deliberate human design may well be peculiar sorts of persons," note social psychologists, "marginal people, perhaps, removed from the centers of power, unable to grasp the conceptions of complicated causal linkages . . . and unwilling to abandon the desire to make simple and clear moral judgments of events."[103]

A 1985 study of suburban Detroit confirmed that "white Democratic defectors express a profound distate for blacks, a sentiment that pervades almost everything they think about government and politics. Blacks constitute the explanation for their [white defectors'] vulnerability and for almost everything that has gone wrong in their lives; not being black is what constitutes being middle class; not living with blacks is what makes a neighborhood a decent place to live."[104]

Most attack works by implying that the opponent rejects the values of the voters. Some of these values were stable for long periods of time. James Truslow Adams noted in 1932, "the persistence of the same topics as subjects for the unfounded slander stories. For over a hundred and thirty years of campaigning these have been almost wholly confined to sexual relations, treatment of wives, drunkenness, and the alleged possession of Negro blood."[105]

At the same time out-groups have been seen to reject the Protestant work ethic. Which group comes to mind when you hear that its members are "lazy and indolent, content either to accept public charity or beg upon the streets but unwilling to do the necessary hard work which the country required"? The same group is blamed for producing a disproportionate number of "criminals." In the discourse of the 1990s, the presumed referent for such attack would be blacks or Hispanics. In the 1830s the referent was "the foreign born."[106]

Visceral identifications and appositions that are the raw stuff of campaigns simplify the world into Manichean dualities and, in their use of the evocative and the visceral, merchandise our hopes and fears. At the same time, they offer ways of seeing that occlude rather than clarify our vision. They are exclusionary, not inclusionary. The terms they adopt are neither contested nor defined. They appropriate rather than argue, abjuring evidence for emotional evocation. They assert. The discursive model they offer is that of visceral adoption. It gains its force by repetition undignified by any invitation to reflect or reformulate. And television's rapidly paced visual telegraphy makes it more difficult to recognize and to counter moves that traffic in audience fears and stereotypes.

The adequacy of available responses to such tactics is the subject of the next chapter.

CHAPTER FOUR

Countering Attacks:
Pitting the Propositional
Against the Primal

From the beginnings of the Republic, politicians and their partisans have recognized that an attack unrebutted is an attack believed. "A falsehood that remains uncontradicted for a month, begins to be looked upon as a truth," wrote William Corbett in *Porcupine's Gazette* in 1797, "and when the detection at last makes its appearance, it is often as useless as that of the doctor who finds his patient expired." But how can one respond to telegraphic, televisual attack that prompts false conclusions?

The comparative power of the negative accounts for the fact that:

- In 1984 and 1988, the first oppositional ads of the presidential campaign aired earlier than they had any time before in the history of televised campaigns.
- In 1988 the proportion of PAC money spent on opposition advertising was higher than it had been in previous years.
- The number of oppositional ads produced increased steadily from 1956 to 1976, jumped dramatically in 1980 and then reverted to the earlier upswinging trend line in 1984 and 1988.
- In most presidential years the most aired ad has been self-promotional; in 1988 the most aired candidate ad was oppositional.

Can primal, illegitimate attacks be blunted with argument and evidence or is response in kind the strategically albeit not ethically advisable countering move? One characteristic of powerful oppositional ads offers

102

a glimmer of hope. Despite their visceral, visual character, oppositional ads also tend to carry a high level of "factual content." Indeed, most oppositional advertising shares four characteristics.

1. The stronger the attack, the greater the amount of specific factual content in the ad. There are notable exceptions. In 1968, for example, an ad for George Wallace showed shouting protesters and burning buildings as it instructed viewers to "Look America. Take a good look. Ask yourself, Why are the anti-American anti-God anarchists also violently anti-Wallace? Want to get rid of them? Vote for a law-abiding God-fearing America and for Mr. Wallace."
2. The stronger the attack, the more likely the ad is to cite multiple sources of support including direct quotation of the opposing candidate.
3. The stronger the attack, the greater the likelihood that the claims will be ascribed to some presumably neutral, nonpartisan authority such as a newspaper.
4. The amount of factual content is higher in oppositional and engaged ads than in self-promotional ads.

Two protections exist against ad pollution: the maligned candidate's use of "free" and "paid" time and the self-protections insulating those not reliant solely on ads for political substance. The first uses what consultants call "free time" against what they term "paid time." Doing this usually means that the attacked candidate responds to the false ad at a press conference. A portion of the press conference is then digested in broadcast and print news. Alternatively, the attacked candidate can respond in a telecast debate.

While of some value, reliance on news and debates is not an ideal solution. First, the audiences for ads and these two other forms differ. Far more people see political ads than watch debates, read about politics in a daily newspaper, or spend dinner with Peter Jennings. Additionally, a debate or news piece will respond to the questionable ad once while the ad itself can air many times. Repetition gives the ad a natural advantage. Moreover, news and debates tend to use words as their weapons. In the contest between evocative pictures and spoken words, pictures usually win. Finally, as I argue in the next chapter, news coverage has more often been part of the problem than part of the solution. Most newscasts in 1988 magnified the power of false advertising rather than minimizing it.

The second protection is a well-informed electorate. "The democratic citizen is . . . supposed to know what the issues are, what their history is, what the relevant facts are, what alternatives are proposed . . . [and] the likely consequences,"[1] wrote Berelson, Lazarsfeld, and McPhee almost forty years ago. Not so, countered Anthony Downs. Because the

Figure 4-1. The telegraphic power of visual communication is well illustrated by these photographs of images from the 1964 campaign. The two pictures of the "Klan" are from an ad that did not air. After Goldwater repudiated the Klan's endorsement, the Democratic strategists concluded that airing the ad would create an anti-Johnson backlash. As a result the ad was shelved.

cost of fully informed voting outweighs the benefits, a rational person instead bases decisions on such informational shortcuts as party identification. If shortcuts yield the same voting decision, then being only minimally informed makes sense.[2]

Cognitive psychologists Amos Tversky and Daniel Kahneman have documented the inevitability of shortcuts in human decision making.[3] Unfortunately, these shortcuts give emotionally compelling data inappropriate weight in the decision-making process. And what televised ads are best at is flooding our consciousness with emotionally compelling data. After seeing William Horton's glowering mug shot and observing the grim circling convicts of the furlough ad, it is unlikely that we will believe that here was an isolated instance, an aberration in an otherwise successful furlough program. Yet those were the facts.

The good news is that citizens "are remarkably accurate in estimating the issue positions of strategic groups in politics, including groups like liberals and conservatives about which one might well suppose the mass public to be ignorant."[4] Those without much political information are also pretty good at determining how well off they are and holding the incumbent accountable.[5]

The bad news is that artful advertising reinforced by candidate speeches can pit evocative visuals and atypical instances against more traditional and more reliable forms of political evidence such as party affiliation and the endorsements of trusted persons and groups. The 1988 presidential campaign provides a case in point. Historically, voters have believed that the Democrats were better for the environment than the Republicans. That belief persisted in 1988. Consistent with that history, the major nonpartisan environmental groups endorsed the Democrat in that election. Overall, despite negative marks for Boston Harbor, for supporting what environmentalists considered overdevelopment of waterfront areas, and for backing incineration over recycling, the evidence and the endorsements suggest that Dukakis had the better environmental record. The recommendations of Bush's Presidential Task Force on Regulatory Relief had been widely condemned by environmentalists who did not approve of delaying removal of lead from gasoline, suspending if only temporarily the federal program for toxic waste control, and delaying fuel-efficiency standards. And Reagan environmental appointees James Watt and Anne Burford remained on the enemies list of most of those in the environmental movement. Overall, there were clear reasons to prefer Dukakis to Bush on environmental matters.

Onto the air went the pollution-clotted Boston Harbor ad. It capitalized on the fact that new information that is vivid and accessible drives out the old and the abstract. Moreover, the sludge and slime appeared where voters were already looking—between popular prime-time programs. Recurrent one-liners by Bush about Boston Harbor reinforced the ad's visuals. The result: Where in mid-summer voters perceived that Dukakis had the better environmental record, by election day Bush had all but closed the gap. The lesson: unrepresentative instances dramatized in ads can override the more traditional and more abstract cues obtained from party, group endorsements, and past candidate performance.

Whether motivated voters or effective counter-advertising can overcome the disabling shortcuts invited by rapidly paced, visually driven, symbolically powerful ads is a difficult question. At some level, awareness helps. Because the purchase of gasoline is no longer an incidental expense, most of us realize that "discount for cash" means "surcharge for credit cards." But the evidence that voters are eager to invest more time in gathering political information is all but non-existent.

What is clear is that if the opposing candidate can purchase comparable air time, a response ad can locate the same audience as the original attack. One tragedy of our current system is that without fundraising prowess or personal wealth, candidates cannot now secure sufficient time to respond effectively to unfair ads.

What is at issue is whether legitimate forms of response do exist to counter ad pollution. A third and final avenue open to the unfairly attacked candidate is counter-advertising, using ads against ads. That protection and its strategic manifestations are the focus of this chapter.

Countering Attacks

Because the simplest and most powerful response to visceral attack is visceral counter-attack, it's tempting to counter an illegitimate ad by displacing with an illegitimate counter-charge. This move does not rebut; instead it attempts at best to replace one horrific image with another, at worst to do unto the other as the other had done unto you, thereby making it difficult for the voter to cast a vote based on the initial attack. Displacement was at work in the Republican response in the 1986 Wisconsin Senate race to the charges of Democrat Edward Garvey that incumbent Robert Kasten (R. Wis.) had been "drinking on the job." Kasten's ad didn't address this charge. Instead, it counter-attacked with another visceral charge. "What would you think of a candidate who pays thousands of dollars to someone who impersonates a reporter and spreads lies about his opponent?" asked the Kasten ad. "There is no place in Wisconsin for Watergate tactics."

Similarly, in September 1990, Republican Jim Edgar attacked his Democratic opponent Attorney General Neil Hartigan with what Edgar's media consultant termed "the bomb." That ad "tacitly encouraged viewers to assume that [a 1968] failure was connected to the current S&L debacle, that depositors lost money and that Hartigan had been guilty of wrongdoing. . . . [T]he S&L had gone under in 1968, depositors were made whole and charges against Hartigan were dropped nearly two decades ago. Not a word of this was in the ad."[6] Hartigan responded by indicting Edgar for a "scandal" in the secretary of state's office. The "scandal" involved low-level workers. More important, it was Edgar who had found the problem and corrected it.

Often these counter-attacks are as illegitimate as the original they seek to displace. How can one respond to use of an atypical instance? With an atypical counter-instance. Late in the 1988 campaign, Dukakis matched the Republicans one menacing killer. He then upped the ante. Where the Republicans argued, in effect, that Dukakis was responsible for William Horton's rape of a woman and assault on her fiancé, the Democrats responded that, in effect, Bush was responsible for the murder of a pregnant mother of two.

The Democratic ad dredged up the story of a convicted federal drug felon who escaped from a halfway house to murder Patsy Pedrin. Both ads argued from the atypical instance. Both deserved to be rejected.

Had the Democratic ad begun airing shortly after the Horton attacks went on the air and had it not relied on a smiling picture of the victim for its visual impact, it might have succeeded. As it was, the Republicans offered a glowering mug shot of William Horton; the Democrats countered with a much less menacing photo of the drug dealer and then undercut the power of their own claim by showing the smiling victim as if she had somehow survived the attack to live happily ever after.

But if the visceral response anchors one end of the advertising continuum, the purely propositional anchors the other. While the visceral lodges quickly in consciousness, the propositional, at least in its usual form, does not. Michael Dukakis learned this in 1988 when he responded to the Bush tank ad's distortions of his record with a five-minute spot in which he talked directly into the camera about George Bush's false ad. Focus groups easily remembered the tank and easily forgot the rebuttal. Harvey Gantt's adteam made the same mistake when it responded to Jesse Helms's visceral, visual claim that Gantt favored racial quotas with a propositional denial by Gantt.

Still, there are alternatives to an eye for eye and a kick in the teeth for a kick in the teeth. If an attack can be anticipated, the most effective action is pre-emption through use of inoculation. Inoculation anticipates the attack, provides a recap of the lines of argument supporting it, rebuts it, and builds a supportive base of evidence to sustain the attacked position. When confronted with the attacking information, the voter is able to recall the defense and by so doing fend off the attack.[7] Inoculation arms the audience with counter-arguments.

Forewarning that manipulation is on the horizon is also effective.[8] So, for example, when listeners are alerted that a speech is designed to persuade them, they are less influenced by it than a group not forewarned.[9] These strategies too are subject to abuse. In the 1990 Texas gubernatorial race, one ad claimed of State Attorney General and gubernatorial candidate Jim Maddox, "If his lips are moving, he may be lying."

Forewarning was used more legitimately in an earlier Texas race. In 1982 Democrat Lloyd Bentsen anticipated attacks by the National Conservative Political Action Committee. He protected himself by pre-emptively attacking NCPAC's credibility. "During the next few weeks you're going to see some distasteful television commercials by some Washington promoters specializing in lies and half-truths. NCPAC has joined James Collins in an attack on Senator Lloyd Bentsen. NCPAC is the same organization that said it could elect Mickey Mouse, that brags the NCPAC can lie through its teeth, and the candidate it helps stays clean. So when you see those ads, remember, NCPAC and James Collins are not trying to build, they're trying to destroy. And that's not the way we do things in Texas."

Successful responses invite audiences to question the legitimacy of the attack and, by implication, the person who has sunk so low. They distance the viewer from the original ad by using humor, testing the plausibility of the ad's claims, and establishing that the ad has gulled the unwary viewer. This is best done by citing credible sources such as respected newspapers or employing credible respondents, by using accurate information, and by inviting central analytic processing of the problematic ad.

In other words, successful responses reframe. Psychiatrists tell us that "people are most influenced when they expect a certain message and receive instead a message at a totally different level."[10] None of the responses I examine in this chapter engages the actual attack. Each instead communicates about the attacking communication. It metacommunicates. And in this communication about communication it invites us to see the attack differently; it reframes. Watzlawick and his colleagues define reframing as a process of altering the meaning attributed to a situation by changing the context or frame through which we experience it.[11] Reframing casts the person who was being controlled as the controller of the situation and its definition. It empowers.[12]

Reframing

In 1978 Senator John Tower of Texas engaged in a classic act of reframing. Tower's opponent was making much of the fact that he had refused to shake his hand. A similar act would prove equally powerful when Clayton Williams refused Ann Richards' hand in 1990. In 1978, Tower appeared in an ad that reframed the meaning of the widely circulated photos. Holding up a newspaper showing the picture, Tower invites us to see the act in a new context. In that context, the act is not one of incivility but of honor. "Perhaps you've seen this picture of my refusal to shake the hand of my opponent," says Tower. "I was brought up to believe that a handshake is a symbol of friendship and respect, not a meaningless hypocritical gesture. My opponent has slurred my wife, my daughters, and falsified my record. My kind of Texan doesn't shake hands with that kind of man. Integrity is one Texas tradition you can count on me to uphold."

In 1983, Republican Bernard Epton faced Democrat Harold Washington in the Chicago mayoral contest. Epton was white, Washington black. Among other things, Epton's radio ads falsely accused Washington of being a "convicted felon" and of having been "disbarred." An unsigned leaflet alleged that Washington had once been arrested on a morals charge. Epton's slogan, widely criticized as "racist" was "Before It's Too Late." "Mr. Epton, while persistently disavowing any race baiting, is nonetheless running a campaign founded on it. His new television slogan, 'Epton—Before It's Too Late,' is disgraceful evidence of either insensitivity or outright exploitation," editorialized the *Chicago Tribune* (March 27, 1983). On Palm Sunday, Washington and presidential hopeful Walter Mondale went to church services at St. Pascal's Catholic Church on the Northwest side. "When they arrived, they found 'nigger die' spray-painted on a wall and were met by a nasty, jeering crowd of perhaps three dozen, some of whom shouted racial epithets as well as 'crook,' 'tax cheater,' and 'baby killer,' referring to the candidates' support of abortion."[13] "The protesters said they opposed Washington because of his pro-abortion stance, although Father Ciezadlo told them that the stands taken by Washington and Epton on abortion are identical," reported the *Chicago Tribune* (March 28, 1983).

Of that encounter, Bill Zimmerman, Washington's media consultant, created two spots. In the first pictures of black and white children together reciting the Pledge of Allegiance were intercut with news footage of the hostile crowd. The spot invites viewers to ask, do these two sets of images belong together? Do they belong in our city?

The second intercuts still after still of traumatic moments in the nation's remembered past. A camera clicks as one picture replaces another. The pictures included images of the Klan, of the Kennedy assassination, the assassination of Martin Luther King, Jr., police beating black civil rights protesters, American soldiers wounded in Vietnam, the scene of the grief-stricken young woman kneeling over the body of a fellow student killed at Kent State, a picture from the Chicago Democratic convention of 1968. As these stills click forward, the announcer notes, "There are moments in our history of which all Americans are thoroughly and profoundly ashamed. One of these moments may be happening now. Here. In Chicago." The videotaped footage from outside the church is frozen on the screen. It then begins to roll forward showing faces contorted in hatred jeering Washington. "When you vote on Tuesday, be sure it's a vote you can be proud of," says the announcer.

The use of the still photos invites us to step back from the moment and set voting in a broader context of the city's and the nation's history.

Figure 4-2. In 1983, Harold Washington was running for Mayor of Chicago against a Republican whose slogan was "Before It's Too Late." His ad producer responded to the racial fears invited by that slogan with an ad rich in historical resonance. It asked voters to consider whether their vote was being cast on a basis that would make them proud.

By asking whether the crowd jeering Washington is analogous to these moments while positing that it "may" be, the ad invites both an emotional and an analytical response. There is not a more powerful instance of "reframing" that I know of in the modern history of televised campaigning.

But for sheer ingenuity, a response by Ken Kramer comes close. "If Tim [Wirth] will try to fool you today, what about tomorrow?" asked a 1986 ad by Rep. Ken Kramer (R. Colorado). Wirth's original ad had used paid actresses to attack Kramer. On the screen of Kramer's response ad run the credits of the actresses who appeared in the first ad. We respond to evidence that we have been deceived with anger. Here the anger is channeled against the presumed deceiver Tim Wirth.

Each of these responsive ads invites viewers to reconsider an earlier judgment. Each works by establishing a context for viewing something controversial. Each metacommunicates—talks about some act of communication—in order to contextualize or recontextualize it.

Taking Umbrage

Some states are less likely to suffer the slings and arrows of outrageous ads simply because consultants have learned that the citizenry there won't tolerate political sleaze. If the unfair attack has occurred in a state un- accustomed to dirty politics, taking umbrage is an effective response. Tolerance levels for attack differ from state to state. An ad that would offend viewers in Minnesota is business as usual in New Jersey and bland in Texas. When former Vermont Governor Richard Snelling moved onto the attack in 1986 against Patrick Leahy he produced a backlash because Vermont is not a state accustomed to strong attack. Leahy's response resonated with voters. A radio ad for him said "[I]t's going to get knee deep around here. Dick Snelling has hired some famous dirty tricksters to foul up the airwaves with a big-bucks, political smear campaign. . . . Do we really have to go through this in quiet, sensible, beautiful Ver- mont?"

In the final days of the Senate races in Minnesota and North Carolina in 1990, similar ads moved on the air against the Democratic challeng- ers. The ads alleged that the challenger was extremely liberal, favored abortion in the final weeks of pregnancy, and supported quotas. In Min- nesota, a state that has had very little exposure to "dirty" campaigning, the attacks backfired. The major newspapers editorialized against them. Community leaders expressed their outrage. The ads helped the candi- date they had been created to hurt. The opposite occurred in North Carolina, a state that six years before had set a record for the total amount spent on suspect oppositional advertising.

The nonpartisan League of Conservation Voters (LCV) has available an ad designed to "take umbrage" at politicians it considers enemies of the environment who masquerade as its friends. This ad was used suc- cessfully against a congressman the LCV had tagged as one of its "Dirty Dozen." When Minnesota's Arlan Strangeland distributed a radio ad praising his commitment to the environment, the LCV responded with the thirty-second television spot "Greenscam." "It's called Greenscam. A politician runs pretty commercials. But he distorts the facts. Pretends to be an environmentalist. Or he covers up his real record by telling you part of the story. The nonpartisan League of Conservation Voters is an authority on who's telling the truth. Or twisting the truth. And this pol- itician is guilty of greenscam [Photo of Strangeland]. Know the facts. Don't let anyone pollute your mind."

Some standards of civility remain in most states. Even in states accus- tomed to high levels of attack, arrogance and rudeness are condemned. After Governor Mario Cuomo refused to debate his Republican chal- lenger Andrew O'Rourke in 1986, O'Rourke managed to drive his sup- port in the polls down with an ad that said "An apology to emperor Cuomo. We apologize for disturbing you with our invitation to debate.

We only thought that since Presidents Reagan and Carter and Ford took the time to debate the issues with their opponents, you would too. But we were forgetting they were only presidents. And you have already elevated yourself a great deal beyond that."

The ad implied that O'Rourke thought himself the equal of presidents. And the public wasn't buying the notion that Cuomo had an ob-

Figure 4-3. Without identifying them as such, Colorado Congressman Tim Wirth used actresses to speak against Wirth's opponent in an oppositional ad. The response invited the audience to focus on the fact that this had been a manipulative ploy.

Figure 4-4. When an ad makes implausible claims, it will be disbelieved and produce a backlash against its sponsor. This ad produced such a backlash.

ligation to debate someone who couched the invitation in terms that seemed instead to invite the choice of pistols.

In the 1988 New Jersey Senate race, an ad for Republican Pete Dawkins alleged that his Democratic opponent Senator Frank Lautenberg planned to serve in the Senate "as long as he can make money on the side." The public and press responded negatively to the claim. Dawkins disclaimed the commercial but the controversy helped Lautenberg win the election.

Implausible attacks will elicit a backlash as well. The electorate in Tennessee was simply unwilling to believe that anyone would approve the actions specified in an ad showcasing a Fidel Castro impersonator. In it, as crates of money are opened and examined, an actor dressed to look like Cuban premier Castro smugly smiles as a narrator says, "When it comes to spending taxpayers' money, Senator James Sasser is a master. Take foreign aid. While important programs are being cut back here at home, Sasser has voted to allow foreign aid to be sent to committed enemies of our country: Vietnam, Laos, Cambodia, Marxist Angola, and even Communist Cuba. You can bet James Sasser is making a lot more friends abroad than he is here in Tennessee." The Castro impersonator lights a hundred dollar bill as he proclaims, "Muchissimas gracias, Senor Sasser."

Nor did Texans take kindly to the unproven allegation that Democratic gubernatorial candidate Ann Richards was a drug abuser. The charge had been bandied about for weeks before one of her primary opponents, State Attorney General Jim Mattox, insinuated it into the rhetorical questions of a television ad that averred, "There's a difference between the youthful mistakes of a college kid and the actions of a forty-seven-year-old elected official. Ann Richards says she hasn't used any mood-altering chemicals since her treatment for chemical dependency. But for three years before that, Richards was an elected public official. That's why reporters and newspapers have repeatedly asked what illegal drugs, if any, did Richards use as a forty-seven-year-old officeholder? Did she use marijuana, or something worse like cocaine . . . . Not as a college kid, but as a forty-seven-year-old elected official sworn to uphold the law?" Within four days, Mattox had dropped seven points in the polls. "That ad created a clear backlash," recalls Richards's media advisor Bob Squier. Richards went on to win both the primary and the 1990 general election.

Finally, when the source lacks credibility and the claim is ridiculous, it will not be believed. This was the case with Lyndon LaRouche's 1976 assertion that "if Jimmy Carter were to be elected on November 2, this nation would be committed to thermonuclear war probably no later than the summer of 1977."

Distancing Through Humor That Invites a Test of Plausibility

By encouraging us to step back and see the situation as funny, humor invites us to reframe.[14] In 1982, through skillful use of humor, Montana Democrat John Melcher neutralized the effectiveness of an attack campaign by NCPAC. The credible source? Cows speaking their mind about veterinarian John Melcher. The wordplay in the ad is clever, the presence of the cows offbeat. The announcer says, "For more than a year now, a pack of East Coast politicos have been scurrying into Montana with briefcases full of money, trying to convince us that our John Melcher is out of step with Montana. Montana isn't buying it, especially those who know bull when they hear it."

The cows then gossip about the campaign. "Did you hear about those city slickers out here bad-mouthing Doc Melcher?" "One of them," responds the second cow, "was stepping in what they had been trying to sell. He kept calling me a steer." The ad is a performative utterance, the fact of the insider cow talk a means of discrediting the city slickers. Is cow number two a steer? "That will come as some surprise to Junior here," she says. What gives the ad plausibility is Melcher's profession.

Before entering the State Legislature, the Congress, and then the Senate, Melcher was, as the announcer reminds us "a veterinarian." In a test of plausibility one of the cows watches Melcher trudge across the pasture and asks, "Now tell me, does that look like a man who is out of step with Montana?"

The Credible Source Who Invites a Test of Plausibility

In 1984, Democrat Norman D'Amours attacked the Republican incumbent Senator Gordon Humphrey in the New Hampshire senatorial contest. At issue was Humphrey's support of the Reagan budget proposal, blocked by Congress, to roll back or delay cost-of-living adjustments in Social Security. The ad featured a grey-haired older woman, Mildred Ingram, who looked straight into the camera and asked, "What do you think about a politician who tries to frighten the elderly? Well, Norman D'Amours is trying to do just that. He claims Senator Humphrey does not believe in Social Security when his own parents are on it, I'm on it, and many of his constituents in New Hampshire are on it. Mr. D'Amours knows this is a lie. Shame on you, Mr. D'Amours."

The ad draws on our assumptions that the elderly are the keepers of communal wisdom, the truth tellers, who have the right if not the obligation to call the younger generation to account. It is believable because Mrs. Ingram is believable. And it invites viewers to test the plausibility of D'Amours's claims.

Attacked as a champion of kiddie porn, Ohio Senator Howard Metzenbaum responded by asking a credible source to scuttle the attack. Metzenbaum's fellow Democrat, Ohioan John Glenn appears on camera looking angry. "In the past I've known George Voinovich as an honorable man. But this new TV ad is the lowest gutter politics I've seen in a long time. To imply that Howard Metzenbaum with four daughters and six grandchildren is somehow soft on child pornography is disgusting." Note that nothing in the response engages the attack. Nor is Glenn engaging in legitimate rebuttal. Nothing about having daughters and grandchildren provides assurance that someone opposes child pornography. Yet the ad succeeds because it invites us to step back and consider the claim.

Capitalizing on the Credibility of the Press

Although use of newspaper opinion as a form of refutation did not begin to dominate responses until 1990, the effectiveness of this strategy had been demonstrated earlier. In Michigan, George McGovern's ad producer, Charles Guggenheim, overstepped the bounds of causal claiming in a 1974 set of spots against Republican Governor William Milliken. The ads blamed Milliken for not acting to ensure that cattle were protected from the chemical PPB. This negligence would result in human deformities for which Milliken was to blame, suggested the ads.

John Deardourff, of the team that had handled Ford's 1976 ads, responded with an ad that recapped the reaction of state newspapers and editorial writers. Deardourff's candidate defeated the Democrat in a tight race.

In 1986, Democrat Bob Graham's bid to unseat senatorial incumbent Paula Hawkins benefitted from press scrutiny of her claims as well. Hawkins had asserted that she had met with Chinese head of state Deng Xiaoping to get his country to stop shipping quaaludes to the United States. When reporters revealed that the meeting had not occurred, Graham's media consultant, Bob Squier, used newspaper headlines exposing Hawkin's deception in an ad that said "two of Hawkin's own aides admit on the record that the meeting never took place and that she never discussed the drug issue with the Chinese leader. If the people who work for Paula Hawkins now say they don't believe her, how can we?"

But our trust in the credibility of newspapers can also be the source of deception. Computers are now able to make up headlines and articles indistinguishable from the real thing. In the 1990 Texas gubernatorial race, an attack ad produced by Squier for Democrat Ann Richards showed a newspaper headline legitimizing one of Richards' charges. But, as reporters were quick to point out, the headline was missing two critical words, "Richards alleges." Squier withdrew the ad and apologized. In the process of moving the headline into the computer, he explained, "Richards alleges" inadvertently had been dropped from the text.

In the same year, Republican consultant Ed Blakely was caught fabricating a headline. "I make no apologies for it," says Blakely. "The headline accurately represented our opponent's actions." Here too the press cried foul.

Disassociation

Rather than questioning the legitimacy of guilt by association, successful responses disassociate. In 1988 when Republican David Karnes attacked Nebraska Democrat Robert Kerrey as a Fonda liberal on foreign policy, the Medal-of-Honor-winning vet responded, "I served in Vietnam, and many friends of mine were hurt as a result of Jane Fonda's visit to Vietnam. So I urge Senator Karnes to associate me with some other liberal that he thinks will hurt me in this campaign or find some other politician to associate with Jane Fonda." Kerrey's argument was helped by the fact that he had lost part of one leg in the Vietnam War, a fact unmentioned in the response but widely known in the state.

Admit Mistakes and Ask Forgiveness

In the 1978 Illinois senatorial race, Democrat Alex Seith faced incumbent Republican Charles Percy. The little known Seith overtook Percy in the polls with tactics that included guilt by association. In one Seith radio ad, an announcer asked, "Do you think Senator Percy is a friend of black people?" The answer: "Well, remember Earl Butz? He was the secretary of agriculture who made a racist and sexually obscene joke about blacks. We can't repeat his words on the air, of course, but they were so offensive that he had to resign. Maybe you are wondering what that's got to do with Senator Percy. Just this—Senator Percy said of Earl Butz . . . 'I wish he were secretary of agriculture still today.' Still today, Senator Percy? Percy wants the black vote, and with friends like this, you don't need enemies. Because Charles Percy tolerates the Earl Butz insult to blacks, more and more people are getting behind Alex Seith for the United States Senate." Percy had called for Butz's resignation as soon as he heard of the joke but he had approved of Butz's agricultural policies.

Seith also faulted Percy for waffling on tax reductions. What turned the race around for Percy was not a direct response to any of these but a public act of contrition. Percy eked out a narrow victory with an apology that invited voters to compare him to his opponent rather than simply cast a "no" vote against him. Surrounded by his family in his living room, Percy spoke directly to the camera. "The polls say that many of you want to send me a message. But after Tuesday, I may not be in the Senate to receive it. Believe me, I've gotten the message: and you're right. Washington has gone overboard. And I'm sure I've made my share of mistakes. But in truth, your priorities are mine too. Stop the waste. Cut the spending. Cut the taxes. I've worked as hard as I know how for you. I'm not ready to quit now. And I don't want to be fired. I want to keep working for you. And I'm asking for your vote."

Of note is the fact that none of these responses is a direct propositional refutation. Each invites some test of plausibility or evidence. Would such moves work elsewhere? The Zimmerman response crafted for Washington could have been used effectively against the two ad hominem Helms ads discussed in the last chapter. Instead, the Gantt campaign engaged in propositional rebuttal. In the process, I suspect, the campaign managed to make Gantt seem defensive, legitimize the charges in the attack ads, and further embed those claims in the audience.

The shaming approach of Mildred Ingram could have worked against the Bush furlough and Boston Harbor ads and against the Dukakis Social Security ad. Dukakis could have pre-empted all attacks on the furlough program by simply making an apology ad or issuing an apology in one of the debates in the primaries. His mistake: supporting a furlough program for first-degree murderers. The statement should have included an apology to Horton's victims and indicated what he had learned from this tragedy.

The natural time to have done so occurred when he signed into law the ban on such furloughs. Such an approach would have made it impossible for Bush to declare as he mistakenly did on the stump that "Dukakis fought tooth and nail" to keep the furloughs for first-degree murderers. The furlough program had already been raised by that point in the campaign by Tennessee's Albert Gore.

A backlash can be created against deceptive claims by vigilant, respected civic organizations, reporters, papers, and stations that offer factual, not strategy-based, ad watches. Additionally, we should expect the press to note violations of the consultants' own "Code of Professional Ethics." In it, they pledge that they will "use no appeal to voters which is based on racism or discrimination and will condemn those who use such practices . . . will refrain from false and misleading attacks on an opponent or member of his family and shall do everything in my power to prevent others from using such tactics . . . will document accurately and fully any criticism for an opponent or his record . . . [and] shall be honest in my relationship with the press and candidly answer questions when I have the authority to do so." [15]

Additionally, we can support the "citizen jury" concept pioneered in 1990 by the Minnesota League of Women Voters. The juries are a revivified form of the Fair Campaign Practices Commission. They involve a representative group of citizens from around a state in the process of eliciting candidate positions and holding candidates accountable for the accuracy of their claims.

The National Association of Broadcasters has urged stations to reject unfair or inaccurate ads brought to them by PACs. Interested citizens can remind stations of the NAB position and reiterate that stations are under no obligation to air PAC ads and can be sued over misrepresentations found in them. Candidates whose records are distorted in PAC ads then should sue both the airing station and the PAC. Such action should encourage stations to exercise greater vigilance in screening such ads.

We should encourage newspapers and television stations to editorialize against false ads. The *Washington Post* demonstrated the power of a strong, clear, recurrent editorial voice when it countered strong NRA ads with a series of editorials supporting gun control in Maryland in 1989.

A dozen and a half states now have on their books laws governing campaign conduct. Some govern only claims about an opponent; others (e.g., Minnesota and Massachusetts) include claims candidates make about themselves. In most instances these laws were enacted as part of the state's corrupt practices act. Wisconsin, both Dakotas, Utah, and Oregon are among the states whose statutes permit removal of a guilty official from office. Interested citizens should encourage their states to enact such statutes and encourage the responsible officials to enforce the law.

The process would be well served if candidates were voluntarily to accept the recommendation of nationally syndicated columnist David Broder that soon after an ad begins airing, the sponsoring candidate take questions on its content and accuracy. Consultants should be expected to air their ads for the press and make available documentation for the ads' claims. In 1990, for the first time, most major consultants were making such information available. This was being done in response to the rise of "ad watches" in newspapers and on television stations.

Candidate debates provide an opportunity for one candidate to hold another accountable for the claims found in the ads. Walter Mondale used this opportunity effectively in the New York primary when he turned to his opponent Gary Hart in a debate and asked why he was saying in his ads that Mondale favored killing kids in Central America. Measures that encourage focused debates with answers longer than ad length also foster candidate engagement and accountability and as such should be encouraged.

Since the candidate with the larger budget has a natural advantage in the ad wars, proposals that take money out of the political campaign equation while providing access to the airwaves should be taken seriously.

I have reservations about the constitutionality and wisdom of the Danforth–Hollings Bill. This bill would require candidates to appear in their own attack ads and would provide response time for those attacked. It would counterbalance PAC and private third-party ads by giving the opposed candidate free response time. This provision would offer an incentive for stations to reject all noncandidate ads. The difficulty with this proposal is its built-in bias toward already well-funded incumbents. Most oppositional ads are produced for challengers. At the same time, it would raise thorny questions about what does and does not constitute an attack. One could spend a lifetime of campaigns contesting whether any of the enthymematic ads I've discussed are "attacks."

Candidates can counter unfair attacks (and even fair ones) by reframing the issue. But candidates aren't the only ones who have the power to frame how we view political campaigns. Many voters get their campaign information through the frame of news, a topic Part II examines.

II

Ads and the News

CHAPTER FIVE

Power of Ads to Shape News

In October 1980 Citizens' Party candidate Barry Commoner, who would garner a quarter of a million votes in the general election, bought air time for a radio commercial that opened with the word "Bullshit!" As the ad itself admitted, it had used that word to secure news coverage for a campaign that had been ignored by the press. ABC complied (October 15, 1980). CBS and NBC ignored the ad. By getting access to ABC network news time, Commoner's ad producer Bill Zimmerman parlayed a $5000 radio buy into free television attention previously denied that campaign. But the coverage ABC gave the ad was hardly a producer's dream. Throughout, Susan King, the network reporter, uses every available moment to convey her personal distaste and that of the network for the ad.

> *King:* "Political commercials you hear on the radio are broadcast from network studios like this one at ABC in New York. Later this month ABC will be forced to carry the Citizens' Party presidential ad which ran across the country yesterday at CBS and NBC radio and which begins with the unprecedented use of vulgarity."
>
> *Ad:* "Bullshit. What? Reagan and Anderson—it's all bullshit."
>
> *King:* "Shocked? Many listeners were when they heard the ad and complained to their local radio station, but when it comes to political advertising, the candidate controls. By law the studio, or in this case the network, is bound to air the politician's message if he is involved in the ad, no matter what the message says."

An expert then agrees that the law requires airing bona fide candidate ads if the candidate's picture appears or his voice is heard. [The "expert" should have added that this requirement goes into effect only when the station has aired an ad for any candidate for that office.]

> *King:* "Section 315 of the Federal Communications Act dealing with political commercials says, 'The licensee shall have no power of censorship over the material broadcast.' "
> *Commoner:* "I think the American public is mature enough to be able to withstand certain messages and register their reaction to that at the polls."

A spokesperson for Commoner decries a situation that dictates that "the only way we can attract attention is to remind people that this campaign is a hollow sham." King closes by noting that the few stations that refused the ad were being sued by the Citizens' Party. The piece ends with King saying, "No matter how uncomfortable the listener is, the candidate has the last word."

News reporting can provide a frame through which viewers understand ads. Conventional campaign wisdom holds that news sets the context for ads. If the news accounts are inconsistent with the ad, the power of the ad is diminished. When the two are consistent, the power of both is magnified. But news can only reframe ads if reporters question the legitimacy of their claims, point out the false inferences that they invite, and so on. Without such reframing by reporters, campaign ads have the potential to shape the visual and verbal language of news, and in recent campaigns they have been increasingly successful.

Eleven years after the Commoner ad aired, network norms for coverage had changed. On September 4, 1991, CBS, NBC, ABC, and CNN news stories all carried an excerpt from a Conservative Victory Committee ad urging Senate confirmation of Supreme Court nominee Clarence Thomas and attacking the integrity of his likely opponents including one who was not even on the Senate Judiciary Committee.

As a result, viewers saw and heard content they would not otherwise have been exposed to on these news programs. "Who will judge the judge?" asked a segment of the ad. "How many of these liberal Democrats could themselves pass ethical scrutiny?" [Pictures of Alan Cranston, Joseph Biden, and Edward Kennedy are shown.] As the charges unfold, they are repeated in print on the screen. "Ted Kennedy, suspended from Harvard for cheating, left the scene of the accident at Chappaquiddick where Mary Jo Kopechne died" [a headline from the *Washington Star* appears] "and this year Palm Beach [on screen, a photo of the front page of the *New York Post* showing a picture of Kennedy in casual wear and the headline "Teddy's Sexy Romp."] "Joseph Biden, found guilty of plagiarism during his presidential campaign. Alan Cranston, implicated in the Keating Five S&L scandal. Whose values should be on the Supreme Court? Clarence Thomas's or Ted Kennedy's" [The headline "Teddy's Sexy Romp" with the attached photo is juxtaposed with a photo of Thomas].

With the exception of CNN's "Crossfire," the news broadcasts did not focus on the accuracy or fairness of the attacks but rather on the potential impact of the campaign on the Thomas hearings. A small Conservative group with a membership of 80,000 had managed to garner over a million dollars worth of network time with an ad that cost $20,000 to produce and just under $40,000 to air on Fox and CNN in the Washington, D.C., area.

In the process of relaying the controversial segments of the ad to their viewers, the networks legitimized the unsupported inference that Kennedy had either engaged in questionable sexual behavior or, worse, was an accomplice in the alleged rape of a young woman by his nephew at the Kennedy Palm Beach home. The headline in the *New York Post* referred to a later discredited report that Kennedy, wearing only an undershirt, had chased a young woman around the Palm Beach residence. As corrected, the report revealed that the Senator had simply appeared in a living room in which a young woman was talking with Kennedy's son. The senator was at the time wearing a nightshirt that went down to his knees.

As the controversy about the ad raged, the *New York Times* ran a still from the ad on its front page. Where in 1980 two of the three networks ignored the Commoner ad, in 1991 all four networks centered coverage on the Conservative ad. Where the frame created by ABC for the Commoner ad distanced the network from it and treated it negatively, coverage of the anti-Biden, -Cranston, -Kennedy ad focused on its strategy and likely outcome.

But what the ABC coverage of 1980 and the 1991 coverage of the Thomas ad have in common is also important. Neither ABC in 1980 nor any of the networks in 1991 examined the legitimacy of the ads' claims. The Commoner ad alleged that there were no substantive differences among the major party candidates; the Conservative Victory Fund ad posited that the morality of those who would determine the qualifications of a Supreme Court nominee was a legitimate subject of inquiry. Until a subsequent charge of sexual harassment surfaced, no questions about Thomas's morality had been publicly raised by anyone.

News can provide a frame through which viewers are invited to see an ad. But 1988 was the year in which ads began routinely to contextualize news. As many have argued, in 1988 the Republicans defined the campaign terrain for Dukakis, for the press, and for voters. Ads played an important role in the Republicans' ability to set this agenda. To the extent that the spots succeeded and their images were used as visual illustration of the power of the Bush appeals, ads were contextualizing news.

Figure 5-1. As the Senate Judiciary Committee was about to convene its hearings on President George Bush's nomination of Judge Clarence Thomas to the Supreme Court, the Conservative Victory Fund aired this ad on Washington, D.C., television stations. By so doing, the group managed to parlay about $60,000 worth of production costs and air time into over a million dollars' worth of exposure on network news.

126

Ads also contextualized news in a second sense. After a viewer has seen the same ad many times, exposure to a small segment of it can evoke the whole ad. My work with focus groups across a twenty-year period suggests that unless the verbal message is highly salient (e.g., the mention of your profession in the ad), reinforced by print on the screen, or repeatedly uttered in the ad, it is not until the third exposure to a typical production ad that the typical viewer is able to recall a substantial amount of the ad's spoken content.

But weeks after exposure to a single ad image, viewers can accurately recall whether or not they have seen it before. The discussion of whether pictures dominate words or words pictures is confused by its assumptions that one invariably dominates the other, that music plays no role in cueing recall, and that the impact of each remains the same with re-peated exposure.[1]

Ads have an additional recall advantage over news. Most ads are "bed-ded" in a sound track that invites emotions consistent with the ad's mes-sage. So, for example, the musical backtrack for an ad about the candi-date's accomplishments is upbeat and often patriotic. When a segment of the ad airs in news, its soundtrack is usually preserved. Lee Green-wood's "I'm Proud to Be an American" hitchhiked into network news in 1984 when the Reagan ads incorporating it were clipped into broadcast news stories. Although network news opens and closes with theme mu-sic, the news segments themselves aren't musically scored.

Moreover, the announcer's voice on the ad is usually more resonant than the reporter's. These factors increase the power of the embedded ad segment and dampen the corrective words spoken by the reporter.

Repeated exposure increases the likelihood that the words and pic-tures will be remembered. When a segment from a remembered ad is then shown on news, two things happen. First, if the segment is able to function synecdochically for the whole ad, the viewer will recall a larger part of the ad than that shown. Second, the audio that is likely to be remembered is not the reporter's words about the ad but rather some form of the audio from the ad itself.

Ads Can Shape the Visual and Verbal Language of News

Critics from Coleridge to Kenneth Burke have recognized the power of naming. For Coleridge, a word doesn't "convey merely what a certain thing is, but the very passion and all the circumstances which were con-ceived as *constituting* the perception of the thing by the person who used the word."[2] One might paraphrase Burke to say that language does our thinking for us.[3] Along these lines, if the language of a candidate's ads infuses the vocabulary of reporters, the candidate has obtained a signif-icant advantage.

In the 1988 general election the Republicans' ads, reinforced by news coverage of speeches and debates, created a pro-Bush vocabulary for reporters. Others had done so, although with less impact, before. In 1976 the Ford campaign succeeded in getting reporters to adopt the language of its most powerful attack ads. Repeatedly, Carter was faced by press queries about being or being perceived to be "wishy-washy on the issues."

In 1980 Carter achieved the same effect when the press accepted the question raised in Democratic ads and speeches, "Is Reagan too reckless to be president?" "Aides acknowledge that Reagan is having trouble shaking the perception that he might be militarily reckless," notes Barry Serafin (ABC, October 20, 1980). "Critics say his proposals border on recklessness," noted John McWethy (ABC, October 28, 1980). So, for example, after the Carter-Reagan debate, Barry Serafin (ABC, October 31, 1980) commented that Reagan's "advisers think that in his debate with Mr. Carter, he went a long way toward assuring a big audience that he would not be reckless." In their only debate, Reagan was able to dispatch the reckless image more by manner than matter. "There you go again" just aren't the words Hollywood usually scripts for Dr. Strangelove.

But where in these earlier campaigns, one side or the other occasionally enticed the press into embracing one of its words or phrases, in 1988 the Bush campaign managed to insinuate an entire vocabulary about the campaign into press coverage. Reporting on the Dukakis record on crime is illustrative. Here the Republicans secured the complicity of the press in renaming convicted murderer William Horton, in redefining the relationship between Horton's Maryland victims, in adopting such words as "torture" and "terrorize" to describe his actions while on furlough, in defining the furlough program's purpose as dispensing "weekend passes," and in talking of the policy as a "revolving door." Each of these acts of naming biased the discussion against Dukakis. Each was inaccurate. To the extent that the Republicans were able to put this language in place, however, they demonstrated the power of ads, reinforced by candidate speeches and campaign hype, to contextualize news.

Although his given name is William, he calls himself William, court records cite him as William, a July 1988 *Reader's Digest* article identifies him as William J. Horton, Jr.,[4] and press reports before the Republican ad and speech blitz name him "William," the Bush campaign and its supporting PACs identified the furloughed convict as "Willie" Horton. Even the crusading anti-Dukakis newspaper that won a Pulitzer Prize for its exposé on the furlough program consistently identifies Horton as William Horton or William Horton, Jr. When the Maryland man stabbed by the furloughed convict contacted the Lawrence *Eagle-Tribune* reporter, he too referred to Horton as William Horton.[5] In his account of the attack in the PAC ad, however, that man, Clifford Barnes, instead identifies the convict as "Willie" Horton.

One might trace the familiar "Willie" to the naming practices of slave-masters, to our patterns of talk about gangsters, or to the sort of benign paternalism that afflicts adults around small children. But whatever its origin, when discussing murder, kidnapping, and rape "Willie" summons more sinister images of criminality than does William. After all, it wasn't J. Eddie Hoover who hunted down Albert (or was it Alfred?) Capone. And during his trial, the person to that point known as Willie Smith was identified by family and attorney as either William or Will. After his acquittal on charges of rape, the family reverted to the name by which he had been known before.

The PAC ad titled "Weekend Prison Passes" as well as the PAC ads featuring Horton's victims all refer to him as *"Willie* Horton." When his mug shot appears on the screen of "Weekend Prison Passes," print under it reads "Willie Horton." Reporters reduced Dukakis on crime to the Republican sculpted image of "Willie Horton." In news reports, *"Willie"* Horton's name was mentioned more often by reporters than by George Bush or any of his representatives. Use of dramatic, coherent narrative increases the likelihood of recall.[6] Once the Horton narrative was embedded in public consciousness, mention of his name should have been sufficient to evoke the entire story.

By the campaign's end, even the Democratic candidates had accepted the Republican identification of Horton. (Bentsen in Rather interview, CBS, October 26, 1988; Dukakis interview with Rather, October 27, 1988; Dukakis in interview with Jennings, November 9, 1988). The most prominent exception occurred before Horton became a stock feature in the Bush stump speech and the subject of PAC ads. On July 8, 1988, in the *Washington Post* Richard Cohen wrote about *"William* Horton's Furlough."

The schizophrenic labeling by the *New York Times* seemed to invite a Woody Allen to shout that the czar and the tsar were the same person. An editorial on June 30, 1988, labels Horton "Willie Horton" as do articles on October 3 and 21. Yet pieces by Robin Toner on July 5 and Martin Tolchin on October 12 refer to him as "William R. Horton." In Tolchin's article, it is Clifford Barnes who refers to Horton as "Willie Horton."[7] The difference between the two sets of articles appears to be that "Willie Horton" is written about by anonymous reporters tasked with inside reporting and given filler space. By contrast, "issue" pieces carrying bylines write of "William Horton." The contrast raises the unconfirmed possibility that the more contact a reporter had with Bush campaign insiders, the more likely the use of "Willie." The hypothesis falters on the editorial presumably written by someone safely anchored to a desk in New York.

In an October 10, 1988, *New York Times* piece, Horton is initially tagged "Willie" and then accorded "Mr. Horton," the *Times'* usual mode of address. "Clifford Barnes is making a radio commercial—to the delight of

George Bush and the concern of Michael Dukakis," says the report. "More than a year ago, Mr. Barnes and his wife [*note:* she wasn't his wife at the time; they were engaged and living together], Angela, were *viciously* attacked in their suburban Maryland home by *Willie* Horton, who had fled Massachusetts while out of prison under that state's furlough program. Mr. Horton broke into their home, *slashed* Mr. Barnes with a knife, and raped Angela Barnes. *Mr. Horton* is now serving two life sentences plus 85 years in prison for the attack. Vice President Bush repeatedly cites the attack and Mr. Dukakis's support for the furlough program to charge that his rival is soft on crime. Mr. Barnes will recount his grim experience in a radio ad for a pro-George Bush group in California, the Committee for the Presidency." About the *Times'* naming of Horton, one *New York Times* reporter observed, "Once when an editor changed his name to William, I argued that no one would know who I was talking about [if he weren't called 'Willie']."

The Republicans also controlled the language that characterized the furlough program itself. The Bush furlough ad describes Dukakis's policy as giving *"weekend furloughs to first-degree murderers."* The PAC ad titled "Weekend Passes" shows pictures of Bush, Dukakis, and Horton as it claims that Dukakis "allowed first-degree murderers to have *weekend passes* from prison. . . . Horton received ten *weekend passes* [a statement reprinted on the screen]. . . ." The ad is tagged *"Weekend prison passes:* Dukakis on crime" (emphasis added).

The press adopted the phrases "weekend furloughs" and "weekend passes" from the Republican speeches and ads that in turn located them in the Lawrence *Eagle-Tribune*. The phrases are inaccurate. Furloughs in Massachusetts ranged from one to seventy-four hours in 1987 and from one to 170 hours in 1986[8] and furloughs could be granted for any day or days of the week. In 1987, the median number of hours of leave per furlough was 19, five less than a full day and 29 less than a weekend. Horton's approved 48-hour furlough began on Friday, June 6, 1986, which means he should have returned to prison while most of us were still enjoying what we usually define as a weekend.

Bush reinforced the notion that these were weekend events by averring that he says to criminals "Make my day!" while Dukakis says "Have a nice weekend." "Weekend" suggests that the furloughs occur frequently when in fact in 1988 as in 1986 a prisoner is permitted no furloughs for the first half of his or her sentence and in 1988 may be furloughed only in the final three years before eligibility for parole or release.[9] In April 1988, Dukakis signed a bill ending furloughs for those who once were first-degree murderers not eligible for parole.

Weekend is a time for recreation. This association suggests that the assault and rapes were leisure activities for the prisoners. Bush implied as much when he asked those in his audience to question Dukakis why he had let "murderers out on vacation" (June speech to Illinois Republican Convention in Springfield).

Figure 5-2. In news, images of convicted killer William Horton and Michael Dukakis were allied. Here a Republican flier is shown on NBC news.

The Bush furlough ad is titled "Revolving Door" and speaks of Dukakis's "revolving door prison policy." Although the visual in the ad itself shows not a revolving door but a turnstile, reporters also adopted the Republican announcer's characterization of the program as a "revolving door" policy. So, for example, Dan Rather asked the Democratic vice presidential nominee "[C]an't a person, or can a person, be deeply concerned about *revolving-door* justice and laxity toward criminals, even when the criminal happens to be someone who is black and still not be a racist?" (CBS, October 26, 1988).

In describing the ad, reporters adopted the Bush language as well. In an article examining inaccuracies in the ads of both campaigns, the *Washington Post*'s Lloyd Grove describes "[A]nother Bush campaign commercial featuring hard-eyed men in prison garb streaming through a *revolving door*" (*Washington Post*, October 31, 1988, p. A8).

So clear was the identification that reporters quote viewers using it. In Texas Bill Cockerill described the ad to a *New York Times* reporter as "the revolving door commercial, implying that they come out as fast as they go in" (*New York Times*, October 22, 1988).[10] Despite the use of the words "turnstile or gate" in all questions to our Texas focus groups, 36 percent of respondents referred to the "furlough ad" as the "revolving door ad."

Here is an instance of the complexity of the visual-verbal relationship. The repeated use of the phrase "revolving door" couples with repeated viewing of the image of the circling actors as convicts to situate the visual-verbal link in memory. "Revolving door" too suggests a frequency and casualness in the administration of the furlough program that did not characterize the Massachusetts system.

From PAC ads made by Horton's victims, reporters adopted the words "slashed," "brutally," "terrorized," and "tortured." "For twelve hours I was beaten, slashed, and terrorized," says Clifford Barnes, "and my wife Angie was brutally raped." "Horton went on to rape and torture others," says the sister of the man killed by Horton. Bush helped set the language in place. On June 24, he stated, "In no other state would a cold-blooded murderer like *Willie* Horton have been set free to *terrorize* innocent people" (emphasis added).

"Slashed," "terrorized," and "tortured" are not the words usually used by reporters to characterize crime. Nor was it the language first used by the national press to describe Horton's actions. Before the furloughs became a campaign issue, on December 2, 1987, CBS aired a segment that "took a hard look today at a standard procedure for many of the nation's prisons. Forty-five states," says Rather, "offer furlough programs which release inmates from prison for limited times to see how they handle freedom." The language of the correspondent is the factual, calm, descriptive language characteristic of crime reporting in network news. "Wiliam Horton did strike again in this Maryland house where Cliff and Angela Barnes lived. He held them hostage for 12 hours. Horton raped her twice, tied her husband up in the basement and stabbed him 22 times." But by June 26 (Adams) and July 20 (Stahl), CBS reporters were calling Horton "Willie" and adopting the tabloid-like language of torture and terror.

Once the Republican language was in place, it became the optic through which the print media saw and invited us to see Horton's actions as well. The *Washington Post* favored the word "terrorized" (October 22, 1988; October 25, 1988; June 23, 1988, "terror"), as did columnist Tom Wicker (*New York Times,* June 24, 1988). *Newsweek* preferred to label "*Willie* Horton" "the Massachusetts murderer who *tortured* a Maryland couple" (October 31, 1988, p. 16). The *New York Times,* which on July 5 described "William Horton" as "a convicted murderer" who "broke into the couple's home, bound and stabbed Mr. Barnes and raped his wife" by mid-October had "*Willie* Horton" "viciously" attacking and also adopted Barnes's word "*slashed* with a knife" (*New York Times,* October 10, 1988, "Convict's Victim Makes an Ad" [emphasis added]).

Academics also embraced the Republican language. "The furlough program was emphasized," writes journalism professor David Myers, "because *Willie* Horton, a black man who had been convicted of first-degree murder, had escaped to Maryland on a *weekend pass,* where he *brutalized* a white man and raped his fiancée."[11]

As interesting is the fact that when offered two different constructions of the relationship of the couple assaulted by Horton, press reports adopt the more incendiary of the two until late in the campaign. At the time of the Horton attack, Clifford Barnes and his fiancée were living together. The first PAC ad to air on the topic says accurately that Horton "kidnapped a young couple, stabbing the man and repeatedly [twice] raping his *girlfriend*."[12] That ad began airing September 9. On October 20 a second PAC ad is aired in California. This spot features Clifford Barnes, who is now married to the woman who was his fiancée at the time of the attack by Horton. "My wife Angie was brutally raped," says Barnes.

The sources that identify "Angie" as Barnes's "wife" at the time of the attack include CBS (December 1987), Cohen in the *Washington Post*, Holman of "MacNeil/Lehrer," and Toner in the *New York Times*. Although in an October 23 ABC report, Joe Bergantino identifies Barnes as her "boyfriend," two days later ABC's Britt Hume identifies Barnes as her husband (October 25, 1988). On NBC (October 28, 1988), this identification was reinforced in what in the next chapter I will define as a "newsad," a segment of news that might as well have been paid candidate advertising:

> *Ken Bode:* "George Bush was here [California] again today. Again talking about crime."
>
> *Bush:* "I believe in safe neighborhoods, and I say I believe it is time for America to take back our streets."
>
> *Bode:* "Like everywhere else the Democrats have been on the defensive about crime. Willie Horton's victims made a campaign commercial."
>
> *Cliff Barnes in ad clip:* "For twelve hours I was beaten, slashed, and terrorized, and my wife Angie was brutally raped."
>
> *Bode:* "But mostly, Bush's tough talk on crime works, because it fits with what Californians see on their news each day."
>
> *Man:* "When you have gang murders in the headlines, day after day, I think the voters understand that there is only one candidate in this race who is truly tough on crime. Only one candidate for President who really supports the death penalty."

My final claim is that the Republican use of Horton shaped the visual portrayal of crime in network news in ways that reinforced the mistaken assumption that violent crime is disproportionately committed by blacks, disproportionately committed by black perpetrators against white victims, and disproportionately the activity of black males against white females. In other words, Republican use of Horton shaped the visuals in 1988 network crime coverage in a way that underscored the Bush message.

James Devitt and I have systematically examined the way in which alleged criminals are portrayed in network news from 1985 to 1989. In 911 scenes of alleged criminals in 530 network news stories, blacks are proportionately more likely than whites to be shown restrained and in actual mug shots—the two visuals shown in the Horton PAC ads. Robert Entman has found the same pattern in local news.[13]

I suspect that this disproportionate exposure to black males in mug shots increases the telegraphic power of the use of the Horton mug shot in the PAC ads. This tendency is then magnified at a statistically significant level in coverage of crime as a 1988 campaign issue ($p = .0011$). This finding raises the question: What subtle chain of inferences or visceral responses might be invited by Senator Jesse Helms's showing of a close-up still photo of his opponent Harvey Gantt?

Our data also provide a baseline telling us how often blacks are likely to appear as "alleged criminals" in news and what visual forms this representation will take. By comparing the appearance of blacks as alleged criminals in crime stories from 1985 to 1989 with appearance in stories about the issue of crime in the 1988 general election, we can determine whether the crime stories of 1988 differed significantly from earlier norms. They do. The increase in the proportion of blacks identified or shown as criminals in 1988 general election stories about crime is statistically significant ($p = .0139$). Moreover, the number of female victims per news story doubled in 1988 stories about crime.

Just as the Bush campaign verbally primed reporters' discussion of crime, so too the issue of Horton subtly primed producers and editors to include more blacks in their covering shots showing presumed criminals. The most egregious example of this occurred October 31, 1988 on ABC. The reporter was Ken Kashiwahara. All of the presumed criminals but one are black or Hispanic. All of those who say that they are afraid are white. Most are women.

To portray a black male who "killed" one white male, stabbed a second, and raped a white woman as a typical criminal is inaccurate. Blacks run a greater risk of forcible rape, robbery, and aggravated assault than whites. Low-income individuals are the most likely victims of violent crime. Men are more likely than women to be the victims of violence, blacks more often than whites.[14] FBI statistics confirm that, unlike robbery, rape and murder in the United States are primarily intraracial not interracial phenomena. In 1988, for example, 11.3 percent of reported rapes involved a black rapist and a white victim.[15]

I do not intend to minimize Thomas and Mary Edsall's claims that a higher percent of the crime committed by blacks is interracial and that in the categories of assault and robbery more than half of the robberies committed by blacks have white victims.[16] Rather, my point is that raising the fear of whites that they are likely to be murdered or raped by blacks is unjustified. It is racist to identify William Horton's actions as somehow typical, as George Bush did when he said that the Horton case had "come to symbolize, and represent . . . the misguided outlook of my opponent."

Moreover, disproportionate portrayal of blacks as criminals plays on racial fears. When discussion of crime in network news occurs in segments in which blacks are visually cast in disproportion as criminals, the news stories themselves are priming both a pro-Bush and a racist response.

In 1988 the power of the Republican campaign to export the visual and verbal language of its ads to news was indicative of a change in the relationship between news and political advertising. Where news once contextualized ads, visually evocative and easily edited oppositional ads backed by reinforcing candidate speeches and pseudo-events now have the capacity to shape the language and pictures of news.

CHAPTER SIX

Adbites, Ad Stories, and Newsads

Black and white images of Senator John Kerry and Massachusetts' outgoing governor Michael Dukakis meld into each other on the television screen. The sound track blends the sounds and theme music of *Poltergeist* and *Jaws*. Rhythmically and ominously the announcer's voice warns, "Tax and Spend. Spend and Tax. Kerry and Dukakis. Dukakis and Kerry. You thought he was gone. But . . . he's . . . baaaacck."

The woman on the screen wearing the red dress looks earnestly into the camera and in a voice edged with concern says, "Harvey Gantt is asking you and me to approve of some pretty awful things. Aborting a child in the final weeks of pregnancy. Aborting a child because it is a girl instead of a boy."

Menacing men in prison garb circle through a turnstile as the announcer notes that Dukakis's "revolving door prison policy gave weekend furloughs for first-degree murderers not eligible for parole. While out, many committed other crimes like kidnapping and rape."

These ad segments appeared in network news more often than any others in 1988 and 1990. The first is a 1990 ad for James Rappaport that aired in Massachusetts, the second, an anti-Gantt ad aired by Jesse Helms in North Carolina that same year, the third a Bush ad from the 1988 general election. "You get a 30 or 40 percent bump out of getting it [your ad] on the news," observes media guru Roger Ailes. "You get more viewers, you get credibility, you get it in a framework."[1] If Ailes is correct, it becomes crucial to explore the types of ads that get into the news and to examine the sort of framework the news is providing.

The first televised ad clip to gain substantial public attention in the history of televised news was oppositional, visually evocative, and controversial. It also carried an intriguing sound track and lent itself well to digestive editing; a single short clip, the segment juxtaposing the counting child with the exploding bomb, could telegraph the message of the whole ad. That ad was the legendary daisy commercial discussed in an earlier chapter.

When replayed on network news, the daisy ad reached a larger audience than it had in its only paid airing. "[W]hile we paid for the ad only once on NBC last Monday night," wrote Johnson aide Bill Moyers to the president on September 13, 1964, "ABC and CBS both ran it on their news shows Friday. So we got it shown on all three networks for the price of one. This particular ad was designed to run only one time."

With the broadcast of this ad in the news, a new category was born: the unpaid ad. As news' interest in political ads has increased, brief clips of ads have become commonplace in political reporting. These ad segments are the visual equivalent of soundbites. But where reporters use soundbites to advance the narration of the news story, ad segments or adbites have the capacity to function simply as "wallpaper," visually illustrating campaign coverage that does not necessarily focus verbally on the ad itself. So, for example, a broadcast news story asserting that this is an unusually negative campaign will often string together adbites with no explicit commentary on any of them. By being situated in the credible environment of news, these ad segments gain both free airing and, as important, the legitimacy that comes from appearing in news.

Ads also appear in stories that focus specifically on the aired ad. In the 1988 presidential campaign and in the statewide races of 1990, these stories most often focused not on the fairness or accuracy of the ad content being shown but on its strategic effect. In these stories, inaccuracies are ignored. The equation is simple: effective equals good. This chapter will focus on adbites and ad stories to argue that in 1988 and 1990 the appearance of a political ad in a broadcast news story usually meant that the power of the ad and its content were being magnified, not analyzed or undercut.

Characteristics of Adbites Found in News

In 1988, 1989, and 1990, the ads most likely to be aired in the morning, evening, late night, and Sunday news and public affairs programs attacked their opponents in a humorous or symbolically powerful or controversial fashion using evocative visual material and an intriguing sound track. Their meaning could be telegraphed without requiring elaboration in easily edited clips. These criteria dictate that news will feature oppositional rather than self-promoting candidate ads.

The result is a skewed public perception of the negativity of campaigns. Sixty-seven percent of the total number of television ads aired in "paid time" in nine statewide races in 1989–1990 were self-promotional, a label I prefer to "positive."[2]

Yet ads that appeared in network news were nearly twelve times (11.7) more often oppositional than self-promotional. In other words, a fraction of 33 percent of the total ads aired captured more than 90 percent of the free national news time devoted to political ads. Why? The oppositional ad segments met two of the three criteria Bush's media advisor Roger Ailes believes attract media coverage. "[T]he media," he says, "are interested in pictures, mistakes, and attacks." Adbites usually provide *pictures* that *attack*. "You try to give them as many pictures as you can. If you need coverage," Ailes concludes, "you attack, and you will get coverage."[3]

Because newspapers cannot use ad clips as a backdrop to words, they are less likely than television to create a montage of ad images. Among other things, this means that fewer ads are treated in print than on television. But like those in broadcast news, those discussed in newspapers are unrepresentatively oppositional. In 1989–1990, print coverage of the nine campaigns in the *New York Times, Washington Post, Los Angeles Times, Philadelphia Inquirer, Dallas Morning News, Chicago Tribune, Richmond Times Dispatch, Trenton Times,* and *Boston Globe* was six times more likely to mention an oppositional than a self-promotional ad.

Three of the four presidential ads that made a memorable and "strong impression" on respondents to the *New York Times*/CBS post-election surveys of 1984 and 1988 appeared not only as ads in ad time but as news. On the Republican side these were the 1984 allegory about U.S.-Soviet relations bearing the message that under Reagan we were prepared for peace and the 1988 furlough ad evoking fears that liberal Dukakis was lenient on criminals. Each appeared in news more often than any other Reagan (84) or Bush (88) oppositional ad in its respective year.

On the Democratic side, the 1984 Mondale attack on the Reagan "Star Wars initiative" was recalled in large part because the familiar lyrics of Crosby, Stills, and Nash's "Teach Your Children Well" were intercut with the reinforcing pictures of children who were in turn intercut with missile launches.

In 1988, what viewers called the "pizza ad" created the strongest impressions of the Dukakis ads. In it a college aspirant is consigned to tossing pizza dough in a fast food outlet because "his family couldn't afford tuition." In a forecast of Dukakis's college support plan, the ad notes that "If a kid like Jimmy has the grades for college, America should find a way to send him."

Each is visually evocative, symbolically powerful, carries an involving audio track, is controversial, and lends itself easily to editing into a use-

Figure 6-1. In 1968, this ad hominem attack on Republican vice presidential nominee Spiro Agnew provoked controversy.

able news clip that digests the central meaning of the ad. Of the four, only the Dukakis pizza ad failed to secure free network news time.

One other criterion occasionally propels ads into national news: skillful use of humor. The first humorous presidential general election ad to secure national news time also was one of the two most controversial ads of 1968. On a television screen, we read "Agnew for Vice President" as the presumed viewer convulses in laughter. As the spot closes, a tag line appears: "This would be funny if it weren't so serious."

The first ad to succeed on this basis is also one that created the conventional wisdom that now says attacks must be answered. In 1984, Roger Ailes produced the "Hound Dog" ads for Mitch McConnell against Dee Huddleston in Kentucky. In them, a pack of tenacious hounds plague a Huddleston look-alike who flees rather than be confronted with his absenteeism or his record. The ad campaign helped retire the incumbent.

Three humorous ads filtered more often than others into national news in 1990. The first two were produced for Minnesota Senatorial candidate Paul Wellstone. The third parodies the quiz-show format by providing contestants with answers to which they must tie the question. The question to every answer is "Who is David Duke?"

Both of the frequently aired Wellstone ads parody the conventions of television and film. In one, Wellstone runs breathlessly from frame to frame showing voters his home, his place of work, and the like to make the point that since he lacks his opponent's money he must get his message out quickly. In the second titled "Looking for Rudy," he employs the conventions of the cult film "Roger and Me" as he wanders into such places as his opponent's headquarters trying to schedule a debate. Short of cash, the Wellstone campaign featured this two-minute ad in press conferences called around the state. The free time secured in Minnesota alone exceeded the paid time.

Adbites Secure Free Air Time

If the ad clips are fair, accurate, contextual, and relevant to the candidates' performance in office, then passing them through to the public in news poses a single concern for those who devote their time to worrying about public discourse. By providing free time to one side, they advantage one candidate's message over another's.

ABC did this on October 29, 1990, when "Good Morning America" closed its news piece on negative ads with 15 seconds of the visual track and 8 seconds of the audio of a self-promotional ad for Governor Mario Cuomo. The Cuomo ad illustrated the reporter's claim that those far enough ahead in the polls don't need to attack. By placing the Cuomo segment, its disclaimer, and tag at the end of the news segment, ABC invited the interpretation that the Governor may even have sponsored the news piece! No mention of the opponent occurred, not even the whisper of his name.

Where the Bush ads that appeared in newscasts provided shots of Bush as active leader (reviewing troops, with Gorbachev) and compassionate caregiver (lifting grandchild, sitting with a child on a swing, feeding his family) most of the positive Dukakis ads found in the news showed the Massachusetts governor as a talking head. On first glance, these differences may not seem great. However, the pattern that they establish— Bush as a visually active and involved leader, Dukakis as talking head— heighten their significance greatly. Visuals portraying activity consistently produce better recall among viewers than do shots of talking heads.[4]

This fact was dramatically illustrated when Dukakis gained news time with an ad ostensibly rebutting the Bush tank ad. In the Bush ad, Michael Dukakis—enveloped in an M1 tank—rumbles into view. The footage is from the Dukakis pseudo-event that I analyzed in the opening section of this book. As the tank circles, the ad's announcer intones: "Michael Dukakis has opposed virtually every defense system we developed. He opposed four missile systems, including the Pershing Two Missile deployment." The announcer's words are reinforced by a print crawl. "Dukakis opposed the Stealth bomber and a ground emergency warning system against nuclear attack. He even criticized our rescue mission to Grenada and our strike against Libya. And now he wants to be our Commander in Chief. America can't afford that risk." As both the Democrats and the press pointed out, the ad seriously misstated Dukakis's record.

But, consistent with his image as the cerebral candidate, Dukakis answered the evocative visuals of the tank ad with words. In the ad of his that got news play, he is shown turning off the tank ad on a television set and saying, "I'm fed up with it. George Bush's negative ads are full of lies and he knows it. I'm on the record for the very weapons systems his ad says I'm against." A talking head could not dislodge memories of the circling tank. By repeatedly replaying segments of the "revolving door" and "tank" ads, the networks reinforced Bush's false claims about Dukakis. The Democrat did not enjoy comparable news access for his most deceptive ad. Only twice did network evening news feature the Democratic ad showing a Social Security card being torn away as the announcer claims that Bush voted to "cut" Social Security. As I noted earlier, since Bush voted only to freeze a cost-of-living adjustment, the use of the word "cut" is inviting a false inference. That inference is propelled by the on-screen image of a Social Security card being torn down to a small fraction of its former self.

Pictures from candidate or PAC ads appeared in 60 CBS, ABC, and NBC evening news broadcasts during the general election campaign.

Those stories showed visuals from Dukakis ads or ads produced by Dukakis supporters for 10.48 minutes and from ads by the Bush campaign or pro-Bush PACs for 12.4 minutes. Of the 155 ad-based images shown, 71 were drawn from ads advancing Dukakis or opposing Bush and 84 from ads advancing Bush or attacking Dukakis.

Because the Bush campaign offered more compelling visuals—its most aired images were action shots, not a talking head—Bush gained more news time in illustrative news pieces not specifically about the ads. So, for example, a piece by Bob Schieffer on the presence and absence of humor in the campaign (October 29, 1988) displays sections of the tank and furlough ad and nothing of Dukakis's.

The power of these ads' claims was magnified on two of the networks. By showing the ad images full screen, ABC and CBS replicated the exposure a viewer routinely has to the ad. Only NBC visually contextualized the ad segments and distanced the viewer from them by showing them appearing on a television set.

Selective, uncritical treatment of ads in news gives a candidate free air time or print space. However, such exposure doesn't always help the aired ad's campaign. By the networks' own admissions, the most aired ad image in news helped Bush and hurt Dukakis. The most aired image from the Dukakis ads, other than that of him speaking directly to the camera, was from the so-called handlers ads. Fourteen percent of the images drawn from the Dukakis ads depicted scenes from the "handlers" series, which showed actors masquerading as Bush advisors lamenting Dukakis's success as a governor and plotting ways to deflect attention from Bush's weak record.

Twenty-three percent of the images shown from Bush ads came from the revolving door ad. Of the revolving door images, the one appearing most often both on ABC, NBC, and CBS evening news (11 images) and in print stories showed "268 escaped" imprinted over the image of the circling convicts. As that number appears, the announcer is asserting that many first-degree murderers escaped.

The press characterized the Bush furlough ad as effective. Where the revolving door stood for the competence of the Bush strategy, the handler's ad stood as an indictment of the Dukakis campaign (cf. CBS, November 3, 1988). On October 15, 1988, Bob Schieffer of CBS described one of the handlers ads as "an attempt by the Dukakis people to do some negative advertising." After a part of one aired, his guest, *Adweek*'s Barbara Lippert, remarked: "That's one of the most denounced ads in political history; nobody likes it. And I think it's very vague; it's abstract, and the problem is that it gives Bush the kind of invulnerability that President Reagan has had, and it looks like one of those ads for the phone company where someone's going to get fired or those strange Nissan engineers who sat around."

To her comments, Schieffer added: "I agree with you. Most people said that ad simply didn't work." On NBC, Tom Brokaw characterized "the Dukakis campaign television commercials" as "a missed message so far, not focused, even confusing, while the Bush commercials have been controversial, but effective by consensus" (NBC, October 25, 1988). As a "handler" ad played, Stan Bernard said, "Then came the wide-criticized Dukakis commercials which dramatized so-called Bush packagers. Some voters complained they didn't know who they [the ads] were for or against."

Although the Bush Boston Harbor ad aired almost as many days and almost as often in paid time as did the furlough ad, it was the "revolving door" spot that viewers told *New York Times* pollsters "made the biggest impression" on them.[5] This was true of Republicans, Democrats, and Independents. Perhaps the furlough ad is more visually evocative. Or perhaps the additional exposure it received in news enhanced recall.

It is unlikely that TV reporters will begin clocking the minutes devoted to each candidate's ads, and campaign discourse probably wouldn't be improved if they did. More important are ways in which news frames the ads it airs.

News Can Legitimize Ad Content

The frequency with which political ads appeared in network news in 1988 prompted former CBS News executive Bill Small to observe, "Reporters have got to find a way to critically analyze political ads. The Roger Ailes of the world are now able to create ads in order to have them air in television news."[6]

Airing claims in news affords them and their false premises a legitimacy they do not have when broadcast in "paid time." We expect television news not to uncritically transmit the propagandistic claims and visuals of one candidate or the other but "to tell it like it is." As the Roper polls tell us yearly, most people get most of their news from television and most consider that news fair and accurate.

Yet, in the case of the Rappaport, Helms, and Bush adbites at the beginning of this chapter, the clips either fail to disclose needed information, invite false inferences, or lie. The first invites an inference unwarranted by any evidence in the adclip itself—that like Michael Dukakis, John Kerry is a "tax and spend" liberal. Without offering evidence, the adclip would have us believe that Dukakis is appropriately identified as a "tax and spend" liberal, that this identification is a negative one, and one that John Kerry legitimately shares. By using the ad to illustrate the "negativity" of the campaign without questioning its content, reporters gave it the opportunity to pass its evocative theme music—which combined the themes of *Poltergeist* and *Jaws*—and its riveting visuals directly into living rooms in news time.

The second asserts that Harvey Gantt favors aborting a child in the final weeks of pregnancy, a position beyond that of *Roe v. Wade*, illegal in North Carolina, and one he does not hold. It also frames support for a woman's right to choose as an endorsement of aborting, and of aborting not a "fetus" but a "child." Not a single network newscast informed its viewers that the woman in the red dress was misstating Gantt's position.

Most Stories About Ads Enhance the Power of the Ads

By airing segments of the Rappaport, Helms, and Bush ads uncontested, news legitimized their false inferences and fudged claims. The reason is simple. Most of the news segments that aired the two 1990 ad clips left the truth or falsity or their claims unexamined. The same was true of the 1988 presidential campaign. From the conventions through the general election of 1988, the *New York Times, Washington Post, Christian Science Monitor, Wall Street Journal, Time,* and *Newsweek* carried 75 articles on the ads. More than 17 percent of the lines in these stories reproduced ad content. Only 1.7 percent of the lines discussed the accuracy of the ads. The focus of the news stories was most often the negativity of the campaigns. From September through election eve, 1988, NBC, ABC, and CBS evening news aired 155 broadcast ad images from the presidential campaign. During only 4 percent of that air time was the accuracy, fairness, legitimacy, or relevance to governance of the images being evaluated.

The 1990 governor's race in Texas provides a good example of reporters' failure to contextualize ads. State Attorney General Jim Mattox, former Governor Mark White, and State Treasurer Ann Richards sought the Democratic nomination, with Richards the winner. Businessman Clayton Williams drew the most votes in the Republican primary. The Republican incumbent did not seek reelection. So, in the general election, two individuals who had never before sought the governorship faced each other. Neither was burdened with the record that comes with having served as a sitting governor.

Those tuned only to CNN, CBS, NBC, and ABC national television news and public affairs programming during the Texas primaries and runoff had multiple opportunities to see clips of five Texas ads. These advantaged Democrat White and Republican Williams, disadvantaged Richards, and both helped (one self-promotional) and hurt (one oppositional) Mattox. Adbites arguing that their sponsors were tough on crime and favored the death penalty aired for Mattox and White. Republican Clayton Williams' ad on youths busting rocks as a solution to drug use was aired as well. On the oppositional side, an anti-Mattox ad sponsored by his primary opponent former Governor Mark White shows a warning stamped in red on a TV set airing a Mattox ad. The announcer notes that "When you see Jim Mattox on TV: watch his lips. If they're moving, he could be lying." In a Mattox ad, the announcer asks rhetorically whether

Ann Richards has used illegal drugs as an elected official. In the general election, national airtime gave Richards the edge by featuring her oppositional synopsis of Williams' gaffes.

Most of the stories about the spots in the nine races focused not on the accuracy of the ads' claims but on their role in the candidate's strategy. In the headlines, we can read a primer on political maneuvering. "Candidates also competing to control images on TV" (*New York Times,* November 4, 1989). "Time Running Out, Giuliani Steps Up Attacks" (*Washington Post,* September 29, 1989). "Media Advisers Tone It Down in N.Y. Race—Lest They Become an Issue" (*Los Angeles Times,* October 15, 1989). "Dinkins Unveils TV Ad Enlisting Aid of Kennedy to Assail Giuliani" (*New York Times,* October 26, 1989). "Democrat Wilder Makes Preemptive Strike in Television Battle" (*Washington Post,* June 1, 1989). "Behind in New Poll, Wilder Hits Coleman on Abortion" (*RTD* September 20, 1989).

Rarely do reporters ask the questions a voter might want answered about the content of the ad. In the 1990 Texas gubernatorial primary, for example, Ann Richards ran a TV spot that showed:

> Still, captioned, black-and-white photos of Mattox and White on screen as the voice-over noted: "Mark White and Jim Mattox want the governor's job."
>
> Newsclip saying "White pushes tax hike" *Voice-over:* "White promised not to raise taxes, but he did."
>
> *On screen:* "Took our tax dollars to line his own pockets."
>
> *Voice-over:* "Then he took our tax money to line his own pockets."
>
> *On screen:* Deed of trust with following words highlighted: "Mark White and Linda Gale White" and "One million one hundred thousand dollars."
>
> *Voice-over:* "No wonder he could afford his own million-dollar mansion when he left the governor's office."

To judge this ad, a viewer should know whether White did raise taxes after promising not to do so, whether some unforeseen but compelling exigence warranted the tax hike, and whether he misused the powers of his office as governor for personal financial gain.

A voter seeking such answers in the *Dallas Morning News* on March 10, 1990,[7] would learn instead that after inviting reporters to meet him at a closed S&L to dramatize the notion that his opponent Ann Richards had not forestalled that financial crisis, White's "strategy abruptly shifted, taking a more ominous tone." "Outside of a closed Oak Cliff bank, just after noon, Mr. White said he had a different agenda to discuss: He demanded Ms. Richards yank her television ads accusing him of building a personal fortune with taxpayers' dollars. 'There is no more blatant lie that's ever been told in the political history of this state,' he said angrily."

Should a reader believe the Richards ad or the White response? The article doesn't say. The *Dallas Morning News* actually provided the answer. It appeared in an article that ran on March 6.

The *Austin American-Statesman* did no better on March 11, 1990.[8] There, a six-column story evaluates the strategies behind the candidates' ads. "As a platoon of convicts trots by under the watchful eye of armed guards, Clayton Williams talks tough on drugs," begins the piece. "Then, with the Texas flag as a backdrop, he discusses restoring the state's business climate. In another scene, Williams addresses a class of graduating seniors. Next, he slams shut a prison door, touting the death penalty for drug pushers. Williams, a millionaire oil man and Republican gubernatorial candidate, has struck a political fortune with his television commercials: They represent one of the most successful advertising campaigns in a race for Texas governor, political consultants say."

No treatment of the fairness or accuracy of the ads appears in this article. Alongside it on the jump page is an uncontextualized summary of "what the candidates are saying in their ads on the final days of the campaign."

This summary includes such statements as Jim Mattox "also accuses his opponents of opposing a state lottery and says he would enact a lottery to fund programs for children." Does he? Would he? And if he would, would it work? "And he says he cares about crime victims and that Ann Richards is soft on the death penalty." Does he? If so, how does that caring manifest itself? Is he different in his caring from the others? What is Ann Richards' position on the death penalty? "Mark White is saying Mattox has not been truthful when he talks about his record on fighting crime and drugs and opposing a state income tax." Are the claims true? "White also says Richards, the state treasurer, has put Texas tax dollars in banks owned by out-of-state interests." Did she? If so, what advantage or disadvantage was there as a result to the state?

It's important for reporters to question the claims in the ads they're covering. But even when they try, it's not always easy. In the strongest 1988 story attempting to contextualize an ad, the distortions in the ad were magnified. On October 19, 1988, Richard Threlkeld, then of ABC, analyzed portions of the Bush tank ad by freezing the images of the ad on the screen as he countered its claims orally. In the ad, the crawl of the words was continuous. Now in the news clip, they were frozen on screen. In the process, they were reinforced.

> *Visual:* Dukakis in tank.
> *Announcer* (as words crawl across screen): "Michael Dukakis has opposed virtually every defense system we developed."
> *Threlkeld:* "In fact, he supports a range of new weapons including the Trident II missile."
> *Announcer* (as words crawl across the screen): "He opposed anti-satellite weapons." Words stay frozen over tank in ad as Threlkeld says "In fact, Dukakis would ban those weapons only if the Soviets did the same. The same principle incorporated in the INF treaty which George Bush supports."
> *Announcer* (as works crawl across in ad and are frozen): "He opposed four missile systems including the Pershing II missile deployment." With

words frozen on screen, Threlkeld adds, "In fact, Dukakis opposed not four missile systems but two as expensive and impractical, but never opposed deploying Pershing II."

Those focus group members who saw Threlkeld's piece were better able than those who had not to recall the *ad's* claims. They could remember that a reporter said some of the ad was false but could not recall what or why.

The visually evocative nature of Bush's ads meant that the ads themselves could thwart broadcast journalists' attempts to use words to counter their distortions. This is true first because on single exposure in most instances viewers recall pictures better than words.[9] It is true as well because when the reporters' words and the accompanying pictures clash, learning declines.[10] Because pictures are processed faster and at a deeper semantic level than words,[11] they are able to "drown out" the verbal statements of reporters who are showing the controversial ad as they debunk its claims.

Network news also sabotaged its own ability to place distortions in context by feeling a need to balance. The Threlkeld piece points out four factual errors in Bush's ad and then notes one error in an ad on Social Security by Dukakis. But the piece concludes by positing equal culpability. "If the government ever gets around to putting a warning label on TV campaign commercials the way they do on cigarettes maybe it ought to read something like this: If in the heat of a presidential campaign you're tempted to buy something one guy says about the other guy in his TV ads, caveat emptor, buyer beware."

I have suggested that visually evocative, controversial, and humorous oppositional ads are securing uncritical play in national news with two likely effects: a campaign gains the benefit of unpaid access to a large audience; and false claims in the ad segment are legitimized by airing without correction in news space and time. More important, legitimizing misleading ads in news rewards rather than punishes the campaign that produced the material. As Threlkeld's piece on Bush's tank ad illustrates, however, framing an ad's claims verbally often is not sufficient to undercut its message. In Appendix II, I show how the Threlkeld piece can be re-edited to increase audience retention of his words and minimize the power of the ad's pictures.

Adbites and ad stories are not the only forms of political advertising found in broadcast news. Increasingly, the shared visual language of news and ads is giving rise to a new genre in political campaigns, the ad created by reporters and news producers.

The Rise of the Newsad

Broadcast news and ads share the conventions of narrative, employ comparable forms of editing, and use similar forms of address. Ongoing sound, whether voice, music or sound effects, creates a sense of continuity between otherwise discontinuous images. We entrust explanation of what we see to a voice—often disembodied, usually male.

So similar had the techniques of ads and news become that in 1980 the Carter campaign pirated a segment directly from an ABC news piece, aired it as a Carter ad, and few noticed. At issue was Reagan's denial that he had made a statement Carter credited to him in their only debate of 1980. The night after the debate, ABC broadcast the following segment:

> *Barry Serafin:* ". . . the President was apparently on the mark when citing a Reagan statement on stopping nuclear proliferation." *Carter from debate:* "When Governor Reagan has been asked about that, he makes a very disturbing comment that nonproliferation or the control of the spread of nuclear weapons is none of our business." *Reagan (old footage):* "I just don't think it's any of our business. Unilaterally the United States seemed to be the only nation in the word that's trying to stop the proliferation of nuclear weapons." *Reagan in debate:* "I would like to correct a misstatement of fact by the President. I have never made the statement that he suggested about nuclear proliferation."

To air it as an ad, the Carter campaign simply deleted Serafin from the piece.

The newsad is not the by-product of ideological bias but rather of identifiable dispositions in the press that need not characterize political coverage, in general, or coverage of political ads in particular. By focusing on illustrating polls and explicating the effectiveness or ineffectiveness of campaign strategy, reporters inadvertently create one-sided story segments that mimic advertising. At the same time, they abandon their role in maintaining the generic range that makes political discourse work in this system.

Origins of the Newsad

Newsads have a complex genealogy that begins when admakers deliberately began appropriating the grammar of news. In the early 1970s, DeVries and Tarrance[12] revealed that ticket splitters got their most influential political information from television news shows, documentaries, and discussion programs.[13] In the 1970s, these scholar-consultants predicted that political advertising would "look less like traditional advertising (i.e., trying to 'sell' candidates) and . . . [would] be more issue and problem oriented. This . . . [would] come about because political media producers—taking cues from studies like this one— . . . [would] structure their commercials using television newscast formats, mini-documentaries, and confrontation situations in simulated press conferences, debates and talk shows."[14]

Whether guided by DeVries and Tarrance or by intuition, admakers increasingly began casting ads in newslike forms. The trend had begun in 1968. It accelerated in 1972. Not only did ads counterfeit news but, wherever possible, time buyers positioned newslike ads adjacent to actual news programming. One consequence was noted when in the mid-1970s, those conducting focus groups found respondents crediting news with material available only in ads.

Since news is more credible than ads, the confusion in form increases the credibility of the ad. When the production capacity once available only to news became accessible to advertisers, the ability of ads to mimic news jumped.

Broadcast news began as a sustained encounter between an anchor and the audience. The function of the anchor was delivering the news copy in front of him. When available, visual illustration was used. By the mid-1960s, reporters had begun to rely on experts who increasingly were shown being interviewed on camera. Comedian Steve Allen pioneered "man on the street" interviews as a comedy form.

The person in the street form was employed in ads to tout Goldwater in '64, Humphrey in '68, and Ford in '76. As a vehicle of attack, it was used with devastating effectiveness to tag Carter as "wishy-washy" in '76; Carter employed the technique more successfully against Teddy Kennedy in the primaries of '80 than against Reagan in the general election. Reagan revived the form against Mondale in '84; Bush used it against Dukakis in '88.

As ads appropriated the formal conventions of news, an additional phenomenon blurred their boundaries. Where political ad campaigns since Stevenson's in 1952 had employed actors, news until recently had not. As some network newscasts simulated incidents to illustrate stories, another distinction vanished.

It is further blurred when news personalities appear in fictional political contexts as Howard K. Smith did in *The Candidate,* when retired politicians appear in product ads, as former House Speaker Tip O'Neill recently has done, when world leaders are shown in ads for cold remedies, and when actors pretend that they are news anchors as one did in an attack ad by Mississippi gubernatorial candidate Mike Sturdivant against his opponent Ray Mabus in 1987 and as former NBC reporter Peter Hackas did in an anti-David Duke ad in 1991. Meanwhile use of actors in political ads became so commonplace that the presence of actors in Reagan's 1984 "Morning in America" series and in the Bush furlough ad prompted no controversy.

The presence of actors in ads was once controversial. When Ford's 1976 California primary ads featured actors, the need to carry the message with hired hands was roundly ridiculed and the ad series shelved. By contrast, the presence of "actual people" in the person in the street attack ads for Ford was applauded.

By 1984, no one thought it strange that real boy scouts were intercut with paid actors from earlier ads—all shown watching a train carrying Ronald Reagan through America. It was not the actors in Dukakis's handlers' ads that evoked criticism but rather the self-contradiction in the use of scripted actors to indict the machinations of the Bush campaign.

Until 1968, the influence was largely of news on advertising. But as the pressure to compete with alternative channels increased, so too did the reliance of news on what to that point had been advertising's grammar: rapid cuts, short statements, visually evocative content. Even when they occurred in their own form of time—news in news programming and ads between program segments—it was sometimes difficult to tell one from the other. Senior CBS News political producer Brian Healy explained why in 1988: "In the 1970s when we looked at commercials and advertising techniques, and the pacing of popular TV programs, we saw that the American mind was capable of handling a lot of different camera angles, quick shots and short bites, because Americans had seen commercials all their lives. So we have borrowed from the advertising techniques of commercial filmmaking to put our spots together."[15]

At the same time, news was advertising itself in the grammar of political spots. Specifically, in their claim that their anchors were trusted, knowledgeable, and ubiquitous, network promos employed language more readily recognized as that used to market candidates.

The blurring of the boundaries between news and ads is facilitated by some of their common features. Like product ads, political spots are brief, usually either thirty or sixty seconds; they assert but do not argue; when they offer evidence it often assumes the form of the example, although not necessarily the representative example; they both personalize and visualize abstract concepts; because they are brief assertions based in dramatic narrative and/or example and rely on what can be shown, they also favor the simple over the complex.

What formerly distinguished news' use of documentary techniques, person in the street interviews, candidates speaking in direct address, endorsements, and exposure of gaffes from similar moves and conventions in ads was the two-sidedness of news and the single-sidedness of ads. But as news focused intensely on unmasking strategy and explaining polls, whole stories increasingly resembled one-sided ads.

When Will Newsads Occur and Why?

Investigative journalism often takes the form of a damning report based on credible evidence. Such reports differ from ads only in that they faithfully offer the investigated person the right to respond. Any report documenting a pattern of candidate activity or a discernible habit of mind will also seem one sided. A number of such stories documented the suspect sources of candidate Reagan's "facts" in the 1980 campaign. Stories examining the distance between a candidate's proclaimed and real past will also be one sided as were several fine pieces of reporting on the claims of candidate Jimmy Carter in 1976.

In each case the form of the news report and the form of attack advertising will be virtually indistinguishable. Both will use a neutral reporter voice. Both will be heavily "factual." Indeed the 1976 Ford neutral reporter attack ads on Carter's Georgia record looked much like news reports on the same subject. If any of these forms of candidate evaluation were to vanish from news, the public would be poorer for it.

The one-sided news stories that trouble me are built either on explicating strategy or on events staged by the campaign that have no necessary tie to the candidate's record or proposed policies. Sometimes, they reinforce inaccurate information. In 1988, for example, misinformation was spread by news segments showing individuals who proclaimed their belief that Dukakis would confiscate their hunting rifles.

Whether the strategy and pseudo-event driven newsads will favor one candidate or the other is not a function of ideological bias but plainly and simply a function of which campaign better manipulates the press. Specifically, newsads will shower down upon (1) the candidate with pseudo-events tied to sound and adbites; (2) the candidate ahead in the polls; (3) the candidate who metacommunicates more effectively than his or her opponent; and (4) the candidate who exercises the most control over live interviews.

Collision of Pseudo-events, Ad and Soundbites

If campaigns choreograph their pseudo-events to evoke the images from ads, news coverage of these staged acts will increase the power of the ad's images and in the process create a newsad. This was a principle well understood by the Bush campaign. An ABC segment aired on October 19, 1988, shows the result.

> *Bush:* "Let me be as clear as President Reagan and I have been with Mr. Gorbachev, peace through strength works. It is the only policy."
>
> *Brit Hume:* "The crowd cheered even the most familiar lines, the message of the day was again on national security where Bush has an experience advantage. Bush also called on his opponent to join him in opposing unilateral U.S. troop cuts in Europe, something Dukakis has never advocated. Bush's national security message is backed here by commercials now running on Detroit TV stations, as well as nationally, that, among other things, associate Bush with the recent INF treaty with the Soviets (commercial cut from that ad)."

The Bush biographical ad showed missiles being destroyed as an announcer intoned, "Where soldiers began destroying hundreds of nuclear missiles with the understanding that we'd destroy some of our own, the first disarmament treaty of its kind, and though most Americans were unaware of the significance of the moment, or realized it was George Bush who led the way, someday their grandchildren will."

On September 8, 1988, ABC's Britt Hume showed what he characterized as "a photo opportunity": "the Vice President watching as a Pershing missile motor burned off its fuel, the first step in the destruction of U.S. missiles under the INF treaty." One of Bush's two soundbites underscored the positive claims in his biographical ad: "The lesson of INF is the age-old lesson that peace comes not through weakness but through strength."

The second sound snippet previewed the attacks of the forthcoming tank ad: "He [Dukakis] wants to cut the MX, the Midgetman, the B-1, SDI and heaven knows what else. He wants to cut out two carrier battle groups and he asks for nothing in return."

The Republicans missed few opportunities to reincarnate the language of their ads. When Bush received the endorsement of a police union, its head, Robert Guiney (PPA president), was quoted on ABC (September 22, 1988) repeating the message spoken by the announcer in the furlough ad. "We know Governor Dukakis well and we can state publicly that he is not a friend of police. During his term as Governor, he has presided over a revolving door criminal justice system. We are ever mindful of his total opposition to capital punishment." Unspoken on ABC was the context for the pseudo-event. Here was a conservative police union that had twice before endorsed Reagan. Overall, Bush was not endorsed by more police unions than Dukakis; but his endorsements were better stage managed to reinforce the claims of his ads.

Standing in Polls

When the polls show that a strategy is working, news reports will ask Why? As the anti-Dukakis newsads on crime and gun control testify, the answer will favor the candidate ahead on that issue. When polls reveal that a strategy has failed, the explanatory newsad will resemble an attack ad.

A pro-Bush segment that appeared in ABC News on October 28, 1988 is illustrative.

> *Jennings:* "In the heart of Texas, George Bush has struck it rich politically by focusing as much as he does on what he says are essential American values."
>
> *Bush:* "I believe that I am on the side of American people and the people of Texas in terms of values."
>
> *Jennings:* "For George Bush in this election year that means being against the American Civil Liberties Union, against gun control and against abortion. And in this election campaign of 1988, George Bush says time and again he is for prayer in school, for the death penalty and wholeheartedly for the Pledge of Allegiance. Those are issues which have been selling well in Texas."

> *Woman:* "I can't support anybody that would even affiliate with the ACLU."
>
> *Woman:* "Prayer in school is important too. I grew up with it and it helped me through school. I don't see why they want to remove it."

In the same newscast and within the same story, a second newsad occurs.

> *Jennings:* "And when it came to the Pledge of Allegiance, Republicans showed their Texas flair for red meat rhetoric. [A class of elementary school children is shown and heard pledging allegiance to the flag.] It doesn't seem to matter here that Dukakis isn't against the Pledge of Allegiance, only against penalizing teachers who will not lead it in the classroom. But for many Texans the pledge issue has become a test of patriotism pure and simple."
>
> *Man:* "What's wrong with the Pledge of Allegiance; it's just showing that you believe and you stand behind your country. I don't hear anything wrong with that."
>
> *Woman:* "I love my country and I don't mind saying the pledge for it."
>
> *Man:* "Every one of us could stand some more patriotism."

Within the structure of this story, the words of the interviewees serve as a rebuttal to the claim Jennings makes about Dukakis's actual position.

Which Candidate Communicates More Effectively About a Newsworthy Charge?

News reporters tend to excerpt soundbites that create a context for viewing the communication of the campaign. For this reason, the candidate better able to metacommunicate is more likely to be the beneficiary of newsads that counter the opponent's charges. A segment appearing on NBC (October 24, 1988) is a good example. Note that it acknowledges the Dukakis charge, rebuts it, and builds a support base for the rebuttal. In short, it inoculates.

> *Myers:* "The Vice President dismissed all the charges as a sign of desperation. He angrily denied that his campaign has been racist, accusations aides claim are designed to build Dukakis' weak support among blacks."
>
> *Bush:* "That is desperation, insidious and outrageous."
>
> *Myers:* "The racism charge is based largely on Bush's criticism of Dukakis' furlough program, under which Willie Horton, a black convicted murderer raped and tortured a white couple while on a weekend pass."
>
> *PAC ad* (anti-Dukakis): "Weekend prison passes: Dukakis on crime."
>
> *Myers:* "Bush's aides say they would have used the Horton case even if he weren't black. And it is ridiculous to suggest talking about law and order is somehow anti-black because blacks are even more concerned about crimes than whites. Bush also brushed off complaints that his campaign commercials lie about Dukakis' record."

   Bush: "And he is upset, not because it is false, but because he is weak
   on crime and defense, and that's the inescapable truth."

Bush and his spokespersons receive a disproportionate amount of time
in this segment. Because they have been attacked, they are being given
the opportunity to respond. By providing communication about the Dukakis communication, in this case communication that attributes the
Democratic claim to a failing candidate's desperation, the Republicans
give us a rationale for dismissing the Democratic assertion. Then, to provide visual anchorage for the Democratic charge and Republican response, the segment shows a part of the questioned ad. The result: an
adbite within a pro-Bush newsad.

   In a later chapter, I will note the pervasive presence and power of
reporters' focus on strategy. By speaking in "insider" terms, the Republican metacommunication capitalizes on the disposition of press and public
to displace discussion of issues (i.e., are the Horton and furlough ads
racist?) with talk about strategy (i.e., why is Dukakis making this move?
Because he is desperate).

   The newsad is a by-product of reporters' fascination with pseudo-events
and focus on strategy, outcome, and polls. The temptations of the well-
crafted pseudo-event are many. It provides pre-packaged visuals. Its
soundbites are tied to the visuals. Point the camera, stand the reporter
up at the beginning and the end, and—presto—an intact news story.

   Creation of pseudo-event and strategy newsads was facilitated at every
turn by the Bush campaign whose televisual choreography, visually evocative soundbites, and pictorially dramatic ads prompted more frequent
and more favorable use of material from the Bush ads and use of material complementary to them. It is ironic that the reporters who indict
political advertising for displacing substance themselves displace substance with stories that use advertising's disjunctive, abbreviated, telegraphic, narrative form to create personae that bear little relationship to
one's ultimate experience of the elected candidate as president.

Which Candidate Better Controls Live Interviews?

During the 1991 Louisiana gubernatorial race, the national broadcast
media built audiences and ratings by providing David Duke one opportunity after another to telecast newsads to the folks back home. As a
result, by November 13, 58 percent of a national sample could correctly
identify Duke. Only 30 percent could identify his opponent Edwin Edwards.[16] That meant that Duke had wider name recognition than any of
the declared Democratic candidates for president!

   Duke transformed national free air time on such shows as "Good
Morning America," "Today," "Crossfire," "Donahue," "Nightwatch,"
"Nightline," and "Larry King Live" into national newsads for his state-

wide candidacy. While Edwards was on the air in Louisiana in paid time, Duke was using national interview time to beam ads of his own back home. Twice during his interview with Larry King on CNN's "Larry King Live" and once on "Nightline," Duke urged viewers to write for more information or send contributions to his Louisiana headquarters. On "Larry King Live," Duke gave the address including zip code. National publicity helps account for the fact that four out of ten of Duke's contributions came from outside Louisiana.[17] Without a single national direct mail effort, Duke managed to receive contributions from all but four states.[18] Duke's tactic forecast Jerry Brown's controversial intrusion of his "800" number into the 1992 Democratic primary debates.

Not only did Duke make appeals for support but he also used national interview time to insinuate false claims into public consciousness. Unchallenged on either "Larry King Live" or "Nightline" was Duke's assertion that the U.S. Post Office drops the test scores of whites and elevates them for blacks. A spokesperson for the U.S. Post Office categorically denies that statement saying that the only score alterations are for veterans who receive an extra five points and disabled veterans who receive ten.

On "Larry King Live," Duke declared that he had letters from billion-dollar-a-year companies eager to come to Louisiana if he were elected; King asked for evidence. The letter Duke read was not from a company wanting to bring jobs to Louisiana but from a bond company that wanted Louisiana's business. King never questioned Duke's response.

Duke demonstrated repeatedly that he could use national television for his purposes. Before agreeing to appear, he elicited a commitment from Donahue not to use the visual capacity of television to make an attack ad out of his appearances. To get Duke to appear, Donahue agreed not to show photos of him in Klan regalia and not to print on the screen statements he had since disavowed. When Duke told a Donahue caller, "I'm here in the Lion's Den," he had little to fear. His prior agreement had bearded the lion.

In each of the nationally televised interviews, Duke's tone was earnest, his demeanor restrained, his voice modulated, his language polite and filled with "Sir" and "Ma'am." As a result, he sounded and looked more like a talk show host than a Hitler or Huey Long. Had early photos and news clips been shown, they would both have bonded Duke to his disclaimed past and asserted visually that his cosmetic transformation was more visible than his Christian one. The Louisiana Coalition Against Racism and Nazism highlighted the visual contrast in full-page ads showing "before" and "after" pictures of Duke under the headline "Some Change Is Only Skin Deep." "He changed his face," said the print ad. "He changed his political image. But he can't change the truth."[19]

More important, earlier clips showed a "hot," intense, more stereotypically demagogic style. The visual and tonal contrast between the Duke of Klansman past and Christian present raises more powerfully than words the question, Who is the real David Duke? and with it the suspicion that there is more to Duke than meets the eye.

If newsads are the bad news, the good is that in 1990, newspapers in major markets, including the *Los Angeles Times,* the *Dallas Morning News,* the *St. Paul Pioneer Press,* and the *Washington Post,* reprinted the transcripts of ads and then analyzed their factual claims and invited inferences.

In some cases, the effect of the ad watches has been dramatic. In the final days of the Minnesota Senatorial contest in 1990, the incumbent began airing a television ad that showed his opponent's face on the screen as the announcer said, "Who is this guy? Who wants the federal bureaucracy to take over the American medical system? Who would take Medicare money from the seniors who need it so much and use it to fund his socialized health care plan? Who would eliminate Medicare coverage while doubling our personal income taxes? Who is he? He's Paul Wellstone. Not too smart for a college professor." Near the ad's end, the hand of an elderly woman covers up Wellstone's picture.

The ad began airing November 2. The next day, the *St. Paul Pioneer Press*'s "Campaign Ad Watch" said that the ad "may be the most misleading political ad to air in the state this year. Portions of it are simply made up, and all of it is distorted." The column, written by Bruce Orwall, then explains that "Wellstone does not want the federal bureaucracy to take over the American medical system. He has endorsed a plan, published in the *New England Journal of Medicine* last year, by a 30-doctor panel that recommended replacing private health insurance companies with a government-operated insurance plan. The doctors involved say it would not be 'socialized medicine' because hospitals, research facilities and doctors would continue to operate privately. If the plan were ever enacted, Wellstone says, Medicare would still be a big part of providing health care to senior citizens; in fact, Wellstone has said repeatedly that he views Medicare as a sacred trust that he would never vote to cut. On top of that, there is no evidence that Wellstone supports doubling income taxes, although Boschwitz believes that would be the net result of Wellstone's proposals."

"Boschwitz, on the other hand, has voted to cut Medicare, as recently as last month, when a 'budget summit' produced a plan that would have doubled the deductible Medicare recipients pay."

By the final week of the 1990 campaign, the Boschwitz campaign was airing more inaccurate ads than any in the nation. To the airwar, the Republican team then added a carefully targeted piece of direct mail. Again the Minneapolis/St. Paul papers swung into action.

On November 1, 1990, a group titled "People for Boschwitz" sent to "Our Friends in the Minnesota Jewish Community" a letter endorsing incumbent Republican Senator Rudy Boschwitz in his race against Democrat Paul Wellstone. The letter noted:

Both candidates were born as Jews and historically this may be a first. But from there on the difference between them is profound.

One, Paul Wellstone, has no connection whatsoever with the Jewish community or our communal life. His children were brought up as non-Jews. He represents a disturbing element in American politics. He was Jesse Jackson's Minnesota State Co-Chairman in the 1988 presidential campaign. Jesse Jackson has embraced, literally and figuratively, Yasser Arafat and has never repudiated that embrace. Jesse Jackson has never disavowed the support of the notoriously anti-Semitic Louis Farrakhan. Jesse Jackson has very recently, on national television, equated Saddam Hussein's brutal invasion and occupation of Kuwait to the Israeli presence in the West Bank. Wellstone has never disassociated himself from any of Jesse Jackson's policies.

The other candidate is Rudy Boschwitz, whose sense of his people was deeply imbued into him by his parents. They brought Rudy to the U.S. at the age of five, just ahead of the Holocaust, in which many of his family perished. His grandfather was a Rabbi as were six preceding generations of Boschwitzs. Because of his intense interest in all things Jewish, Rudy is known as the "Rabbi of the Senate". . . .

On the Metro News Page of the *Minneapolis Star Tribune,* columnists condemned the letter. Wellstone's media advisor rushed the headlines into a rebuttal ad. "Boschwitz accentuates the negative," said one. "Is Boschwitz trying to stir up a little fear?" asked another. "Boschwitz's smiley face turns ugly," announced a third. On election day, the *Minneapolis Star Tribune* broke with tradition to run an editorial denouncing the Boschwitz mailing as "the lowest political blow of them all." Calling it "the shameless letter," the paper argued that voters should be outraged by Boschwitz's tactics that "grossly stretch the bounds of truth and propriety."[20] In a state known for its citizen activism and political literacy, the news reports carried additional power. Although heavily outspent, Wellstone won.

In fall 1991, the press in Pennsylvania monitored the Wofford-Thornburgh Senate race more carefully and with clearer effect than any Senate race in recent memory. In both Pittsburgh and Philadelphia, the major papers checked the candidates' "facts," set claims in historical context, and exposed both sins of omission and commission in political ads and speeches. So, for example, when Thornburgh claimed that Wofford's national health care plan would cost 300,000 Pennsylvanians their jobs or "experience other severe impacts," reporters contacted the authors of the study Thornburgh had cited. They had not seen the Wofford plan. Their study of the Kennedy and Mitchell plans did not necessarily generalize to Wofford's, reported the two. Thornburgh's claim and the study's authors' denial was carried throughout the state. When Wofford attacked Thornburgh for spending taxpayers' money for a "junket" to Hawaii, the papers corrected the claim by noting that Thornburgh had delivered a speech that fell within his duties as Attorney General and had remained on the island only a few hours.

The state's major newspapers as well as the *New York Times* checked the accuracy of another of the ads. "You decide," said an early Thornburgh ad. "Dick Thornburgh was a highly acclaimed prosecutor. Harris Wofford was a liberal college president who led the school to big budget deficits." Reporters asked the Thornburgh campaign for proof and sought out confirmation from the current president of Bryn Mawr. President Mary Patterson McPherson disputed the Republican claim and documented a reduction in the school's indebtedness under Wofford. "Each year from 1972 to 1978, he added to the college endownment," she added.[21] The *Philadelphia Daily News* asked Thornburgh's camp for documentation and reported that even Thornburgh's data "shows Bryn Mawr's deficit shrinking, both in size and as a percentage of the budget, during Wofford's tenure."[22]

Wofford's counter-advertising and the vigilance of the press turned the race into "Truth or Consequences." "While my opponent was Governor Casey's Secretary of Labor and Industry," said Republican Richard Thornburgh on the stump and in his ads, "the number of people out of work increased by 100,000." By contrast, while he was governor, Thornburgh noted, the state had added 500,000 new jobs. "Neither Mr. Thornburgh, nor his advertisement mentioned that about 400,000 manufacturing jobs were lost in Mr. Thornburgh's administration," noted an article in the *New York Times*, "or that unemployment almost reached 15 percent at the height of the 1982 recession in his first term."[23] On similar grounds, the *Philadelphia Inquirer* found both campaigns doctoring their claims about jobs and joblessness.

Another Republican ad declared: "Adnan Kashoggi. Notorious big-arms dealer. What kind of man would solicit money from him. Harris Wofford," The facts? In 1977 when Wofford was president of Bryn Mawr College, Kashoggi tried to establish a Middle Eastern Studies department at Bryn Mawr, Swarthmore, and Haverford. When a student-faculty committee recommended that the school accept money only for purposes that Kashoggi couldn't influence, such as scholarships and books, he withdrew the offer.

On October 31, 1991, the *Philadelphia Inquirer* editorialized against that ad. "Our candidate for the worst negative ad? The 30-second Thornburgh [ad] that laughably strains" to link Wofford to "notorious big arms dealer" Adnan Kashoggi. " 'Late hit' doesn't begin to describe it. This is an ad from another planet." The Pittsburgh papers joined in the condemnation.

"What the newspapers said enabled us to blunt any negative attack by Thornburgh," notes Wofford strategist Bob Shrum. "If they would make that claim, they would be willing to say anything. That ad was so far over the line that I think the papers would have editorialized against it even if they hadn't been doing adwatches. Our final rebuttal ad was a general rebuttal that we produced the Thursday before the election. We didn't know what they would air at the last minute. So that ad used the comments of the papers to rebut and then returned to the health care issue."

Local stations including WFAA in Dallas, KVUE in Austin, WCCO in Minneapolis, and KRON in San Francisco have followed the lead of their print cousins. The results in the Texas gubernatorial race were clear. Under the caption "KVUE 24 Truth Tests," Carol Kneeland at the Austin station took a Clayton Williams ad to task for "doubling the state budget to claim government had grown by more than it had." Williams pulled the ad. As I noted in an earlier chapter, Ann Richards' media advisor, Bob Squier, was cited for "distorting a newspaper headline by leaving off words attributing to her its negative comments about her opponent." To avoid a repeat of that embarrassing incident, Squier now compares all headlines in ads to the original.

As interesting is Kneeland's claim that the adwatch helped rather than hurt the station economically: "[M]ore than one candidate said they bought more time on our station because they thought the Truth Tests were attracting more politically aware viewers to our newscasts." Displaced by the focus on facticity in the candidates' ads and speeches was the kind of coverage that is the focus of the next chapters. "[W]e avoided the horse race stories about who's ahead, who's behind and what's the latest campaign strategy, the stuff journalists and campaign insiders find fascinating," Kneeland says, "but which is not all that revealing to a voter trying to decide how to vote based on issues and character." How reporters have covered and could cover politics is the subject of the two chapters in Part III.

III

News Coverage
of the Campaign

CHAPTER SEVEN

The News Media as Sounding Board

Throughout 1988, a group of experts diligently instructed American citizens in the sometimes arcane art of politics. The principles are not complicated. They include:

- Doing or saying something inconsistent with past words or deeds invites negative press coverage.
- Lowering expectations is standard front-runner strategy.
- In political campaigns it is advantageous for a candidate to be pictured with respected foreign leaders.
- A "photo opportunity gaffe" occurs when the setting undercuts the visual message (e.g., condemning foreign ownership while in a plant owned by non-U.S. residents).
- Momentum matters. The ways to shift momentum include effective use of attack, "winning" a debate decisively.
- Voters vote the top of the ticket.
- When faced with a scandal, secure the resignation of the person producing the scandal and ensure that public revelation of the scandal and the resignation appear in the same newscast.
- If your candidate misspeaks in a debate, "clarify" his or her position as soon as possible the next morning to remove the potential gaffe from the media agenda.
- "[I]nspecting fire damage in a presidential manner doesn't get you on the air until you get to be president."

- Polls affect how a campaign runs. When a candidate is "up" in the polls, it is easier to raise money and staff morale is high.
- When you are ahead, you play it safe.
- When candidates lead in the polls, they worry about being perceived as arrogant and overconfident.
- Candidates who are about to lose can still draw large, enthusiastic crowds. The presence of such crowds should not be taken as an indication of impending victory.
- Candidates believe that symbols win more votes than substance.
- If you are ahead near the end of a race, avoid words or deeds that could incite controversy. At the end of a campaign, those ahead in the polls adopt the motto: no news is good news.

Neither the Republican nor Democratic National Committee dispensed this sage advice. Nor did it come from campaign consultants wooing prospective clients. Instead these principles were disseminated by Dan Rather, Tom Brokaw, Peter Jennings, Lesley Stahl, Lisa Myers, Sam Donaldson, and the other reporters on the morning, evening, and late night news programs. The same principles can be culled from newspaper reports.

These precepts instruct viewers and readers in how to interpret campaign phenomena. The relationship between the diagnosis and the prognosis in these statements is clear. Clear as well is the focus on explicating rather than assessing candidate engagement, differentiation, and accountability.

These principles also guide viewers and readers to ask some questions and not others. "Who is going to win?" is a central question here. "Who is offering a compelling understanding of the state of the nation, the challenges it faces, and the directions it should take?" is not. So, for example, as the February 16, 1992, CNN Democratic candidates debate was about to begin, viewers were given this preview.

> *CNN Commentator Catherine Crier:* ". . . Eleanor Clift, political correspondent for *Newsweek* magazine and syndicated columnist Jack Germond of the *Baltimore Sun*. Jack, we're just moments away from the start of the debate. What should we be listening for?"
>
> *Jack Germond:* "Well, I think they're going to try to do two things: They have to try to establish that they are presidential and electable, because a large number of New Hampshire Democrats are undecided still. And secondly, they would like to be on the winning side of whatever soundbite comes out of this debate and that's used over and over again in the last thirty-six hours of the campaign."
>
> *Catherine Crier:* "What do you think, Eleanor?"
>
> *Eleanor Clift:* "Well, I think there's going to be a lot of pressure on Senator Paul Tsongas. Until now he's been treated with deference because nobody took him seriously. Now he's the new front runner, and it's unclear whether his appeal is personal—that he's the uncandidate of the year—or whether it has to do with his message, which is pain and sacri-

fice. The others are advocating sugar pills for the economy, and I would expect they're going to try to draw him out on the specifics of his message, which in the past have really been death for Democrats in the modern era of feelgood politics."

Catherine Crier: "So the pre-debate bottom line: Who has the most to gain? Who has the most to lose?"

Eleanor Clift: "Well, I think the two front runners are really in the most precarious positions. Senator Tsongas would like to sit on his lead. And I think Governor Bill Clinton is going to have to shed his front runner's caution. He's now the underdog, and I would expect he's going to take some risks to reassure voters about his candidacy."

Catherine Crier: "Jack, do you agree?"

Jack Germond: "Yeah, I think there's also high stakes for Harkin and Kerrey because one of them has to finish third, one fourth probably. And finishing fourth is no good."

Catherine Crier: "Real quickly. Last interchange before the vote on Tuesday night. Do we expect the gloves to come off at all?"

Jack Germond: "It wouldn't. . . . I would expect there'll be some tough stuff, yeah."

Catherine Crier: "What do you think?"

Eleanor Clift: "Well, I would watch Senator Harkin who is the attack dog in this group."

Catherine Crier: "Okay, we'll be watching. Thank you both. And now it's time. Tonight's debate among the five major Democratic candidates is about to get underway."

The Focus on Strategy

"We celebrated Roger Ailes for his craft as a maker of television ads that created a picture of Michael Dukakis as a friend of murderers and rapists," recalled *New York Times* columnist Anthony Lewis in late November 1988. "There were lots of stories about the superiority of the technicians on that side: value-free stories. . . . I do not think the press should be cheering the corrupters for their efficiency."[1]

As rhetorical theorist Kenneth Burke observes, as "we are using language, it is using us."[2] The language through which the press reports on politics assumes that the American electorate selects a president through a process called a "campaign" seen as a "game" or "war" between a "front runner" and an "underdog" in which each "candidate's" goal is "winning." Candidates' words and actions are seen as their choice of what they presumably envision as a means to victory. So enmeshed is the vocabulary of horse race and war in our thoughts about politics that we are not conscious that the "race" is a metaphor and "spectatorship" an inappropriate role for the electorate. Press reliance on the language of strategy reduces candidate and public accountability.

Both during "campaigns" and in election post mortems, a single perspective—the strategy schema—is the "'script" or "story form" through which reporters, scholars, and occasionally politicians most often invite us to view political elections.

In the jargon of social psychology, "a schema is an abstract or generic knowledge structure, stored in memory, that specifies the defining features and relevant attributes of some stimulus domain, and the interrelations among those attributes."[3] Social and cognitive psychologists have called them "interpretants," "frames,"[4] "cognitive maps,"[5] "scripts,"[6] or "knowledge structures."[7] Because they mediate cognition, we are largely unaware of the schemas that shape our sense of ourselves and the world.

Schemas influence how we perceive new information, how we remember old information, and how we relate the old and new. These pre-existing categories can function as prototypes, determining the features desired in an ideal incumbent president.[8] In the process of cognition we activate schemas, apply them, alter them, reject them.

Schemas simplify, organize, and enable us to process the world without confronting each situation anew. Once triggered, a schema helps us to fill in consistent information that has not actually been provided by an observable event. We store the inferred along with the observed. After the information has resided in memory for a while, we have difficulty distinguishing one from the other.[9]

Individuals who have clear knowledge structures about a specific area of inquiry are known by cognitive psychologists as "schematics"; those who have not developed such knowledge structures are termed "aschematics."[10] A person may be aschematic about politics because he has no interest in it, lacks experience processing political information, or lacks the ability to develop an elaborate knowledge structure. Without exposure to political information and experience in processing it, we cannot develop schemas to sort it.[11]

In the language of social psychology, the strategy schema is an event schema. Event schemas are scripts that assume that sequences of actions are predictable means of achieving some knowable goal in a specific situation.[12] If I invite you to lunch at a local restaurant, we both expect waiters, menus, entrees, a check, and the like. And we expect them to appear more or less in that order. Only in the world of *Monty Python* does the check appear before the entree.

The strategy schema has the advantage of being a "story." As such, it employs a structure native to news, which reduces happenings to "stories." The narrative structure also pervades television, from the minidramas of housewives faced with ring around the collar to the larger dramas of Murphy Brown's pregnancy.

In the strategy schema, candidates are seen as performers, reporters as theatrical critics, the audience as spectators. The goal of the performer is to "win" the votes of the electorate projected throughout the performance in polls. The polls determine whether the candidate will be cast as a front runner or underdog, whether the candidate will be described as achieving goals or "trying" to achieve them, and how the candidate's staged and unstaged activities will be interpreted. In the strategy schema, candidates do not address problems with solutions but "issues" with "strategies." The language of the strategy schema is that of sports and war. This vocabulary lets reporters, candidates, and the public ask, Who is winning and how? The posture invited of the electorate by this schema is cynical and detached.

The story line of the strategy schema encourages voters to ask not who is better able to serve as president but who is going to win? "[W]inning and losing are presented as all-important," writes political scientist Doris Graber, "rather than what winning and losing mean in terms of the political direction of the country in general or the observer's personal situation in particular. Taking its cues from the media, the audience accepts election news as just another story rather than as an important tale that will directly affect its own welfare in real life." [13]

News coverage "primes" or "cues" viewers and readers to see, store, and analyze "campaigns" through the strategy schema. The results are reflected in the way voters talk about "campaigns." So, for example, political scientist Thomas Patterson found that in 1976 the "game" was the subject of voter conversation more often than the substantive elements of the campaign. [14] When 106 focus group respondents in a total of nine states [15] were asked weekly for twelve weeks during the 1990 general election to list what, if anything, they had learned about their statewide campaigns in the past week from watching local and national news, 73 percent of the responses dealt with campaign strategy or who was where in the polls and why.

So pervasive was strategy discussion that it even wormed its way into the Dukakis election eve telecast. In this half-hour broadcast, Michael Dukakis responds to questions asked of him by voters from across the country. Some offer him strategic advice such as, "You need to be real clear and real strong in your comments." Others question his strategy. "Why weren't you playing hardball when he was playing hardball?" "I'd like to know why it takes him so long to respond to the lies that come out in Bush's speeches?"

At the same time, they assume that what they have seen of Dukakis in the campaign may not be the real person, that campaign actions are scripted for effect and can be modified by a simple act of will. "When you were asked that question in the debate about your wife being raped and murdered, why was your answer so cold?" "I just want to know why Dukakis doesn't seem to let his emotions show through, he doesn't seem to want anyone to know who he is."

The questioners have been taped earlier by producer Bob Squier. The fact that the questions were asked, that Squier included them in the candidate's last half hour on network television, and that Dukakis took them seriously enough to answer them suggests the extent to which the strategy schema has made its way into the contours of political discourse.

Why the focus on strategy? Increasingly, scholars agree with an explanation offered by political scientists Michael Robinson and Margaret Sheehan. "For a host of reasons, objective journalism has, for a century and a half, defined news as *events,* as happenings," they note. " 'Horse races' happen; 'horse races' are themselves filled with specific actions. Policy issues, on the other hand, do not happen; they merely exist. Substance has no events; issues generally remain static. So policy issues, or substance, have been traditionally defined as outside the orbit of real news." [16]

Other factors also come into play. Strategy was the native tongue of those reporters who once were campaign insiders. In 1988 the guild of former campaigners now covering campaigns included: ABC's Jeff Greenfield, NBC's Ken Bode, CBS's Diane Sawyer, CNN's Pat Buchanan, ABC's George Will, MacNeil/Lehrer's David Gergen (also of *U.S. News*), NBC Vice President Timothy Russert, and independent producer most frequently seen on PBS, Bill Moyers. Chris Matthews, the Washington Bureau Chief for the *San Francisco Examiner,* is former press secretary to Democratic House Speaker Tip O'Neill. In 1988 he doubled as a regular political consultant appearing on CBS news as did Rep. Jack Kemp's former press secretary John Buckley. Syndicated columnists Jody Powell and William Safire also led earlier lives in presidential service.

The revolving door turned both ways. Reporters who gave up pen or mike for government appointments carried into the bureaucracy an insider's understanding of how the news could be shaped. The first presidential campaign to carry large numbers of reporters and producers into candidate service was Nixon's in 1968. Patrick Buchanan had been an editorial writer for the St. Louis *Globe-Democrat;* Ray Price had performed the same function for the New York *Herald Tribune.* Nixon's television advisers in 1968 included Frank Shakespeare, formerly a CBS Vice President, and Roger Ailes, formerly of the "Mike Douglas Show." Nixon's 1968 campaign communication coordinator was a former *Time* editor, James Keogh.

Following the lead of Theodore White, whose *Making of the President* series reshaped journalists' conception of the available means of story construction, many of the nation's top reporters envision the campaign year ending with a best-selling book answering the question "Who Won and How?" Their titles reveal the strategy schema simmering below the story line: *Portrait of an Election* by Elizabeth Drew, *Marathon: The Pursuit of the Presidency, 1972–1976* by Jules Witcover, *Dasher: The Roots and Rising of Jimmy Carter* by James Wooten, *The Road to the White House* by a team from the *New York Times, The Quest for the Presidency: The 1988 Campaign* by Peter Goldman, Tom Mathews, and the *Newsweek* Special Election Team, *The Winning of the White House 1988* by the editors of *Time* magazine, *Road Show* by Roger Smith.

Alongside these are the more arcane works of those of us who call the university home. Like reporters, academics reinterpret the polls, analyze how the campaign agendas were formed, and account for the strategies behind the candidates' use of news, advertising, and the debates.

Schemas in Recent Campaign History

Campaign history also has something to do with the nature and scope of the strategy focus. To underscore his claim of being an outsider who would reform Washington, Jimmy Carter ran in 1976 on a rhetoric of self-conscious symbols. He carried his own luggage, wrote his own thank-you notes, and spurned hotels for pull-out couches in the homes of his supporters. His actions invited reporters to account for this aberrant behavior.

In spring 1976, a second candidate entered the forum in a campaign also built from self-conscious symbols. California governor Edmund G. (Jerry) Brown, Jr., had abjured the governor's mansion for an apartment near the capitol and the governor's limousine for an old used car. He too carried his own luggage and flew coach. Both were arguing performatively that theirs would not be imperial presidencies.

At the same time the post-Watergate, post-Vietnam press was scrutinizing candidates with unprecedented care to determine whether any among them would lie about his conduct of public policy while secretly sanctioning illegal activities. But neither the press nor the public knew what verbal or behavior signs were the outward manifestation of an inward disposition to deceive. One thing was clear, however. The press would identify anything that looked like manipulation. So, for example, it was repeatedly noted that Ford was trying to look presidential as he campaigned from the Rose Garden in 1976.

In 1976 and 1980, countervailing forces created pressure to cover policy proposals as well. These forces conspired to ensure that campaign coverage would stress substance and not merely semblance. In the primaries, Carter's opponents capitalized on his lack of familiarity with Washington by claiming that he was "fuzzy" on the issues. Such a claim requires evidence. When his adaptations to dissimilar audiences in Iowa prompted the initial charge, abortion was the instance most often mentioned. With unemployment approaching 7.9 percent and inflation in double digits, candidates in 1980 were naturally expected to answer the question, What would they do differently? Nonetheless, in his 1976 interview with *Playboy*, candidate Jimmy Carter would sound much like Bush advisor Robert Ailes did at the end of the 1988 campaign. Carter averred that "[T]he traveling press have zero interest in any issue, unless it's a matter of making a mistake. What they're looking for is a 47-second argument between me and another candidate or something like that. There's nobody in the back of this plane who would ask an issue question unless he thought he could trick me into some crazy statement."[17]

Corroboration that the campaign had substance came from reporters themselves. When, on "Campaign Countdown," Walter Cronkite asked Lesley Stahl about claims that the 1980 campaign had been issueless, she replied: "The candidates are discussing the issues, but we aren't reporting them. They are old news." Illustrative is CBS's treatment that year of a speech on the economy that the Democrats purchased time to air. On two network news segments, CBS noted that the speech was in preparation and would air the next Sunday evening. But reporting on the speech in CBS evening news was limited to this observation. "The medium: network radio. The message: the economy is looking up. President Carter took to the airwaves today in his campaign for re-election. Lee Thornton reports." *Thornton:* "The paid political broadcast was part of an effort to breathe fresh life into the Carter campaign—15 minutes on network radio, the first of a series of three such addresses. The subject of the President's speech was the economy, but the address also included some restrained talk about the choice before the voters. A Carter advisor said this was a way for the President to talk to voters at greater length and in more coherent fashion than he is able to in brief news reports." Nothing of the substance of the speech is quoted. Ironically, the news report includes this excerpt: "Too often in political campaigns, the focus is on the contest itself, debates about debates, charges and counter charges among candidates, the endless speculation about who is ahead. Too often the meaning of the election, the real decision facing the country is lost or forgotten" (CBS, October 12, 1980).

In 1990, similar judgments can be made about coverage of statewide races. In a joint appearance at a luncheon before members of the Greater Dallas Crime Commission on October 11, 1990, Texas gubernatorial candidates Clayton Williams and Ann Richards delivered speeches differentiating their positions on how to deal with crime in the state. At the dais, Williams approached Richards and said, "Ann, I'm here to call you a liar today." Richards responded that she was sorry to hear it. After charging that she had lied about her opponents in the spring primaries and was lying about him in the fall campaign, Williams said, "I'm gonna finish this deal today, and you can count on it." As he stepped back, Richards extended her hand. Williams refused to shake it.

That evening, local news focused not on the statements on crime but on the spurned handshake. The exchange became the center point in a Richards ad against Williams. "[I]t was a great day for reporters on the scene," wrote Dave Denison who covered the race for the *Boston Globe*. "They were rescued from the task of doing speech coverage or issues coverage. They had a dramatic incident with front-page and top-of-the-news appeal. All the reporters who were there, including myself, felt they had gotten a good show."[18]

Candidates as Performers

"My concern is for our business," noted *New York Times'* Anthony Lewis after the 1988 campaign. "There were times in this campaign when we looked like theatre critics—critics interested only in the artfulness of the scenery, not in the message of the play."[19]

"It was floating political theatre," said CBS's Bob Schieffer of Bush's trip to Boston Harbor, "and the plot was simple: show that, while Dukakis talks about cleaning up the environment, Boston Harbor just gets dirtier" (CBS, September 1, 1988). While they're most often the most informative parts of campaigns," notes Schieffer, "debates are a lot like watching a good play, especially since it's the first time the main actors are sharing the same stage." Democratic consultant Bob Beckel agrees. "It's the greatest act in American politics, and it's called the presidential debate, act one, Sunday night" (CBS, September 24, 1988).

"Lowered expectations aside," says CBS's Bill Whitaker, "everyone in the campaign agrees Dukakis needs to give a stellar performance Sunday" (CBS, September 24, 1988). It is "staged" (CBS, September 21, 1988), a "staged love-in," said Betsy Aaron of Dukakis, Bentsen, and Jackson in mid-September (CBS, September 15, 1988). The candidate's advisors are called "choreographers" and "handlers," and Bentsen is described as a "senior senator who could have stepped out of central casting" (CBS, September 30, 1988).

The performance criteria ask not what you are but how you seem or appear. So, for example, a deputy manager of the Bush campaign says of his candidate's debate performance: "He wants to come across as presidential, to have command of this subject matter and to avoid costly errors" (CBS, September 23, 1988). After the first debate Dan Rather observed that Bush "came across as he wanted to, and that is firm and in command. In Michael Dukakis's case, the sense, the feel, here in the room was that he accomplished at least one of his purposes, which was to come across as someone steady, reliable, who knows at least what he's talking about, whether you agree with him or—or not" (CBS, September 25, 1988).

In the process of evaluating the "performance" of the candidates, critics set in place criteria for assessment. If a focus on performance/promise were governing their perspective, they would ask: What is the candidate's record in dealing with this sort of problem? In dealing with the sorts of problems a president faces? Did the candidate address the problems facing the country? How well? Which candidate has proposed more viable solutions? A strategy focus provides a different optic: How effective were the strategies? In the process an effective strategy implicitly becomes a "good" strategy.

One danger in seeing candidates as actors is that they will be lured by our expectations into becoming the person they pretend to be. One might

Figure 7-1. In colorful ads that resembled documentaries, incumbent president Richard Nixon was shown meeting world leaders and busily fulfilling his presidential obligations. This image was designed to minimize public belief that Nixon would have had either the time or the inclination to be involved in Watergate. Meanwhile, ads for Democrats for Nixon argued that Nixon's opponent, George McGovern, wasn't up to the job.

argue, for example, that as president JFK OK'd the Bay of Pigs operation to preempt claims from the right that he was insufficiently tough on
communism. A former aide makes a related claim about Kennedy's 1960
opponent. "His personal failure," wrote speechwriter William Safire of
his former boss Richard Nixon, was that "he was concerned too much
with how he would be perceived, occasionally creating a mask that became the man."[20]

The Reporter as Theatre Critic or Campaign Consultant

Reporters and experts are cast in this "performance" as "critics." The
results are strange. So, for example, NBC's Lisa Myers (September 19,
1988) notes that the Bush campaign "is a campaign of carefully staged
events and carefully crafted images." Reporters compare the candidates
to actors and the campaign's staged events to television shows. "Bush's
law-and-order message has taken him to more police stations than Cag-
ney and Lacey put together," noted CBS's Eric Engberg (CBS, October
22, 1988). "And today it was the real CHIPS of the California Highway
Patrol who provided the backdrop of another show of blue power. Bush
started at the training track for the future Broderick Crawfords, then
got more than a hundred endorsements from California lawmen."

Reporters also publicly advise candidates on how to improve their self-
projection and staging. "Bush needs to overcome the impression that
he's a bad candidate [not needs to overcome *being* a bad candidate but
needs to overcome the *impression*]: easily rattled during a 1980 debate
with Ronald Reagan, too flip after a debate with Geraldine Ferraro in
1984. . . . And Bush must work to overcome one other negative—the
idea that despite his resume and his war record, he's somehow not decisive, not forceful, not a Commander-in-Chief." The critic/consultant
was Bruce Morton (CBS, October 12, 1987). "Unless you're Harry Truman—and Dukakis is not—the strategy of giving them hell runs the risk
of sounding shrill and unpresidential," notes ABC's Sam Donaldson on
September 12, 1988.

At other times the critic patronizingly tells us things we ought to be
able to observe for ourselves. "Simon is a plain man. No high-flown eloquence, no glitz. Plain speech. That plainness finds an echo here. A lot
of Iowans are plain people too" (Bruce Morton, November 23, 1987).
"Dole is trying to soften his hatchet man image" (Bob Schieffer, November 9, 1987). "Say one thing for Gephardt, he looks the part and his
family is campaign poster classic right down to the loyal dog" (Bob
Schieffer, October 22, 1987).

At other times, a reporter's seemingly therapeutic insight cries out for
evidence. "But when Bush tries to be himself, his words and actions often
make him sound like an elitist," observes ABC's Carole Simpson (March
8, 1988).

Sometimes the critic/consultant appears to be running a school for as-piring campaign consultants. Bruce Morton observes (CBS, September 13, 1988): "In the trade of politics, it's called a visual. The idea is pic-tures are symbols that tell the voter important things about the candi-date. If your candidate is seen in the polls as weak on defense, put him in a tank."

Before evaluating the success or failure of a strategy, reporters often tell us how it is supposed to work. So, for example, on September 21, 1988, Bruce Morton explains and illustrates how the "message of the day" works. "Sometimes, it's just staging, what are called visuals. This is a show at the Los Angeles Police Academy meant to reinforce an anti-drug speech that day. Sometimes it's cosmetic as it was when Dukakis switched from a red sweater to a suede jacket for a tour of Yellowstone National Park." Indeed, Dukakis's aides report that his sartorial switch from sweater to jacket came at the prompting of a network news corre-spondent.

If candidates are seen as performers and reporters as critics, then re-porting about the reports of the critics is a natural press topic. The sil-liness of it all was exposed on "Nightline" September 26, 1988, by a person with credentials both as a newspaperman and political insider. That program focused not on the substance of the first presidential de-bate but on post-debate polls, spin control, the tenor of press coverage, and the meaning of it all for the two campaigns. In this context, ABC correspondent Jeff Greenfield asked former Nixon aide and *New York Times* columnist Bill Safire, "Why should anyone think that this debate would have any effect in showing or turning that [pro-Bush] trend?" First Safire mocked the tone with which Greenfield had promulgated his predictions. "I think the estimates delivered—hats off to you, in a very authoritative way—are cockeyed. Who knows what the estimates are? They're estimates, but they're out of touch with reality." Then he an-nounced that the emperor and his court had no clothes, "Tonight, on this program, we're covering the coverage of an event. That's like taking a picture of a statue of a man. We're twice removed from reality. I don't agree with the basic premise of your—of your question, which is that the media, the pundits, the thumbsuckers, the spin meisters, determine what people think about the candidates. I think we're flattering ourselves."

What Safire called for was an end to the cheap shots and a focus on "some big things like what [difference] will this decision make to the Supreme Court, or what would having a Democratic president mean in Washington when you'd have both Democratic Congress and White House?" To that, liberal commentator and *New Republic* editor Michael Kinsley added, "The biggest decision facing the country is what we're going to do fiscally about the deficit. And that's a question which both campaigns are running from as fast as they can. So the hope of really getting serious about the most important issue is nearly hopeless."

Two commentators have grabbed the agenda and dragged it back to the problems facing the country and the decisions that the next president will have to make. How long can this line of inquiry sustain itself? Greenfield responds to Kinsley's observation about the deficit by asking, "Well, Michael Kinsley, it seems striking to me that even Michael Dukakis's most loyal supporters are now going around saying, 'You know, the guy just isn't giving us the juice we need.' Is that an example of what Bill Safire would call a superficial, media-driven irrelevancy, or is it a real problem?" "No, I think it is a real problem," says Kinsley and back to talking about pictures of the pictures of statues go the discussants.

The Role of Polls in Strategy Reporting

Polling data often provide the trip wire that activates the discussion of strategy in news. Activation looks like this. The words are Barry Serafin's on ABC, October 4, 1988. "[T]he Vice President [Bush] was back to the tried and true, the one liners that in California, for example, have helped him erase a double digit deficit in the polls." The piece then plays a litany of Bush soundbites.

In 1988 there were "10 national polling organizations in the field, and a new poll was reported every second day on average during the final months of the campaign."[21] Nearly a third of the network news election stories aired during the 1988 primaries made note of poll results.[22]

Pollsters are augurs. What they forecast is victory or defeat. These prophesies determine how reporters treat the candidate. "Coverage of candidates and their campaigns differs qualitatively depending on their relative standing [in the polls]," writes Democratic pollster Harrison Hickman. "Stories about candidates doing well in polls usually focus on what they are doing *correctly*—the policy positions, campaign strategies, and personal qualities that put them at the top of the preference rankings. Coverage of candidates doing badly in polls usually focuses on what they are doing *wrong*—various factors that put them behind front-runners."[23]

Words are outward signs instituted by polls to determine place. In the primaries the amount of news space or time a candidate receives is a function of standing in the polls; the symbolic moments chosen to stand for the campaign as a whole are determined in part by the reporters' reading of the polls' divinations. Among other things, this means that candidates ahead in the polls are more likely to see segments of their ads run in news to illustrate the effectiveness of their communication strategies. Polls also shape the nouns, verbs, and adverbs that reporters choose to characterize a candidate's discourse and behavior.

Polls and Nouns

The implied nouns in poll-driven reporting are win, place, and show. In starker terms, this is a world of front runners, underdogs, and also rans. "Dole, running far behind Bush, used some of his toughest language."

"Pat Robertson, who slipped back into third place in South Carolina, was in Louisiana today trying to shore up his religious base" (ABC, March 7, 1988). "In this our final report, ABC's Carole Simpson on the Republican front runner George Bush" (ABC, March, 8, 1988). In a news segment in which Sam Donaldson notes that Bush "is still on top 50 to 47," Jackie Judd (ABC, October 10, 1988) reports that "Michael Dukakis took his underdog campaign to New York City's Columbus Day parade."

The campaign is going to the dog races. "Front runners" work to maintain their lead. "Underdogs" try to come from behind. If polls show a drop in popularity, the candidate is said to lose ground.[24] "Front runners" and contenders receive more press space than minor candidates and "also rans." The nature of their coverage differs as well.

The "front runner" and the "underdog" are pegged in the "pack" by their place in the polls. Each tag carries baggage. True to his name, the "underdog" campaigns "doggedly." Where the "front runner" is plagued only by the possibility of overconfidence, the "underdog" is doggedly desperate. Where "front runners" shore up, persuade, appeal, and stride, "underdogs" can't seem to sidle up to active verbs. If one were to believe network news, front runners are exempt from Murphy's Laws. "Front runners" are shown in symbolic moments underscoring their competence. "Underdogs," to mix the metaphor, can't pitch, stage pseudo-events, get their planes on schedule, or their cars on the road. They struggle.

Polls and Adverbs

But nouns aren't all an "underdog" has to bitch about. Whether a candidate is described as striding briskly or struggling is not a function of the person's orthopedic agility but rather a metaphoric register of his or her standing in the polls. In July, when he is ahead in the polls, Dukakis's travel through seven states in three days is characterized by saying, "Michael Dukakis maintains a brisk pace on and off the campaign trail. Very early this morning he got some exercise with his wife Kitty" (NBC, July 30, 1988, Bob Kur). On October 25, after Peter Jennings notes that "The latest *Los Angeles Times* poll finds that Bush is ahead in California by 11 points," Sam Donaldson reports that "Michael Dukakis struggled on today in an effort to shake off the negative image George Bush's advertising has so effectively created around him." On October 12, 1988, Dan Rather concluded a summary of a poll by noting "Only one of three voters (30%) believes Quayle is qualified for the presidency, and if it became necessary for Quayle to assume that office, nearly two out of three voters (63%) said they would be downright worried." The damage in the polls is reflected in the adverb in the next sentence. "Aides to Bush have been *furiously trying* to limit the damage by keeping Quayle on a tight leash" (emphasis added).

Polls and "Trying"

As he drops in the polls, the relationship between the candidate and active verbs becomes more tenuous. Candidates who are behind in the polls or "lose" a debate no longer directly act; instead they try. On October 10, 1984, after the first Mondale-Reagan debate, Lesley Stahl reports: "Today, a show of stamina. The president walking when normally he would take his limousine. Campaigning among ethnic groups. Mr. Reagan *tried* to regain the offensive, swinging hard at Mondale on taxes and defense."

In 1988 on ABC more so than on CBS and NBC, those behind in the polls suffer "tries" as well as tribulations. After reporting that Bush is the forecast choice of 59 percent and Dole of 22 percent of the likely Super Tuesday voters, Peter Jennings adds, "Again today Senator Dole *was trying* to cast himself as an activist and George Bush as passive." "Our latest ABC News-*Washington Post* poll shows that Bush has a nearly two to one lead over Dole in next Tuesday's battleground, Illinois," reported Peter Jennings on March 1. As ABC's Barry Serafin reports, "Dole was campaigning there today while his campaign staff *tried* to figure out exactly what to do." Serafin then observes, "Dole today visited a rehabilitation hospital while *trying* to figure out what to do about his campaign."

In summer, when polls showed him trailing Dukakis, it was Bush who was "tried." Bush is "*trying* to make capital punishment a major campaign issue," said Lisa Myers in June (NBC, June 22, 1988). "One line of negative campaigning and attack," noted Dan Rather in July, "to *try* to portray Dukakis and the Democrats as soft on crime" (CBS, July 20, 1988).

Down in the polls before the first debate on ABC (September 21, 1988) Dukakis "*tried* to project a certain jaunty confidence." Still behind in the polls as the second debate approached, ABC forecast that "Tonight he'll [Dukakis] *try* to project more warmth, more likability" (October 13, 1988). Donaldson closes: "Dukakis, the man behind, knows he must win this debate."

On October 19, ABC's Peter Jennings notes that "George Bush said he would continue to campaign as if he were the underdog even though the latest ABC News poll out today shows that Bush continues to maintain a lead over Michael Dukakis of about seven points. . . . Our first report tonight is from the Dukakis campaign, where today the Governor, who campaigned in the midwest, was *trying to* set the record straight on the position he takes regarding crime."

One might surmise that "trying to" is an indication that Dukakis but not Bush has been distracted by his opponent's message. But that interpretation is set aside when Brit Hume reports (October 26, 1988), "In Detroit to address a business group, Bush wanted to get back to his theme of the week, prosperity, which has been obscured the past two days by his defense of his TV ads." So Bush's message has been blurred as well.

But, ahead in the polls, Bush will act, not try. "But today, Bush also defended [did not *try to defend*] his plan to cut the capital gains tax and assailed [did not *try to assail*] Michael Dukakis for calling it a 40 billion dollar bonus for the rich."

Occasionally the meaning of all of this "trying" is made explicit. Candidates behind in the polls work hard at things but don't actually accomplish them. If they did, the polls would presumably reflect that. "Michael Dukakis worked hard today to energize traditional Democratic strength" (Donaldson, ABC, October 28, 1988). "Later in Warren, Michigan, Dukakis worked hard on the blue collar vote" (same broadcast). Working hard is contagious. "Governor James Blanchard and other top Democrats are working hard for Dukakis but still the polls show him behind here" (Donaldson, same broadcast).

When Dukakis' claim that the Bush campaign was "negative" began to resonate in the polls, he momentarily put Bush in a "trying position." Bush *"tried* to deal with increasingly aggressive talk from Mike Dukakis, charges by the Dukakis campaign of outright lying and racist overtones," noted Dan Rather (CBS, October 14, 1988). "Bush *tried* to put [Dukakis's charges of racism and negativity] behind him early" (emphasis added), observed Bob Schieffer (CBS, October 24, 1988).

Polls Determine When Your Performance Will Be Taken Seriously

On October 17, 1980, incumbent president Jimmy Carter was trailing challenger Ronald Reagan in the polls. On that day a freight train jumped its tracks and stopped near Carter headquarters in Plains, Georgia. Sander Vanocur has just concluded an analysis of blue-collar defections from the Democratic ticket with the words "And for that reason, any defection, whether it's votes for Reagan or people who just stay home, spells potential trouble for Jimmy Carter." ABC anchor Max Robinson continues, "Well, trouble of another kind did materialize at President Carter's campaign headquarters in Plains, Georgia, today. It came in the form of a surprise visit from several freight cars which jumped the tracks early this morning and wound up precariously close to the President's headquarters at the old depot in downtown Plains. No one was hurt, but late today police were still trying to move those cars." In this context, the crumpled wreckage is juxtaposed with the crumbling Democratic party plagued by defections. But the symbolic tie is not made directly.

Throughout 1984, in Shakespearean fashion, the broadcasters' sense of the external world seemed to mimic the internal state of the two campaigns. During 1984, Mondale never led in the polls. On September 4, 1984, Susan Spencer of CBS noted, "A rally last night in Long Beach had done little to cheer anyone up. The sound system failed." But Mondale briefly changed the chemistry of the campaign with his command of the facts and the agenda in the first presidential debate. That was reflected on October 8, the day after the first Mondale-Reagan debate

of 1984, when Sam Donaldson of ABC reported, "The presidential mo-
torcade rolled slowly and painfully out of Louisville this morning, its
occupants well aware that the heavyweight debating champ had stubbed
his toe on Walter Mondale."

By 1988, polls determined whether a candidate's staged visualizations
of his messages would play or fail. Such moments were treated as synecdochic commentary on the campaigns. On Friday, September 23, 1988,
Dukakis tossed a baseball back and forth to Red Sox outfielder Ellis Burke.
The "photo-op" took about twenty minutes. At one point he missed the
ball. "In my broadcast tonight, guess what picture appeared when I reported that Dukakis had spent today preparing for a debate in an election that he says is about competence," asked ABC's Sam Donaldson in
a daily diary. " 'Ooops,' I said—as he missed the ball. Campaign staffers
and partisan supporters dislike these harmless visual touches, but they
are fun. Let the record show that I apply them equally wherever I find
them—to Carter, to Reagan and now to Dukakis." [25]

But as Donaldson himself admits later in the diary, such visuals are
not harmless. When the right front tire on Dukakis's limousine blows
out on the New Jersey turnpike, September 29, the Democratic trip director tries to block the press from photographing it. "I'm sure that our
safety wasn't his first concern," says Donaldson. "Think of the fun a TV
camera could have had with that one. A picture like that just cries out
'loser.' " [26]

And when a candidate is ahead in the polls, as Bush was from Labor
Day through the election, such incidents as failure of the air condition-
ing on the press bus (September 5), his limousine overheating and
steaming (October 3, 1988), and his repeated mistelling of the Horton
story, do not become the synecdochic moments through which the press
invites us to see his campaign.

Nor was ABC, as Donaldson avers, an equal-opportunity symbolizer.
ABC, which in 1988 offered the most poll-driven coverage, was the only
of the networks to show Dukakis throwing a gutter ball in a bowling alley
October 17. On NBC Chris Wallace showed Dukakis knocking down most
of the pins as the crowd applauded. Here the success at bowling provides a counterpoint to the problems in the campaign. "In these tough
times," says Wallace, "it's the kind of encouragement that keeps the candidate going." "When you are losing," said Bruce Morton on CBS,
"everything is a symbol, whether you throw a gutter ball or knock down
some pins."

The coverage of Bush's Labor Day events in 1988 and Mondale's in
1984 is instructive. At the time in 1984, Mondale was behind in the polls.
By contrast, Bush had just closed a 17-point lead and was perceived by
the press to be "surging."

When the Democrats attracted small crowds at the first parade of the
day in 1984, the press quickly read symbolism into the snafu. But four
years later when the Republicans failed to draw a large crowd no such
leap to interpret was evident. "It was a good picture," noted CBS's Bob

Schieffer, "of the Disneyland 'backdrop.' [B]ut the crowd was not large, for Labor Day; and, at an earlier stop in San Diego, things did not go at all as campaign choreographers had hoped. The crowd was small; and, even though Bush's people tried to block them from sight, there were almost as many Dukakis signs as Bush signs. Even so, Bush used tough language, as he argued that Dukakis would weaken America's defenses" (CBS, September 5, 1988). Why did one small crowd symbolize impending doom while the other was simply reported as a fact? The answer lies in Schieffer's final comment. "But the real good news for the Bush team this Labor Day is a poll published by the *Los Angeles Times,* which shows Bush holding an astonishing 32-point lead here in heavily Republican, heavily populated Orange County. If that kind of lead can hold, then Bush can probably carry California, until now considered a toss-up state." Yet twelve days later CBS reported that polls in California showed the race a "dead heat" (CBS, September 17, 1988).

The Role of Issues in the Strategy Schema

Within the strategy schema, the candidates and the country do not confront problems but "issues." "When Americans watch politics now, in thirty-second snatches or even in more satisfactory formats like "Nightline" or "The MacNeil/Lehrer NewsHour," they understand instinctively that politics these days is not about finding solutions," writes *Washington Post* reporter E. J. Dionne, Jr. "It is about discovering postures that offer short-term political benefits. We give the game away when we talk about 'issues,' not 'problems.' Problems are solved; issues are merely what politicians use to divide the citizenry and advance themselves."[27]

Issues are treated by most reporters as if they had an existence independent of the candidates' and reporters' construction of them. In fact, problems become "problems" when defined as such. Problems become "issues" when a candidate, the press, or polls say that they are considered important in determining which candidate will win. Since the Savings and Loan situation was not defined by Bush, Dukakis, the press, or the polls as an "issue," it remained undiscussed in any serious way by the candidates in the 1988 "campaign."

Nor did reporters ask what access they had to the candidates in 1988 to ask probing questions that advanced the issue agenda and held the candidates accountable for their claims. If they had, the S&L crisis would have emerged in the issues agenda of 1988. In late September 1988, Representative Schumer (D. NY) charged George Bush with responsibility for the S&L crisis. It was, he said, an environment in which "fat cats ran wild."[28] On October 8, the *New York Times* reported that Texas's second largest bank had posted a $525 million loss for the third quarter and would need federal help to survive. "In the last two years," said the article, "eight of the ten largest banking companies in Texas have either been sold or put up for sale."[29] On October 15, the *Dallas Morning News* reported that eleven Texas institutions had been consolidated and sold in a transaction that would cost the FSLIC 1.3 billion dollars.[30] Florida's second largest S&L showed a 69-million dollar loss. To solve its solvency crisis, Florida's Financial Security Savings was taken over by federal regulators.[31] Meanwhile, the *Des Moines Register* reported on an October 14 trial that disclosed that Iowa's Capital Savings and Loan Association had been considered desperate since 1982.[32]

By election eve 1988, bailing out the Iowa savings institutions had cost $250,000,000 with an estimated $100,000,000 more needed. A week before the election, CBS's Brady reported that "Nearly a thousand savings and loans are losing money—that's depositors' money, insured by Uncle Sam, who's got to pay it back. It could add up to $60 billion for a government already deeply in debt. . . . Losses are so huge in fact they've wiped out much of the insurance safety net for the entire industry." Brady also noted that "in a period of unprecedented bad news, [top S&L officers] have spent a small fortune" to have their annual meeting in the "paradise" of Hawaii.

When Bush met with reporters on Air Force 2 en route to Stockton, California, on October 15, 1988, a reporter's transcript of a tape of the exchange reveals the comparative importance the reporters and the Vice President attached to the Savings and Loan issue and campaign strategy. And in Vice President Bush's compliment, "Nice try," to a reporter who was trying to pin down a cost of the S&L bailout, it reveals as well the extent to which both Bush and the reporter are aware that Bush has successfully ducked the question. Following that answer, questions from the reporters shift back to strategy.

> *Bush:* "Things seem to be moving in the right direction . . . let's keep on going. A guy asked me yesterday, 'Are you overconfident?' . . . I said no. I have no sense of overconfidence at all. . . . Let's keep moving, keep going ahead . . . get the message out; I've got to still define differences . . . so I don't think you'll see any change of game plan or anything like that."
>
> *Question:* "What about the 'Say goodnight, Mike' signs, etc.?"
>
> *Bush:* "I don't think so. I think some people feel very excited about it. They are not out. . . . They're not the candidate. They're not out running for president. They're not out there facing what I have to face every day. I think there was a lot of enthusiasm amongst our people . . . at Loyola yesterday, which is good. But I think for me to project what I don't feel, some kind of overconfidence, would be totally counter-productive. And I don't intend to do that, and I won't do that."
>
> *Question:* "Prediction on how much you win by?"
>
> *Bush:* "No. That would be the worst thing I could do. I don't think anybody's contemplating any changed strategy or change in schedule or change of message or any of those things. It's simply not going to work that way."

Question: "Is it going to stay as negative in the last three weeks?"

Bush: "I don't think it's been that negative. That's your assessment, perhaps, and others, when you say that, but I'm gonna keep on keeping on, and say what I think, and not be diverted from what I think by some that might be critical of it. . . ."

Question: "Criticism from columnists that you are running for national sheriff? Do you have any thoughts on whether the crime issue has been overstressed?"

Bush: "No. If I thought it had been overstressed I wouldn't keep stressing it. I read some of the columnists, but I can't shape a campaign by what some liberal columnist thinks . . . conservative columnist . . . I've just gotta do what I think."

Question: "George Will said you're running for national sheriff. . . ."

Bush: "George Will. . . . I'm not focusing anything past November 8."

Question: "Savings and Loan problems?"

Bush: "I think they ought to do what we asked Congress to do. It would be a good place to start. And reassure the depositors that they are in no jeopardy at all. All of these stories ought to have that right up in the front of every one of them."

Question: "Dole has talked about a $50 billion bailout."

Bush: "I don't . . . I have no plan for a $50 billion bailout. . . . We need to keep working out of the difficulty and to be sure that the funds are available for these takeovers . . . and to protect the depositors."

Question: "How much will it cost?"

Bush: "I don't know. Nobody knows. Nobody knows."

Question: "They are saying $50 billion."

Bush: "Well, they are saying. Who's saying?"

Question: "Bob Dole for one."

Bush: "Well, he's got his opinion. And I don't, I don't have a figure. Nice try, though."

Question: "How do you feel now, compared to how you felt leaving Iowa in January?"

Bush: "Leaving Iowa?"

Question: "Yeah, when you lost there."

Bush: "Yes, I feel better. I don't look forward beyond November 8. . . . unifocus."

Question: "Can you honestly look at us and tell us you're not the clear front runner right now?"

Bush: "You know, I don't think in those terms. I can't conceal the fact that I felt good after the debate. And I'm not trying to make you believe that. But, things can change too dramatically. You're talking to a guy that maybe some here thought was out of the race from time to time. So, why in the hell would should I now turn around and think everything is roses."

Question: "Do you think if there is a turnaround it's more likely to come from a mess up on your part rather than something Dukakis does?"

Bush: ". . . but I'm not going to mess up. I made a mistake about Pearl Harbor, but I'm not gonna mess up."

By February 1992, Congress had authorized $105 billion in spending on failed S&Ls and the administration was seeking another $55 billion.

Where the issue and strategy foci had led somewhat interconnected lives in earlier campaigns, in 1988, stories on policy issues increasingly stood in pristine isolation from reports on the ongoing campaign. At the same time, polling reports were absorbed in strategy coverage. Since both originally focused on performance and both saw as their goal predicting who would win and explaining how, the fit was natural. The process of creating this more perfect union of polling and punditry was jeopardized only by their different metaphoric embodiments. Where the strategy schema relied on the language of appearance, scripts, and performance, the polling schema centered on winning and losing votes. The language of war transcended this metaphoric divide.

The merger granted that two different realities operate simultaneously in a campaign. At one level, empirical markers indicate public acceptance at the moment or in a particular state. At another level, a candidate who is "ahead" in the polls can fail to "act like" a front runner. Insiders and experts are quoted as relaying the world of "is." Is the candidate presidential? Intelligent? Informed? Reporters work in the role of appearance. Does he or she appear presidential, informed, intelligent?

The language of war emerged as a dominant metaphor in 1988 in part because it encompasses the vocabulary of strategy with its tactics, positioning, attacking, victory, and defeat and the language of performance with its discussion of the "theatre of war" "expected performance of troops" requirement that a battleplan/script be followed, and its positioning of the audience as a spectator not a participant.

The Role of Metaphors in the Strategy Schema

In a schema whose central question is, "Who will win?" and the secondary question, "How?" sports, game, and war metaphors are all but inevitable.[33] It is, after all, the arena of sports that contributed such pieties as "Whether you win or lose doesn't matter, it's how you play the game" and "Winning isn't everything, it's the only thing." When two teams "face off," each has winning as its goal. Sports reporting leads with the question, Who is going to win? and wraps up its coverage by indicating who accomplished this feat. The winner doesn't then qualify for anything other than the right to compete in the same game in the play-offs, the world series, the Super Bowl. The focus of journalists is on the process of winning—on the "campaign" not "election."

Elsewhere I argue that metaphors tend to cluster in predictable ways that enable speakers to mix facets of those clusters. Lawton Chiles's statement about the 1984 presidential debates is illustrative. "It's like a football game," he noted, "Mondale can't get the ball back with one big play. But the American people love a horserace. I would advise him not to knock Reagan out." Chiles first identifies "the game," then an unlikely Mondale strategy, next he reiterates that the American people don't like an "uneven" contest; finally he advises Mondale on how to achieve the desired outcome strategically. There is a pattern to the statements. Only a purist would observe that the metaphor is mixed. We know what he means. We understand the metaphoric range within which he and we discuss each of the sports. We understand the interchangeability of the metaphoric elements in each cluster. In other words, we share domain-specific schemas for each of the sports and a general schema of "talk about games." Because the end of the strategy schema is accounting for who won, and the goal of the sports schema is providing a language to account for who will win, the two schemas merge in our discussion of politics.

Yet the very facets of the metaphor that suit it for sports smother a serious coverage of a "campaign." By "winning" the presidency a person qualifies not to run for some higher office but rather to govern the country, a process requiring skills untested in campaigns as we now construct them.

Increase in Language of War

Interestingly, the shift in 1988 press reports from the game language that dominated the reporting of the past decade to "war" metaphors is in some ways constructive. We after all engage in war in order to achieve some goal other than "winning." However, in the afterglow of the Gulf War, the "goals" for which we had presumably fought were overshadowed by the fact of "victory." As victory parades commemorated the heroism of American troops, the person whose rule in Iraq we pledged to end remained in power, the country we pledged to free remained undemocratic, and thousands of refugees remained homeless. Perhaps the appropriation of "war" metaphors for political ends has redefined our sense of the appropriate "end" of war, rendering ironic Clauswitz' observation that war is politics by other means.

Ironic too is the language in which reporter Thomas Oliphant expressed his plea for reporters and editors to control their obsession with campaign tactics. "If there's a lesson in 1988," he said, "it takes the form of an appeal to editors . . . 'Stop me before I kill again.' We do like to do the tactical pieces, the horse-race coverage. . . . Don't let us. Ruthlessly cut it out."[34]

Throughout the 1988 campaign reports gave new meaning to "The Battle Hymn of the Republic." In mid-August 1988, Bob Schieffer of CBS asked Republican consultant Stu Spencer, "What kind of campaign is this going to be?" Spencer replied, "No prisoners taken." Before the first debate of the 1988 general election, President Ronald Reagan concurred, indicating that he had advised his heir apparent to "Take no prisoners" (ABC, September 21, 1988).

Reagan and the Republican consultants were not alone in seeing politics as war by other means. Were he to win the Texas primary (ABC, March 6, 1988), "it would be as big as the third world war," noted Pat Robertson. In this world of kill or be killed, Robert Dole goaded George Bush (ABC, March 9, 1988), "Here's a chance, George, to finish me off, right here in Illinois" (ABC, March 11, 1988). "[W]ith the lead he has he ought to just come out here and blow me away," said Dole two days later.

In the primaries, ads were "bombarding TV viewers" (CBS, March 6, 1988); Democrats "continued to bash each other with nastier and nastier ads" (CBS, March 7, 1988); the campaigns ran "search and destroy missions"; candidates "shot it out" (September 22, 1988), "holding back no ammunition" (NBC, October 6, 1988). The Democrats tested (ABC, April 1, 1988) "new strategies for cutting down the Reverend Jesse Jackson." The Bush campaign branded a Dole attack ad "the killer commercial" (ABC, March 5, 1988). Ads were also described as "hand grenades" (ABC, March 9, 1988).

During the primaries, Dukakis lacked "fire" in his delivery (CBS, April 6, 1988). His campaign (ABC, March 29, 1988) "under fire for lack of fire, Dukakis decided no more Mr. Nice Guy when it comes to Jesse Jackson." But by fall Dukakis's offensive was offensive. In the first debate he came across as a "cut-and-slash candidate because he spent too much time criticizing the Reagan defense build-up and not enough time explaining his own" (CBS, September 14, 1988); Bentsen was Dukakis's "main weapon" in "the must-win battleground of Texas" (CBS, November 1, 1988).

The primaries were seen as battles, the states hosting them as battlefields, and opponents as "targets," with the Dallas debate "the Fort Sumpter of the Democrats' southern conflict" (ABC, February 19, 1988). The battles also had a chronology. Dukakis "took the first shot across his bow" (ABC, February 18, 1988). "The truce declared in the verbal warfare between Republican presidential candidates Bob Dole and George Bush broke down today . . . slinging the most arrows was Senator Robert Dole" (ABC, January 16, 1988). Occasionally, candidates would declare "cease-fires," only to resume attack when provoked (ABC, January 16, 1988).

In the final hours of a "campaign's" life, candidates faced a "do or die" situation and tried desperately to "breathe new life into" a "dying presidential campaign" (ABC, March 12, 1988). Such moments of "life or death struggle" were reminiscent of "the Roman coliseum" (ABC, September 25, 1988). It was at such a point that the Republicans began to "wage a war of attrition" (CBS, October 23, 1988) against the Democrats. Those who did not do well in primaries were labeled "the wounded." Poor "showings" in primaries "could be fatal" (ABC, March 6, 1988). Hart's campaign "crashed in flames" (ABC, March 11, 1988).

The presence of such metaphors is rendered more jarring when juxtaposed with the real thing. Following the news segment in which Reagan recommended that Bush take no prisoners was this lead by Peter Jennings: "When we come back, arson and gunfire break out again in the Soviet Republic of Armenia."[35]

The "war" that we are watching is not one into which we can be drafted or by which we can be wounded or killed. Instead, it is a ritualized spectacle and we, its spectators.

The Cynicism of the Focus on Strategy

The strategy schema assumes that a candidate's expressions of caring, the stressed features of his or her biography, and the problems and solutions the candidate offers are all the calculated product of strategic choice. Those who believe that the candidates are motivated by selfless conviction see reports framed by the strategy schema as disdainful invitations to public cynicism. Those who believe that candidates are consummate sophists see strategy reports as realistic revelations of the fundamental Machiavellianism of those who seek public office.

The cynicism, suggest reporters, is in the campaigns and in the electorate. "To appeal to an increasingly alienated electorate," writes the *Washington Post*'s E. J. Dionne, "candidates and their political consultants have adopted a cynical stance which, they believe with good reason, plays into popular cynicism about politics and thus wins them votes."[36]

While that is undoubtedly true as far as it goes, the cynicism is in the reporting as well. Refusing to take candidates' words and actions as anything other than crass ploys to influence votes invites public cynicism. Even if pandering is the intent of candidates, their words entail commitments for which they will be held accountable once elected and as such should be treated seriously. Whether the Star Wars Initiative was promoted or opposed by the president made a difference in how tax dollars were used, for example. And no one seriously doubts that Walter Mondale and Michael Dukakis would have placed different justices on the Supreme Court, with palpable differences in human lives. These are practical differences that do matter. Treating campaigns as little more than meaningless posturing tends to obscure them.

If reporters believed that candidates were saying things of importance to the nation, why would they instead use precious news time to ask about polls? Not only do polls and strategy talk distort but they distract as well. "In Philadelphia, Bush went to mass with Cardinal John Krol," noted ABC's Mike Von Fremd (October 30, 1988). "And while he was posing for cameras, enjoying the autumn breeze, it was clear that things weren't quite falling into place. The Vice President was asked if his internal polls that show his lead is slipping are right." *Bush:* "One, I don't think they are. And two, I'm not going to say anymore about it." In late October, Sam Donaldson notes of Dukakis, "But even if people are listening to what he says now, the polls show he's still losing ground. Are you depressed about the polls, Governor?" *Dukakis:* "Feel good, feel good, Sam." "How can you, sir?" asked Sam Donaldson. "Things go well," says the Democrat. Donaldson then observes, "Candidates who appear to be losing can't quit" (October 26, 1988). The polls have both generated and capped this story segment.

The strategy schema is problematic because it disengages the electorate from the election and minimizes the accountability of the candidates in seven ways. First, the electorate can know who is ahead, why, and what strategies are necessary for each to win without knowing what problems face the country and which candidate can better address them in office. The strategy schema asks questions that position its audience as campaign consultants not knowledgeable voters.

Second, the strategy schema invites audiences to critique a campaign as if it were a theatrical performance in which the audience is involved only as a spectator. It asks whether a candidate "seems," "looks," or "appears" presidential and whether his strategies are coherent, resonant, and unobtrusive, whether he is running an effective campaign. Once we have answered these questions and hence drawn a reasonable inference about who will win, the strategy schema invites us to no further involvement in the campaign.

Third, the strategy schema displaces such questions as, Is the candidate's rhetoric, including speeches, ads, statements in debates, and statements by surrogates, fair, accurate, and relevant to governance?

Fourth, the strategy schema minimizes the educational value of a campaign's most informative moments, those that occur in mass exposure to general election presidential debates. Blinded by the strategy schema, reporters reduce debate coverage to three questions, Who won? Why? and What impact will the debate "performance" have on the outcome of the election? This constricted focus on unanswerable and silly questions reduces the panorama of information gathered by all segments of the viewing public to irrelevant data.

Fifth, the strategy schema invites voters to trust presumed "experts" rather than themselves. It is experts who take and report the meaning of polls, "experts" who tell us who "won" and "lost" debates, "experts" who evaluate the strategic successes and failures of the candidates. Reliance on experts reduces the personal accountability of the viewing, reading, listening, thinking voter. Reliance on experts certified in news increases our vulnerability to other forms of "expertise" such as that carried by the unseen announcer in political ads.

Sixth, reliance on the strategy schema means that campaigns are shifting from communication to metacommunication, thereby reducing the informational content available to voters. Seventh, the strategy schema is cynical. It takes nothing at face value. Its world is Machiavellian. And since it assumes that most candidates are pandering sophists, it minimizes the disposition of the press to elicit or the viewer to discern the important differences the candidates would bring to the process of governance.

The strategy focus takes time and space that could be spent dispensing richer information. Yet, shifting from the strategy schema does not necessarily sacrifice the useful information voters garner from it. A performance/promise or problem/solution focus would require that reporters be prepared to cover issues not focused on by the candidates and to try to get the candidates to address them as well. Press focus on strategy means that reporters are more likely to concentrate on the issues on which the candidates focus in speeches, ads, and debates than on those treated only in passing (as was our changed relations with the Soviet Union in 1988), or ignored, as, for the most part, was the emerging S&L crisis was in that campaign. So, for example, what the members of the "Moscow intelligentsia" who are experts at the U.S.A. Institute noticed "about the 1988 presidential campaign was neither the personalities of the candidates nor their tactics, but what had been ignored or evaded. This was the issue the Soviet policymakers believed was central, and it consumed them night and day. The issue was the ending of the Cold War."[37]

Strategy coverage does little to help the country confront what Conservative theorist Kevin Phillips describes as "a critical weakness in American politics and governance—the frightening inability of the nation's leaders to face, much less define and debate, the unprecedented problems and opportunities facing the country."[38]

CHAPTER EIGHT

Solutions or Strategy?

Two moments in the 1980 campaign illustrate the differences between a focus on strategy and a focus on problems, candidates' proposed solutions, and their relevant performance in the past. The first occurred on the morning of the New Hampshire primary. On the Democratic side, Senator Edward Kennedy (D. Mass.) was facing incumbent president Jimmy Carter. As New Hampshire voters were drinking their morning cup of coffee, Tom Brokaw was interviewing Kennedy on NBC. Were a therapist eavesdropping on the conversation, she might ask, Can this relationship be saved? After all, their goals are fundamentally incompatible. Brokaw wants to know what Kennedy will do if he loses to Carter in New Hampshire; Kennedy wants to persuade New Hampshire Democrats that his proposed policies are preferable to the Georgian's.

"If you lose in New Hampshire, how can you possibly survive as a candidate?" queries Brokaw. Kennedy responds: "I'm hopeful that we'll do well" and swings into a discussion of inflation and the cost of fuel. "Can you survive?" persists Brokaw. In Maine the caucuses were closer than the polls predicted, says Kennedy. "Can you run second in New Hampshire and go on?" asks Brokaw who is now becoming something of a nag. "I believe we're doing increasingly well in the issues that we're raising . . . ," says Kennedy, not answering the question. After all, voters in New Hampshire "don't really want to rubber stamp the policies that have not worked."

Brokaw tries again, "If you run second 24 hours from now . . ." In-

189

terrupting him and in obvious irritation, Kennedy responds, "Maybe we can talk at that time but the important point now is that people can make a difference up here. They can vote for change. They can reject high rates of inflation, high fuel bills, high costs of living at the supermarket."

Unasked by Brokaw was, How would Kennedy bring down inflation, the cost of fuel and groceries? Had he been president from 1976 to 1980, what would he have done that Carter had not?

A very different news piece was broadcast on CBS Evening News in late October the same year. After interviewing both presidential candidates, CBS's Walter Cronkite devoted segments on consecutive evenings to their answers (October 22–23, 1980). One night the questions asked about the appropriate role of the federal government. The problem with assuming that a soundbite's length suggests its intellectual richness is evident in the amount of substance in these abbreviated answers.

> *Cronkite:* "In what areas can the federal government improve on the work of local government or the private sector? Welfare?"
> *Reagan:* "Better handled at local and state level."
> *Carter:* "Yes, I think the federal government should take over more of the responsibility for financing the welfare system than in the past."
> *Cronkite:* "Health?"
> *Reagan:* "I don't believe in a nationalized health service."
> *Carter:* "And I would like to see a nationwide program for the prevention of disease and for the catastrophic health insurance."
> *Cronkite:* "Energy—federal, local, or private initiative?"
> *Reagan:* "I think private initiative, and I think that the federal government is largely responsible for the present energy crisis."
> *Carter:* "That ought to be the private enterprise system. We have deregulated the energy program over a phased period of time to prevent an economic shock and we have taxed the excess profits for the oil companies with the windfall-profits tax."
> *Cronkite:* "Reagan opposes a windfall-profits tax. Carter created the Departments of Energy and Education: Reagan would do away with both. . . ."

News Schemas

Politicians invite us to understand politics through schemas that serve their interests. Scholars who study agenda setting have confirmed the power of broadcast news to make some topics seem more important than others and to influence the criteria through which viewers evaluate office holders and candidates. When asked to identify the most important problems facing the country, respondents usually report those things recently featured in the news. In assessing how well a leader is doing, viewers consider the topics highlighted in news more important than other topics.

In short, television news primes our sense of what topics are important and shapes the criteria by which we assess the competence of our leaders.[1] By focusing on the dramas of individuals and their victims, for example, rather than on analyzing and contextualizing larger social problems, network evening newscasts deflect blame from political parties, politicians, policies, and social factors and onto the individual.[2] As a result, politicians are not only held less responsible for the existence of a problem but also less accountable for alleviating it.[3]

The press can, if it chooses, invite us to see campaigns through a structure that better serves our needs as a democracy. This chapter asks: What do we know of politics and how do we know it? What should we know of politics and how can we know it? How can we increase the accountability of the press, the public, and politicians in political campaigns? It argues that a press focus on strategy should give way to a focus on problem-promise-performance.

Two decades of research concluded that political news reports concentrate not on policy discussion or on the past performance of those seeking the office but on the strategy, gameplan, and horse race of campaigns.[4] In the most exhaustive study of the 1988 general election campaign, political scientist Bruce Buchanan found that 9.7 percent of the 7574 broadcast and print stories coded focused on policy issues, 19.2 percent on candidate qualifications, and 36.1 percent on campaign horse race.[5]

In the last chapter I argued that the optic created by a focus on political strategy presupposes that the campaign is a performance enacted through strategies designed to ensure victory. The viewer is a spectator observing the "sport" of politics. If the voter is invited to judge the "contest," it is to answer the questions, Who is the better campaigner? Who is running the more effective campaign?

By contrast, the problem-promise-performance approach relates the performance of the candidates to their promises and sets the solutions the candidate offers against the problems the voter sees as important. So, for example, in 1976 a voter would ask whether to grant Jimmy Carter's claim that government had become unresponsive to peoples' needs. If so, we have a "problem." She would then evaluate Carter's promise to reorganize the government to produce cost savings and greater efficiency by asking, (1) Would such a move solve the problem and (2) Does Carter's performance as governor suggest (a) this solution will work and (b) that Carter knows how to implement the solution. Since the number of individuals employed by state government did not decrease under Carter, bonded indebtedness increased, and the state's bond ratings did not improve, she might conclude that even if the solution could solve the problem, the performance did not justify the promise. Since Ford had a track record as president, one could then search it for comparable information.

Asking who better understands the challenges confronting the country and is better suited to address them here determines who would be better able to serve as president. This frame situates the viewer not as a spectator but as a judge whose vote has electoral consequences which, even if they do not determine outcome, provide a means of interpreting the "will of the people."

The strategy focus defines campaigns as contests; the problem-promise-performance schema as quests to "find" the "solutions" to the "problems" that trouble the country and to "find" the candidate whose past best forecasts a disposition and ability to solve them. Where, in the first, the language of sports and war focuses on "opponents" to be overcome, in the second a "quest" "searches" for "solutions" that will transform a troubling situation. One focuses on winning, the other on finding and solving.

Where one invites voter passivity, the other forecasts voter activity. The solution schema would ask, What are the central problems of concern to us as voters? What has each candidate said and done to find and implement solutions to these problems? Which candidate is better suited by temperament and training to address them and comparable problems and challenges that may arise? How can I know that? If I agree to support one candidate in her quest, will my support help produce the outcome I seek?

The two structures pivot on fundamentally different questions. Where the strategy schema asks, Who has campaigned better? and Who will win? The solution schema asks, Who has more effectively combatted problems of social concern? Uncovered, created, found solutions? It may be that the candidate who "will" win is not the candidate who has found solutions. The quest schema invites us to join the "better" quester in seeking, finding, and implementing solutions. Among the steps in that process is casting a vote.

Content analysis of news coverage isn't the only source of the conclusion that the dominant schema through which politics is presented and processed is strategic. As I indicated earlier, most of what survey respondents can recall without prompting focuses on the horse race.[6] After the 1984 New Hampshire primary, respondents could discuss Gary Hart's chances of winning his party's nomination but one-quarter of those comfortable with making such an assessment couldn't summarize his position on such important and discussed matters as cuts in social programs.[7]

Because they set up very different questions, the two approaches produce dissimilar reporting on presidential debates, candidate advertising, candidate speeches, and the person of the candidate.

Differences in the Approach to Debates

The focus on solutions suggests that a debate answer will "play well" if it addresses the problem at hand and provides arguments whose evidence invites assent from voters to the claim that there is a reasonable, acceptable solution. So, for example, on CBS Morning News (October 29, 1980) Charles Kuralt asks "business columnist" Jane Bryant Quinn how well each candidate "fared in explaining his economic program for the country." Although her answer is colored with "strategy" language, Quinn answers from a problem-promise-performance perspective. The presupposed problem: high inflation, interest rates, unemployment, and an expanding budget deficit. Is Reagan's "promised solution viable?" "[H]ow do you [Reagan] put it all together, your program to raise military spending and cut taxes to keep government programs on an even keel and still balance the budget," asks Quinn and answers that she concurs with candidate John Anderson's earlier assessment of Reagan's solution. Reagan will use "mirrors." "He has a five-year economic projection, which is a page and a couple of lines of numbers that he put out about a month ago," notes Quinn, but he has not successfully answered the question. "[Y]ou keep saying you're going to cut spending. Where are you going to cut it?" "Once again," notes Quinn, "we come back on the programmed answer. 'Nothing has to be cut except fraud and waste,' And," she adds, "I don't think that this answer is playing either." "For good reason," says Kuralt.

What of Carter's promised solution? His problem, says Quinn, is inflation. His performance belies his promise and raises serious questions about his ability to solve the country's economic problems. "How does he account for the terrible inflation that has happened during his regime? And he falls back on the answer that it—it has to do with oil. And this answer isn't playing, either. Certainly, part of it has to do with oil. But part of it has to do with the enormous amount of spending that he put through when he first came in as President. He did it to create jobs, and it was a noble purpose, and he created, as he said last night, the highest number of jobs ever. But he has reaped some inflation for it. And so, he was trying to fob off the inflation problem by pointing to Reagan and saying, 'Well, you know, his tax cut program is inflationary, so don't think about my inflation.' . . . [B]oth of them were ducking a real discussion of these issues, saying we have some fundamental problems that both of us will have to deal with. None of them easy."

The strategy approach asks who won the debate and what strategies accounted for that outcome. Bob Schieffer employed the strategy focus when he noted, "On ABC, Howard K. Smith, who moderated the 1960 debate as well as last night's encounter, saw this debate as a lost opportunity for both men. ABC also invited viewers to call in their opinions on who won. Seven hundred thousand called in, and Reagan won that. . . . The headline in the *New York Times* reflected much of the newspaper reaction around the country. *The Detroit News* said the only real winner was the phone company, since it made several hundred thousand dollars on the ABC telephone bill. But while most newspapers we surveyed saw it as a draw, many found significance in the fact that Reagan wasn't kayoed—a view summed up by syndicated columnist David Broder, who wrote, 'Mr. Carter accomplished all of his objectives except his most important—destruction of Ronald Reagan's credibility as a potential President'."

The overriding question for those preoccupied with strategy is, Who won? In 1980, CBS designated Bruce Morton "poll watcher." After Cronkite indicates that the CBS overnight poll puts Reagan as the winner of the debate 44 to 36 percent, Morton answers that question this way. "Reagan people were a little firmer. We had very few Reagan people whom we polled switching over to Carter. Relatively more Carter people—still not a lot—but more—saying 'Gee, Governor Reagan sounded pretty good.' But you need a lot of caution with this. After the Reagan-Anderson debate we did a poll, and Governor Reagan bobbed up briefly and then settled about back to where he'd been. And I think the lesson is that these things take time; that there's a first reaction and a second reaction, and how it will affect people a—a week from the debate, which is to say Election Day, is something we just don't know yet."

The pervasiveness of the strategy focus was evident to an observer who watched as the press surrounded Geraldine Ferraro's advisors after her vice presidential debate with George Bush in 1984. Their questions concerned not issues but performance. "Questions focused almost exclusively on the candidates' debating styles and on how their performance would affect the horse race. 'Did Bush's stridency surprise you?' Beckel was asked. 'Didn't Mrs. Ferraro look uncomfortable up there? What was her finest moment? What would this mean in the polls?' Asking a question on substance was pointless in that mob atmosphere. One reporter who did got nowhere."[8]

Differences in Approaches to Ads

A solution approach to ads asks the same questions that Quinn asked of the candidates' debate answers in 1976. By those criteria, most ads fail. On the assumption that a candidate's disposition toward truth telling is an important indication of character and that factually inaccurate content can distort policy promises and performance, analysis of ads should focus on accuracy and fairness and ask whether ad claims have been taken from context. When an ad speaks to a matter of public policy, this, if nothing else, will help clarify the nature of the problem or the proposed solutions. The analysis of the Bush tank ad that Richard Threlkeld did for ABC in 1988 illustrates this approach.

Similarly, when a National Conservative Political Action Committee ad against Idaho Senator Frank Church claims, "These silos aren't filled with missiles anymore. You see, Senator Frank Church has almost always opposed a strong national defense," CBS shows Church responding, "Well, there were just a few things wrong with that commercial frankly speaking. First of all, I didn't empty the missile silo. It was emptied by the Air

Force, when the Titan missile became obsolete and was replaced by a more reliable missile, the Minute Man, which I supported" (CBS, October 11, 1980). Ideally, CBS would have gone one step further and indicated whether Church was telling the truth.

A strategy focus treats strategic intent rather than the viability of an ad's promise or its accuracy or fairness. So, for example, in 1980 Jeff Greenfield explained that "some ads are designed specifically for one region" (CBS, October 10, 1980). An excerpt of an ad showing Carter's speech at Tuscumbia, Alabama, follows. Greenfield adds, "This Carter ad is designed to shore up the President's southern base by linking his roots to a strong defense policy, an issue which Reagan hopes to use to challenge Carter on his home turf."

In 1988, *Newsweek* did for ad coverage what AAA guides did for restaurants and voiceless critics in underfunded newspapers did for movie reviewing. In a segment titled "Video Politics," the magazine rated the presidential ads "for effectiveness (not truth) on a scale of one to five stars."[9] Dukakis's "Real Answers" rated a single star and status as "The Blob" of political ads. "Another weak national ad," lamented *Newsweek*. "The warm, 'I'm-not-packaged' Dukakis talks about America 'getting out of shape.' Text eloquent, but energy level low. Lighting so poor the press nicknamed this ad 'Shadows.' " Verdict: One star.[10]

If not *Gone With the Wind*, Bush's "The Harbor" was at least the original *King Kong*—It merited three stars. Why? "Sewage oozes," writes *Newsweek*, "crud floats in Boston Harbor, which (the ad says) Dukakis 'had the opportunity' to clean up but 'chose not to.' Slick. This ad is damaging Dukakis in coast-conscious California and New Jersey."[11]

Polls permit reporters bent on tracking strategy to ask whether an ad addresses a matter considered important to the electorate and if the ad is working. So, for example, on October 6, 1980, CBS Evening News aired clips from person-in-the-street Carter ads. In it, Californians are shown saying:

> *Man 1:* "Reagan scares me."
> *Man 2:* "He shoots from the hip."
> *Man 3:* "As a governor, it didn't really make that much difference because the State of California doesn't have a foreign policy."

Lesley Stahl contextualizes the ad this way: "But as for attitudes about Reagan as governor, our poll of the California electorate shows that a wide majority of the people have a positive view." The screen shows the claim "Reagan as Governor: good job, 56%; bad job, 24%."

The Different Approaches to Speeches

A problem-promise-performance focus employs segments of a candidate's speech to determine how well the aspirant has defined the prob-

lem, the adequacy of the solutions proposed, and whether the candidate's background documents an ability to effect such solutions. In the
process, such reporting summarizes key ideas and, if their accuracy or
fairness is in doubt, offers alternative interpretations or adjudicates the
claims. This perspective also invites consideration of the position of the
opponent on that issue by comparing and contrasting the two. So, for
example, Morton Dean notes that Reagan "also accused the President of
stealing his prescription for curing the ailing steel industry. 'Mr. Carter's
big plan,' said Reagan, 'is the one I recommended a couple of weeks
before he decided to say it.' " Then, Dean adds, "The plans are similar"
(CBS, October 2, 1980). The report tells us that the plans are similar
without specifying how.

The more usual means of contesting the accuracy of a speech's claim
is to turn to experts. For instance, when in early October 1980, Reagan
claimed that Mt. St. Helens "has probably released more sulfur dioxide
into the atmosphere" than "ten years of automobile driving," Bill Plante
replayed Reagan's statement and then noted, "The Environmental Protection Agency points out that automobiles do not emit sulfur dioxide."
"Sulfur oxides that are emitted by Mt. St. Helens add up to about what
one major power plant does over the course of a year," says an EPA
administrator. To check on Reagan's statement that "the oxides of nitro-
gen in decaying vegetation may benefit tuberculosis patients," Plante quotes
a physician at the Center for Disease Control saying, "To the best of our
knowledge, there is no scientific information to support that in terms of
human studies." Plante then "presses" Reagan aides for sources and is
told they must have come from the candidate's own reading.

The press believes that its role is to "cover" a campaign. The metaphor
presupposes that the press reports what the candidate is saying and doing.
When candidates adopt a problem-promise-performance perspective,
reporters presumably will mirror it. CBS raises the question of court
appointments in 1988 when Dukakis "repeatedly called Vice President
Bush's judgment into question, asking voters to consider what kind of
appointments Bush would make to the Supreme Court." The report
contextualized the claim by noting that three liberal judges were in their
late seventies or early eighties. "[W]ith three extremely senior justices,"
says Rita Braver, "the next president of the United States could have a
major impact on the court." The candidates or their representatives then
distinguish the candidates' philosophies on judicial appointments. Bush
asks whether Dukakis would take the advice of the ACLU.

A Dukakis representative says that Dukakis would look for "a profound commitment to our Constitution, including its Bill of Rights and
its provisions on commitments on civil rights." A Bush spokesperson says
the Vice President would appoint someone who would not be a judicial
activist but would instead ask what the statute books say. Braver notes,
"Bush and Dukakis appointees would be likely to vote differently on
affirmative action, abortion and civil liberties" (CBS, October 9, 1988).
By fall 1991, Bush had the opportunity to name two justices to the court.

Because it concentrates on problems and the candidates' qualifications to respond to them, a focus on "substance" also asks what the candidates aren't saying. Jeff Greenfield (CBS, October 28, 1980) fantasized that he

> heard Jimmy Carter acknowledge that the China breakthrough of which he speaks so proudly actually began under the Administration of an official non-person, Richard Nixon. I thought I heard Governor Reagan acknowledge that the economic dilemmas of which he speaks did not begin on January 20, 1977, but worsened under an Administration whose advisors are now advising him. I thought I heard Jimmy Carter acknowledge that the increases in defense spending he speaks of repudiated his own 1976 pledge to cut defense spending by five to seven billion dollars, and that he himself tried to renegotiate the SALT II treaty, a step he now describes as fraught with danger. I thought I heard Governor Reagan concede that the easy rhetoric of a thousand banquets was a poor guide to shaping defense policy, and that the doubts many Americans have about his prudence are due as much to his own words as to those of his opponents. And I thought I heard both candidates point to the realities that have gone all but ignored in this election, to the spread of crime that will produce 2,000 homicides this year in our greatest city, to the joblessness and hopelessness of the poor that's creating a permanent underclass generation after generation, to the disappearance of critical farmland under rapacious developments.

A strategy focus settles instead on the presumed intent or effectiveness of a candidate's speech. "The Carter campaign, seizing on Ronald Reagan's rejection of the new League of Women Voters debate proposal, believes it has him on the defensive on that issue," said Walter Cronkite on September 26, 1980. "White House spokesman Jody Powell said today that Reagan's cloak of self-righteousness on the debates has been removed."

Polls flesh out the strategy approach by explaining speech acts as a form of capital offered to voters in the name of securing votes in needed states. Accordingly, Bruce Morton explains why Carter is campaigning in California. "Two reasons for attacking the other guy's strength: Carter might win California—though polls show him trailing—and his people think he has a chance in Oregon and Washington; besides he'll worry Reagan; make Reagan spend time campaigning to protect his base, instead of working in close states elsewhere" (CBS, October 2, 1980).

Why Prefer a Problem-Promise-Performance Approach?

By setting spectatorship not participation as the goal, the focus on strategy circumscribes the relationship between viewer and viewed. Since the purpose for which people expect to use information affects what they process and how they process it,[12] the strategy schema minimizes audience involvement in more traditional forms of democratic participation such as voting. It also reduces the likelihood of recalling information more relevant to the process of governance than strategic concerns. What we remember of available communication is a function of our goal in processing the data. Burglars focus on different information about two boys' activities at one of the boy's homes than do potential buyers of that home, for example. [13] And when asked to determine whether someone should be hired for a specified job, we focus on traits relevant to the job and discount those that seem irrelevant. [14]

If we assume the desirability of the model of governance built on active citizenship, the implications of seeing prospective voters as spectators are troubling. "Politics was a spectator, not a participant, sport for our panelists," noted Graber about the individuals whose patterns of news consumption she studied. "This detached attitude had several consequences. It prevented people from exerting themselves to keep up with the news and encouraged them to process it in ways that were quick and effortless. It led them to scan the news haphazardly and made them ignore much of it totally. It also explained why our panelists, most of the time, neglected to pass judgments about the events that came to their attention and why they rarely thought about solutions to problems." [15]

There is one other reason for preferring a problem-promise-performance to a strategy structure. The structure of the first is the argument, of the second, the narrative. Pivoting on the state of the nation and required solutions finds expression in a structure that more closely approximates the essay. Instead of telling a story, this form compares and contrasts, educes evidence, argues. Centering a report on the means and schemes of the campaigns invites reporters to produce newslike soap opera. Its form is narrative. The candidates are performing characters whose words cannot be trusted—reporters reveal their secrets. And occasionally, consistent with the grammar of soap operas, candidates, indeed even presidents, claim to suffer amnesia.

If one wants to weigh alternatives, narrative permits us to apply tests of identification, internal coherence, and plausibility. Argument invites us instead to apply tests of evidence. Bush's campaign pledge not to raise taxes was compelling narrative. "My opponent won't rule out raising taxes. But I will. The Congress will push me to raise taxes, and I'll say no. And they'll push, and I'll say no. And they'll push again, and I'll say to them: 'Read my lips. No new taxes'." It does not answer the question, How will you pay for needed social programs, retain a commitment to every weapon on the drawing boards, cope with the deficit and not raise taxes? The answer, of course, was, You won't.

The turnaround on taxes was not an aberration. The hero of Bush's campaign narratives bore little relationship to the person who governed from 1989 to 1992. In a campaign speech in Lees Summit, Missouri, October 10, 1988, and in the second debate, Bush was Prince Valiant protecting the average honest taxpayer from invasion of hordes of Dukakis-dispatched IRS agents. "[T]his idea of unleashing a whole bunch, an army, a conventional force army of IRS agents into everybody's kitchen—I mean, he's against most defense matters, and now he wants to get an army of IRS auditors going out there. I'm against that," declared Bush. "I oppose that." And in Lees Summit, "Politicians used to promise a chicken in every pot. Now this guy wants to promise an IRS agent in every kitchen. We don't need that. The American people are honest. I'm for a taxpayers' bill of rights." Between narrative and governance fell reality. On March 20, 1991, IRS Commissioner Fred Goldberg, Jr., informed Congress that "overdue collections were up 20 percent as a result of hiring 2,788 new Internal Revenue Service enforcement personnel." He also indicated that "he had rejected Bush administration orders to increase audits of low-income taxpayers and ease pressure on corporations." And, reported *The Dallas Morning News,* "the administration has balked at a taxpayers' bill of rights."[16]

If the strategy and problem-promise-performance schemas are really discrete cognitive structures, as I hypothesize that they are, swathing policy issues in strategy talk will result in inappropriate storage and interpretation of the issue content. As Iyengar and Kinder have found, unless content is explicitly tied to a leader in news, viewers don't tend to make the connection.[17] Strategy coverage fails to tie either problems or proposed solutions to candidates in a very useful way.

I do not wish to suggest that campaign reporting supplies no useful information to voters but rather that the utility of that information could be increased were it structured schematically to focus on the problems and opportunities facing the country and the background and temperament of those who would face them.

IV

Accountability, Engagement, and Democracy

CHAPTER NINE

Argument, Engagement, and Accountability in Political Discourse

Reasoned argument is by no means dead in American politics. As the last echoes of the choruses of academics were bemoaning the discourse of the 1988 campaign, the congressional debate over whether to authorize U.S. entry into a Gulf War took place. In it, the very members of Congress elected in the vacuous campaigns of 1984–1990 delivered thoughtful speeches that engaged the ideas of others, examined evidence, and moved with care to warranted conclusions. Within the same period, the confirmation hearings on Supreme Court nominee Souter and the congressional deliberations over the Brady Bill confirmed that the discourse over the Gulf War was not aberrational.

What characterized the War, Souter, and Brady Bill debates was argument, statement, and proof. And in the aftermath of the war, the testing of the original arguments persisted. New evidence lent weight to some claims and diminished the cogency of others. Saddam was on the verge of developing nuclear capacity, argued some. Others suggested that such a possibility was at least a decade away. By summer 1991 evidence uncovered by U.N. inspectors confirmed that nuclear capacity was nearer at hand than many had supposed. American missiles had eliminated Saddam's nuclear capacity, asserted U.S. briefers during the war. Not so, said the later evidence. In the war debate, some argued that the president had forecast no postwar structure for peace. In the aftermath of the war, that view gained credibility.

In these three debates, the discussants engaged the claims of those in disagreement with them. In the intersections of their arguments, both issues and our understanding of them were advanced. The members of Congress spoke a language of good will, presuming the integrity of those in disagreement. Rarely were the motives or integrity of those in disagreement impugned.

Clear in these debates was the multisidedness of the issues before the country. Although one would ultimately vote for or against continued sanctions, for or against an authorization of war, for or against the confirmation of Judge Souter, for or against the Brady Bill, the arguments pro and con did not parse neatly into two dichotomous positions. Yet, despite the complexity of the issues at stake, one did not need Dan Rather, Tom Brokaw, Bernard Shaw, or Peter Jennings to help us follow any of these three debates.

But before anyone could herald a new Golden Age and scout the horizon for a Pericles or Elizabeth Cady Stanton, the debate over the so-called "quota bill" sunk back to rhetoric as usual, summoning in the discussants nightmares or ecstatic visions of how their remarks would play in thirty-second campaign ads.

The norms of public speech as public spectacle treat assertion as if it constitutes argument, while the strategy perspective that pervades campaign coverage deprives the public of an ability to judge the legitimacy of candidate discourse. And candidates have no interest in providing a corrective since they have nothing to gain and everything to lose by taking clear stands on controversial policy issues. As political scientist Benjamin Page argues, taking a liberal position will alienate conservatives, taking a conservative position will alienate liberals, and taking a middle-of-the-road position will alienate both. Accordingly, candidates focus on "matters of consensus," de-emphasize controversial issues, and remain vague or ambiguous when they do take a stand.[1] Bush's 1988 communication director, Roger Ailes, agrees. At the Harvard debriefing after that election, "The MacNeil/Lehrer NewsHour's" Judy Woodruff suggested, "So you're saying the notion of the candidate saying 'I want to run for President because I want to do something for this country' is crazy." Ailes replied. "Suicide."[2]

Increasingly, campaigns have become narcotics that blur our awareness of problems long enough to elect the lawmakers who must deal with them. In the 1990 Pennsylvania gubernatorial campaign, the Republican nominee tried unsuccessfully to persuade voters that the state was facing a major revenue shortfall. After being re-elected in a feel-good campaign, the Democratic incumbent responded to the crisis with the largest tax increase in the state's history. In New Jersey the 1989 race for the governorship centered on whether the Democrat had ties to the mob or the Republican had dumped "toxic" waste on his own property. There too the elected governor faced the need to put through unpopular tax increases. And in 1988, with both parties neck deep in complicity, the costly S&L crisis was all but ignored in a presidential campaign awash in

Boston's Harbor's sludge, oceans of red, white, and blue bunting, and the well-marketed anguish of William Horton's victims. After Bush's election, voters learned that the savings had gone to Bush's son as well as four influential Democratic senators; by contrast, the loans would be paid off in tax dollars for longer than anyone cared to forecast.

Candidates divert public and press attention from legitimate issues by calculated strategies of distraction. The disposition to divert attention is not limited to magic acts and political campaigns, however. How many today know that over half of the U.S. "Patriot Missiles" missed their intended targets in the Gulf War of 1991? How many are aware that U.S. soldiers bulldozed Iraqi trenches burying thousands of "the enemy" alive? How many are aware of the role of faulty equipment on the U.S.'s Apachi helicopters in the deaths of U.S. soldiers by friendly fire? Instead most of us recall the handful of repeated scenes of missiles hitting presumably strategic sites, the triumphant homecoming parades, the flood of patriotism that washed over advertising and news. By focusing our attention on one set of visually evocative images and denying the media access to the others, the Bush administration successfully shunted aside troubling questions as well as pictureless revelations of faulty Patriot missiles and deaths by "friendly fire."

A campaign composed of publicized broadcast speeches, advertising, debates, citizen call-in programs, press conferences, press interviews with candidates, and analytic recapitulative news invites an office seeker to engage in extended argument that defines its terms, locates policy positions in an historical context, compares them to the available alternatives, argues the comparative advantage of the proposed policy, and then uses dramatic personal appeals to anchor it in the citizenry.

While not a guarantor that a campaign will be engaged and substantive, when both major candidates participate in a full menu of discourse, the odds of finding specificity and substance go up. When this mix is present, ads enable the candidates to digest claims argued elsewhere while appealing to their chosen audiences unfiltered by reporters or editors. When complemented by expository speeches, debates, and press conferences, the telegraphy of ads is useful. The expository forms give the ads substance to digest. The debates and press conferences can hold candidates accountable for the claims made in other generic forms. All of this changes when campaign discourse is transmogrified into ads.

In the political world of 1988, candidates conceived all forms of public communication as parts of a choreographed whole. In successful campaigns, each amplifies the other to create a single sense of the candidate and his opponent, a single set of simplified messages, driven home through frames of reference forged in the electorate early and reinforced throughout the campaign. In 1988, in other words, the once broad menu of discourse was reduced to ad McNuggets.

Whether viewers are increasingly being influenced by ads or are increasingly willing to disclose such influence is difficult to know. Whatever the cause, by late October 1988 one in four voters told the *New York Times*/CBS News Poll that the campaign ads had helped them choose between the candidates.[3] When the substance of policy distinctions has been laid out in speeches, engaged in press conferences, panel interviews, citizen call-ins, and debates, then spot advertising can convey similarities and differences in its necessarily abbreviated form. But in 1988, this was not the case.

Television has accustomed us to brief, intimate, telegraphic, visual, narrative messages. Candidates are learning to act, speak, and think in television's terms. In the process they are transforming speeches, debates, and their appearances in news into ads. At the same time, a focus on explaining polls and divining strategy is producing in news what one would ordinarily call ads. This accumulation of tendencies is changing the way in which candidates attack and defend and minimizing the protections a vigilant press can maintain against distortion, deception, and distraction in political discourse.

The Speech as Ad

In recent campaigns, survival of the briefest has become the political norm. The hour-long political speeches of radio days have given way to thirty-second ads and ten-second soundbites. Where an hour-long speech was accepted as usual on the stump in the nineteenth century, today's presidential candidate will deliver an average stump speech in under seventeen minutes.[4] Increasingly, nationally *broadcast* political discourse and our exposure to it come in bite-size morsels. That is true of answers in debates, which have dropped to one and two minutes; candidate soundbites in CBS, ABC, and NBC evening news, which Dan Hallin argues dropped to 9.8 seconds in 1988;[5] and presidential campaign ads, which have dropped in modal length from thirty minutes in 1952 to thirty seconds in 1988.

As C-SPAN viewers are aware, politicians often fail to structure ideas into coherent speeches or bridge them with transitions. Rather than building arguments, their campaign speeches have adapted to the demands of the press and the dispositions of the mass public by stringing together one-liners and anecdotes. No camera crew will have to look long for a soundbite; no intricate argumentative structure will drive viewers away.

Texas State Treasurer Ann Richards' speech at the 1988 Democratic Convention is illustrative. It contains her memories of summer nights listening to the grownups talk; one letter from a constituent; references to granddaughter Lily—the visual tie to the Democratic attempts to identify themselves with the future by aligning themselves with children; and thirty-second soundbites. The speech alternates between identification and apposition. I am like you. I care; we Democrats care. George Bush isn't like you; he doesn't care. We've had to work for what we've gotten; he hasn't. "Twelve years ago, Barbara Jordan, another Texas woman, made the keynote address to this convention and two women in 160 years is about par for the course. But if you give us a chance, we can perform. After all, Ginger Rogers did everything that Fred Astaire did. She just did it backwards." CUT. "For eight straight years George Bush hasn't displayed the slightest interest in anything we care about. And now that he's after a job he can't get appointed to." CUT. "He's like Columbus discovering America. He's found child care. He's found education." CUT. "Poor George. He can't help it. He was born with a silver foot in his mouth." CUT.

The best way to teach the structure of most contemporary political persuasion is to invite students to examine Jay Leno's monologues. "Moving right along here" is more of a transition than links the disjunctive soundbites in much public speech.

"The young people who do speeches for major politicians," claims Reagan and Bush speechwriter Peggy Noonan, "[don't write] a serious text with serious arguments, they just write soundbite after soundbite."[6] Noonan did little more. Her speeches for Reagan at Point de Hoc and after the *Challenger* explosion are storytelling, not argument; the convention acceptance speech she crafted for Bush, little more than uplifting description and assertion.

In prime-time television, we grant the hypothetical reality of the characters on the screen. From its first moments, we recognize the characters who populate "Murphy Brown" as surely as we do those on "Designing Women." We accept the compression of days and weeks into half-hour programs. The time usually spent sleeping, eating, and getting from place to place no longer exists in this telegraphed world. We grant that it is representative as well. Even though interrupted by commercials and station breaks, we do not question the reality it posits. We grant it a coherence it intrinsically lacks.

Adopting a telegraphic line from actor as gunslinger Clint Eastwood, nominee George Bush sounded tough and decisive at the Republican convention on August 18, 1988, when he said, "The Congress will push me to raise taxes, and I'll say no, and they'll push, and I'll say no, and they'll push again, and I'll say to them, 'Read my lips. No new taxes.' "

In this snippet, we see operating the form that has come to characterize American televised discourse. The statement is digestive and short. It telegraphs a familiar persona. It reduces that abbreviated telegraphic message to a narrative captured in the primal archetype of physics: force and resistance to force. The verbal form suggests a defense of principle. As important is the fact that the words were repeated throughout the campaign in news. In the process, they gained the repetitive force of advertising in the credible context of news.

When abbreviated discourse is unanchored in traditional speech, it tends to deal in simplifying identifications and appositions that caricature the complexity of issues. Although it occurs in a speech, "Read my lips" is such a simplifying telegraphic statement. That fact supports my earlier claim that campaign speeches have now become soundbite-filled ads strung together with transitions.

"Read my lips. No new taxes" can warn a celluloid gunslinger that Boot Hill is in his immediate future; it cannot of itself articulate an economic philosophy or an argument for how one can meet government's promises without new revenue.

Such soundbites function as do such abbreviated viscerally visual forms as torn Social Security cards or menacing convicts. Both sacrifice two of the preconditions of ethical judgment: the time to consider options and with it the ability of a conscious agent to grant informed consent.

Debate Answers as Ads

The late 1980s witnessed a trend toward adlike candidate responses in debates. In the debates of the 1988 presidential general election, the candidates' one- and two-minute answers to reporters' questions repeated the claims and evoked the images of their ads. Out of the 1988 debates came two attack ads, one Democratic, one Republican. The Democrats replayed the exchange between vice presidential candidates Bentsen and Quayle that culminated in Bentsen's claim that Quayle was no John Kennedy. Dismissive laughter was added to the ad's audio track. The Republicans paid for time to air and rebut Dukakis' denial that he had raided his state's pension fund to balance the budget.

Where the Kennedy-Nixon debates anchored themselves in references to candidate speeches,[7] the Dukakis-Bush debates tied themselves to evocation of newscast pseudo-events and ads. The presence of a live, candidate-picked audience transformed answer after answer into ad material. Just as laugh tracks once cued audiences to chuckle at the "right" moments of sit coms, the laughter and boos signaled responses to debate answers.

In political campaigns, the interrelation among news, advertising, and debates is prismic. Each reflects, refracts, or refocuses the other in seemingly endless turns. From Dukakis in his tank to Quayle claiming kinship with JFK, clips from news and debates slip into ads to magnify one's own successes or indict an opponent. In news, reporters recount strategies behind ads, posit their effectiveness, and occasionally note the accuracy and fairness of an ad's claims. To underscore supposedly decisive moments, segments of debates replay in ads and news.

Speaking in soundbites requires a capacity to digest and simplify; those issues or discussions that defy digestion into sound and sightbites are not the stuff of which television or winning campaigns are made. Whatever else one says about Gary Hart in 1984, he offered some thoughtful, substantive alternatives on defense policy. Indeed, he had written a book and delivered a number of major speeches outlining proposed reforms in a level of detail uncharacteristic of most modern political discourse.

When, in a March 1984 primary debate, Walter Mondale turned to him and said, "When I hear your new ideas, I'm reminded of that ad, 'Where's the beef'?," the Minnesotan had used the rapier of the sound-bite to skewer Hart. Hart's incapacity in that moment was in part a function of the forms in which contemporary discourse traffics.

In the seconds left in the likely sound clip, Hart couldn't articulate his defense alternatives. "Vice President Mondale cleverly has picked up the slogan from a fast food chain and tried to suggest that there are no ideas or issues when he knows full well that they are in the form of a book, in the form of strategy and position papers—quite detailed, quite elaborate," responded Hart feebly. "The fact of the matter is that other candidates or the press or whomever really isn't interested quite often in what industrial policies are, what these detailed ideas are." In that brief telegraphic moment, substance was dispatched by the slogan of a hamburger chain. Later, we learned that Mondale had not even seen the Wendy's ad that propelled "Where's the beef?" into the national vocabulary. He had been handed the line by an aide.

Unsurprisingly, in such an environment, most of the questions asked by debate panelists in the 1988 presidential debates were answered by neither candidate. The likelihood that a question would be answered increased as the controversiality of the question decreased. So, for example, when ABC's Peter Jennings asks Dukakis, "Where would you get the money to devote to the inner cities?" and "Can you be specific about the programs not only you'd reinstate, but the more imaginative ones you'd begin?," it was predictable that the Democrat would duck the first question and parlay his accomplishments in Massachusetts to answer the second.

One can divide the presidential debate questions into those that spoke to matters the polls said were of concern to the electorate and those unmentioned as important. Of the forty-eight questions asked of the two presidential candidates in the two 1988 presidential debates, seventeen addressed matters not reflected in the polls. The candidates responded to nine (53 percent) of these in a way that answered the question and differentiated their positions. On those matters listed as important in the Gallup Polls, the candidates answered and differentiated their positions on only six (19.3 percent).[8] Aware of shortened attention spans and public acceptance of disjunctive messages, consultants now routinely counsel candidates not to answer the question asked but to answer instead the question they wished had been asked.

Interview and News Conference Answers as Ads

The Bush-Brokaw interview on NBC on October 31, 1988, provides an illustration of the interview answer as ad.

Brokaw: "Your campaign has had a good deal of success on the whole law and order issue in the course of this campaign. That surprise you? Given the fact that in your administration, Michael Deaver and Lyn Nofzinger, who had both served in it, were convicted? We have the National Security Adviser, John Poindexter, who has been indicted. Oliver North has been indicted. You had a top environmental administrator who was convicted. Given all of that, have you been surprised that you've been able to do as well in the law and order thing?"

Bush begins to answer the question and then, catching himself, delivers an adbite instead: "No. Because I think the law and—I'll tell you, one of the most moving moments in this campaign for me personally, not just sound bites or backdrops, was when Matt Byrnes, the Lieutenant, ex-Lieutenant on the New York Police force, handed me the badge of his fallen son. And he was doing it because I think he knows I am committed to backing up the local policeman, the guy with the badge, out on the cutting edge in the neighborhood."[9]

"Candidates give their prepared message of the day, regardless of the question. This detracts from the give-and-take of the information process," lamented network correspondent Harry Smith. "We get accused of reducing the campaign to soundbites, but when we *do* ask a serious question, the candidates are so trained to speak succinctly that soundbites are all we get."

For Brokaw's viewers, Bush recreates a story played out on an earlier newscast, recalled in an earlier debate, and viewed again in the Bush election eve program. The message: Bush is tough but caring. Its effect: to displace Brokaw's question about indictments and convictions in the Reagan-Bush administration. There is no propositional relationship between Brokaw's question and Bush's answer.

When faced with a question about his commitment to the confirmation of his Supreme Court nominee, Bush used the same technique more bluntly. "Any questions that you ask me will be answered with the statement, 'I support Clarence Thomas,' " he said.[10] Similarly, H. Ross Perot ducked a question about whether he was liberal or conservative by inviting "Today" viewers (May 18, 1992) to "Read the book *On Wings of Eagles* by Ken Follett. It tells you all about me, more than you want to know." Unrevealed was Perot's role in shaping the book.

Questioning by Citizens as Ad

With a little help from friendly consultants, candidates' responses to citizen questions also can become the raw stuff of ads. In 1980 the Republican team that had handled the Ford account in 1976 signed on to work for the presidential campaign of Tennessee Senator Howard Baker. The campaign's most memorable spot was also its most manipulative. In it Baker is shown saying to a large crowd, "America must resolve that she's not going to be pushed around. That doesn't cause a war. That stops a war." As the audience applauds, Baker acknowledges an Iranian student holding a handful of pamphlets. The camera angles are set to magnify the height of the field's shortest candidate.

Angrily, the student exclaims, "When the Shah's army killed more than 60,000 Iranian people with their U.S. equipped weapons, why weren't you raising your voice of support of international law?" Baker stares determinedly at the student who continues, "And [the] United States government shipped a hundred and fifty thousand barrels of oil for the Shah's army to kill the Iranian people. Why weren't you concerned about international law?"

Leaning into the podium, his hand thrust forward in a decisive gesture, Baker in close-up responds, "Because, my friend, I'm interested in fifty Americans, that's why." Applause begins to build on the audio track. "And when those fifty Americans are released, then I'm perfectly willing to talk about that." The applause builds to a crescendo. The crowd stands, apparently giving Baker an ovation. At the podium, Baker smiles. There was only one problem. The ovation had not occurred at the end of the answer but instead had been intercut by the adteam.

Soundbites as Ads

In 1988 the candidates reached the largest number of viewers in environments in which assertion was the norm. From Labor Day until election eve, each presidential candidate had eight opportunities five days a week to gain access to a national audience on morning, evening, and late night network news. With the exception of "MacNeil/Lehrer," what was most likely to be excerpted from the candidate's speech of the day was a dramatic attack on his opponent set in a visually reinforcing environment. The major speeches of the campaign that lacked such moments, including Bush's major speech on agricultural policy and Dukakis's major speech on defense, received no network news treatment.

With the exception of candidate interviews, network news is somewhat like the peg boards used to assess children's hand-eye coordination and spacial processing. These boxlike fixtures contain holes of various sizes and shapes. The child is handed a bag of cut-out blocks. The goal of the exercise is getting each block inside the box through the appropriate hole as quickly as possible. The strategy schema provides holes for blocks that are small and help construct the narrative that answers the question, Who is winning and why? The hole demands short statements that do not require additional contextual explanation from the reporter, do not require additional editing, and will be compatible with the reporter's story line. Any pithy attack on the opponent will do.

In 1978 I was invited to appear on network television for the first time. Wanting to do a good job, I was particularly careful in the pre-interview to define my terms and lay out the available evidence for my arguments. After talking with me for more than a half hour, the producer of the segment laughed and said, "Look professor, I know you are an expert in this area. That's why we want you on the show. But when we say you are an expert, it means you are an expert. You don't have to tell us how you got to your conclusions, just give us the bottom line." In the fourteen years since that experience I have learned that a soundbite is actually an assertion. Whether it is warranted by evidence or not cannot usually be known by the reader or viewer. By certifying the interviewee as an "expert," reporters ask their audiences to take the existence of evidence on faith.

Network news accustoms audiences to assertion not argument. Over time, it reinforces the notion that politics is about visceral identification and apposition, not complex problems and their solutions. It also accustoms politicians and quoted academics to think and speak in assertions.

Speechwriters produce and candidates deliver what is rewarded with newsplay. Over time, assertion—not argument—has become the norm for candidate speeches. Indeed, the goal of the campaign comes to be getting the same soundbite into the soundbite hole of each of the networks. Interestingly, that soundbite is not necessarily the thesis of the speech. More often it is an attack on an opponent.

If the goal of a speech is producing a widgetlike soundbite in a prefabricated environment, then some facets of argument fall to the wayside. One does not dare note the legitimacy of anything the opponent has done or said. Doing so runs the risk that that moment of equanimity will be the one played on news. Banned too is discussion of substantive similarities between candidates. One does not accurately summarize the case for the other side, even if only to rebut it. Nor ought one to tie evidence to one's claims lest in the process the claim expands beyond the size of the soundbite slot and as a result is shunted aside. "Stepping on your own message" is shorthand for letting the reporters or the opposing campaign shape the content of your soundbite. As those who watched C-SPAN and the "MacNeil/Lehrer NewsHour" are aware, both Dukakis and Bush delivered important, cogent, well-argued speeches on the stump in 1988. In some instances their central claims and the rationale behind them did reach the nation's living rooms through network evening news. More often, they did not.

When I argued earlier that all forms of campaign discourse were becoming adlike, I meant in part that they were substituting assertion for argument and attack for engagement.

I don't mean to suggest that short assertive statements are necessarily superficial. When a voter is fully informed about an issue and needs only to know whether the candidate is of like mind, such assertions as "I favor *Roe v. Wade*" or "I favor the death penalty for drug lords" are useful and efficient. But if the voter is seeking an understanding of the rationale that has led the candidate to this conclusion or is trying to determine which position to embrace, soundbites aren't very helpful. They can tell a voter *what* a candidate believes, but not *why*. And many issues are too complex to be freeze dried into a slogan and a smile.

Transforming telegraphic assertion into argument requires data and a link between the data and the claim. Engagement goes a step further by differentiating between the espoused position and that of one's opponent and arguing the comparative advantages of one over the other.

Since ads usually do digest the positions being taken in other public settings, one might justifiably ask, What's lost in a world in which everything's an ad? Perhaps the country that created the assembly line has simply found a more efficient way to do politics.

In fact, when a candidate is ducking the challenges created by debates, press conferences, and interviews, the answer is that there is little in the speeches or the campaign not found in the ads. But the cost is high. In such circumstances, the likelihood that campaign rhetoric will prophesy conduct in office plummets.

In 1968, for example, Richard Nixon told the Republican convention that "for those who are able to help themselves, what we need are not more millions on welfare rolls, but more millions on payrolls in the United States of America." That line was a mainstay of his fall stump speech. Minus the phrase "for those who are able to help themselves," he repeated it in an often aired telelvision ad.

His major radio address on welfare reform dealt in similar generalities. He favored incentives for "families to stay together," he said, and wanted to supplement "welfare checks with part-time earnings." Unanswered was "How?"

In mid-May of that campaign year, he noted that he did not foresee recommending "a guaranteed annual income or a negative income tax." Yet in early August of his first year as president, Nixon offered the nation an income maintenance plan. Had Nixon argued for such a course during the 1968 campaign, its chances of becoming law would have increased. By the end of Nixon's second year in office, the plan was dead.

What is lost when a speech is simmered down to an ad is a clear relationship between the appealing claim and its public policy incarnation. Again the Nixon 1968 campaign is illustrative. In his acceptance speech and on the stump, Nixon promised to appoint to the Supreme Court "men who are for civil rights, but who recognize that the first civil right of every American is to be free from domestic violence." When edited for a television ad, the tie between freedom from domestic violence and appointments to the court was lost. Yet the public policy implications of the promise would hand Nixon two of the major defeats of his first term in the form of repudiation of his nominations of Clement Haynesworth and Harrold Carswell to the high court.

When candidates are ducking position-taking, our hope for answers resides in tenacious reporters not preoccupied with questions of strategic intent and effect. In 1968 candidates were still expected to answer the questions they were asked. Although candidate Nixon was shielding himself from conferences with the national press corps, as well as from the Sunday interview shows and debates, he was being interviewed regularly by local reporters. These interviews pinned him down on the issue of federal cessation of aid to segregated schools.

In a September 11 interview with WBTV in Charlotte, North Carolina, Nixon's rambling answer to a question about his position on cut-offs concluded by noting that he supported *Brown v. Board of Education*'s ban on segregation. He then added that "when you go beyond that and say that it is the responsibility of the federal government and the federal courts to, in effect, act as local school districts in determining how we carry that out, then to use the power of the federal treasury to withhold funds in order to carry it out, then I think we are going too far. In my view, that kind of activity should be very scrupulously examined and in many cases should be rescinded." A week later in an interview in Anaheim, California, the agreement to rein in federal activity was modified. Queried about whether he would ask Congress to rescind Title VI of the 1964 Civil Rights Act, thereby eliminating the title authorizing cut-offs in school aide, Nixon responded, "Certainly not." What he had actually said in North Carolina, he claimed, was that funds should be withdrawn if a freedom of choice plan was a "subterfuge for segregation."

Whether Nixon was telling two different audiences what they wanted to hear, I can't say. What is clear is that Leon Panetta, Head of HEW's Office of Civil Rights, couldn't determine from Nixon's campaign rhetoric what the administration's policy was supposed to be. "The trouble," he wrote, "was that no one really understood what Nixon said or promised during the campaign, and his statements were shrouded in ambiguity and controversy."[11] What was missing in 1968 were argument, engagement, and accountability.

Argument and Engagement

It was through a process of trial and error that the country came to defend the free play of argument in politics. The Sedition Act of 1798, passed by the Federalists, made it a Federal crime to "write, utter or publish . . . any false, scandalous and malicious writing . . . against the government of the United States."[12] During the election of 1800, Federalist Secretary of State Timothy Pickering used this act to prosecute opposition Republican newspapers. The government "depends for its existence upon the good will of the people," argued defenders of the Act. "That good will is maintained by their good opinion But, how is that good opinion to be preserved, if wicked and unprincipled men, men of inordinate and desperate ambition, are allowed to state facts to the people which are not true, which they know at the time to be false, and which are stated with the criminal intention of bringing the Government into disrepute among the people."[13]

By contrast, the Republicans held that in the clash of ideas, true opinion would prevail. The state could not be so menaced by words, they argued, as to justify the harm that could result from their suppression. After that brief experiment in limiting political debate, the founders came out for a free and open exchange of ideas.

The ideal was amply precedented. The philosopher Immanuel Kant termed it "the transcendental principle of publicness."[14] "Let Truth and Falsehood grapple," argued Milton in "Areopagitica," "who ever knew truth put to the worse in a free and open encounter."[15]

The argument for what some have called the "marketplace of ideas" also drew strength from the theorizing of two of the fathers of the revolution: Benjamin Franklin and Thomas Jefferson. In his 1731 "Apology for Printers," Franklin noted that "both Sides ought equally to have the Advantage of being heard by the Publick."[16] In 1801, Jefferson's inaugural reflected his support for the concept, "If there be any among us who would wish to dissolve this union or to change its republican form," he wrote, "let them stand undisturbed, as monuments of the safety with which error of opinion may be tolerated, where reason is left free to combat it." The protections of political speech that govern contemporary politics are a legacy of this view.

Today, if it has aired ads for any candidate in a federal race, there are only four grounds on which an FCC-licensed television or radio station can refuse a political ad for a bona fide candidate. The ad can be barred if its length differs from the time purchased. For example, in a thirty-second slot, a station would not have to air a twenty-six- or thirty-two-second ad. An ad must meet the technical broadcast requirements of the station. So, for example, the audio track cannot break into technically unacceptable noise levels. To enable listeners or viewers to hold those who sponsored the ad accountable for its content, the ad must bear an identifying disclaiming notice or tag. And the ad may not be obscene. A copulating couple may not be shown even in the missionary position. Unless it violates the law, the U.S. government cannot proscribe or penalize any speech of a candidate campaigning for office.

This does not mean, of course, that political speech has consistently and invariably been protected. Eugene Debs was jailed for his opposition to World War I. Indeed, he ran a presidential campaign from his prison cell.

But overall the distance is not great between the sentiments of Jefferson and the 1964 Supreme Court, which in *New York Times v. Sullivan* praised the United States' "profound national commitment to the principle that debate on public issues should be uninhibited, robust, and wide open, and that it may well include vehement, caustic, and sometimes unpleasantly sharp attacks on government and public officials."[17]

Nonetheless, there has been a longstanding tension between confidence in the deliberations of the community and fear that in the heat of passion the public will embrace a course of action not in its own interest. "As the cool and deliberate sense of the community ought, in all governments and actually will, in all free governments, ultimately prevail over the views of its rulers," noted Madison in *Federalist* number 63, "so there are particular moments in public affairs when the people, stimulated by some irregular passion or some illicit advantage, or misled by the artful misrepresentations of interested men, may call for measures which they themselves will afterwards be the most ready to lament and condemn."

The likelihood that the public will be misled is minimized if the candidates' views are available and tested by each other and by the press, if they are expected to engage in warranted argument, and if they accept responsibility for defending their own claims and the claims others offer on their behalf.

Of course, none of this ensures that most citizens or most voters will pay a whit of attention. But it would increase the probability that those who are interested have "adequate" if not "equal" "opportunities for discovering and validating, in the time permitted by the need for a decision, what his or her preferences are on the matter to be decided."[18]

The size of the United States, the heterogeneity of its population, and the complexity of its role in the international community mean that the kind of deliberative discourse envisioned by Aristotle is beyond our reach. Indeed any whisper of Aristotle or Athens in a book about political rhetoric invites the charge of polis envy. But that does not mean that we can't aspire to an Athenian ideal characterized by argument and engagement.

What Aristotle prized was argument; yet argument has a double meaning. On the one hand it means reasoned discourse, or "the organizing process of disciplined thought."[19] On the other, it signals a clash between two sets of reasoned claims. The first is an "utterance of a sort of communicative act," the second "a particular kind of interaction."[20] For the sake of clarity, I am calling the first "argument" and the second "engagement."

Engagement is a process of comparison that enables audiences to determine which argument has the greater force. It emanates from what debate theorists call "clash" and "extension." Clash pits two competing argumentative positions against each other in a fashion that invites the audience to select the more persuasive. Extension is response to response. It carries the argument forward, clarifying in the process the implications of the cases built for each side.

In traditional terms, the purpose of argument is demonstrating the truth or legitimacy of a proposition. This is done by weighing the evidence and determining how well it supports the proposed claim. "Unless [an] assertion was made quite wildly and irresponsibly," notes philosopher Stephen Toulmin, "we shall normally have some facts to which we can point in its support: if the claim is challenged, it is up to us to appeal to those facts, and present them as the foundation upon which our claim is based."[21]

Postmodernism aside, at some level, political discourse presupposes the existence of brute, verifiable facts. "Freedom of opinion," as Hannah Arendt notes, "is a farce unless factual information is guaranteed and the facts themselves are not in dispute. In other words, factual truth informs political thought."[22] There either are or are not homeless on our streets. The rate of unemployment has either increased since 1988 or it has not. William Horton either did or did not kill someone while on furlough from a Massachusetts prison. George Bush either did or did not say in the 1988 campaign "Read my lips. No new taxes."

The first test of any political claim then becomes: Is it factually accurate? In the 1992 Georgia primary, an ad by Republican Pat Buchanan failed this test. "In the past three years the Bush Administration has invested our tax dollars in pornographic and blasphemous art, too shocking to show," said the announcer as scenes of leather-clad men appeared on the screen. The problem with the ad is straightforward. The film being shown was funded by a state arts council under the Reagan, not the Bush administration. The ad fails on other grounds as well. The film being shown is an atypical instance of arts funding. Most NEA funding supports such noncontroversial instances of high culture as the Chicago Symphony and Pavarotti on PBS.

Facts and shared beliefs are the substance of argument and commonly shared norms determine the appropriateness of their use. But facts alone are not the self-sufficient stuff of argument. Argument also builds from such communal premises as education is a social good. Assumed as well is a common sense of the "rules of argument." Testimony from those who are self-interested is suspect. Evidence must not be sundered from context; relevant evidence must be disclosed, not suppressed. Like items should be compared to like. A plan that is offered may legitimately be tested by asking whether it meets the need and whether the advantages that follow from it outweigh the disadvantages.

Beyond the communal pale are name calling or ad hominem attack and guilt by association. To all of this, argument theory adds an additional caution: Proof can be counterfeit. The persuasiveness of fallacies "comes from their superficial resemblance to sound arguments; this similarity lends them an air of plausibility."[23]

In two centuries of political speech, we have developed public norms for appropriate discourse and additionally some sense of the ideal to which it should aspire. The presence of these norms is evident in the exchange between George Bush and Dan Rather at the start of the 1988 primary season as surely as in the congressional debate over entry into the Gulf War, and the confirmation hearings of Justice David Souter to the Supreme Court and Robert Gates to head the CIA.

These dissimilar environments produced discourse that assumed that both sides had a right to be heard, that argument should be backed by proof, that the fairness and accuracy of the evidence should be subject to scrutiny, that the context from which evidence emerged should not be distorted, that those who are attacked have a right to reply, that in the process of engaging in argument consensus could emerge, and that those making claims should be held responsible for them. The exchanges presuppose that those on opposing sides will grant the good will and integrity of their opponents. They assume that those involved in the discussion will not be swayed by specious claims or attacks that appeal to prejudice rather than reason, and that the end of the engagement is a judgment to which each side commits itself and for which it is accountable.

An alien viewing these public discussions would assume from the Bush-Rather exchange that the Vice President disapproves of selective use of evidence and resents having statements taken out of context. Viewers of the Gates confirmation hearing would hear Gates as well as his supporters and opponents agree that "distorting" or "slanting" evidence is wrong. At issue for all concerned was whether that is what Gates had done.

When these norms are honored, areas of disagreement and agreement are clarified. The collective understanding of an issue is advanced. The commitment of all participants to the legitimacy of the system is reinforced. The community is better for the experience; and reason, not rancor, is the order of the day.

All of this is of concern because, in the 1988 presidential campaign, argument, engagement, and accountability fell short both of the norms set in previous campaigns and of the standards to which we should hold discourse. Indeed, mapping the patterns of campaign discourse shows that there has been a marked falloff since the days when the half-hour speech was the norm for the televised campaign. To help make sense of the charts showing these changes, let me contrast the claims made by Stevenson in 1956 with those made by Johnson in 1964.

In 1956, Adlai Stevenson staked his candidacy on two policy proposals: an end to the military draft and an end to major nuclear testing. He might have said, "Read my lips. No nuclear testing." Instead, by providing a rationale for his claims, he invited audiences to follow the line of thinking that led to his conclusion. Envisioned by the speeches was a thoughtful, concerned electorate.

A professional army would be cheaper, Stevenson argued, and, in an age of technological warfare, more efficient. Nuclear tests were polluting the air and water and thus endangering the planet. We already knew what we needed to about the weapons and now had the wherewithal to monitor Russian compliance without onsite inspections. So, he reasoned, we could and should end testing.

What remained unvoiced is as important as what Stevenson said. Nowhere in his speeches did the Democrat impugn the integrity or intelligence of his opponent. Nor did he imply that Eisenhower relished contaminating the air and groundwater or gloried in conscripting young adults. In other words, Stevenson attacked a position not a person.

Stevenson's speeches *engaged* opposing arguments. And in the *clash* of opposing views, the addresses clarified definitions and points of agreement and disagreement. Contested by the Democrat, for example, were the counter-claims that we would not be able to fill a professional army and would be sabotaged by the Russians who would capitalize on a test ban to overtake us militarily.

By 1964, argument and engagement on the issue of a nuclear test ban had been reduced to assertion and attack. "We are told to regard as fruitless the search for lasting agreements, such as the test ban treaty," Lyndon Johnson stated in his nationally telecast election eve speech. "We are attacked for our restraint in the use of our mighty power." The choice he posed was both Manichaean and misleading. "Shall we move forward, innovating where necessary, but building on the programs and the policies that are nourished by progressive men of both parties? Or shall we strip the house to the foundation, throw aside the work of decades, discard the wisdom of a generation of trusted leaders, and strike off in an uncertain and, I believe, a deeply dangerous direction?"

Complementing these appositions was an ad that seemed to say that Barry Goldwater wanted to kill children. "Do you know what people used to do?" asks the female announcer as a child is shown licking an ice cream cone. "They used to explode atomic bombs in the air. Now, children should have lots of vitamin A and calcium but they shouldn't have any Strontium 90 or Cesium 137. These things come from atomic bombs and they're radioactive. They can make you die. Do you know what people finally did? They got together and signed a nuclear test ban treaty, and then the radioactive poisons started to go away. But now, there is a man who wants to be president of the United States, and he doesn't like this treaty. He's fought against it. He even voted against it. He wants to go on testing more bombs. His name is Barry Goldwater and if he's elected, they might start testing all over again." The visual and the visceral had replaced the invitation to reasoned response.

Where Stevenson acknowledged the reasons for testing and argued that they could be accomplished in other ways, the Strontium 90 ad simply assumed that testing was an unmitigated evil. Where Stevenson laid out and rebutted the case for the other side, the ice cream ad attributed Goldwater's position to "dislike." Where Stevenson granted the good will and integrity of those who disagreed with him, Johnson's ad implies that Goldwater would willingly harm a child. Instead of engaging Goldwater's position, the ad parodied it.

Neither Johnson nor Stevenson's positions were tested in debate with their opponents. Had debate occurred, both would have been subjected to forms of scrutiny unlikely in the monologic form of even the best intentioned speech. Debate pits arguments against each other. In the process it discloses the chain of reasoning that warrants one conclusion over another. It also invites the reasoned assent of the community. "In the absence of debate," wrote Walter Lippmann, "unrestricted utterance leads to the degradation of opinion. By a kind of Gresham's law the more rational is overcome by the less rationale, and the opinions that will prevail will be those which are held most ardently by those with the most passionate will."[24]

Discourse can be seen as oppositional or self-promotional. Because it lays out both one's own and one's opponent's positions, engaged discourse is both self-promotional and oppositional. But it doesn't end there. Engaged rhetoric is built on clash and extension. It provides the basis for comparing and contrasting candidate positions.

Before valorizing argumentatively based differentiation, engagement, and accountability as criteria to which campaign discourse should aspire, let me note one strong tendency in contemporary discourse that runs counter to engagement. The ritualized condemnation of "negativity" in political discourse, particularly political advertising, that has been a mainstay of campaign coverage since the first NCPAC ads aired in 1980, is confused and confusing. By their nature, campaigns combine the self-promotional and the oppositional, the case for voting for one person and one position rather than the other.

Propositionally legitimate, fair, accurate, contextual, oppositional claims that differentiate one candidate from another are the basis for comparative judgment. By its nature, such discourse will focus on comparing and contrasting and in so doing will direct its attention to the opponent's record and positions. Unfortunately, scholars and reporters alike have come to regard any form of oppositional discourse as "negative" and hence illegitimate. Apart from the energy lost to the GNP in collective handwringing, what is troubling about this rush to rid the body politic of the oppositional is the fact that self-promoting ads (usually called "positive") are the more typical repository of false claims.

Moreover, since candidates do not usually purchase air time to reveal their own failings or the weaknesses in their positions, such fault lines will remain unexplored if not raised by the opposing candidate or the press. By dispatching all analysis of an opponent's record, we risk driving engaged comparison and contrast from campaigns entirely.

Consultants prefer the word "comparative" to "negative" or "oppositional." And if their ads were, in fact, comparative, I would agree. But most of what the pundits term "comparative" are simply indictments. The Bush harbor ad does not compare Bush's and Dukakis's records on the environment any more than Dukakis's Social Security ad compares their records on the vote to freeze the cost-of-living adjustment; both ads are simply oppositional. Lost in the noncomparative indictments are Bush's comparatively worse record on the environment and the fact that

Dukakis had taken the same position as Bush on the need to freeze the Social Security cost-of-living adjustment.

An analysis of the most aired ad in each general election from 1952 through 1988 is revealing.

    1952: (SP) Man from Abilene
    1956: (SP) Man from Libertyville #2
    1960: (SP-E) Kennedy Speech to Houston Ministers
    1964: (OPP-E) Social Security ad
    1968: (SP) What Manner of Man—HHH
    1972: (OPP) McGovern defense plan
    1976: (SP) Ford biographical ad
    1980: (SP-E) Reagan five-minute bio
    1984: (SP-E) Morning in America
    1988: (OPP) Revolving door furlough
    (SP) = Self-promotional; (E) = Engaged; (OPP) = Oppositional

Note that in 1988 the most controversial candidate ad was also the ad aired most frequently in the campaign. When the accuracy of the inference it invited was challenged, the Bush campaign defended the ad and continued to run it. By contrast, the 1964 campaign's two most controversial ads aired a single time each. One showed a child licking an ice cream cone as the announcer implied that Goldwater wanted to poison children with the Strontium 90 from bomb tests. The other is the daisy commercial. The same was true in 1968. That ad intercut Humphrey with scenes of poverty and violence. Note also that in only two campaigns was the most aired ad oppositional.

As a general rule, oppositional ads are not aired nationally. Instead they are concentrated in key states. So, for example, in 1952 the Republican oppositional spots were aired at saturation levels in 49 counties in 12 states at a cost of almost $1.5 million. By contrast, most of the speeches delivered in that campaign were nationally aired. In 1964, the Democrats concentrated their spot buys in 17 states. Heaviest saturation: Texas, 1345 spot buys; California, 823; New York, 410. Johnson's speeches were nationally aired. In 1972 McGovern began with 16 priority states in 52 media markets. By the second week of the campaign, that number had increased to 21 states. In 1988, the Republicans aired their oppositional ads in selected spot markets and their self-promotional ads nationally. PAC ads are almost exclusively aired market by market.

Of course, there is no reason that paid time has to be limited to spot ads. For all practical purposes, however, in the 1988 campaign, that's the way it was. The modal length of aired candidate and party paid television was thirty minutes in 1952, five minutes in 1956 and 1960, sixty seconds in 1964, 1968, 1972, and 1976. In 1980 it was five minutes for the Republicans but sixty seconds for the Democrats; it dropped to thirty seconds for both parties in 1988.

Interestingly, as I will argue in the next chapter, the most engaged campaign of the 1980s momentarily halted the trend toward shorter ads. Those who assert that ad purchases have steadily gotten shorter forget that in the 1980 general election the Reagan campaign purchased 73 five-minute network time slots. Most (60) were used to air the five-minute Reagan biographical documentary. By contrast, the campaign purchased only 43 sixty-second network slots.[25] In mid-September, the five-minute documentary made up 75 percent of the purchased air time for the Reagan campaign. Five-minute ads were also the dominant mode in 1960.[26]

Two speeches by Stevenson in 1956 contrast oppositional and engaged oppositional campaign discourse. On October 19, 1956, Adlai Stevenson indicted Eisenhower's handling of the Suez situation without indicating precisely what he would do differently. The speech opposed but failed to engage. The trouble, according to the Democrat, was that instead of adjusting its policies "to new conditions," the administration "has remained tied to old methods, old thinking, and old slogans." The claim invites specification of the alternative course. Instead, Stevenson noted that "I have no slick formula, no patent medicine, to cure our problems. The difficulties which face American policy-makers in all parts of the world are deep rooted and complex. And this will continue to be so regardless of who wins in November." He wanted, he said, to re-examine the military establishment and Selective Service, to meet the challenges of the underdeveloped parts of the world, and to revitalize NATO. None of this indicated what he would have done differently in Suez or how like situations might be prevented in the future.

Stevenson's speech of October 19 was an oddity in that campaign year. On November 1, the Democrat did his case more justice. In a broadcast from Buffalo, New York, he argued that had he been president he would not have pressed the British "to evacuate their great military base without making provision for international control of the canal; he would have opposed arms shipments to Egypt and at the same time would have armed Israel. At the same time, he approved Eisenhower's attempt to "check military action."

More usual in recent campaigns is the absence of engagement Reagan complained of mid-way through their only 1980 presidential debate, when he said "I know that the President's supposed to be responding to me, but sometimes I have a hard time connecting what he's saying with what I said or what my positions are."

When candidates fail to engage, the press ought to sort the confusions out. Unless the viewer has an independent source of evidence gathered on her own, the following news report provides no intelligent basis for judgment of the competing claims.

> *Dukakis:* "The price of housing in this country has raced ahead of young people's wages and has made it impossible for them to buy homes in the

communities that they grew up in." [Has it? A reporter focused on strategy won't intrude to say.]

Bruce Morton (reporter, CBS): "Dukakis reminded the enthusiastically Democratic audience of something George Bush said during the debate."

Bush: "Now, how does that grab ya for increasing housing? Housing is up." [Is it? The reporter isn't telling.]

Dukakis: "And he's right, my friends. Housing is up. It's up so much, it's almost out of sight for the average family *(applause)* (CBS, October 10, 1988).

Later Morton states, "Home ownership has declined during the Reagan years, he [Dukakis] said." [Has it? We have no way of knowing from the report.]

Dukakis is sundering Bush's claim from context. What the Republican nominee is saying is that the number of federally funded housing units has increased. But Dukakis takes "up" to mean "cost" not "available units."

Who is telling the truth? Both are. Federally supported housing units have increased. But most of the increase is based in filling commitments set in place in the Carter administration. From 1980 to 1988, federal funding of low-income housing dropped by $25 million a year.

Depending on the region of the county addressed, Dukakis is correct as well. The ability of young couples to afford a home has eroded. The problem here is that the terms of dispute are not being defined.

Without agreed upon definitions, the argument cannot be engaged. It is possible, for example, that an increase in the number of available units has occurred but that their rental cost is above the means of those requiring housing. (The difference between Dukakis and Bush is telegraphed but not made explicit in their first debate. The Democrats would rehabilitate or build more low-cost units and subsidize the rental of them; the Republicans would provide the poor with vouchers and expect them to locate housing on their own.)

One hundred percent of the discourse in a campaign—including speeches, debates, and answers to press questions—could be oppositional; 100 percent could be self-promotional. Both forms of discourse have a place in a campaign. Engaged discourse takes a position, provides evidence to justify that position, and differentiates the position from that of the opponent. As Chart 9-1 in Appendix I indicates, the percent of total paid time that engaged dropped in 1988 to the lowest point in the last thirty-six years of broadcast campaigning. My assumption that longer forms of communication, specifically the 5-, 15-, and 30-minute speech, are more likely than spot ads to produce engagement is based in historical fact. If one sums the minutes of paid engaged discourse in the general elections from 1952 through 1988 to ask what forms produced engagement most often, one finds that the likelihood of engagement increases as the length of the speech increases (see Chart 9-2).

Accountability

Accountability presupposes accessibility. Until the fall campaign of 1984, it was axiomatic in political circles that a candidate far ahead in the polls would duck debates. LBJ had done so in 1964 as had Nixon in 1968 and 1972. In 1984 Reagan changed all that by acceding to public pressure and the need to dispatch fears about his age. In the process, he "institutionalized" presidential debates.

But the underlying tendency remains. Candidates ahead in the polls are less accessible to the press than those behind. They hold fewer press conferences (see Chart 9-3) and are less likely to take questions on the Sunday interview shows (see Chart 9-4). And when those whose polling numbers are lagging expose themselves to press scrutiny, they are more likely than the front runners to be asked "strategy questions." At the same time, the average number of nationally publicized press conferences held by the candidates dropped in 1984 and 1988 to an all-time low (see Chart 9-5).

Candidates are also exercising increasing control over the format of general election presidential debates. This control has wrested from the press its principle means of holding candidates responsible for their claims. Since the format forbade follow-up questions, it was only by "breaking" the rules that the press panel in 1988 was able to repeatedly ask Republican vice presidential nominee Dan Quayle what he would do first if he learned that he had just ascended to the presidency.

Press conferences can hold candidates accountable for the accuracy, fairness, and contextuality of claims as well as their cost and practicability. By mid-October 1988, however, the form had all but disappeared from the campaign.

Accessibility

By 1988 the Republican nominee had perfected the art of not answering the question asked. When a person in a crowd called out to Bush, "What about the deficit?" He responded, "Deficit. Let me tell you what about it. I don't think you're paying too little in taxes. I think the government's spending too much. I will not raise your taxes. I'm not going to raise them. Get the same pledge out of that Democrat" (ABC, September 6, 1988).

By late September, the press was pointing out Bush's inaccessibility. "Polls show Bush behind in Illinois," noted Britt Hume on ABC, "and he apparently thought getting out among the people would be just the thing. Did that also mean that he would answer reporters' questions? Not today. After all, you can carry this accessibility stuff too far" (ABC, September 28, 1988).

In one of the many debriefings that followed the 1988 campaign, Hume sighed, "I'd like to tell you anecdotes about what it's like to cover George Bush up close, but I never got close enough to George Bush."[27] Print reporters were equally frustrated. "They would say over their earphones, 'Reporters on the right' and the Secret Service would steer Bush to the left to keep him out of our shouting range," observes *Washington Post* correspondent David Hoffman.

Avoiding the press is politically feasible because it carries no penalties. "In fact, Dukakis campaign officials say that before they isolated their candidate the campaign suffered greatly for being accessible. Mr. Bush would launch attacks and Mr. Dukakis, confronted by reporters, would answer. He looked defensive, Mr. Bush looked in control. Mr. Dukakis plummeted in the polls."[28]

As a general rule, the candidate ahead in the polls is less accessible to the press than the trailing candidate. Typically, the winning presidential candidate in the television age has been less accessible than the losing candidate and has answered fewer questions posed in press conferences and debates. This pattern is troubling because it raises the possibility that the candidate most likely to win is least likely to tell us what he will do in office.

In general, unless they are behind in the polls, as Ford was in 1976, incumbents provide less access to the press, have fewer press conferences, and favor fewer debates than challengers. When the polls indicate that the outcome is unclear, as they did in 1960, 1968, and 1980, both campaigns become more accessible. In 1988, the candidate behind in the polls was asked markedly more strategy questions than the leading candidate. (see Chart 9-8). As candidates fall behind in the polls, the number of strategy-based questions they will be asked by the press increases. So, for example, in 1980 John Anderson held more press conferences than his opponents and was asked proportionately more strategy questions than Carter or Reagan.

If press conferences are to produce engagement, reporters must ask questions of public importance and press the candidates to answer them and both major party candidates must give reporters access in some form. If one candidate is highly accessible and the other inaccessible, the accessible candidate is penalized. Years in which the candidates (or, in the case of 1980, their senior advisors) were comparably accessible increase the amount of substantive clash on the issues with a resulting increase in the attentive public's ability to differentiate the candidates. Senior reporters who covered the campaigns from 1960 through 1988 and insiders who participated in the campaigns agree that the press had comparable access to both candidates in 1960, 1976, and 1980. In 1964, 1968, 1972, 1984, and 1988 the eventual victor was less accessible than the eventual loser.[29]

If judged by whether the candidate is repeatedly and intelligently pressed to answer important questions, the interview program is far more successful than the press conference or the debate. This is the case, in part, because neither follow-up by the reporter nor the length of a candidate's answer is artificially constrained. When a candidate is far behind in the polls, the questions here as in press conferences turn increasingly to strategy. But, with that factor controlled, as David Broder observes, over all, the percent of questions based in strategic concerns has not changed markedly since the early days of television.[30]

It is on "Meet The Press" that vice presidential nominee Geraldine Ferraro is asked and complains about being asked whether she "could push the nuclear button" (NBC, January 14, 1984). In the same forum, vice presidential nominee George Bush is called to account for remarks that Governor Reagan made before B'nai B'rith, attacking "Carter for providing fighter planes to Saudi Arabia and tanks to Jordan," when in the past both Republican and Democratic administrations have done likewise. And in a Sunday interview, David Broder asked President Carter a question that otherwise would have been asked at the Iowa debate that Carter did not attend. The question: "[W]e still have 5.8% unemployment; inflation has risen from 4.8% to 13%. We still don't have a viable energy policy. Russian troops are in Cuba and Afghanistan. The dollar is falling; gold is rising, and the hostages after 78 days are still in Tehran. Just what have you done, sir, to deserve renomination?" (NBC, January 20, 1980).

In the interview shows, candidates are held accountable as they are nowhere else for their statements in speeches,[31] news conferences, and ads. Indeed, the only serious public confrontation between the press and a member of the Democratic ticket over the daisy ad occurs on "Meet the Press" on September 20, 1964, when Vice President Humphrey is asked, "Senator Humphrey, recently you warned the American people that the Republicans—and these were your words 'may appeal to passion and prejudices and to fear and bitterness in the campaign,' and you pledged that the Democrats' campaign would be conducted—and again these were your words—'with honor and dignity.' In view of that, why did the Democrats use the TV spot showing a little girl counting daisies and then being blown to bits by a nuclear blast, with the voice asking that you vote for President Johnson? Would you say that was an appeal to 'passion' and 'fear'?" Humphrey responds that he did not approve of the spot and suggested that it be withdrawn.

Questions candidates are squirming away from, such as busing in 1972, are raised. The meanings and resonances of phrases such as "law and order" are probed. In 1968, the candidates' differences on Vietnam are explored on the Sunday shows. And on the May 3, 1992 "Meet The Press," independent presidential contender H. Ross Perot disclaimed his assertion that the government could "easily" save $100 billion by cutting Social Security and Medicare benefits for "folks just like" him.

The interviews that produce the highest level of candidate accountability attract the smallest audience. Spot ads, which cumulatively reach the largest audience, now duck candidate responsibility for most claims.

Accountability: The Case of the Disappearing Candidate

A key element in legitimate oppositional discourse is the accountability that comes from personal utterance of the message. Since Aristotle's time, we have known that the ethos or credibility of the rhetor both affects and is affected by the message. To increase accountability, some have proposed that advertised attack be carried only in the voice of the attacking candidate. Others have argued that candidates should accept questions from the press on all new ads shortly after they begin airing.

The trend away from candidate accountability for oppositional ad claims is clear. The oppositional claims in most of the Republican spot ads of 1952 were made by Ike. In 1964, the oppositional premises LBJ voiced in his ads were enthymematic. By 1988, George Bush was voicing none of his oppositional ads. That instead is the function of the faceless announcer. Only in the ad's final frame does a matchbook-sized picture of Bush appear in the bottom left of the screen. It is there to meet the FCC-stipulated condition for a lower purchase rate for ad time.

The horizon is not quite as empty as the absentee claims would suggest. Most PAC money is spent on self-promotional rather than oppositional material. But in the last decade there does appear to be an increase in PAC-sponsored attacks and a decrease in the *number* of purely oppositional ads by candidates. This decline in the number aired has not been followed by a decline in the percent of purchased air time devoted to oppositional ads.

Any campaign can speak in seven possible voices: the candidate's, a surrogate for the candidate, an "ordinary voter," a neutral reporter, a newspaper clipping or other presumably authoritative source, an unnamed advocate, and an anonymous source. The first holds the candidate most accountable, the last, the least.

In 1952 the major party nominees and their running mates were the principal speakers in 73 percent of the paid half-hour time slots. In 1956, 90 percent; in 1960, 88 percent. By 1988, each candidate was appearing in only a single half hour of paid national time. In that general election, the presidential candidates voiced less than 20 percent of the claims in their ads.

Unlike debates, speeches, and press conferences, with the major exception of the 1952 Republican campaign, oppositional spot ads seldom show the nominees "attacking." Congressional proposals to mandate that attack be spoken by the attacking candidate are an attempt to increase accountability as was the 1992 FCC requirement, beaten back by the parties, that ads orally identify sponsorship.

Candidates Speaking for Themselves

As television became the country's dominant mass medium, candidates' comfort with it and with advertising on it increased. In 1952 both Eisenhower and Stevenson recoiled at the intrusion of "spot advertising" into their campaigns. Both doubted that complex ideas could be communicated in thirty- or sixty-second snippets. Both felt uneasy talking to a camera lens instead of a visible audience. Unlike Stevenson, Ike personally appeared in spot ads in 1952. By 1956 Stevenson had seen the light.

From 1952 through 1960 the bulk of broadcast political ads for presidential contenders consisted of the candidate speaking directly to the viewing audience or the viewing audience eavesdropping on the candidate as he or she addressed a rally. In 1956, in a concession to television's visual nature, both Republican cabinet members and Stevenson's running mate underscored their key ideas with visual aids.

Neither Eisenhower nor Stevenson had any major television experience before the 1952 campaign. By contrast, their successors in 1960 had used television ads and, in Kennedy's case, a television documentary in their races for the Senate. Additionally, Nixon had salvaged his political career through the nationally televised Checkers speech and had appeared in ads for Ike in 1956. For Kennedy and Nixon, televised advertising was a political fact of life. Both talked to a camera with greater ease than their predecessors had.

From 1952 through 1976 candidate attack raised little public concern. In 1980 that changed. The National Conservative Political Action Committee targeted liberal Senators. And President Jimmy Carter's strident appeals established that a candidate could overstep the public's tolerance for attack. Jimmy Carter's claim that Reagan would rend North from South, black from white, Jew from Gentile, is widely credited with contributing to his downfall. Not until 1988 would such strong rhetoric be spoken by a candidate.

The shift from candidate-delivered attack to televised assault by surrogates began in 1952 when Stevenson's anti-Republican ads were delivered by actors. The strongest attacks ever since (with the exception of the final ten days of the 1976 general election campaign, when Carter personally delivered hard-hitting attacks on Ford in his ads) have been in spots that do not feature the speaking beneficiary.

Surrogates

Throughout most of the nineteenth century when the office was supposed to seek the presidential candidate rather than the candidate the office, candidates did not have to face the delicate task of retailing their public sense of humility to the public while wholesaling claims of their political merits to the kingmakers. In public, surrogates spoke on their behalf. And even after candidates took to the stump, there were some things simply too self-serving to say of yourself.

In both the nineteenth and twentieth centuries, testimonial ads by those who knew the candidate filled this need. As early as 1952, prominent citizens such as Senator Estes Kefauver, nationally known for his investigation of organized crime, praised Stevenson's record as a crime fighter in Illinois and attacked the Republicans. Similarly, it was more credible for Harry Belafonte to tell viewers that John Kennedy had a strong commitment to civil rights than it was for Kennedy to make that assertion himself. In 1964, it was more believable for Senator Margaret Chase Smith to testify that Barry Goldwater had voted for Social Security than for Goldwater himself to shoulder the claim.

But surrogates had baser uses as well. The strongest attacks in a campaign traditionally have been made by someone other than the candidate. In 1969 Republican vice presidential nominee Spiro Agnew called Democratic nominee Hubert Humphrey "squishy soft, soft on inflation, soft on Communism and soft on law and order" and averred that the Democrat was beginning to look "a lot like Neville Chamberlain." Neither claim found its way into the Republican ads.

In February 1972, Nixon aide H. R. Haldeman responded to a proposal by Democratic candidate Edmund Muskie by stating in a TV interview that such "critics are consciously aiding and abetting the enemy of the United States."[32] That same year the incumbent president instructed one of his aides to create "savage attack lines" against McGovern that would portray the Democrat as "a fanatical, dedicated leftist extremist."[33] Senator Hugh Scott of Pennsylvania was among the speakers carrying Nixon's case. He labeled McGovern the candidate of "acid, abortion, and amnesty."[34] That claim was not found in advertising either.

If an attack by a surrogate creates a backlash, the surrogate, not the candidate, presumably absorbs it. A number of studies have documented the advantages of attack by someone other than the benefitting candidate.[35] Accordingly, it was retired general P. X. Kelley, not President George Bush, who told Texas and Georgia voters that Bush opponent Pat Buchanan's opposition to Desert Storm disqualified him from the presidency. "I took it personally," said Kelley in a thirty-second Bush ad. "I served with many of the marines who fought in Desert Storm. The last thing we need in the White House is an isolationist like Pat Buchanan. If he doesn't think America should lead the world, how can we trust him to lead America?" The day the ad went on the air, Bush's spokesman Marlin Fitzwater explained that "the new Bush ads were part of a strategy against Buchanan that consists of using surrogates and paid advertising to counter him in states where the conservative challenger is directly opposing Bush, but which leaves Bush himself above the fray."

In the age of television, with few exceptions, the most hyperbolic claims have been made by surrogates. In 1988, for example, it was a Republican senator, not the presidential nominee, who claimed without corroboration that, as a college student, the Democratic nominee's wife had burned a flag.

More outrageous by far than claims made in person are those made in the first surrogate medium—print.

The most inaccurate claim of Iowa senator and presidential hopeful

Tom Harkin's campaign occurred not on the airwaves but in print. In South Carolina, Harkin's supporters distributed a flier juxtaposing two photos: one showing the Democrat shaking the hand of Jesse Jackson; the other a photocopy of his rival Bill Clinton in discussion with Georgia Senator Sam Nunn at a prison-like boot camp for offenders who elect that option to longer term incarceration. Most of the inmates standing at attention in the background are black. The flier says, "While Tom Harkin and Jesse Jackson are fighting for social and economic justice, Bill Clinton has been fighting for a national police force." Nothing in Clinton's record or rhetoric suggests that he favors a national police force.

Because an unseen voice routinely narrated its pictures, television accustomed us to this surrogate who was less accountable than those who visibly spoke on the candidate's behalf. With the first political radio broadcast, the paid announcer entered politics. As political newsreels entered theaters, the unseen voice followed. In a 1952 TV spot, the newsreels' authoritative voice moved to television to tout "The Man from Abilene."

Personal Witness Ads

In the shadow of Watergate, newslike personal witness ads emerged as a form of attack in 1976. In them, citizens claimed that Carter was "too wishy-washy" or noted that he didn't do much as governor. To underscore that these were actual citizens voicing unscripted opinions, these Ford oppositional ads identified the speakers' hometowns. By adopting the conventions of the news interview, such ads appropriate the credibility of that form. To be effective, the testifiers must sound unrehearsed.

Because those testifying are not actors and are expressing actually held opinions, they seem divorced from either candidate. Their statements seem less like attacks than the same comments would in a production spot or an ad voiced by the candidate. A number of American commonplaces nurture our disposition to approve of this form of attack, among them, "I may not agree with what you say, but I'll defend your right to say it," and "Everybody's entitled to an opinion." In 1980, both sides used personal witness ads.

Personal witness ads survived in 1984. In that campaign the Reagan strategists refined the form by displaying the speakers' names as they spoke and by contrasting the testimony of a worker in 1980 with testimony of that same worker in 1984. In 1988, the Republican's ads featured disenchanted Massachusetts voters.

The Neutral Reporter Ad

Another form of newslike attack that emerged from the ashes of Watergate was the "neutral reporter" ad. In both 1976 and 1980, the majority of ads directed against the opponent used either persons in the street or "neutral reporters." A neutral reporter ad sets forth a series of factual statements and then invites a judgment. These "rational" political ads offer factual data, suggest or stipulate a conclusion, and warrant that conclusion. So, for example, an ad for Ford in 1976 noted that Carter had promised to do for the federal government what he had done for Georgia. To test Carter's claim, the ad invited us to look at the record. It then provided data on the size of government, bonded indebtedness, and other matters that appeared to contradict what Carter had been saying.

In 1980 the majority of Reagan's anti-Carter ads on the economy followed this form. Ad after ad simply recounted the inflation rate for such items as sugar and bread or such categories as housing and transportation. Repeating the formula Ford had used against him, Carter responded with an ad that showed the California state seal as an announcer noted that Reagan raised taxes and increased the size of government in California. One entire set of Carter's ads in 1980 simply juxtaposed Reagan's statements with details about his record.

The majority of the attack ads produced by and for the independent PACs in 1980 fell into the neutral reporter category. The most common form simply quoted a promise Carter made in 1976 and documented that he had not kept it. Of these, the most cogent were the National Conservative Political Action Committee's ads that replayed Carter making promises in the Carter-Ford debates; after Carter promised something, the frame froze. Evidence then appeared on the screen documenting that the promise had been broken. One ad compared the rate of inflation in 1976 and in 1980; another compared the size of the budget deficit during both years.

In 1990, neutral reporter ads relied more heavily than they had in the past on newspaper clips as a form of evidence. The reason? The advent of adwatches meant that newspapers were a natural source of seemingly credible oppositional material indicting the opponent's ads.

The Unidentified Advocate

Most televised ads that link unrelated visual images are part of a broad category of attack ads called concept or production spots that are narrated by an unidentified voice. In these attack ads, the sponsoring candidates are but a whispered presence.

By 1960 presidential candidates had realized that one of the ways in which they could damage their chances of winning was to appear unpresidential by attacking their opponent directly. The result was the unnamed advocate. In these ads, a resonate, usually male, voice invites a partisan interpretation of evocative pictures. In both tone and visual content, these differ from neutral reporter ads.

In a calm tone employing disinterested language, the reporter seems bent on simply stating fact; the tone and language of the ad suggest that it is spoken by a neutral nonpartisan custodian of truth; by contrast, the persona speaking in the unnamed advocate ad is a partisan whose value-laden language reveals an intent to persuade. In the 1960 Democratic spots attacking Nixon, an unseen announcer asserted that those who wanted underpaid teachers and inadequately supplied schools should vote for Nixon, but those standing for strong education should vote for Kennedy.

Just as music does not underscore broadcast news, it usually doesn't occur on the soundtrack of the neutral reporter ad. In contrast, the unnamed advocate is aided in making his case by mood music that invites the audience to accept the advocate's claims.

The visuals in the two types of ads differ as well. In neutral reporter ads, the visuals are ostensibly "objective." They include graphs, charts, government reports, pages of newspapers. In contrast, the unnamed advocate relies on such highly evocative visuals as exploding bombs, ringing red telephones, and circling convicts. In neither form does the sponsoring candidate appear as a central character. So small is the picture of the sponsoring candidate in these ads that most people don't even notice it on the bottom of the first or last frames.

In 1964, concept spots asserted that Barry Goldwater would wreck Social Security; the most dramatic and most often aired ad showed a Social Security card being ripped in half. By contrast, Johnson made five-minute speeches about the need to protect Social Security, never mentioning Goldwater by name. In 1968, a Democratic concept spot showed Agnew's name on the television screen while on the soundtrack a man convulsed in laughter. In 1972 a man on a girder high above a city was the focus of a Republican ad that suggested that McGovern wanted to put half the country on welfare. In 1972 attack ads were disassociated from their sponsoring candidate not only by their form but also by their tag. These spots were sponsored not by the Committee to Re-Elect the President but by its offshoot, Democrats for Nixon.

The unnamed advocate disappeared from the 1976 campaign as did attack ads using guilt by visual association. As the memories of Watergate dimmed and honesty receded as a criterion by which presidential candidates would be tested, unnamed advocate ads returned in force in 1984. In the bloody Democratic primaries Mondale attacked Hart in ads whose central characters included a red phone and a handgun. An ad for Hart countered with a burning fuse and the hyperbolic charges that Mondale favored using our boys as "bodyguards" for dictators and as "trading chips."

In the 1984 general election, the red phone reappeared for Mondale. Also on the scene was a roller coaster meant to dramatize the impending collapse of the Reagan recovery. The Reagan campaign contributed an ad featuring a bear in the woods whose existence was questioned at the end of the ad by the announcer. In place of the neutral reporter ads' careful logic, 1984 saw a Reagan ad that reduced Mondale's plan for the future to raising taxes and Reagan's to growth, trimming waste, and adding jobs.

Unidentified advocate ads were a staple of the 1988 Republican presidential campaign. In vibrant color on oil-like water floats an accumulation of waste. Midway through the ad a sign warning RADIATION: HAZARD: NO SWIMMING is superimposed over the scene. The announcer indicts Michael Dukakis's environmental record.

The 1988 Bush campaign's most discussed spot was a black-and-white unnamed advocacy spot. The scene: a prison. Convicts circle through a turnstile as the announcer charges the Massachusetts governor with vetoing the death penalty and furloughing convicts.

The Anonymous Attack

From the country's beginnings, the basest attacks appeared in unsigned print. In 1781, Benjamin Franklin complained to Robert Morris that the public "is often niggardly, even of its Thanks, while you are sure of being censured by malevolent Criticks and Bug-writers, who will abuse you while you are serving them, and wound your Character in nameless Pamphlets; thereby resembling those little dirty stinking insects, that attack us only in the dark, disturb our Repose, molesting and wounding us while our Sweat and Blood are contributing to their Substance."[36]

Those who claim that politics is cleaner now than it was in the nineteenth century are usually marshalling evidence that compares toucans to tangerines, unsigned print ads to televised claims. But if one compares print to print one finds as much that is disreputable in today's campaigns as in the past. For example, among the unsigned fliers of 1988 was one caricature of Bush as Hitler.

Most of the instances illustrative of the dirty campaigns of yesteryear recall attacks that were unsigned. So, for example, an open anonymous letter was dispatched in the final days of the successful Harding campaign. "When one citizen knows beyond the peradventure of doubt what concerns all other citizens but is not generally known, duty compels publication," said the letter. "The father of Warren Gamaliel Harding is George Tryon Harding, second, now resident of Marion Ohio, said to be seventy-six years of age, who practices medicine as a one-time student of the art in the office of Doctor McCuen, then resident in Blooming Grove, Morrow County, Ohio, and who has never been accepted by the people of Crawford, Morrow and Marion Counties as a white man." Labeled a "foul, eleventh hour attack," by the *New York Herald,* the letter was circulated throughout the country.[37]

Even today the most scandalous claims are carried in unsigned fliers. In 1988, a leaflet bearing no disclaimer was circulated at gatherings of conservative Republicans. "In 1970, Mike Dukakis proposed legalizing sodomy and sex with animals," it read. "Was it bad values or just bad judgment?" Comic books showed terrified animals running from a trench-coat-clad man. Under the right of free petition requirement of the Massachusetts state constitution, in 1970 Dukakis had introduced a bill to change the state's "blue laws." The bill would have repealed provisions concerning "crime against nature, either with mankind or a beast." The bill failed to survive committee.

Federal law requires that all literature distributed and all material broadcast in federal campaigns contain a disclaimer indicating who is paying to distribute the material. The law assumes that the motives of those producing material are a factor in judging it and that those responsible should be held accountable for the claims the material makes.

What of the Voter?

To this point I've focused on the responsibilities of the press and the politicians with scant attention to the voter. What does it profit a campaign after all if it argues, engages, and accepts accountability for claims if the price of such responsibility is the inattention of voters and defeat at the polls?

To what extent did voters in 1988 pay attention to the available substance? "Frontline" aired biographies of the candidates, the "MacNeil/Lehrer NewsHour" broadcast long portions of candidate speeches and cogent summaries of the similar and dissimilar positions of the candidates, Koppel interviewed both Dukakis and Bush on "Nightline," and exemplary interviews of the candidates were done on the morning news shows. Moreover, in 1988, C-SPAN alone aired over a thousand hours of political programming.

There was much more substance to the 1988 campaign than the media's treatment of the studies of soundbites would suggest. Worth noting is the fact that an inverse correlation exists between substantive programming and audience. At some level, this finding isn't surprising. After all, the audience for the first Dukakis-Bush debate was smaller in net numbers than that for the first Kennedy-Nixon debate.

Much has been made in the past two years about the "shrinking soundbite." Misgeneralization from two studies advancing that claim has been rampant. What the University of California, San Diego, communication scholar Dan Hallin and Harvard's Kiku Adatto analyzed was not all "news" but network evening news.

Even that analysis was carefully circumscribed. Neither treated anything on CNN, the broadcast networks' morning news shows, the Sunday interview shows, or "Nightline." Adatto excluded weekend news and statements by the vice presidential contenders; Hallin excluded all broadcast interviews with the candidates. Although it is broadcast in the evening, is clearly news, and airs nationally, both excluded the "MacNeil/Lehrer NewsHour."

If one takes the total profile of network news for 1988, the average length of a quoted statement by a presidential candidate is substantially higher than 9.8 seconds (see Chart 9-6). The 8.2 rating garnered by the first hour of the Koppel interview approaches the audience usually attracted to a single network news show. More important, unlike the strategy-driven evening news coverage, Koppel's questioning created a context for understanding Dukakis's answers and invited sustained attention to a limited number of topics.

The comparison both Hallin and Adatto make to 1968 has led to the mistaken conclusion that voters had less access to candidate discourse in 1988 than before.[38] The claim that the norm for network news in 1968 was 45 seconds reveals that if length is the yardstick, substance must have been up in 1988. The fact of presidential and vice presidential debates in 1988 means that the largest audience of the campaign was exposed to more one- and two-minute answers by the candidates than to any other time length.

Because most evening news is narrative, not argument, and focuses on strategy, not substance, substance indeed is in short supply in 1988 network evening news. But it is up elsewhere. Because it played extended portions of the candidate's speeches on a regular basis, devoted quarter-hour segments to analysis of both candidates' positions on issues, and brought in experts to explicate and defend the Democratic and Republican positions, the "MacNeil/Lehrer NewsHour" was the home for the argument, engagement, and accountability in the campaign. The professional community recognized the excellence of this effort with the Peabody Award.

But in a sense the concern about shrinking soundbites is on target, because it is also true that, with the exception of the presidential debates and the Koppel interview with Dukakis, the programs with the shorter soundbites have the larger audiences. Moreover, the programs with the longer soundbites attract the more educated (see Chart 9-7). (Since in most markets "MacNeil/Lehrer" airs in the same or a closely tied time block as network news, viewers seem to be choosing one over the other.)

Kernell offers one reading of the present and future. As politicians strain to reach their audiences, "policy questions become oversimplified and stylized to satisfy the cognitive requirements of a largely inattentive national audience."[39] But there is an alternative view. As cable brings C-SPAN into a larger number of homes and innovations such as those tried by CNN under the Markle grant in 1992 proliferate, perhaps access to an educated, interested audience will elicit adaptive substantive discourse.

The extent to which candidates provide what the public wants was nowhere clearer than in the New Hampshire primary of 1992. Faced with a state that had lost 50,000 jobs in four years and a citizenry crowded with those fearful of losing their jobs and homes, the Democratic candidates responded with a higher level of policy substance than has characterized any early primary in recent memory. Ads inched back from thirty to sixty seconds. In their spots, candidates carried their own messages. Half-hour programming reappeared. And "MacNeil/Lehrer" hosted a candidate debate that provided a model of argument, engagement, and accountability.

Cynics claim that attack attracts and strategy sells. Perhaps. What is important is that substance exists and that those who want it can get it, that campaigns offer the electorate the opportunity to weigh the options before the country and to embrace one over the other knowing that what is said and promised in the campaign will be mirrored in office. By tolerating any less we do our leaders and ourselves an injustice.

In the opening months of the 1992 primaries, two statements indicated better than any others the cost the country and the president had paid for the lack of argument, engagement, and accountability in the 1988 campaign. The director of the conservative Heritage Foundation stated that we had elected George Bush and gotten Michael Dukakis, and former president Ronald Reagan was reported to have told an aide that he didn't know what George Bush stood for. A mean and meaningless campaign had produced a rudderless presidency. Politics *(praxis)* and practical reason *(phronesis)* had been sundered. Our task is finding a way to put them back together again, reconstructing a polis in which we can take pride. Asking whether we've done that in the past and how we can do it in the future is the task of the next chapter.

CHAPTER TEN

The Good, The Bad, and The Ugly: 1960–1988 and Beyond

Claims that campaigns aren't doing what they ought are often mistaken for dissatisfaction with the person elected. If voters ultimately do vote in what they and political scientists perceive as their best interest, what difference does the process that got them to that point make? When the structural theories of political scientists are borne out year after year in the vote—with peace and prosperity, for example, producing a majority for the incumbent—why worry about the process?

An alternative position holds that how we elect is as important as who we elect. The process of election, goes this line of reasoning, either provides or denies citizens the opportunity to ratify their own futures by participating in a discussion of the challenges facing the country and the ways and means of addressing them. Out of open discussion of the ends and means of national policy, a campaign can forge a consensus. In the clash of alternatives will emerge a stronger final plan and a better president. And one to whom even those who voted for the loser can pledge allegiance.

The focus on process does not preclude a careful weighing of the persons who ask to be entrusted with the power of the presidency. By displaying who they are and how they think in news conferences, interviews, and debates and by inviting head-to-head comparison and contrast in debates, candidates disclose the dispositions and habits of mind that they will bring to bear on the unpredictable future.

If we are in fact electing the right candidates, then an engaged campaign won't change outcome. But it could better project the who, what, and how of governance. In the process, it would invite citizens to commit themselves to policies that will affect their lives. And, as my grand-mother was fond of saying, what's the harm in that?

In the past, some campaigns have done this better than others. The 1960 contest revealed Kennedy's legislative prospectus but not the some-times fragile state of his health. By contrast, the 1964 campaign sup-pressed discussion of the most controversial issue of its decade, the war in Vietnam. In 1972, the failure of the campaign was not in its forecast of the future but in concealment of corrupt use of presidential power. If knowing who, what, and how are objectives, then the recent 1980 campaign looks pretty good. It did after all accurately forecast both the aspirant and his agenda. By contrast, on every count, the campaign of 1988 was impoverished. The George Bush who emerged from the Oval Office after the Inaugural bore scant resemblance to Bush the cam-paigner. Gone was the gun-slinging persona crafted by his handlers. Ab-sent as well were the tightly constructed, tightly scripted sentences. Back was a higher voice pitch! What we saw in the campaign was, from the perspective of some, thankfully, not what we got in the White House.

At the same time, since the campaign had prophesied little of the what and how of presidential policy, Bush entered the Oval Office bound to little more than supporting the death penalty for drug kingpins and opposing all new taxes. The rest was a tabula rasa. Just as the candidates in 1964 had suppressed discussion of the most costly policy of that de-cade, so too in 1988 there had been no talk of the staggeringly expensive S&L bailout, of its causes and cures, or of ways to ensure that the mis-takes that led to it were not repeated.

As interesting is the fact that Kennedy in 1960, Johnson in 1964, and Nixon in 1972 used engagement on some issues to deflect public atten-tion from others that might have swayed voting decisions against them and later would bear importantly on the victor's conduct in office. In each of these election campaigns, the public desire to know was damp-ened, public attention diverted, and candidate lies believed. In each case, evocative advertising played an important role in the deflective process. In two instances the candidates closed off the access of the press and public by skirting debates. In all three, reporters failed to press the can-didates effectively on a key issue. Of particular note is the fact that dis-traction was the by-product of *the* television age's most engaged cam-paign, a campaign in which candidate accessibility reached an as yet unrivalled peak. In short, engagement itself can distract.

1960: Engagement and Distraction

In his widely televised September 12, 1960 speech to the Houston min-isters, Democratic presidential candidate John F. Kennedy both reiterated his commitment to the separation of Church and state and declared that "The real issues in this campaign have been obscured—perhaps deliberately, in some quarters less responsible than this." They had been. But not only in the ways hinted at in that speech. The 1960 Democratic campaign was built on two false claims. Not long after the election, the falsity of the first was acknowledged by Kennedy's Deputy Secretary of Defense, Roswell Gilpatric. Indeed, in preparation for the 1964 campaign, Kennedy asked an advisor to explain to him "how we came to the judgment that there was a missile gap?"[1]

Where candidate Kennedy predicated his foreign policy on a presumed missile gap, President Kennedy could locate no such gap. As Nixon had claimed, the U.S. enjoyed a substantial advantage. Not wanting to lull the Soviets into exercising their nuclear muscle against an enemy that thought it was underprepared and wanting to warn the Soviets to keep their hands off Berlin, in October 1961, Gilpatric, in a well-publicized speech, concluded that the United States held the strategic nuclear advantage.

The speech instead was read with alarm in the Soviet Union. Decades later, Sergo Mikoyan, whose father advised Khrushchev, revealed that the Soviet leader had "worried about the possibility that somebody in the United States might think that a seventeen-to-one superiority would mean that a first strike was possible."[2] Since the Soviets lacked long-distance ICBMs, it could redress the imbalance only by stationing shorter range missiles beyond Soviet borders. Cuba was a natural choice.[3] So redressing one deception of the Kennedy campaign contributed to the Cuban Missile Crisis.

Once the crisis began, a major campaign cover-up became relevant. Contrary to his denials, Kennedy suffered from a serious disease whose treatment included use of mood-altering medication. The two deceptions intersected in the thirteen days of the Cuban Missile Crisis.

The superhuman endurance required by Kennedy's reported actions in the Pacific lent credibility to his claims about Soviet military might, countered claims of Addison's disease, and set him apart from primary opponent Hubert Humphrey who had been unable to serve in World War II, from convention opponent Lyndon Johnson, an older man with a questionable war record who since had suffered a heart attack, and from his Quaker opponent whose health in the 1960 campaign seemed more fragile than Kennedy's.

Minnesota's Hubert Humphrey had not served in World War II because of a physical disability that resulted in a deferment. Television appeals in the West Virginia primary reminded voters that Kennedy is "the only veteran in the West Virginia primary." In that primary, some prominent Kennedy supporters falsely labeled Humphrey a "draft dodger." "We were stressing Kennedy's record as a war hero, of course," notes Kennedy aide Larry O'Brien, "and we hoped the voters would contrast it with Humphrey's lack of a war record. But the Roosevelt incident went beyond that."[4] When told of remarks Humphrey had supposedly made about him, Franklin Roosevelt, Jr., who was campaigning for Kennedy, leaked correspondence between Humphrey and his World War II draft board to the press. At the same time he called Humphrey a "draft dodger." The contrast between a "draft dodger" and a PT-109 hero was clear.

Kennedy's stress on his own youth and "vigah" invited a focus on LBJ's health and age. In 1955, the older man had suffered a heart attack. As I noted earlier, Johnson's military service consisted of a single bombing run in which he participated as an observer. If the choice was Johnson versus Kennedy, the story of PT-109 implicitly pitted the war-ducking Johnson against a naval hero.

PT-109 also worked against Republican nominee Richard Nixon. As he admitted in the Checkers Speech, Nixon wasn't entitled to any special kudos for his efforts in World War II. He was merely there "when the bombs were falling." And the Republican's need for hospitalization midway through the 1960 fall campaign put him in no position to raise health as an issue.

At the same time, PT-109 served to counter claims that the Massachusetts' senator suffered from Addison's disease. As his campaign for the presidency was being planned, Kennedy dispelled fears that he suffered from a disabling illness by noting that "During the war I contracted malaria in the South Pacific, along with water exposure and a series of fevers. Diagnosis showed that this stress was accompanied by a partial adrenal insufficiency, though there was no tubercular infection or other problem. From 1946 through 1949 I underwent treatment for the malaria—the fevers ceased—there was complete rehabilitation and I have had no special medical care, no special checkup, no particular difficulty on this score at all. . . ."[5]

In an effort to block Kennedy's nomination, Texas Senator Lyndon Baines Johnson officially entered the race on July 5. The Texan's supporters raised questions about Kennedy's health. In early July 1960, two representatives of Citizens for Johnson whispered to reporters that Kennedy had Addison's disease. The Kennedy campaign responded with a carefully worded medical report denying Addison's disease and attributing his "minor" adrenal insufficiency to his "malaria."

That summer, Kennedy got liberal supporters to block stories about his reliance on medication to control the adrenal problem.[6] Their success is interesting in light of the inconsistencies in their claims. Where aides denied his use of cortisone, Kennedy himself told reporters that when he "worked hard" he "frequently" took medication similar to cortisone. Opponents worked hard to draw public attention to the inconsistencies but without effect.[7]

In the final week of the general election campaign, the issue was revived when one of FDR's sons, a Nixon supporter, sent both candidates a telegram asking for disclosures about their health. The move was transparent. While Nixon was asked for details about his knee injury, Kennedy was asked to document the extent of his adrenal insufficiency "and what drugs" he was taking to compensate.

What made the charge of Addison's disease seem implausible was the story of PT-109, which used the conventions of drama to involve us in an heroic narrative: man against nature; man's selfless devotion to his fellows; courage in service of conviction.

"In one of World War II's most dramatic stories," noted a 1960 Kennedy print ad, "the PT boat skippered by Lt. John F. Kennedy (USNR) was rammed by a Japanese destroyer in the 1943 battle for the Solomon Islands. Severely injured and lost nine days in the jungle, Lt. Kennedy called on his remarkable qualities of leadership and endurance to lead his eleven shipmates to safety. He saved one of the men by placing a line from the man's life preserver between his teeth and swimming five miles. For his heroism he was twice decorated. His Navy citation stated that his 'courage, endurance and leadership' were 'in keeping with high traditions of the United States Naval Service.' "[8]

The narrative's plausibility was tested during Kennedy's repeated hospitalizations while in the Senate. The press accepted the story. Throughout his Senate career hospitalizations were attributed to surgery "required by the wounds he [Kennedy] suffered during World War II as commanding officer of a motor torpedo boat."[9]

In the Wisconsin primary, members of Kennedy's PT-109 crew appeared in a television rally. A half-hour documentary ad aired in the Wisconsin primary included an account of the PT-109; a five-minute general election ad focused exclusively on the events surrounding the sinking of the boat and Kennedy's role in the rescue of its crew. That ad had a Kennedy crewmate recounting the young lieutenant's heroism in the Pacific. Lapel buttons and tie clasps cast as likenesses of PT-109 were distributed to campaign volunteers. And throughout the Kennedy presidency, when the president was puffy and yellow-skinned from Addison's disease, when pain drove him to his famous rocker, all his staff had to say to provide protective cover was: bad back, PT-109.

The PT-109 ad and its accompanying *Reader's Digest* tale distracted the American people from what should have been an issue in the 1960 campaign—Kennedy's health. It did so by a skillful blend of fact and fiction.

Some believe that John Kennedy should have been court-martialed over PT-109. Why, after all, hadn't the young lieutenant, who was in charge of the boat, set up a watch to ensure that an oncoming destroyer would be spotted? Only paternal intervention saved JFK from punishment. Instead of a court-martial, he received a naval award. His father had the foresight to realize the utility of a picture showing his son receiving a Navy citation for bravery. His staff was clever enough to ensure as well that a major author, John Hersey, wrote up the PT-109 story for

Reader's Digest. During the 1960 primaries and general election, thousands of copies of the article were distributed. And later, Kennedy partisans ensured that a docufilm of the events was made.

The story of PT-109 helped elect a president who required cortical steroids to relieve the symptoms of Addison's disease. The disease is due to a defect in the hormone that enables us to survive stress. Cortical steroids compensate for the defect; in overdose, they produce euphoria. When properly administered, they produce a simple sense of optimism or buoyancy.[10]

Kennedy confidants remain silent on the question of Kennedy's use of medication during the missile crisis. In the Hawks Cay Conference on the crisis's twenty-fifth anniversary, those who had sat around the White House conference table at that time were asked about the "effects of crisis-induced stress and pressure on your deliberations. . . . Was there any use of drugs or medication, and if so, what were their effects?"[11] The question went unanswered.

Yet as Russian ships approached the American blockade off Cuba, Robert Kennedy watched his brother whose "face seemed drawn, his eyes pained" and remembered the times when JFK "was ill and almost died."[12] Contrary to reports by Kennedy stalwarts that "[h]e was as calm as an iceberg throughout" the crisis,[13] oral histories by participants recount that in the meetings Kennedy was not the unemotional presence hagiographers made him out to be. Rather, he was "clipped" and "tense."[14]

At the point in history at which the United States stood on the brink of "world wide nuclear war,"[15] tapes of the meetings[16] reveal that the president was sometimes confused about the nature of Khrushchev's offer,[17] sometimes militant ("We're certainly going to do number one; we're going to take out these, uh, missiles"[18]), sometimes angry,[19] sometimes preoccupied with finding a peaceful way out. What role, if any, his use of cortical steroids played in these mood changes is unknowable. That he admitted to using cortisone-like medication when working hard is known. That cortisone affects mood is also known. Whether knowledge of Kennedy's disease and its treatment would have altered the course of the century's closest election is unknowable. Unknowable as well is whether Richard Nixon would have responded differently than Kennedy to the exigencies now known as the Cuban Missile Crisis.

With the missile gap and JFK's health the exceptions, Kennedy and Nixon compared their positions in ways that clarified their similarities and differences and distinguished the ends and means of their policies. The candidates engaged each other's arguments and by so doing advanced the issue agenda. They accepted responsibility for the positions they took, and for the tactics of their campaigns.

Not only did Kennedy and Nixon debate each other four times but they also participated regularly in press conferences and interviews. Kennedy took questions on television from the Houston ministers; on election eve, Nixon took questions from around the country. In other words, in the 1960 campaign, the candidates engaged each other in argument and were also responsive to questions from the press.

Recalls nationally syndicated columnist David Broder, "In the 1960 campaign, Kennedy provided plenty of access and manipulated the hell out of the press. Nixon was reputed to be inaccessible but there was a central dialogue and exchange furnished if not by Nixon then by Bob Finch or Herb Kline and others who spoke for Nixon. There was a dialogue through the press in that campaign."[20]

As important was the content of the candidates' discourse. Each contender devoted over 40 percent of his speaking time to discussing problems facing the country and the goals and solution he would pursue if elected.[21] Nightly on the week before the election, Nixon detailed his presidential plans in fifteen-minute televised speeches. Not counting newscasts, the networks devoted over forty-one hours to campaign programs. Over half were sponsored by commercial advertising.[22] In 1960, the modal length of spot ads was five minutes. Most of the 60-second spots were direct lifts from longer ones. Over 75 percent of the ads show the candidates making their case. In the ads, the candidates specified their differences on Medicare, federal aid to education, the minimum wage, and public works for the unemployed. At issue in the ads as in the speeches was whether U.S. military strength and prestige had declined under the Eisenhower administration.

The result was engaged discourse in which the candidates held themselves and each other responsible for their claims. For example, on October 28, 1960, NBC News reported: "Mr. Nixon accused his opponent of making 'the most disgraceful, irresponsible statement of the campaign on the Nation's economic health.' The Democratic nominee in Detroit on Wednesday had said that the economy appeared to be slipping into its third recession in the last eight years. But Mr. Nixon today declared that the same newspapers which reported this statement also carried stories saying that new car sales were running at a record high in early October."

Broadcast reports regularly synopsized ongoing matters of dispute. On October 18, 1960, Edward P. Morgan reported that "The political plot over whether a Negro would be appointed to a Nixon-Lodge Cabinet thickened today. Henry Cabot Lodge made the pledge in Harlem last Wednesday, reneged in Virginia next day, after distress from southern Republicans was reported and after Vice President Nixon said he would select only the best people without regard to race or any such test. The two running mates conferred in Hartford, Connecticut, Sunday. Today in Albany, New York, Lodge flatly predicted that Nixon would put a Negro on the cabinet. Asked to comment, the Republican presidential candidate again declined to endorse." Meanwhile, says Morgan, a Democratic Congressman charged that the highest "Negro appointment" in the Eisenhower administration was as Assistant Secretary of Labor and, alleged the congressman, he was "thrown out in order to give a job to

Lodge's son." Morgan, who has checked the sequence, notes that Lodge's son was appointed the day of the resignation but adds, "There were reports at the time that Labor Secretary Mitchell had asked Wilkins to quit. Wilkins claimed he was quitting for personal reasons. He died two months later." Lodge then denies the allegation. The news segment concludes by noting that "Senator Kennedy said yesterday that pledging to appoint a man only because of his race or nationality or religion was 'the worst sort of racism.' "

When a candidate misrepresented his opponent's position, that fact was noted. When Nixon declared that Kennedy "would have sliced off free territory—Quemoy and Matsu—and given it to the Communists" and "might well plunge this hemisphere into war by his advocacy of assistance to anti-Castro Cubans," ABC's Edward Morgan observes, "He completely ignored Kennedy's own version of these positions" (October 24, 1960).

On the stump, the candidates contested each other's statements of fact. "On Tuesday in Charleston, West Virginia, Nixon demanded Kennedy retract a false primary campaign statement that some 17 million Americans go to bed hungry every night. Subsequently the Senator qualified that to read 'undernourished' " (ABC, September 30, 1960).

From the first week in September until the week before the election, the candidates averaged 1.2 network news interviews a week. The questions were direct and comprehensive. NBC aired a one-hour-a-week special called "The Campaign and the Candidates." On it on October 15, David Brinkley asked Richard Nixon if he could straighten out something for him. "On this matter of the rate of economic growth, my records or research say that in 1954, when Stevenson warned you that the Soviet economy was growing at a rate faster that ours, you used the phrase, 'spreading pro-Communist propaganda, as he attacked with violent fury the economic system of the United States.' Then before the Newspaper Publishers' Association, you called upon the members to ponder the sobering fact that the Soviet economy is growing faster than ours. Now it would seem that your position today is somewhat different."

On CBS, Walter Cronkite did long interviews on the candidates' family history and political background.

The reporting conventions of 1960 dictated that every major speech by a candidate be summarized. In place of polls, the number of seconds of audience applause and the size of the crowds were used as indicators of impact. But this sort of information was an incidental not a central part of the report.

Despite its failure to forecast the Bay of Pigs invasion, its seemingly irrelevant dispute over Quemoy and Matsu, its fake missile gap and its fictions about Kennedy's health, the 1960 Kennedy-Nixon campaign produced the most robust, engaged, accountable discourse of any in the history of television.

1964: Ducking the Major Issue

In 1964, both an ad showing a Social Security card being torn in two and the daisy ad telegraphically encouraged viewers to read fears of Republican nominee Barry Goldwater into their texts. Each served to distract the press and public from the larger questions raised by U.S. involvement in Vietnam. In this case, the distraction would prove both costly monetarily—for, despite Johnson's assurances to the contrary, the country could not finance both guns and butter—and personally—in more than 260,000 U.S. casualties and 58,152 U.S. lives.

Like Kennedy, Lyndon Johnson understood the power of distractive ploys. As a Southerner whose civil rights record was more moderate than that of his fellows, Johnson saw how other Southerners used the race issue to deflect voters' attention. Campaigning in the South in 1960 the Democratic vice presidential nominee told an aide, "If you can convince the lowest white man that he's better than the best colored man, he won't notice you picking his pocket."[23]

Inside the White House in 1964 aides debated about whether Johnson should publicly make the argument for U.S. involvement in Vietnam. On June 2, 1964, a staff memo probably authored by Johnson aide Bill Moyers summarized the questions the "public" was asking about Vietnam:

> 1. Why are we in South Viet Nam?
> 2. Why have we been unable to train South Vietnamese to do their own fighting after ten years of instruction? (The North seems capable of producing winning fighting men.)
> 3. Why can't we win the war?
> 4. Why can't we turn the war over to the 'locals' and get out?
> 5. What happens if we pull out of South Viet Nam? Why is it important to 'stand and fight' in this part of the world?
> 6. Why can't we turn the war over to the UN? We did this in Korea, yet we are going it alone in South Viet Nam. Why?[24]

The memo argues that from a "public opinion standpoint" the United States should "Stay where we are now. Do what we have been doing—and NOT involve ourselves in the North." Central to this strategy is "[C]ommunication with the public so they understand what we are doing and why. Put this course of action on a non-partisan basis. Unless we can extract the issue from politics, we are hard put to follow it through. If we can persuade some Republican leaders of stature and influence to join this line, we can tab the others as extremists and malcontents—and thereby stabilize our plan of action for some time to come. The benefit here is our *standing above* politics, and convincing the public that the lne [*sic*, line] we follow is in *their best interests*."[25] The public's questions went unanswered, the speech ungiven in the 1964 campaign.

The war in Vietnam was a matter of ongoing presidential and congressional concern throughout 1964 and, as such, a legitimate topic for discussion in the fall campaign. Between November 1963 and September 9, 1964, eleven bipartisan meetings of the congressional leadership were called by the president to enable General Taylor to report on the progress of the "Vietnamese army" against the "Communist Viet Cong." Taylor briefed reporters as well.[26]

When one of these meetings coincided with a Johnson speech on "peace" in mid-June 1964, Assistant Secretary of State Fred Dutton wrote Johnson White House aide Bill Moyers about ensuring that briefings in Washington not contradict the president's speeches on the road. "[A] look at the front pages of the principal California papers, and the attached two in the East," noted Dutton, "shows that while the President's primary subjective news emphasis for his Friday night speech was 'peace' (even though peace through strength), a high Administration briefing in Washington the same day sharply emphasized the possibility of increased U.S. military involvement in Southeast Asia. The President's speech lead and the briefing can logically be reconciled; but for most of the newspaper-reading public they appeared to be somewhat inconsistent."[27]

As the fall campaign approached, "contingency drafts" of what would become the Tonkin Gulf Resolution had already been prepared by the administration.[28] CIA Operation Plan 34A authorizing South Vietnamese naval strikes against North Vietnam had been approved by Johnson in February. One such strike occurred the day before the supposed second attack in the Gulf on the *Maddox*. Yet when in a press conference June 2, 1964, reporters asked whether there was substance to a claim by Representative Melvin Laird of Wisconsin that "the administration is preparing to move the Viet-Nam war into the North," Johnson responded "I know of no plans that have been made to that effect."[29]

On August 2, 1964, the *U.S.S. Maddox* fired on two Vietnamese patrol boats that were approaching her and the *Turner Joy* at high speed. The "attack" occurred in daylight. There were no U.S. casualties. Two nights later on August 4, the two destroyers reported that they were being attacked by torpedoes. All the torpedo reports came from a fresh sonarman who probably mistook the sound of his ship's own propellers for attacks. The enemy was not sighted visually. Nor did any enemy boats register on *Turner Joy*'s sonar.

In a cable to the Pentagon, the commander on the bridge of the *Maddox* characterized the attack as "doubtful" and urged "complete evaluation before any further action."[30] Even as Lyndon Johnson was solemnly assuring the country that the United States had suffered "open aggression on the high seas," no confirmation was in hand. Nor would it later emerge. Three days later, the Congress OK'd "all necessary steps" in South East Asia.

Johnson had obtained congressional authorization to pursue the war by transforming feeble evidence into an assertion of armed assault against the United States. After repeated questioning at four press conferences, the press failed to determine the specific nature of the alleged attack and the possible motives of those initiating it. Reporters let the matter drop. "There was only one *New York Times* reporter on the campaign plane who persistently asked questions about Viet Nam," recalls Johnson's press secretary Georgy Reedy.[31] Trustingly, the public, the press, and the Congress accepted fiction as fact.

In his statement to the American people August 5, 1964, the president said that "On August 2 the United States destroyer *Maddox* was attacked on the high seas in the Gulf of Tonkin by hostile vessels of the Government of North Vietnam. On August 4 that attack was repeated in those same waters against two United States destroyers. The attacks were deliberate. The attacks were unprovoked. The attacks have been answered." Only the last of these three statements was true. There was no confirmed attack. And if there had been, it probably would have been in response to the secret U.S.-supported bombing raids from Laos.

The press bought Johnson's story. On August 4, the *New York Times* reported, "President Johnson has ordered retaliatory action against gunboats and 'certain supporting facilities in North Vietnam' after renewed attacks against American destroyers in the Gulf of Tonkin."[32] When in early October, reporters raised the possibility that U.S. policy in Vietnam was being shaped by Johnson's campaign agenda, Secretary of State Dean Rusk issued a flat denial.[33]

By securing the Tonkin Gulf resolution, Johnson neutralized the traditional Republican charge that the Democrats are "soft on defense." At the same time, the Tonkin Gulf "incident" rallied Congress and the public behind the president. By taking Vietnam out of the domain of partisan dispute, Johnson could ensure both that Democrats would not be blamed for Kennedy's false claim in 1960 that the country had a missile gap, and that partisan probing of U.S. activity would not turn up Kennedy's authorization of CIA operatives to infiltrate North Vietnam to gather intelligence and sabotage the "enemy." The nature and extent of the covert operation would be revealed with the publication of the Pentagon Papers in 1971. The Pentagon Papers would also confirm that the CIA had backed the generals who overthrew the South Vietnamese president on November 1, 1963. At the time of its occurrence, the Kennedy Administration denied that it had supported the coup that resulted in the death of President Diem.

Johnson's success in making Vietnam a non-issue is evident in the falloff in press interest from early August to late September of that campaign year. Of the eleven major questions asked at the August 8, 1964 press conference, four concerned matters other than Vietnam. By the press conference of August 15, only three of sixteen major questions pertained to Vietnam, two of them about Goldwater's misconstrual of Johnson's authorization of weapons in Vietnam to mean "any [presum-

ably including nuclear] weapons." Not a single question in the news conference of September 5 focuses on Vietnam. The press conference of
September 21 spent more time clarifying Johnson's campaign travel plans
than repeating earlier questions about the probable motives of the ships
that presumably had fired on U.S. destroyers.

The same pattern appears in Johnson's telecast speeches. Neither
Tonkin Gulf nor Vietnam is mentioned in either Johnson's acceptance
speech at the Democratic convention or in his nationally broadcast election eve address. The conflict garnered a bare two sentences in the telecast campaign address of October 7.

And on the second front, through judicious juxtaposition of narratives, Johnson invited the inference that he would not escalate. Here is
the verbal equivalent of assertion by visual association. In a nationally
televised half-hour speech aired on CBS the evening of October 7, Johnson encased his response to the Tonkin Gulf incident in earlier U.S.
responses that did not escalate into war. "Truman met Communist
aggression in Greece and Turkey. [Note that Johnson does not invoke
Korea.] President Eisenhower met Communist aggression in the For-
mosa Strait. President Kennedy met Communist aggression in Cuba. And,
when our destroyers were attacked, we met Communist aggression around
Vietnam." Having introduced Tonkin Gulf with a litany of non-escala-
tory successes, Johnson segues out of the series with assurance about his
and our peaceful resolve. "But each of these presidents has known that
guns and rockets alone do not bring peace. Only men can bring peace.
They have used our great power with restraint—never once taking a
reckless risk which might plunge us into large-scale war."

In an October 2, 1964, issue of the New York Times James Reston quoted
Lyndon Johnson saying, "We don't want our American boys to do the
fighting for Asian boys. . . . We don't want to get tied down in a land
war in Asia. So what are we doing? We are staying there and supplying
[the South Vietnamese] with some of the things that we have. . . . We
have 20,000 men out there advising and helping them . . . but we are
not about to start another war and we're not about to run away from
where we are."[34]

"I can tell you," Secretary of State Dean Rusk told reporters on October 8, 1964, "and I hope it is not an indiscretion—that the President has
made it very clear to his own principal advisors that the decisions that
are required with respect to South Vietnam have nothing to do with the
American elections."[35] At the same press conference, Rusk declared that
"we are not concealing anything or postponing or marking time or refusing to make the decisions that are required."

The public queries Johnson heard about Vietnam came from campaign audiences and local reporters. "We still have our problems in Vietnam," noted Johnson to a conservative audience in New Hampshire September 28. "Every day some one jumps up and shouts and says, 'Tell us
what is happening in Vietnam and why we are in Vietnam, and how did

I get you into Vietnam.' Well, I didn't get you into Vietnam. You have been in Vietnam 10 years."

Vietnam was not an issue in the 1964 campaign. Johnson and his aides supressed public focus on Vietnam with narratives of decisive presidential action that had achieved U.S. ends without war and by distracting the public with claims that Goldwater would risk nuclear war. The strategy was set forth in a memo filed as if it were written by CBS president Frank Stanton July 28, 1964, and found in the files of Johnson aide Bill Moyers. "The frustrations arising from Vietnam and Cuba disappear when confronted by the threat of nuclear war," says the memo.[36]

So effective were the Democrats in setting their agenda that it displaced both warranted concerns about Vietnam and Goldwater's alternative discussions of other issues. "I went to Florida to speak about the quality of life, our loss of freedom, and the growing violence disfiguring American society," recalled Goldwater. "The reporters ignored what I said and wrote that I should have discussed Social Security and my plans to abolish it."[37]

Little more than a month after Johnson was sworn in as a president elected in his own right, the *New York Times* would write, "A great debate on the Vietnamese conflict is now raging all over the United States. It goes from the White House, Congress and the Pentagon to every home, office, factory and farm."[38]

Barely a decade later, U.S. helicopters ferried the last fleeing U.S. representatives from the roof of the U.S. embassy in Saigon. So powerful is the memory of that war in national consciousness that as President George Bush embarked on the military campaign in the Gulf in winter 1991, he repeatedly assured the American people that this would not be another Vietnam. After the United States had withdrawn from the Gulf, the president could testify that our quick engagement and presumed success meant that he had kept his word.

Goldwater and Johnson differed importantly on the conduct of the war. Goldwater advocated a quick end to it achieved either by withdrawal or by victory through full commitment of U.S. force. In short, he stood foursquare behind the Eisenhower Doctrine. Johnson favored gradual increases in U.S. troop strength. Neither position was debated in the campaign of 1964. In an environment in which the legitimacy and conduct of the war were being questioned by Johnson's own advisors, the American people deserved to be party to such a discussion.

The Lessons of 1960 and 1964

Kennedy and Johnson entranced the public with a shell game. As our attention focused on their mesmerizing stories and anxiety-producing attacks, central issues slipped out of sight. The lesson is that campaigns can engage without necessarily engaging central issues of biography and policy.

1972: Pushing the Press Off the Playing Field

If engagement is the goal, then 1972 was a disaster. "Mr. Nixon and Mr. McGovern conducted their campaigns for two different audiences, never joining issues in one central place, but setting up their tents, offering different music, on different terrains of American culture, inviting Americans to divide,"[39] wrote Theodore White of the 1972 campaign.

The charges that would eventually send Richard Nixon back to San Clemente, his second term unfinished, were set forth by his 1972 presidential opponent and discounted by the electorate. Twenty-one months after his landslide victory over George McGovern, Richard Nixon resigned. In the absence of candidate debates and press conferences, it is very difficult to engage an issue and hold the nonresponsive candidate accountable. Nixon's strategy was facilitated by attacks on the credibility of the press.

To displace Watergate, the Nixon campaign used a three-pronged strategy: Dismiss allegations about Watergate as self-serving Democratic propaganda put out by McGovern's camp followers in the liberal press, construct a sense of Nixon's presidency so pervaded with presidential activity that any claim to involvement in a petty burglary would seem farfetched, duck press contact and foreswear debates.

In summer 1972, a group of presumed burglars were caught inside the headquarters of the Democratic National Committee in a hotel complex known as Watergate. Throughout the fall, two cub reporters from the *Washington Post* uncovered detail after detail tying the break-in to those running the Nixon presidential re-election campaign. The networks carried denial after denial from the Nixon high command. When asked why he was not investigating the charges, Attorney General Kleindienst replied, "About all I've seen is what I would characterize generally as hearsay and speculative reports in some of the newspapers. . . . as of right now, any evidence that has come to us would not indicate the violation of a federal law" (ABC, October 24, 1972). Nixon's campaign manager, Clark MacGregor, claimed that the *Washington Post* was "operating at least in close philosophic and strategic and tactical co-operation with the McGovernites" (ABC, October 25, 1972).

Throughout the fall, McGovern tried and failed to make Watergate an issue. As the campaign progressed, the Democratic challenger increasingly focused on the corruption issue. His ads aggregated the shards of evidence in an attempt to forge an inference that the evidence did not yet sustain.

In late October, McGovern followed up with a half-hour nationally telecast speech on corruption. Nixon refused to engage the issue. Midway through Nixon's second term, McGovern's charges would be verified to the satisfaction of enough Members of Congress to vote articles of impeachment against the incumbent.

"My own observation about this campaign is that there was little importance given issues, at least in the minds of the voters," said McGovern aide Ann Wexler at the end of the 1972 campaign. "There was always something else that was occupying them."

Haunting the press in its pursuit of Watergate was the unease produced by the revelations of the Pentagon Papers that had been secured by reporters and published in 1971. Press and public awareness of the duplicity of Kennedy and Johnson lent plausibility to the hypothesis that eventually led to articles of impeachment.

The Contrast Between 1980 and 1988

Interesting in a period of widespread soul searching about what's gone wrong with the ways we elect our leaders is the evidence that a recent televised campaign argued, engaged, and accurately predicted the winner's conduct in office. The contrast between the campaigns of 1980 and 1988 is instructive.

"[T]here was nobody who was in a non-comatose state in 1980," recalled analyst Mark Shields in 1988, "who did not know what Ronald Reagan intended to do as president. He laid it out in graphic, specific details. . . . It was a clarifying election. This [1988] is not a clarifying election. . . . Ronald Reagan ran to do something in 1980, and he had a vision of what he intended to do, and I am hard pressed, having covered this campaign [to know] what the first three official acts would be of Vice President George Bush if he was elected President of the United States, what legislative proposals, how they take form."[40]

In 1980 there were two debates, one between Reagan and Independent John Anderson, the other between Reagan and Carter. In paid half-hour slots in four key states, including his native Texas, Republican vice presidential candidate George Bush took questions from voters "live and unrehearsed so that you can know where he and Ronald Reagan stand on the political issues of the day." In 1980 the modal length of Reagan ads was five minutes. As an incumbent whose record was known, Carter did not require longer ads.

After a series of well-publicized gaffes, Reagan's campaign closed off most press access to the candidate. By the beginning of the second week of October, reporters were complaining on the air that Reagan had held only two press conferences since late in August (CBS, October 9, 1980).

By the third week in October the Republicans had learned how to dodge challenges by Carter and set in place the press buffers that would function throughout two terms of the Reagan presidency. When asked about Carter's charge that the Californian's "unspecified ideas about ending the hostage crisis were much like Richard Nixon's 1968 so-called secret plan to end the Vietnam War," Reagan responded, "I know he's— I know he's saying that, and I'm just not going to discuss it anymore, because it's doing nothing but trying to keep the campaign away from the real issue, which is his failure as a President" (CBS, October 23, 1980).

But Reagan still consented to do one-on-one interviews and the campaign continued to make experts available to talk with reporters about Reagan's proposals. On October 16, in an interview with Reagan, for example, Barbara Walters noted that all of the United States' allies support SALT II and asked, "Have you or your advisers talked with them and seen how they feel about your point of view?" By asking whether one can legislate morality on such matters as abortion, Walters elicited a response that Reagan would repeat in subsequent debates. "I happen to believe from all the study that I have been able to do, all the information I have been able to get, that when you interrupt a pregnancy you are taking a human life, and so it isn't a question of legislating someone's morality. It is a question of do we, in our reinterpretation of morality, have the right to take an innocent human life that can't defend itself" (ABC, October 16, 1980). Walters interviewed Carter and Anderson as well.

On radio Carter delivered three fifteen-minute speeches on the economy and foreign policy. One of these speeches, aired October 19, compared the two candidates' positions on the SALT II Treaty, which Carter favored and Reagan opposed. The same day, Reagan responded in a half-hour televised speech pledging to negotiate a better treaty. In that speech, Reagan forecast the philosophy that would in fact guide his presidency. "The way to avoid an arms race is not simply to let the Soviets race ahead. We need to remove their incentive to race ahead by making it clear to them that we can and will compete if need be."

Carter responded the next day. "If Governor Reagan had the last word last night on the war and peace issue," reported Sam Donaldson, "President Carter got in the first word this morning, portraying Reagan as a naive man in wanting to threaten the Soviet Union with a nuclear arms race." The statement of Carter's that is then shown advances the argument. "Imagine for one moment," says the President, "that President Brezhnev made a speech and said the Soviet Union is ready to launch a nuclear arms race against the United States unless the Americans made additional concessions. How would I or any president of the United States respond to that? We would match them missile for missile, and SALT would be replaced by a new nuclear arms race. It is extraordinarily naive to expect that the Soviet Union would meekly accept what we would immediately and totally reject" (ABC, October 20, 1980).

In the process of this exchange, those who listened to the Carter speech or saw segments of it carried in the news learned that Carter had put in place the military capacity to ensure that the United States could respond to an oil shutoff in the Middle East. Ten years later that action would seem eerily prescient.

That afternoon, the Reagan campaign made available its team of foreign policy experts to take questions from the press about the Reagan proposal. The group included former Secretary of State Henry Kissinger; his predecessor, William Rogers; former Secretary of Defense Elliot Richardson; and Georgetown University Professor Jeane Kirkpatrick. Again the issue discussion moved forward.

In 1980 the press was still tracking the candidates' arguments well enough to know when they had and had not been engaged. On October 24, Reagan delivered a half-hour nationally telecast speech on the economy that defended his tax-cut plan and pinned the blame for high interest rates, inflation, and unemployment on Carter. Carter responded in a talk at the National Press Club arguing that Reagan could not balance the budget while increasing defense spending without cutting programs. In that speech, Carter forecast that Reagan's proposals would add $130 billion to the 1983 budget deficit. After summarizing these claims, CBS turned to the response of the Reagan "truth squad" and noted that "The participants, New York Congressman Barber Conable and former Nixon Assistant Treasury Secretary Charles Walker offered little to rebut what Mr. Carter said, and not much about specific costs of Reagan's programs" (October 14, 1980).

Campaign coverage included straightforward summaries of the candidate's differences on the issues. So, for example, ABC's John McWethy capsulized the record this way. "While allowing small increases each year, he [Carter] did make some cuts. He killed the B-1 bomber, vetoed plans to build a nuclear aircraft carrier, delayed decisions on a new MX missile system. Now Carter is pushing for 5% more defense money above and beyond inflation, the largest increase in military spending since Vietnam." And Reagan? "Reagan wants a bigger shipbuilding program, more nuclear weapons, a stronger civil defense. He applauds President Carter's efforts to develop a rapid deployment force that can respond to crises in the world, but Reagan questions just how strong and ready to fight any American force can be without substantial pay increases" (ABC, October 28, 1980).

McWethy concludes: "If elected, Ronald Reagan would kill the SALT II treaty and try for a new agreement. President Carter would push for a ratification of SALT II and use it as a basis for further negotiations. Carter will push for 5% real growth in defense spending, the largest boost since Vietnam. Reagan, though he has refused to offer any specifics, will urge even higher defense spending. Carter will continue registration for the draft. Reagan says he will not. Governor Reagan strongly favors higher military pay. Under Carter the increases would be smaller. Real differences between the candidates. Jimmy Carter's record is one of restraint on defense spending and use of military force. Ronald Reagan's history is one of urging higher levels of defense spending and tough military responses to Soviet aggression. Fundamental differences in the philosophies and approaches to defense" (ABC, October 28, 1980).

McWethy lays out and compares each candidate's positions. The next evening Dan Cordtz does the same thing for the contenders' economic positions.

The campaign both informed the public about Reagan's positions and forecast his presidency.[41] His exchanges with Carter and with reporters advanced public understanding of his positions and prompted him to take such new positions as offering treaty negotiations with the Soviets. The policy outcomes of the election were not a surprise. Reagan had clearly forecast a military buildup, a tax cut, and a move away from governmental regulation. Carter had accurately forecast that Reagan couldn't do this and balance the budget. Reagan promised that his fiscal philosophy would bring down inflation and unemployment. Four years later, voters agreed that it had. Additionally, Reagan promised to appoint the first woman to the U.S. Supreme Court and did. At the same time he held to his opposition to abortion and the Equal Rights Amendment.

In 1988, conscientious viewers of network news who faithfully watched the debates and ads and searched in vain for telecast candidate press conferences or well-publicized policy speeches could not forecast with the certainty they would have had in 1980 or 1960 how the winner would handle the economy, treat defense, cope with the mounting S&L crisis, or adjust to changing world relations. Former Reagan staffer David Gergen, of *U.S. News & World Report,* observed, "Traditionally when we talk about a mandate in this country, we mean what is it a president is going to try to do, what are the initiatives he's going to try to undertake when he gets into office? And the Bush people have been very opaque on that question, so much so that there's a lot of talk now in the Bush campaign that if he wins that during the transition period, he might give some speeches laying out more completely before he is inaugurated, a real break from tradition, laying out what he wants to do as president."[42]

When asked in one of the debates what he would eliminate from the current military budget, Bush listed three pieces of equipment that had already been cut. At issue was whether or not the United States should engage in the conventional build-up that Dukakis favored and eliminate a number of weapons systems, which Dukakis also favored. In place of a serious discussion of defense alternatives, network news treated its audience to one-liners that strained to be humorous. Network time was given Arnold Schwarzenegger's claim that "Michael Dukakis is the real terminator" and Dukakis's objection to Bush's "new baloney." In network news in 1988, sophomoric throw-away-lines were immortalized as soundbites. On October 24, Bush said:

> [W]e've been strong and I will not allow this country to be made weak again. My opponent's views, my opponent's views on defense are the

standard litany of the liberal left, no MX, no Midgetman, no SDI, and cancel two carrier task forces. What a program. I wouldn't be surprised if he thinks that Naval exercise is something you find in Jane Fonda's workout book. No, the fact is we're living in a tough world and we can't afford to be governed by blind negative ideology against weapons.[43]

The only portion of this statement that found its way into evening news was the claim about Jane Fonda!

What was dismal about this campaign was the absence of clear expository statements of record and position by candidates in paid television and radio time, engagement on those issues in the debates, in press conferences, and in news, and candidate accountability for the claims of their own campaigns. Instead of candidate engagement that both advanced the issues and our understanding of them, the Republican presidential campaign of 1988 devolved to what *New York Times* reporter Mark Green called "*slur du jour.*" Meanwhile, the Democrats struggled to find a central theme and to carry it through the strategy-driven filter of network news.

Not only was engagement down but so too was candidate accountability. In past years, presidential candidates have aired suspect ads and made questionable claims in speeches. But, for the most part, when the misleading inferences or unfair appeals were pointed out by the press, the statements stopped; when they appeared in an ad, the ad was withdrawn.

So, for example, when the press found out that the bills had been paid by an insurer, the Kennedy campaign of 1960 pulled back an ad implying that a citizen being interviewed by the candidate faced a pile of unpaid hospital bills. In 1964, the controversial daisy commercial aired only once; when criticized, a 1968 ad juxtaposing Humphrey with violence outside the Democratic convention and death in Vietnam was withdrawn; in 1980, the Reagan campaign re-edited an ad to correct a misattribution of a newspaper quote.

When illegitimate ads stayed on the air, it was because the press failed to point out their inaccuracy, unfairness, or distortions. This was the case both of the Kennedy ad that edited clips of a sweating, shifty-eyed Nixon into an extended clip of Kennedy's opening statement of the 1960 debate and true as well of the PT-109 ad.

Not so in 1988. When confronted by the press with one gigantic false inference in the furlough ad and a series of misstatements of Dukakis' positions in the tank ad, Bush, his campaign manager, and his campaign team stood by the claims, sandbagged them with the assertions of presumed experts, and counter-attacked. When asked about the charges that his ads distorted the Democrat's record, Bush said that "his campaign had 'complete documentation' for its advertisements assailing Dukakis over a Massachusetts prisoner furlough program—which has now been curtailed—and on defense issues." Dukakis is upset, said the Vice President, "not because it's false but because he is weak on crime and defense, and that's the inescapable truth" (Associated Press, October 25, 1988). "The record on the essential opposition, the opposition to these essential military programs is no lie, and we have, for your understanding, we have complete documentation for those who want to see it, and he is upset, not because it's false, but because he is weak on defense, and that's the inescapable truth."[44]

"The [Bush] campaign flooded reporters with detailed fact sheets and carefully prepared charts outlining how it said Dukakis was trying to be misleading, and trotted out former Sen. John Tower of Texas, Gov. John H. Sununu of New Hampshire and Sen. Arlen Specter of Pennsylvania to carry the charge," reported the *Los Angeles Times* (October 24, 1988). "But when reporters challenged some of the facts in Bush's fact sheets, Specter at one point had to admit he wasn't sure of some of his statements and said he couldn't vouch for the accuracy of the fact sheet."

The charts and handouts did not establish the Republican claim that the Bush ads were a simple exercise in truth telling. In support of the tank ad's claim that Dukakis opposed the D5 Trident II missile, the fact sheet cited a report in the *Washington Post* (October 13, 1987), saying "Development, procurement, expansion of the D5 really depend on our negotiations with the Soviets." To document the Democrat's opposition to the Stealth Bomber, the Republicans misread this statement found in the *Boston Globe* (September 27, 1987): "[Dukakis] would not necessarily favor deployment of the new D-5 missile system on Trident nuclear submarines or development of Stealth technology for strategic bombers." The Republican's second source indicates why this is misleading. "I don't know that you need modernized B52s, B1s, the Stealth, cruise missiles. I mean, all of those are just one leg of the triad" (*Washington Post*, September 13, 1987).[45]

Those responsible for the fact sheet distributed to the press apparently assumed that reporters wouldn't bother to question the supposed "evidence" offered in support of the tank ad's assertions. In this case, Republican confidence in reporters' trusting natures was well placed. Only on "Meet the Press," the Sunday after the press conference, does a reporter, Chris Wallace, explicitly quote from the original Dukakis interview in the *Washington Post* to challenge Republican strategist Charles Black's defense of the ad.

The Republican fact sheet distributed to the acquiescent press at that news conference sunders two of Dukakis's statements from the very contexts that establish that the tank ad is deceptive. In the interview with David Broder cited to establish Dukakis's opposition to the D5, Dukakis sets out the conditions under which he would oppose that missile system. "Development, procurement, expansion of the D5 really depend on our negotiations with the Soviets. If we can seriously negotiate deep cuts in strategic weapons and a comprehensive test ban treaty and a flight-test treaty, then obviously that will have an impact on any new system. . . . If we don't, then I think the D5 becomes something that we should develop." The same interview makes clear the Democrat's commitment to the Stealth bomber. "Our development of the Stealth should continue, but I don't know that you need modernized B52s, B1s, the Stealth, cruise missiles. I mean, all of these are just one leg of the triad and don't even take into account the fact that we've got . . . a virtually invulnerable sea-based capacity and land-based capacity." Broder's summary of the interview confirms the Democrat's position. "Dukakis said he would continue development work on the Stealth bomber and the D5 Trident submarine-launched ballistic missile. . . . "

Even the creator of the PAC ad featuring William Horton concluded that the Bush tank ad's claims about Dukakis could not be justified.[46] And on October 21, 1988, former Reagan White House advisor, David Gergen, stated on the "MacNeil/Lehrer Newshour" that "The Bush campaign has charged in its advertising that Dukakis is against the Stealth bomber, and that's just not true. And they've said he's against all these defense systems, and the Dukakis people, you know, say with some reason, hey, we're for a lot of these things, this ad is taking it way beyond the facts."

Yet network news showed former Senator John Tower standing in front of a chart documenting switches in Dukakis's positions on defense as if the fact of the chart constituted proof. And the *Washington Post* failed to provide even the correcting context offered by the *Los Angeles Times*. Said the *Post*, "Armed with charts and sheafs of paper, [the experts defended] the three Bush campaign commercials slamming the Massachusetts governor's positions on military issues, a furlough program for state prison inmates and his record on the cleanup of Boston Harbor" (October 26, 1988, A14). The form of proof—stacks of paper, sizeable charts—was taken for actual proof.

Since press reports were simply pairing the Dukakis and Bush claims that the other side was lying, there was no reason for Bush campaign director James Baker to back off when pressed by Lesley Stahl about one of the ads the next Sunday on "Face the Nation" (October 30, 1988).

> *Stahl:* ". . . 268 murderers did not escape. Your campaign had that pointed out to them that this was misleading . . . why have you not corrected that?"
> *Baker:* "I don't admit that it's misleading, and I don't admit that it's incorrect. Let me simply say to you—"
> *Stahl:* "You don't admit that saying 268 escaped while the announcer says 'murderers' is misleading?"
> *Baker:* "I do not admit that is misleading."
> *Stahl:* "Why not?"
> *Baker:* "No ad is run by our campaign that is not checked by legal and by the research people for accuracy with respect to the facts."
> *Stahl:* "I'll tell you something . . . in my business as a television reporter, if I say something and put words on the screen that conflict, that's inaccurate."

Baker: "Well, we make our judgments with respect to that; you can make yours. There is a procedure. If the other side thinks it's inaccurate, they can file a complaint with the Federal Election Commission, which they have not done. My position is that the ad is absolutely accurate."

Baker's claim about the FEC is incorrect. Dukakis's recourse is filing a libel suit. The reason Dukakis didn't is best explained by Craig Shirley, one of the founders of the PAC that sponsored the Horton ad. "We would have loved a libel suit," he told me. "It would have increased public attention on the furlough program."

Confirming the adage that the best defense is a good offense, at the conference defending the ads, the campaign "showed off a new advertisement, to be broadcast in cities around the country, stating that Dukakis deliberately misled '62 million Americans in the last debate.' This accompanies an excerpt from the second presidential debate in which Dukakis said he never raided the Massachusetts pension fund to balance the budget." But that ad also misled, recalls Tom Rosensteil who covered the press conference for the *Los Angeles Times*. "The ad cites as its proof a report in the *Wall Street Journal*. In fact, the report was contained not in the news story but in an editorial from the *Journal's* strongly conservative opinion page, and it differed in certain facts from recent news reports."

The Democrats proved less guilty of deception in advertising, but when caught at it were no more willing to "fess up." Bush had voted to "cut" Social Security, argued Dukakis's aides. "That's what freezing the cost-of-living adjustment would do!" they said. Lost in their defense was the fact that on the screen in the controversial ad was a Social Security card being torn back to a fraction of its original self, a visual image hardly suggesting a "freeze."

In the general election of 1988, the debates embraced the form of ads, only a small percent of the ads engaged the claims of the other side in a fair, accurate, contextual way, and the candidates denied reporters and citizens the ability to use public, publicized questioning to hold them accountable. Meanwhile, reporters on the bus functioned as theatre critics or campaign consultants, not as surrogates for the public. As a result, the level of engagement between the candidates fell below that of even 1972 and 1964, years without presidential debates. The level of candidate accountability for the rhetoric of the campaign dropped to the bottom of the scale as well.

If we assign a weighting of .5 to each nationally televised general election debate, each nationally telecast citizen call-in, and each campaign in which 30 percent or more of the advertising on one side engages the other, we can begin to construct a sense of range of discourse available in the campaign of the broadcast age. Since it takes two press conferences or two nationally broadcast speeches, one by each major candidate, to volley positions back and forth, I have assigned each set of speeches or press conferences a weighting of .5. What is interesting about the resulting chart is the extent to which it comports with our general sense of which campaigns best forecast the presidencies of the winner (see Chart 10-1).

An Assessment of the Best and Worst of Times

Asking what it was about the 1960 and 1980 campaigns that produced engagement on policy and useful predictions about governance is instructive. Both were close elections. And in close elections, the press and the candidates behave differently. Both candidates see advantage in providing the press and public with access. Increased as a result are well-publicized news conferences with the national press, participation in interview shows, and willingness to debate. At the same time, when the race is close the press makes better use of the access it is given. Press questions are more likely to focus on substance than strategy; and one candidate is not burdened with a greater percent of strategy questions than the other.

When an opponent begins to close in the polls, the "front runner" becomes more accessible. So, for example, in the final weeks of both the 1968 and 1988 campaigns Nixon and Bush, who had been ducking such press contact, agreed to network interviews, Nixon on the Sunday interview shows, Bush on network morning and evening news. Close races also create incentives for candidates to engage in a broader range of discourse and to employ engaged forms more frequently.

If the matters at issue are central to governance, differentiating one's stands from those of the opponent is a useful means of informing voters. The longer the statement, the more likely it is to compare and contrast candidates' positions, providing either oppositional evidence discrediting the opponent's stand or supportive evidence for one's own side or both. So, for example, speeches are more likely to engage than spots, the longer soundbites of "MacNeil/Lehrer" more likely to engage than those on other network evening news. Unfortunately, the number of nationally broadcast general election messages fifteen minutes or longer has declined dramatically in recent years (see Chart 10-2) as has public attention to programs, speeches and discussions about campaigns (see Chart 10-3), the number of hours of convention programming aired on the three commercial networks (see Chart 10-4), and viewed there (see Chart 10-5), and the number of hours of candidate sponsored programming on election eve (see Chart 10-5).

The presidents elected in 1960 and 1980 did so with campaigns filled with five-minute not thirty- and sixty-second ads. In these campaigns, the contenders delivered major nationally broadcast policy speeches. And the greater press access that came with the closeness of the race meant that the clash of opposing positions both advanced arguments and deepened understanding of their rationale and implications. At the same time, enhanced contact with press and public caught and corrected distortions that candidates put out about their records or recommendations.

Since there is no way to engineer close races, how can we encourage the argument, engagement, and accountability that come with longer forms of communication and with access to the press? And how can we invite the press to use access to the candidates to advance our understanding of the who, what, and how of governance rather than the "why" and "with what effect" of campaigning?

Some of the answers are structural. By throwing candidates into states as dissimilar as Georgia, Colorado, and Maryland in a single week, we ensure that the messages reaching the national audience will fragment. Because the South Dakota primary was unpaired with that of any other agricultural state, the farm policies the candidates discussed in that debate seemed irrelevant to most of the rest of the nation. They were lost, as well, in media reports that covered strategy because there was not enough similarity in policy focus across the primary states to build stories on substance.

When the resources of the entire candidate field are concentrated on one homogeneous state such as New Hampshire, the discourse naturally focuses on that state's concerns. With New Hampshire in economic crisis in winter 1992, the candidates had no choice but to lay out their economic plans. There was little room for distraction. The quality of the discourse was high. Ads inched upward in length. Thirty-minute ads reemerged. Three of the candidates distributed detailed print policy statements. The debates were substantive and distraction was low.

When the candidates' focus shifted to campaigning in a handful of states with no marked similarities, the discourse quickly became meaner and more meaningless. With resources spread across the larger number of media markets and no single natural policy focus upon which to build the redundancy that is central to retention, the sensible strategic thing to do is exactly what the candidates did: roll out the unengaged attacks.

One way to increase the amount of focused, engaged discourse in the primaries would be to cluster states that share similar problems and challenges. One set of primaries might occur in states grappling with decaying cities (e.g., Pennsylvania could be added to Michigan and Illinois). This would solve a problem for the candidates and the press.

If one week's primaries were in states that raise cotton, cows, and corn, the candidates could focus their debates, speeches, ads, interviews, and press conferences for that week on farm policy. The interests of voters in those states would invite candidates to concentrate their resources on discussing parity pricing, subsidies, the relationship between farm policy and international trade, use of agri-products as alternative fuels, and combatting U.S. and world hunger through use of American-produced grain.

The level of engaged oppositional advertising would undoubtedly be high but in an environment in which all forms of communication are focused on the same topic so too would candidate accountability for distortion. And the shared topic area would make it easier for the press to structure stories on problems and solutions rather than strategy.

In 1980, Ronald Reagan argued that we were creating a disincentive to work by taxing wealth. Momentarily adopting his philosophy might lead us to ask, How do we reward candidates for engaging in a broad menu of discourse and, as a result, for accessibility to public and press? Since broadcast speeches attract small audiences, we must find a way to provide an incentive for candidates to deliver such speeches, accept invitations to be interviewed and conduct press conferences and also provide incentives for voters to watch. Elsewhere,[47] I have proposed that the press, civic organizations, and schools set the expectation that citizens will watch two thirty-minute speeches by each candidate, one delivered on national television on Labor Day, the other on election eve. In the intervening time, the candidates would participate in four debates in various formats, and appear in nationally telecast press conferences after each debate. They would also appear weekly in five-minute time slots provided to major party candidates who agree to deliver a statement on a specified weekly topic. The topics would be determined by non-candidate polls. So, for example, the topic for the first week after Labor Day would be the topic listed by the largest percentage of the surveyed public as most important to it. By noting major items on the congressional agenda, experts could add to the list of topics.

Because the airwaves are publicly owned, the networks, their affiliates, and the unaffiliated stations could contribute a powerful incentive by providing free national airtime for these rhetorical acts. In 1988, both presidential candidates accepted offers to be interviewed in morning and evening news although the front runner ducked CBS and "Nightline." Similarly, in March 1992, three of the Democrats and one Republican accepted the offer by the Discovery Channel of twenty minutes of time to deliver a speech. One might also tie acceptance of federal campaign financing to an agreement to participate in debates.

However, if debates are to engage and hold candidates accountable for the statements they make, the format has to change. To minimize risk, both Democratic and Republican candidates have insisted on short answers with no press follow-up. Longer answers with provision for reporters to follow up would do much to eliminate the debate-ads that now masquerade as debates. Because the 1976 debates followed a three-minute first answer, two-minute second answer with follow-up by the questioner, reporter Jack Nelson could say to candidate Jimmy Carter, "Governor, I don't believe you answered my question about the kinds of people you would be looking for [on the] Court, the type of philosophy you would be looking for?" Where Carter had ducked the question the first time, when pressed he responds that in the Burger-Warren tradition he would appoint those who tip the balance toward human rights.

Banning the studio audience would help as well. Alternatively, if the experiments undertaken in the primaries of 1980 and 1984 are any indication, removing the buffer of the press panel would also increase engagement and accountability in debates.

To ensure that the candidates both address each other and the issues of primary concern to the public, the press would cover campaigns in ways that increase candidate accountability and decrease the rewards for pseudo-answers, pseudo-events, and for transforming all available forms of communication into ads. The importance of reporters in the equation was acknowledged by the man who choreographed the visuals for the Reagan presidency, Michael Deaver, who noted: "The candidates aren't going to change. The media are going to have to force the change by the type of coverage they do, they insist upon."[48]

The portends are varied. On the one hand, on a live radio interview show *San Francisco Examiner* reporter Chris Matthews asked Bill Clinton, "What was it like having an outhouse." Laughing, Clinton responded, "It was O.K. except in the winter when it was cold, and in the summer sometimes when there were snakes down the hole." An inveterate seeker of insight about primal candidate experiences, Matthews inquired, "How did you go at night with those snakes?" "You made real sure you wanted to go bad," responded the candidate to audience laughter. "I don't believe I agreed to do this." (May 29, 1992, San Francisco).

On the other, in the Democratic candidates' debate on PBS (January 31, 1992), Jim Lehrer asked: "Senator Tsongas, the experts say that all of the discussions that you and everybody else have about health care in the United States always avoid the real issue, which is allocation of resources, rationing, or whatever. In other words, we cannot afford to pay for the health care system that our science and medical profession can provide. Are they right?" His follow-up questions asked Tsongas to define managed competition, queried Kerrey about the mandated nature of his proposal, pursued the question, "How do you manage costs under your plan?", and parried an answer by asking "But that's going to lead to rationing and allocation, is it not?" The exchanges clarified the different approaches the two candidates would take to national health insurance.

By giving voters the information they need to judge candidates' messages on their accuracy, fairness, and contextuality and relevance to governance, reporters also make it possible to penalize sleaze and reward substance. So, for example, in the 1992 Georgia primary, voters surprised those who had assumed that the South surfeits with "Bubbas" eager to vote their prejudices. Viewers penalized Republican hopeful Patrick Buchanan for an unfair attack on incumbent president George Bush.

The ad showed scenes from the film *Tongues Untied* as print scrolled up the screen saying, "In the past three years the Bush Administration has invested our tax dollars in pornographic and blasphemous art, too shocking to show." Voters spotted the irony. "If it's so shocking, what's

Figure 10-1. In the 1992 Georgia primary, challenger Patrick Buchanan ran an ad alleging that George Bush had funded pornography. Evidence from focus groups suggested and a CNN-Gallup survey confirmed that the ad created a backlash against its sponsor. Voters were unwilling to believe that Bush was responsible for the expenditure which had, in fact, occurred during the Reagan administration.

his business in showing it in my living room?" asked an angered focus group member. "He's using my money to put that junk on the air just like what he says George Bush did," noted another. What the voters are referring to are the semi-clad men in leather shown dancing on the screen.

"This so-called art has glorified homosexuality, exploited children, and perverted the image of Jesus Christ," says the ad. "He thinks we're going to vote for him because we are Christians," said a middle-aged man in one of the groups. "And because some of us believe that homosexuality is wrong," added another. "I know George Bush is a good Christian," noted the first. "He would not have approved of anything that profaned Jesus Christ."

"Even after good people protested, Bush continued to fund this kind of art," states the ad. "I heard on television that that wasn't true," said a seventy-three-year-old retired school teacher. "I even made it on tape and freeze frome (sic) [laughter] my television set. When you go up and look I don't even know what it is. All I saw was a bunch of butts [laughter]." "The thing that really offended me," said a college student, "was putting George Bush's picture right on the film as if he had made it himself." "What matters to me," said a middle-aged male construction worker, "is that that ad doesn't tell the truth." "Bush didn't support that film. It happened under Reagan. This kind of advertising is what's wrong with politics." "But it does tell you a lot about Buchanan," said the college student. "Yeah," responded the construction worker. "He's a low life." "If that's all he's got to say about what he'd want to do when he is president, he hasn't got much more to say," commented a secretary.

"How, what makes you think the ad is untrue?" asked the focus group leader. "It was on the news," said the construction worker. "CNN," said the school teacher. "No, it was one of the other ones," added the construction worker. "It said that that film was funded by someone else while Reagan was president and that what the agency [National Endowment for the Arts] does now is funds symphonies and opera." "I just didn't believe junk like that. Who would believe that the president would attack Jesus Christ," observed a cop. "That's interesting," said the woman who had tried to get a better look at the ad. "I believe if you can't say something nice, don't say something at all."

The thirty voters in these three groups had been selected to ensure that their demographics matched those of the state; all said they were undecided three weeks before the primary. The night before balloting, each group was asked whether the Buchanan ad had made them more or less likely to support Buchanan or hadn't changed their inclination at all. Seven said that the ad had made them less likely to support the Republican insurgent. A week after the balloting in Georgia, a CNN-Gallup poll confirmed that the NEA ad had created a backlash against Buchanan. Indeed, 23 percent said that the ad had increased the likelihood that they would vote for Buchanan's opponent, George Bush. A misleading ad by Democratic contender Paul Tsongas created a similar effect.

Ten chapters ago, I argued that in 1988 the Republicans exploited quirks in the electorate and conventions of the press to give an atypical instance—the "drama" of William Horton—a power unwarranted by the data. By 1992, the press had learned one lesson of 1988. As a result voters rejected a drama-filled but atypical instance of arts funding that played on fears of gays.

Where the press had abetted the Horton story, it discredited the tale of a president funding pornography. On CNN (February 28, 1992), Brooks Jackson pointed out that the film had been funded by the Reagan, not the Bush, administration at a total cost to the tax payers of $5000. NBC's Lisa Myers went a step further (March 3, 1992) to note that the film was not typical of NEA projects.

As she made this claim, Myers displaced the ad's images with shots of the Chicago Symphony and Pavarotti on PBS. These, she argued, were more representative of the Endowment's mission and expenditures. Both

NBC and CNN distanced audiences from the ad by boxing it on the screen and dampened the power of the ad's visuals by imposing the words "misleading" or "false" over the ad copy in appropriate places.

Data had triumphed over drama, substance over strategy. Argumentation, engagement, and accountability had other noteworthy moments in 1992 as well.

Earlier I argued that the 1988 general election debates were worrisomely ad-like. By contrast, the 1992 MacNeil-Lehrer, Jennings, and Donahue primary debates proved more substantive than any in recent memory. The educator-philosopher John Dewey would have been pleased with the extent to which, occasionally with the gentle encouragement of the moderators, each Democratic contender "follow[ed] an argument, graspe[d] the point of view of another, expand[ed] the boundaries on understanding, [and] debate[d] the alternative purposes that might be pursued."

The bad news is that the audiences for these exchanges were equaled by those for "trash" television. In the low point of the primary campaign, a woman who claimed, without persuasive evidence, to have been Bill Clinton's mistress told a tabloid TV interviewer that she rated the democrat a nine on a ten-point scale of lovers.

Tabloid television was not the only new genre added to the traditional political mix in 1992. As my earlier discussion of the gubernatorial candidacy of David Duke noted, live radio and television talk shows now provide candidates with access to large and, some fear, largely uncritical, audiences.

Responding to the competition provided by "Oprah" and "Geraldo," by 1992 the once serious talk shows had moved to include "sex" and "scandal." Of Jerry Brown, Phil Donahue asked, "You went to Africa with Linda Ronstadt. Did you go anywhere else with anybody else?" Donahue's questions of Bill Clinton focused on whether the Arkansan had or hadn't had affairs.

Midway through Donahue's assault on Clinton, an exasperated candidate and an audience member both said, "Enough." "We're going to sit here a long time in silence, Phil. I'm not going to answer any more of these questions," said Clinton to rising audience applause. "I've answered 'em until I'm blue in the face. You are responsible for the cynicism in this country. You don't want to talk about the real issues." As the crowd voiced its approval, an audience member agreed. "Given the pathetic state of most of the United States at this point . . . ," she said, "I can't believe you spent half an hour of air time attacking this man's character. I'm not even a Bill Clinton supporter, but I think this is ridiculous."

In penance, Donahue devoted his last show before the New York primary to an uninterrupted discussion between Democratic contenders Jerry Brown and Bill Clinton. The worst of times had given way to the best. The exchange proved as substantive and more civil than any in the campaign. And it reached an audience not usually attracted by PBS and C-SPAN.

The emergence of the talk show as a site of both substance and silliness suggests a system in transition. By providing callers and audience members with direct access to candidates, the format enfranchises. Participation rather than spectatorship is invited by its interactive form. Moreover, it attracts an audience otherwise largely inaccessible to candidates.

But because the hosts range from dedicated partisans to entertaining lightweights, a skillful candidate can transform many of these opportunities into interview- or news-ads. And while callers ask useful and often important questions, most are unskilled in follow-up. The opportunity to ask a second question is usually not provided, in any event. In other words, while potentially productive, the talk show form is not likely, of itself, to elicit a high level of argument, engagement, and accountability. And on the horizon is a candidacy capitalizing on public disdain for the traditional news media and disaffection with the forms of politics as usual.[49]

Whether the rise of H. Ross Perot is a symptom of the problem or a solution remains to be seen. But if history is a guide, such questions can best be answered by campaigns that engage in argumentation rather than assertion, differentiation rather than vilification, substantive engagement rather than storytelling. The public and the body politic are ill-served if discourse is driven by drama rather than data and if reporters concentrate on fathoming the candidates' strategic intent and its effect rather on the problems facing us, the qualifications of those who would lead and the legitimacy of the solutions they offer.

All of this is possible if the public will adopt the posture of the angered member of the Donahue audience and insist that candidates and reporters restore the relationship between campaign discourse and governance.

Appendix I

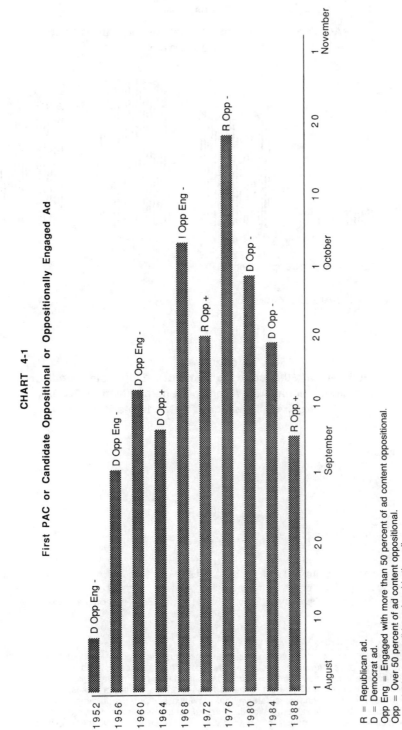

CHART 4-1

First PAC or Candidate Oppositional or Oppositionally Engaged Ad

R = Republican ad.
D = Democrat ad.
Opp Eng = Engaged with more than 50 percent of ad content oppositional.
Opp = Over 50 percent of ad content oppositional.
+ = Ad favors candidate ahead in the polls.
– = Ad favors candidate behind in the polls.

CHART 4-2

PAC Expenses in Presidential Races: Oppositional and Supportive

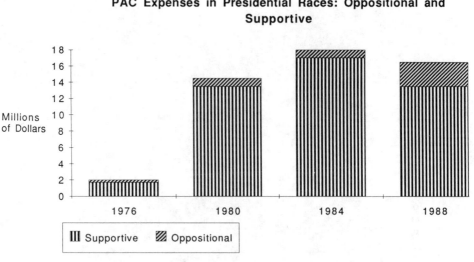

Source: Federal Election Commission

CHART 4-3

Number of 30-second to 5-minute Self-Promotional and Oppositional Ads Aired in General Election For or Against Presidential Candidates*

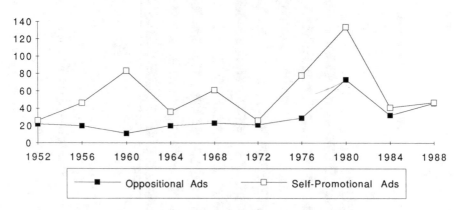

* If more than 50 percent of the ad focuses on the record of the opponent without providing comparative information about what the sponsoring candidate would have done or germane information about the sponsoring candidate's record, the ad is oppositional. If more than 50 percent of the ad focuses on the record, promises, or philosophy of the sponsoring candidate without providing comparative information on the opponent, the ad is self-promotional. If the ad compares relevant facets of both candidates' records or promises, the ad is engaged. Chart 9-1 shows the percent of paid time that engages. As it indicates, ads rarely engage.

CHART 9-1

Percentage of Total Paid Air Time by Candidates That Engaged

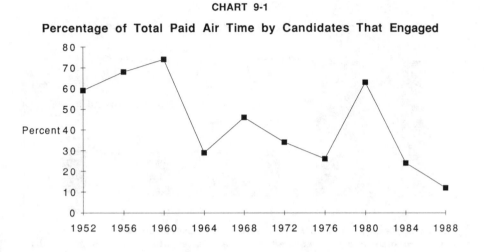

CHART 9-2

Percentage of Total Paid Engagement in
Paid Speeches and Paid Spot Ads

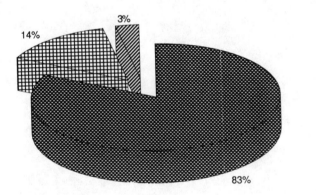

Speeches (5,15,30 min.)

Spot ads (60 sec. or shorter)

Engaged in 60 sec. or less spot ads
in which candidate speaks

CHART 9-3

Number of News Conferences Held by Candidates

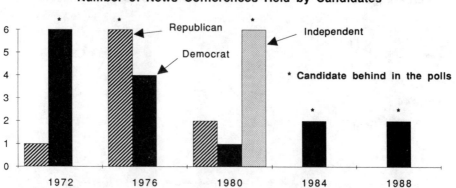

News conferences include only those open to national press which lasted 30 minutes or more and were covered in at least three large circulation papers that were geographically dispersed.

CHART 9-4

Total Number of Questions Asked of Democratic and Republican Candidates, 1960-1988, on "Face the Nation" and "Meet the Press"

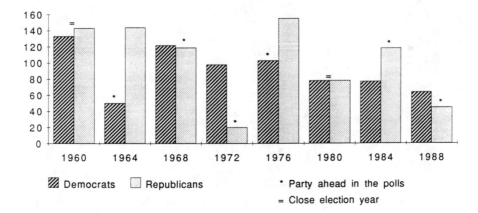

■ Democrats □ Republicans   * Party ahead in the polls
                                     = Close election year

CHART 9-5

Total Number of News Conferences Held by All Candidates, 1956-1988*

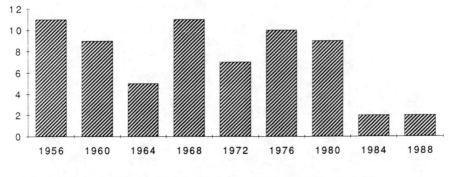

* General election. 1968 total includes Wallace. 1980 total includes Anderson.

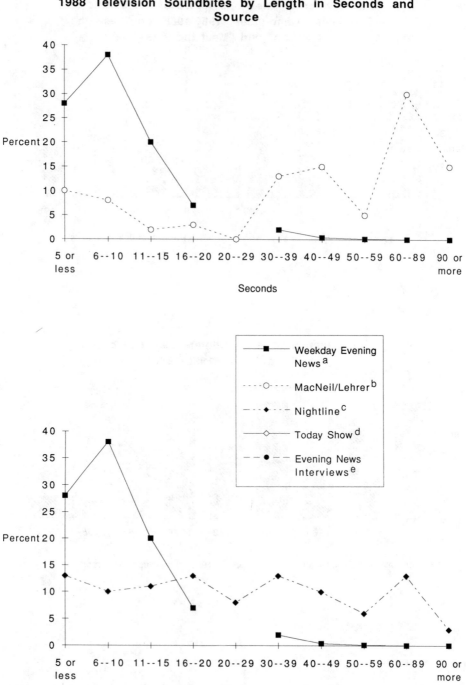

CHART 9-6 a, b

1988 Television Soundbites by Length in Seconds and Source

CHART 9-6 c, d

1988 Television Soundbites by Length in Seconds and Source

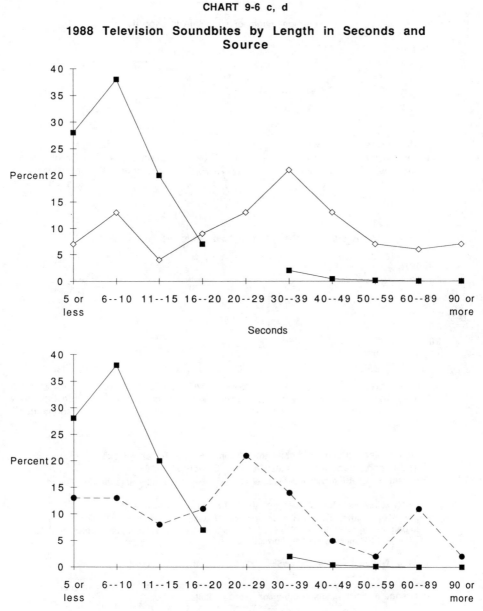

a from Kiku Adatto, "Sound Bite Democracy: Network Evening News Presidential Campaign Coverage, 1968 and 1988," Tables 1 and 2. (Category 29 seconds or less not available.) Presidential candidates on ABC, CBS, and NBC weekday evening news.

b Robert MacNeil and Jim Lehrer interviewing Michael Dukakis, October 31, 1988.

c Ted Koppel interviewing Michael Dukakis, October 25, 1988.

d Bryant Gumbel interviewing Michael Dukakis; Bryant Gumbel interviewing George Bush.

e Twelve network newscasts between July 13 and November 4, 1988.

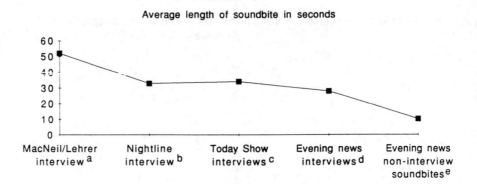

CHART 9-7

Average length of soundbite in seconds

Average number of households watching (in thousands)

a Robert MacNeil and Jim Lehrer interviewing Michael Dukakis, October 31, 1988.

b Ted Koppel interviewing Michael Dukakis, October 25, 1988.

c Bryant Gumbel interviewing Michael Dukakis; Bryant Gumbel interviewing George Bush.

d Twelve network newcasts between July 13 and November 4, 1988.

e from Kiku Adatto, "Sound Bite Democracy: Network Evening News Presidential Campaign Coverage, 1968 and 1988," Tables 1 and 2. Presidential candidates on ABC, CBS, and NBC weekday evening newscasts.

Source: National Custom Analysis, Nielsen, January 6-12, 1992.

Note: I was unable to obtain comparative data for these programs. The four-year difference in time makes comparison more difficult.

1988 Television Interview Soundbites by Length in Seconds and Source

Length of soundbite in seconds	Adatto[a]		Evening news[b]		Today Show[c]		MacNeil/Lehrer[d]		Nightline[e]	
	n	%	n	%	n	%	n	%	n	%
5 or less	202	28	6	19	3	7	4	10	10	13
10 or less	470	66	8	25	9	20	7	18	18	23
15 or less	612	86	8	25	11	24	8	20	26	34
20 or less	660	93	9	28	15	33	9	23	36	47
29 or less	—	—	17	53	21	46	9	23	42	55
30 or more	15	2	15	47	25	54	31	78	35	45
				100%		100%		101%		100%
40 or more	4	.5	13	41	15	33	26	65	25	32
50 or more	1	.1	11	34	9	20	20	50	17	22
60 or more	0	0	9	28	6	13	18	45	12	16
90 or more	0	0	2	6	3	7	6	15	2	3
Average soundbite	10 sec.		40 sec.		34 sec.		52 sec.		33 sec.	

[a] From Kiku Adatto, "Sound Bite Democracy: Network Evening News Presidential Campaign Coverage, 1968 and 1988," Tables 1 and 2. Presidential candidates on ABC, CBS, and NBC weekday evening newscasts.

[b] Three network newscasts: Dan Rather interviewing Lloyd Bentsen; Dan Rather interviewing Michael Dukakis; Tom Brokaw interviewing George Bush.

[c] Two "Today Show" segments: Bryant Gumbel interviewing Michael Dukakis; Bryant Gumbel interviewing George Bush.

[d] Robert MacNeil and Jim Lehrer interviewing Michael Dukakis, October 31, 1988.

[e] Ted Koppel interviewing Michael Dukakis, October 25, 1988.

Audience Size Compared to Soundbite Length

	Average number of households watching[a]	Average length of soundbite
"MacNeil/Lehrer" interview[b]	11,790,000	52 sec.
Nightline interview[c]	14,830,000	33 sec.
"Today Show" interviews[d]	17,040,000	34 sec.
Evening news interviews[e]	23,580,500	40 sec.
ABC, CBS, and ABC weekday evening news soundbites	68,800,000	10 sec.

[a] According to Nielsen data for January 6-12, 1992.
[b] Robert MacNeil and Jim Lehrer interviewing Michael Dukakis, October 31, 1988.
[c] Ted Koppel interviewing Michael Dukakis, October 25, 1988.
[d] Two "Today Show" segments: Bryant Gumbel interviewing Michael Dukakis; Bryant Gumbel interviewing George Bush.
[e] Three network newscasts; Dan Rather interviewing Lloyd Bentsen; Dan Rather interviewing Michael Dukakis; Tom Brokaw interviewing George Bush.
[f] From Kiku Adatto, "Sound Bite Democracy: Network Evening News Presidential Campaign Coverage, 1968 and 1988," Tables 1 and 2. Presidential candidates on ABC, CBS, and NBC weekday evening newscasts.

278   Appendix I

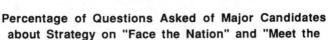

CHART 9-8

Percentage of Questions Asked of Major Candidates about Strategy on "Face the Nation" and "Meet the Press," 1960-1988

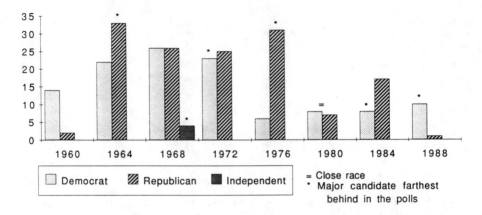

CHART 10-1

Range of Engaged Discourse

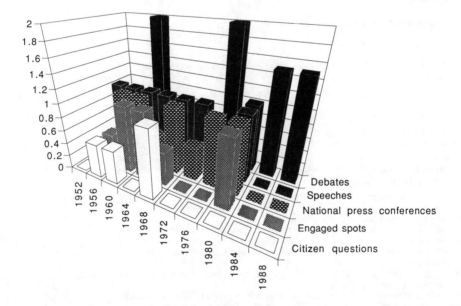

Note: A weight of .5 was given to each nationally televised election debate, each nationally telecast citizen call-in, each campaign in which 30 percent or more of the advertising on one side engaged the other, and each *set* of speeches or press conferences (one by each major candidate).

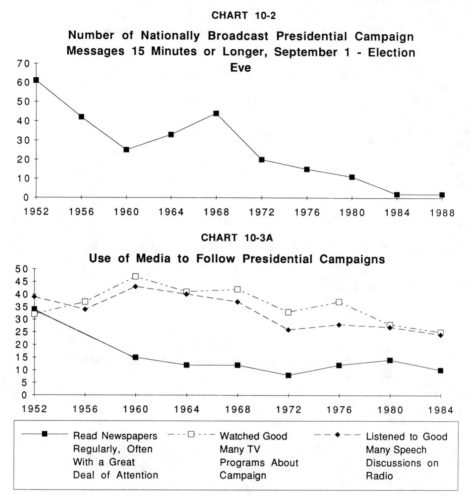

CHART 10-2

Number of Nationally Broadcast Presidential Campaign Messages 15 Minutes or Longer, September 1 - Election Eve

CHART 10-3A

Use of Media to Follow Presidential Campaigns

| ■ Read Newspapers Regularly, Often With a Great Deal of Attention | □ Watched Good Many TV Programs About Campaign | ◆ Listened to Good Many Speech Discussions on Radio |

Source: National Election Studies, University of Michigan

CHART 10-3B

Number of Hours Democratic and Republican Conventions Aired*

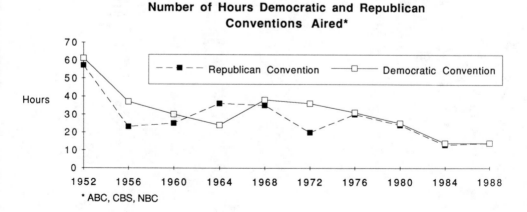

Hours

■ Republican Convention   □ Democratic Convention

* ABC, CBS, NBC

CHART 10-4

Average Number of Hours Conventions Were Viewed*

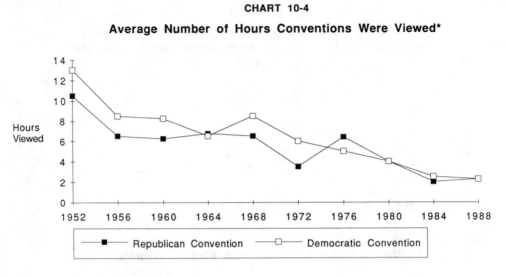

* ABC, CBS, NBC

CHART 10-5

Hours of Late Afternoon and Election Eve Paid TV*

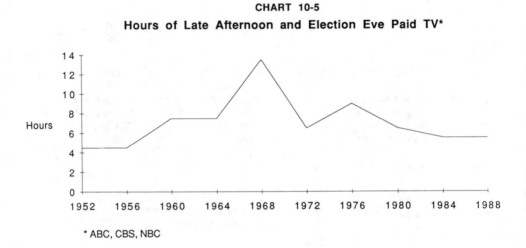

* ABC, CBS, NBC

Appendix II

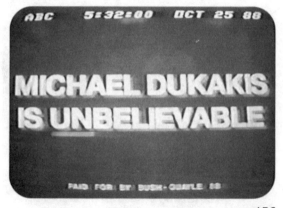

ABC

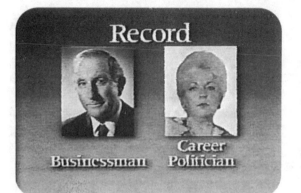

WFAA

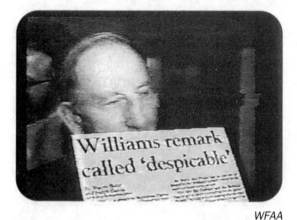

WFAA

(Ads run full screen in news.)

THE PROBLEM

1. Unless the viewer has had sufficient exposure to an ad to recall it from that context, an ad that is aired full screen in news without a disclaimer will be remembered as news rather than as an ad.

2. By airing ads in news, reporters increase the likelihood that they will: a) inadvertently advantage one candidate over another in a given race; b) pass through an ad's unexamined misinformation in the credible environment of news.

The ads most likely to be aired in news are oppositional, visually evocative, symbolically powerful, verbally interesting, controversial, and/or humorous.

3. Ads have natural recall advantages over regular news.

A. News reports do not use music to cue responses.

B. News relies more heavily on the spoken word than do ads; evocative visuals are more readily recalled than evocative words. When a reporter uses words to counteract the pictures, filtered audio, and cueing music of ads, the corrective words are likely to be over-ridden by the power of the ad. (Threlkeld's analysis of the tank ad for ABC in 1988 is illustrative.)

C. Ads are replayed; news reports are broadcast a single time.

D. Ads reach a much larger audience than does news.

E. "Low involvement" individuals are exposed to and influenced by ads; higher involvement individuals are more likely to attend to news.

4. By focusing on their strategy and effect (not on their fairness, accuracy or relevance to governance), most news stories magnify the power of the aired ads. The story on ads most likely to air will discuss the "negativity" of the races being run across the country.

I f reporters are to focus on fairness and accuracy, they require a visual and verbal grammar that will permit their message to get through. When treating ads in strategy stories, reporters should, at least, not advantage distortive ads. Yet this is precisely what occurred in 1988 when the most often aired ad image in news showed circling convicts as a print overlay reported "268 Escaped." This segment of the Bush furlough ad invited a false inference; the same occurred in 1990 when news coverage of "Woman in the Red Dress II" repeatedly carried to the nation the false Helms claim that "Harvey Gantt favors abortion in the final weeks of pregnancy."

RECOMMENDED RESPONSE: In ad watches, preview, distance, disclaim, displace, recap

A. *Preview*: Create a category of story that carries the expectation that it will treat the accuracy of political ads. Give it a title, a logo, and a regular place in the news broadcast. The station's most credible reporter should have this as a regular beat.

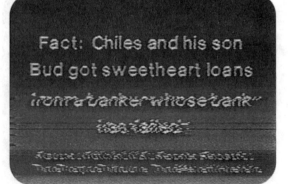

ABC, "Good Morning America"

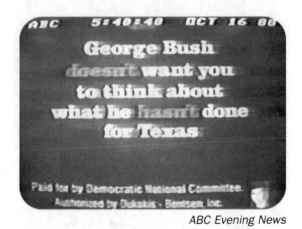

ABC Evening News

PREVIEWING   *ABC Evening News*

DISTANCING   *Experimental—Not Aired*

DISTANCING   *Experimental—Not Aired*

DISTANCING   *CNN Headline News*

B. *Distance*: In these stories, distance the audience from the manipulative advertising

1) By boxing the ad content in a television screen

a) squeeze zooming the screen to upper screen left; or

b) canting the screen.

1) This undercuts some of the evocative power of such images as David Duke and the burning cross and the meld of Dukakis and Kerry in the Rappaport ad.

2) Set the boxed ad distinctively off from its background so that it does not look like a regularly broadcast ad.

a) Setting the boxed ad into a background with a horizon line is the clearest way of defining the ad as "not endorsed news content."

b) The background should provide a clear contrast to the ad content.

3) Some stations run the ad full screen before squeeze zooming to box it. Others begin by boxing it and then move to full screen. The former technique is effective because it lures the viewer into the ad and then distances. The latter distances and then heightens the ad's power by giving it full screen play.

4) It is possible at the most manipulative points in an ad to increase the audience distance, i.e., move to squeeze zoom at first manipulative point, cant screen at second; run a red or yellow line from disclaimer through ad content at third.

C. *Disclaim* the content of the ad.

1) By using contrasting print in a distinguishable font size and color (yellow or red test well against most content) to identify the ad as

a) a political ad

b) sponsored by a specified party, candidate, or PAC (Independent expenditure); each should have its own identifying logo, e.g., "Bush (R) Advertisement" "Dem. Party Advertisement" "$ I.E. Conservatives for Victory (pro Bush)."

c) and holding this ID in place throughout the entire ad segment. (Note: a pulsing disclaimer is very effective at reminding viewers that they are watching an ad. But this visual also makes viewers very angry. It is visually too intrusive!)

2) This ID or disclaimer should intersect the content of the ad. If the disclaimer does not intersect the boxed ad, viewers perceive that it is part of the ad itself.

a) An ID or disclaimer can be printed into the visual field of the ad.

b) It can do this by including a red line that runs from the disclaimer through the ad.

3) The disclaimer should not be in a color of print used in the ad and should not be in a font size or type style used in the ad.

4) If the ad includes print, the disclaimer gains maximum

DISCLAIMING   *C-SPAN*

DISCLAIMING   *ABC, "Good Morning America"*

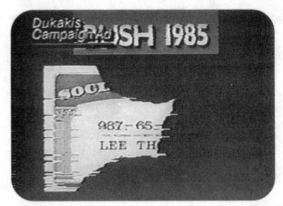

DISCLAIMING   *ABC Evening News*

DISCLAIMING *WFAA*

DISPLACING *WFAA*

DISPLACING *WFAA*

persistent attention in upper screen right.

5) If the ad does not include print, disclaimer gains most persistent attention in upper screen left.

6) Disclaimers at the bottom of the screen are easily ignored.

D. *Displace*

1) Verbally.

a) By putting print corrections on screen

1) by documenting the source of the corrections

b) By having reporter speak the corrections as they are synopsized on screen. When the reporter uses words against ad print and pictures, the reporter's corrections are lost.

c) We are not accustomed to "reading" television. Print corrections that are syntactically complex and/or contain multiple sentences are more likely to be ignored or discounted than those that are simple and appear in single statements.

d) When two sentences or phrases are needed, separate them into two visual units.

2) Visually.

a) by rolling the ad's image off the screen or

b) by wiping the ad's image or

c) by squeeze zooming the ad's image or

d) by putting the universal warning sign over the ad's image or

e) by displacing the ad's images with corrected images or

f) by showing the full context from which the distortive print or picture is drawn.

3) Vocally.

a) Fade down the audio so that reporter can talk over it.

b) Segment the ad into units broken by corrective print and words so that ad's power can't build.

E. *Recap.* Audiences will see the manipulative ad many times, the corrective news once. Using a clearly recognized format, a clear forecast, a clearly structured presentation, and a clear recap will increase the likelihood that the news critique will inoculate against the distortive ad.

EXAMPLE
RECOMMENDED
RESPONSE:

In strategy stories or stories about negativity in the campaigns, use verbal and print forecasting to disclaim ads that are propositionally false, out of context, or invite false inferences. For example, "This year's races are dirtier than ever. Some candidates are accusing their opponents of holding positions nobody holds." (Cut to Woman in Red Dress II.) She says: "Harvey Gantt would have us believe some pretty awful things. Aborting a child in the final weeks of pregnancy." Reporter: "Other ads disclose no evidence for their questionable claims." (Cut to Rappaport ad against Kerry.) Ad says, "Tax and Spend, Spend and Tax. Kerry and Dukakis. Dukakis and Kerry. . . ."

DISPLACING   *Experimental—Not Aired*

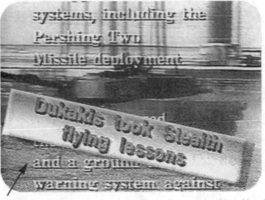

DISPLACING   *Experimental—Not Aired*

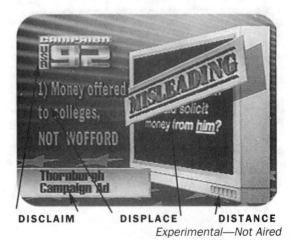

DISCLAIM   DISPLACE   DISTANCE
Experimental—Not Aired

Notes

Introduction

1. Paul Abramson, John Aldrich, and David Rohde, *Change and Continuity in the 1988 Elections* rev. ed. (Washington, D.C.: Congressional Quarterly Press, 1991), 47. Interviews cited without date took place within the last year.

2. Speech at the University of Pennsylvania, October 22, 1990.

3. The differences between Dukakis and Bush had been on the public record for a year to the day of the tank ride. "I think there are serious questions about our conventional equipment: tanks, antitank weapons, support for troops in the field," Dukakis told the *Washington Post*'s David Broder in a September 13, 1987, interview. "Secondly there are persistent reports of problems with ammunition, levels of supplies, medical equipment, these kinds of things. Thirdly, there are unquestionably all kinds of communication problems between and among our services in the field." In his stump speeches, Dukakis pledged: "Lloyd Bentsen and I are going to keep tank production up and we're going to invest in the new technologies we'll need to stop Soviet tanks."

As Charles Krause of the "MacNeil/Lehrer NewsHour" demonstrated, reporters who wanted to compare the two candidates on defense could do so easily. Their similar positions can be synopsized in a single soundbite that of itself discredits the claims of the tank ad. "Despite their differences, both Dukakis and Bush agree on some big weapons projects. For example, both would deploy the next generation of Trident missiles on nuclear submarines. Both candidates also support continued funding for the super secret Stealth bomber, called the B-2." Delineating their differences, which Krause also did, took just under a minute.

4. Sound bite is found in "Nightline," October 10, 1988. ABC.

5. Eric Schmitt, "Bush Is Reported Ready to Cut Back on Stealth Planes," *New York Times,* October 25, 1991, 1.

Chapter 1

1. I have compiled these figures from Table 4, p. 15, of "1989 Annual Statistical Report of the Furlough Program," Massachusetts Department of Correction, January 1991.

2. Those who read newspaper accounts of the furlough program learned that Horton was the only furloughed Massachusetts first-degree murderer who committed a violent crime. Most furloughed escapees committed auto theft. A quarter of the reported escapees hadn't escaped at all and had returned voluntarily but more than two hours late from the furlough. See Kathleen Hall Jamieson, "For Televised Mendacity, This Year Is the Worst Ever," *Washington Post,* October 30, 1988, C1, C2.

3. Dave McNeely, "Bush, Dukakis Commercials Becoming Hottest Campaign Issue," *Austin American-Statesman,* October 25, 1988, B3.

4. Maureen Dowd, "Bush Portrays His Opponent as Sympathetic to Criminals," *New York Times,* October 8, 1988, 9.

5. Gerald M. Boyd, "Bush's Attack on Crime Appeals to the Emotions," *New York Times,* October 11, 1988, 12.

6. Mike Hailey, "Crime Victims Condemn Dukakis," *Austin American-Statesman,* October 11, 1988, B3.

7. See also: J. P. Robinson, D. Davis, H. Sahin, and T. O'Toole, "Comprehension of Television News: How Alert Is the Audience?" Paper presented to the Association for Education in Journalism, Boston, 1980.

8. "MacNeil/Lehrer NewsHour," November 8, 1988.

9. "Top Democrats Accuse Bush Campaign of Inflaming Racial Fears," *New York Times,* October 24, 1988, 10.

10. One study found that crime was the third largest category of news covered by newspapers. Sanford Sherizen, "Social Creation of Crime News: All the News Fitted to Print," In *Deviance and Mass Media,* ed. Charles Winick (Beverly Hills: Sage, 1978), 208, 215.

11. Kathleen Hall Jamieson and Karlyn Kohrs Campbell, *Interplay of Influence: News, Advertising, Politics and the Mass Media,* 3rd ed. (Belmont, Calif.: Wadsworth, 1992), 33.

12. "Ad Executive to Stand Trial in Accident," *Milwaukee Journal,* August 22, 1985.

13. Lawrence Sussman, "Ad Executive Questioned in Hit-And-Run," *Milwaukee Journal,* July 5, 1985; Neil Rosenberg and Mary Ann Esquivel, "Hit-and-run Victim Gets Rehabilitation," *Milwaukee Journal,* July 31, 1985; Maureen O'Donnell, "DA Urges Community Service for Ad Man," *Milwaukee Journal,* April 28, 1986.

14. "Ad Executive Found Guilty in Hit-Run," *Milwaukee Journal,* March 12, 1986.

15. "Cycle Victims Settle with Frankenberry," *Milwaukee Journal,* January 5, 1988.

16. Maureen O'Donnell, "Frankenberry Given 90 Days," *Milwaukee Journal*, July 11, 1986.

17. "Frankenberry Leaves Jail Daily," *Milwaukee Journal*, June 18, 1986.

18. "MacNeil/Lehrer NewsHour," September 16, 1988.

19. Thomas Byrne Edsall with Mary D. Edsall, "Race," *The Atlantic* 267:5 (May 1991), 77.

20. Edelman, *Political Spectacle*, 73.

21. Kinder and Mendelberg, 20.

22. Only those who indicated that they had not yet made a firm voting decision were included in the groups. One hundred individuals, ten per group, were included in the study. Two of the groups met weekly. Eight met once the first week in September and once the third week in October. By the third week in October, seven individuals had dropped from the study or were not attending regularly. I have since redesigned this procedure to include CS for C-SPAN, S for a speech attended, TAD for TV ad, RAD for radio ad, and M for magazine.

23. Stephen Hess, *The Washington Reporters* (Washington, D.C.: Brookings, 1981), 49, 18.

24. Cf. Hayden White, "The Value of Narrativity in the Representation of Reality," in *On Narrative*, ed. W. J. T. Mitchell (Chicago: University of Chicago Press, 1981), 23; Paul Ricoeur, *Time and Narrative*, trans. Kathleen McLaughlin and David Pellauer (Chicago: University of Chicago Press, 1984–86), Volume 1, 74ff.; Jerome Bruner, *Actual Minds, Possible Worlds* (Cambridge, Mass.: Harvard University Press, 1986). I do not wish to imply that narrative is an illegitimate way of knowing or that narrative necessarily works in service of our predispositions and fears. As Bennett and Edelman note, "If stories can be constructed to wall off the senses to the dilemmas and contradictions of social life, perhaps they also can be presented in ways that open up the mind to creative possibilities developed in ways that provoke intellectual struggle, the resolution of contradiction, and the creation of a more workable human order" (W. L. Bennett and M. Edelman, "Toward a New Political Narrative," *Journal of Communication*, 35 (1985), 161–62).

For a discussion of rhetorical functions of narrative, see W. R. Fisher, *Human Communication as Narrative* (Columbia: University of South Carolina Press, 1987); C. M. Condit, "Crafting Virtue: The Rhetorical Construction of Public Morality," *Quarterly Journal of Speech*, 73 (1987), 79–97; W. G. Kirkwood, "Storytelling and Self Confrontation: Parables as Communication Strategies," *Quarterly Journal of Speech*, 69 (1983), 58–74; W. F. Lewis, "Telling America's Story: Narrative Form and the Reagan Presidency," *Quarterly Journal of Speech*, 73 (1987), 280–302; M. C. McGee and J. S. Nelson, "Narrative Reason in Public Argument," *Journal of Communication*, 35, (1985), 139–55; R. C. Rowland, "On Limiting the Narrative Paradigm: Three Case Studies," *Communication Monographs*, 56 (1989), 39–54; V. W. Turner, "Social Dramas and Stories about Them," *Critical Inquiry*, 7 (1980), 141–68; B. Warnick, "The Narrative Paradigm: Another Story," *Quarterly Journal of Speech*, 73 (1987), 172–82.

25. See E. T. Higgins, J. A. Bargh, and W. Lombardi, "Nature of Priming Effects on Categorization," *Journal of Experimental Psychology: Learning, Memory, and Cognition* 11 (1985), 59–69. This heuristic is also well explored in S. Popkin, *The Reasoning Voter* (Chicago: University of Chicago Press, 1991).

26. R. Lau, "Negativity in Political Perception," *Political Behavior*, 4 (1982),

353–77; R. Lau, "Two Explanations for Negativity Effects in Political Behavior," *American Journal of Political Science* 29 (1985), 119–38.

27. K. Kellermann, "The Negativity Effect and Its Implications for Initial Interaction," *Communication Monographs* 51 (1984), 37–55.

28. B. Reeves, E. Thorson, and J. Schleuder, "Attention to Television: Psychological Theories and Chronometric Measures," in *Perspectives on Media Effects*, eds. J. Bryant and D. Zillmann (Hillsdale, N.J.: Lawrence Erlbaum, 1986), 251–79.

29. J. Newhagen and B. Reeves, "Emotion and Memory Response for Negative Political Advertising: A Study of the 1988 Presidential Campaign." Paper presented to the Association for Education in Journalism and Mass Communication, Washington, D.C., 1989.

30. M. A. Shapiro and R. H. J. Rieger, "Comparing Positive and Negative Political Advertising." Paper presented to the International Communication Association, San Francisco, 1989. See also J. Schleuder, M. McCombs, and W. Wanta, "Inside the Agenda Setting Process: How Political Advertising and TV News Prime Viewers to Think About Issues and Candidates." Paper presented to the Association for Education in Journalism and Mass Communication, Washington, D.C., 1989.

31. S. Kernell, "Presidential Popularity and Negative Voting: An Alternative Explanation of the Midterm Congressional Decline of the President's Party," *American Political Science Review* 71, (1977), 44–66.

32. Christopher Jepson and Shelly Chaiken, "Chronic Issue-Specific Fear Inhibits Systematic Processing of Persuasive Communications," In *Communication, Cognition, and Anxiety,* ed. Melanie Booth-Butterfield (Newbury Park, Calif.: Sage, 1990), 61–84.

33. A. Lang, "Involuntary Attention and Physiological Arousal Evoked by Structural Features and Emotional Content of TV Commercials," *Communication Research* 17 (1990), 275–99.

In processing messages we rely not on statistically warranted inferences but on rules of thumb, or heuristics, that have certain predictable biases. These rules of thumb carry nonprobablistic presuppositions about how things work. Even after explanations show the operation and unreliability of a heuristic, we continue to apply it. Understanding their form and mode of operation has become an important concern of scholars of communication.

Computers, by contrast, rely on algorithms. An algorithm is a solution procedure which, if followed correctly, yields a correct answer.

The rule of thumb most relevant to my concerns here is the availability heuristic. Ease of retrieval increases the likelihood that we will misjudge the probability of the event occurring. Because airplane crashes are presented in vivid detail and kill a large group at one time, for example, a single plane crash is likely to be better remembered than reports of hundreds of passenger car accidents. From this, some mistakenly conclude that it is safer to ride in a car than to fly. In the words of Tversky and Kahneman, the availability heuristic evaluates "the frequency of classes or the probability of events . . . by the ease with which relevant issues come to mind" ("Availability: A Heuristic for Judging Frequency and Probability," *Cognitive Psychology* 5 [1973], 207–232, at 207.)

34. J. A. Easterbrook, "The Effect of Emotion on the Utilization and the Organization of Behavior," *Psychological Review* 66 (1959), 183–201.

35. R. B. Zajonc, "Social Facilitation," *Science* 149 (1965), 269–74.

36. C. J. Neweth, "Differential Contributions of Majority and Minority Influence," *Psychological Review* 93 (1986), 23–32.

37. E. J. Johnson and A. Tversky, "Affect, Generalization, and the Perception of Risk," *Journal of Personality and Social Psychology* 45 (1983), 20–31.

Chapter 2

1. Quoted in David Cushman Coyle, *Ordeal of The Presidency* (Washington, D.C.: Public Affairs Press, 1960), 67.

2. *Correspondence . . . Jackson,* III, 426.

3. Coyle, 199.

4. *A Rhetoric of Motives* (Berkeley: University of California Press, 1950; 1969), 26.

5. Thomas Kessner, *Fiorello H. La Guardia* (New York: Penguin Books, 1989), 407.

6. Washburn, 181.

7. Donald English, *Political Uses of Photography in the Third French Republic 1871–1914* (Ann Arbor: University of Michigan Research Press, 1984), 12.

8. Stanley Kelley, Jr., *Professional Public Relations and Political Power* (Baltimore: Johns Hopkins University Press, 1956), 135.

9. Felknor, 115.

10. David Donald, "The Folklore Lincoln," in Nicholas Cords and Patrick Gerster, *Myth and the American Experience* (Beverly Hills, Calif.: Glencoe Press, 1973), 45.

11. November 11, 1802.

12. In Kessner, *La Guardia,* 122.

13. Hone, 493.

14. G. Salomon, "Television Is 'Easy' and Print Is 'Tough': The Differential Investment of Mental Effort in Learning as a Function of Perceptions and Attributions," *Journal of Educational Psychology* 76 (1984), 647–58.

15. R. Horowitz and S. J. Samuels, "Reading and Listening to Expository Text," *Journal of Reading Behavior* 3 (1985), 185–98.

16. E. Thorson, B. Reeves, and J. Schleuder, "Message Complexity and Attention to Television," *Communication Research* 12 (1985), 427–54; B. Reeves, E. Thorson, and J. Schleuder, "Attention to Television: Psychological Theories and Chronometric Measures," in *Perspectives on Media Effects,* J. Bryant and D. Zillmann, eds. (Hillsdale, N.J.: Lawrence Erlbaum, 1986); A. Lang, "Involuntary Attention and Physiological Arousal Evoked by Structural Features and Emotional Content in TV Commercials," *Communication Research* 17 (1990), 275–99. Evidence from EEGs indicates that our response to some of these formal features is involuntary. Indeed, Reeves et al. (1986) suggest that these features "derive their attentional value through the evolutionary significance of detecting movement."

17. Thorson et al., 1985; M. L. Rothschild, E. Thorson, B. Reeves, J. E. Hirsch, and R. Goldstein, "EEG Activity and the Processing of Television Commercials," *Communication Research* 13 (1986), 182–220.

18. G. B. Armstrong and B. S. Greenberg, "Background Television as an Inhibitor of Cognitive Processing," *Human Communication Research* 16 (1990), 355–86.

19. D. Drew and T. Grimes, "Audio-Visual Redundancy and TV News Recall," *Communication Research* 14 (1987), 452–61.

20. M. Clynes and N. Nettheim, "The Living Quality of Music: Neurobiologic Basis of Communicating Feeling," in *Music, Mind, and Brain, The Neuropsychology of Music*, M. Clynes, ed. (New York: Plenum Press, 1982); S. Hecker, "Music for Advertising Effect," *Psychology and Marketing* 1 (1984), 3–8; A. Mitchell, "Current Perspectives and Issues Concerning the Explanation of 'Feeling' Advertising Effects," in *Nonverbal Communication in Advertising*, S. Hecker and D. Stewart, eds. (Lexington, Mass.: Lexington Books, 1988); E. Thorson and M. Friestad, "The Effects of Emotion on Episodic Memory for Television Commercials," in *Cognitive and Affective Responses to Advertising*, P. Cafferata and A. Tybout, eds. (Lexington, Mass.: Lexington Books, 1989); J. Edell and K. L. Keller, "The Information Processing of Coordinated Media Campaigns," *Journal of Marketing Research* 26 (1988), 149–63.

21. V. C. Ottati and R. S. Wyer, Jr., "The Cognitive Mediators of Political Choice: Toward a Comprehensive Model of Political Information Processing," in *Information and Democratic Processes*, J. A. Ferejohn and J. H. Kuklinski, eds. (Urbana and Chicago: University of Illinois Press, 1990), 186–216.

22. P. Lang, "The Cognitive Psychophysiology of Emotion: Fear and Anxiety," in *Anxiety and the Anxiety Disorders*, eds. A. Tuma and J. Maser (Hillsdale, N.J.: Lawrence Erlbaum, 1985).

23. R. B. Zajonc, "On the Primacy of Affect," *American Psychologist* 39 (1984), 117–23. See also R. Batra and M. L. Ray, "Advertising Situations: Implications of Differential Involvement and Accompanying Affect Responses," in *Information Processing Research on Advertising*, R. J. Harris, ed. (Hillsdale, N.J.: Lawrence Erlbaum, 1983).

24. Roger D. Masters, *The Nature of Politics* (New Haven, Conn.: Yale University Press, 1989), 61–68.

25. C. K. Atkin, L. Bowen, O. B. Nayman, and K. G. Sheinkopf, "Quality versus Quantity in Televised Political Ads," *Public Opinion Quarterly* 40 (1973), 209–24; C. K. Atkin and G. Heald, "Effects of Political Advertising," *Public Opinion Quarterly* 40 (1976), 216–28; S. H. Surlin and T. F. Gordon, "How Values Affect Attitudes Toward Direct Reference Political Advertising," *Journalism Quarterly* 54 (1977), 89–98.

26. Times Mirror Center for the People and the Press, "The Age of Indifference: A Study of Young Americans and How They View the News," June 28, 1990, 28.

27. S. Chaiken, "Communicator Physical Attractiveness and Persuasion," *Journal of Personality and Social Psychology* 38 (1979), 1387–97; R. E. Petty, J. T. Cacioppo, and D. Schumann, "Central and Peripheral Routes to Advertising Effectiveness: The Moderating Role of Involvement," *Journal of Consumer Research* 10 (1983), 135–46.

28. R. E. Petty, J. T. Cacioppo, and M. Heesacker, "The Use of Rhetorical Questions in Persuasion," *Journal of Personality and Social Psychology* 40 (1981), 432–40.

29. R. E. Petty and J. T. Cacioppo, "The Effects of Involvement on Responses to Argument Quantity and Quality: Central and Peripheral Routes to Persuasion," *Journal of Personality and Social Psychology* 46 (1984), 69–81.

30. Ottati and Wyer, op. cit., 214.

31. Tim Curran, " 'Attack' Ad May Preview '92 GOP Tactics," *Roll Call*, November 4, 1991, 35.

32. October 31, quoted by *Campaign Hotline,* November 1, 1991, 15.

33. Tim Curran, "Allen Clobbers Slaughter in Virginia Special, 62–35%," *Roll Call,* November 7, 1991, 13.

34. H. P. Grice, "Logic and Conversation," in P. Cole and J. L. Morgan, eds., *Syntax and Semantics,* Vol. 3: *Speech Acts* (New York: Seminar Press, 1975), 41–58; D. A. Norman and D. E. Rumelhart, eds. *Explorations in Cognition* (San Francisco: Freeman, 1975).

35. R. J. Harris and G. E. Monaco, "Psychology of Pragmatic Implication: Information Processing Between the Lines, *Journal of Experimental Psychology, General* 107, (1978), 1–27.

36. Daniel M. Wegner, Richard Wenzlaff, R. Michael Kerker, and Ann E. Beattie, "Incrimination Through Innuendo: Can Media Questions Become Public Answers?" *Journal of Personality and Social Psychology* 40:5 (1981), 822–32.

37. S. M. Miller, "Monitoring and Blunting: Validation of a Questionnaire to Assess Styles of Information Seeking Under Threat," *Journal of Personality and Social Psychology* 52 (1987), 345–53; M. P. Zanna and J. M. Olson, "Individual Differences in Attitudinal Relations," in *Consistency in Social Behavior: The Ontario Symposium,* Vol. 1 (Hillsdale, N.J.: Lawrence Erlbaum, 1982), 75–103.

38. A major focus of the studies of processing has asked when people would process messages systematically or centrally, a mode of processing that requires attention, understanding, and elaboration upon the content of the message. Central processing is likely to occur "as a result of a person's careful and thoughtful consideration of the true merits of the information presented in support of an advocacy." Peripheral processing is likely to occur "as a result of some simple cue in the persuasion context (e.g., an attractive source) that induced [attitude] change without necessitating scrutiny of the central merits of the issue-relevant information presented" (Richard E. Petty and John T. Cacioppo, *Communication and Persuasion: Central and Peripheral Routes to Attitude Change* [London: Springer-Verlag, 1986], p. 3). This model of persuasion presupposes that as our motivation or ability to process an argument decreases, peripheral cues become more powerful in effecting persuasion; correlatively, under argumentative scrutiny, peripheral cues are less powerful. Motivation, interest, and involvement determine how we will process information.

39. D. Axsom, S. Yates, and S. Chaiken, "Audience Response as a Heuristic Cue in Persuasion," *Journal of Personality and Social Psychology* 53 (1987), 30–40; S. Chaiken, "The Heuristic Model of Persuasion," in *Social Influence: The Ontario Symposium,* M. P. Zanna, J. M. Olson, and C. P. Herman, eds., Vol. 5 (Hillsdale, N.J.: Lawrence Erlbaum, 1987), 3–39.

40. R. E. Petty, T. M. Ostrom, and T. C. Brock, eds., *Cognitive Responses in Persuasion* (Hillsdale, N.J.: Lawrence Erlbaum, 1981).

41. Clark and Clark.

Chapter 3

1. Eliot R. Smith, "Content and Process Specificity in the Effects of Prior Experiences," in *Advances in Social Cognition,* Thomas Srull and Robert S. Wyer, Jr., eds. Vol. 3 (Hillsdale, N.J.: Lawrence Erlbaum, 1990), 48.

2. *Psychopathology and Politics* (New York, 1960), 184.

3. This argument is persuasively advanced by Joseph R. Gusfield.

4. Billington, 210, in Lipset, 54.

5. Seymour Martin Lipset and Earl Raab, *The Politics of Unreason* (New York: Harper & Row, 1970), 144.

6. Evans and Novak column quoted by Jody Powell, 268.

7. M. Horwitz and J. M. Rabbie, "Individuality and Membership in the Intergroup System," in H. Tajfel, ed., *Social Identity and Intergroup Relations* (New York: Columbia University Press, 1982). This summary of Horwitz and Rabbie appears in Elisha Y. Babad et al. *The Social Self: Group Influences on Personal Identity* (Beverly Hills, Calif.: Sage, 1983), 109.

8. M. Rothbart and O. P. John, "Social Categorization and Behavioral Episodes: A Cognitive Analysis of the Effects of Intergroup Contact," *Journal of Social Issues* 41 (1985), 81–104.

9. Ibid.

10. See, for example, Paul Sniderman, *Personality and Democratic Politics* (Berkeley: University of California Press, 1975).

11. John L. Sullivan, James E. Piereson, and George E. Marcus, "A Reconceptualization of Political Tolerance: Illusory Increases, 1950's–1970's," *American Political Science Review* 73 (1982), 93.

12. Ibid.

13. Michael Wallace, "The Uses of Violence in American History," in Nicholas Cords and Patrick Gerster, *Myth and the American Experience* (Beverly Hills, Calif.: Glencoe Press, 1973), 407.

14. William Leuchtenburg, "Progressivism and Imperialism: The Progressive Movement and American Foreign Policy, 1898–1916," in Cords and Gerster, *Myth and the American Experience*, 208.

15. M. J. Heale, *American Anticommunism: Combating the Enemy Within, 1830–1970* (Baltimore: Johns Hopkins University Press, 1990), 12.

16. Caro, 48–49.

17. September 23, 1984. Charlotte N.C., transcript from audio tape.

18. *West Virginia State Board of Education v. Barnette*, 319 U.S. 642 (1943).

19. The candidate was Michael A. Musmanno. See Beers, 271.

20. Felknor, 78.

21. Bennett, 103.

22. Hofstadter, 21.

23. Loucks, 106.

24. Quoted by Kessner, *LaGuardia*, 104.

25. Cf. Morse, *Foreign Conspiracy against the Liberties of the United States*, 59–106; Morse, *Imminent Dangers to the Free Institutions of the United States*, 12–28.

26. The book was published in New York by Howe and Bates, 1836. For a discussion of its circulation and impact see Allen Churchill, "The Awful Disclosures of Maria Monk," *American Mercury* 27 (January 1936), 94–98.

27. Billington, 104–17.

28. Quoted by Peter Shaw in *American Patriots and the Rituals of Revolution* (Cambridge, Mass.: Harvard University Press, 1981), 16.

29. See *Congressional Record*, February 15, 1913.

30. Smith, *Campaign Addresses, 1928*, 53–57.

31. "The Southern One-Party System and National Politics," *Journal of Politics* 4 (February 1942), 80.

32. Published by Knopf, 665–75.

33. See Julius Marcus Bloch, *Miscegenation, Melaleukation, and Mr. Lincoln's Dog* (New York, 1958).

34. Franklin and Moss, 227.

35. *Washington Post,* November 5, 1898.

36. Frederick L. Hoffman, "Race Traits and Tendencies of the American Negro," *Publication of the American Economic Association* 11 (August 1896), 241 ff.

37. Fredrickson, 274. This section of this chapter is indebted heavily to Fredrickson's important book.

38. Cited by Fredrickson, 274–75.

39. See N. S. Shaler, "The Negro Since the Civil War," *Popular Science Monthly* 57 (May 1900), 38–39.

40. Felknor, 52.

41. Stanley Cohen, *Rebellion Against Victorianism: The Impetus for Cultural Change in 1920s America* (New York: Oxford University Press, 1991).

42. Catledge, 104.

43. Fulbright, 90.

44. Interview, September 21, 1978.

45. Charles P. Taft, "Campaign to Stop the Campaign Smear," *New York Times Magazine,* October 12, 1958, 11, 82–84.

46. *Washington Post* and *Times Herald,* January 9, 1957.

47. Felknor, 74.

48. Black and Black, 286–87.

49. Quoted by Goldfield, 179.

50. *Washington Post* (August 5, 1987), A20.

51. Letter to Benjamin Rush, February 2, 1807, in *Dialogues of John Adams and Benjamin Rush, 1805–1813,* John A. Schutz, ed. (San Marino, 1966), 76.

52. Kessner, 407.

53. *Constructing the Political Spectacle,* 84.

54. Ibid., 84.

55. Pack, 100.

56. *Scoundrel Time* (New York: Little, Brown, 1976).

57. Jesse Helms, letter to supporters, August 2, 1983.

58. Finlay, Holstoi, and Fagen, 19.

59. Snider, 136–37.

60. Quoted by Schieffer and Gates, 268.

61. *The Advancement of Learning,* W. A. Wright, ed. (Oxford: Clarendon Press, 1900), 201.

62. Ann Devroy and Tom Kenworthy, "GOP Aide Quits Over Foley Memo," *Washington Post,* June 8, 1989, A10.

63. Donald Strong, "Alabama: Transition and Alienation," in *The Changing Politics of the South,* William Havard, ed. (Baton Rouge: Louisiana State University Press, 1972), 439.

64. Ibid., 189.

65. Quoted by Zatarain, 17.

66. AP, "Profile: David Duke," *Ruston Daily Leader,* November 15, 1991, 5.

67. AP, "NAAWP Still Operating Out Of David Duke's Office," *Alexandria Town Talk,* November 16, 1991, D-10.

68. Ibid.

69. "Rally: Duke Says All Must Work Together," *Town Talk,* November 11, 1991, A-2.

70. "Debate," *Sunday Advocate,* November 3, 1991, 4A.

71. Robert Morgan, "Campaign Issues Overshadowed," *Alexandria Daily Town Talk,* November 16, 1991, D1.

72. James Varney, "Runoff Turns to Racial Issues," *Times-Picayune,* October 24, 1991, A-9.

73. Marsha Shuler, "Past Dominates Debate," *Sunday Advocate,* November 3, 1991, 1.

74. Mark Schleifstein and Sheila Grissett, "Religious Leaders Doubt Duke's Christianity," *Times-Picayune,* November 13, 1991, 1.

75. "Duke Speaks at Local Rally," *Alexandria Daily Town Talk,* November 11, 1991, 1.

76. John Margolis, "Edwards Bandwagon Too Full?" *Alexandria Daily Town Talk,* November 13, 1991. Opinion page.

77. Mark Lorando, "WDSU Reporter Flooded by Calls for Grilling Duke," *Times-Picayune,* November 8, 1991, A-8.

78. AP, "Profile: David Duke," *Ruston Daily Leader,* November 15, 1991, 5.

79. Anthony Lewis, "Politics of Hate Come Calling," *Alexandria Town Talk,* November 12, 1991. Opinion page.

80. Cited by Frances Frank Marcus, "White-Supremacist Group Fills a Corner in Duke Campaign," *New York Times,* November 14, 1991, B12.

81. "(Same Old) New Duke," *New York Times,* November 13, 1991, A25.

82. "The Voiders: Who They Are and What They Think," *Times-Picayune,* November 10, 1991, 1.

83. AP, "Contributions Come Pouring In," *Town Talk,* November 16, 1991, A2.

84. "Time for Some Changes," Julie George. Colfax, in *Alexandria Daily Town Talk,* November 16, 1991, A6.

85. Lavina Perry, Forest Lawn in "Campaign Forum," *Town Talk,* November 15, 1991, A-9.

86. James D. Lawson, Tioga, "Campaign Forum," *Town Talk,* November 11, 1991, A-7.

87. Joseph Baker, "Duke Past Fine with Supporters," *Times-Picayune,* November 15, 1991, B-9.

88. Kevin Bell and Chris Adams, "Time for Peace, Duke Foes Say," *Times-Picayune,* November 17, 1991, A-6.

89. Richard J. Neathamer, "Duke Has Good Ideas," *Times-Picayune,* November 15, 1991, B-9.

90. Ibid., A-4.

91. Ibid.

92. Thomas B. Edsall, "Mississippi Win Boosts GOP in South," *Washington Post,* November 7, 1991, A32.

93. Ibid.

94. D. L. Martin, "Racial Voting in 1990: Helms v. Gantt for U.S. Senator in North Carolina and Legislative Term Limitation in California." Paper presented to the American Political Science Association, Washington, D.C., August 29–September 1, 1991.

95. Ibid., 2.

96. Information on impact provided by Gantt's pollster Michael Donlon.

97. D. R. Kinder and L. M. Sanders, "Mimicking Political Debate with Survey Questions: The Case of White Opinion on Affirmative Action for Blacks," *Social Cognition* 8 (1990), 73–103; L. Bobo and J. R. Kluegel, "Modern American Prej-

udice: Stereotypes, Social Distance, and Perceptions of Discrimination Toward Blacks, Hispanics, and Asians." Paper presented to the American Sociological Association, Cincinnati, Ohio, August 1991.

98. T. E. Nelson and D. R. Kinder, "Framing and Policy Debate," Paper presented to the American Psychological Association, Boston, August 10–14, 1990. See also Chapters 12 and 13 in P. Sniderman, R. A. Brody, and P. E. Tetlock, *Reasoning and Choice* (Cambridge: Cambridge University Press, 1991), 223–60.

99. D. R. Kinder and T. Mendelberg, "Cracks in Apartheid? Prejudice, Policy and Racial Isolation in Contemporary American Politics." Paper presented to the American Political Science Association, Washington, D.C., August 30, 1991, 9.

100. Ibid., 9–10.

101. Ibid., 13.

102. P. M. Sniderman, M. G. Hagen, P. E. Tetlock, and H. E. Brade, "Reasoning Chains: Causal Models of Policy Reasoning in Mass Publics," *British Journal of Political Science* 16 (1986), 405–30.

103. G. S. Wood, "Conspiracy and Paranoid Style: Causality and Deceit in the Eighteenth Century," *William and Mary Journal* 39 (1982), 401–41. Quote is at 441.

104. Quoted by Edsall and Edsall, *Atlantic Monthly,* 56.

105. James Truslow Adams, "Our Whispering Campaigns," *Harper's Magazine,* September 1932, 447–48.

106. Billington, 194–95; in Lipset et al., 48.

Chapter 4

1. Berelson, Lazarsfeld, and McPhee, 308.

2. Downs, 100.

3. A. Tversky and D. Kahneman, "Judgment Under Uncertainty: Heuristics and Biases," *Science* 185 (1974), 1124–31. The early work in this area was done by H. Simon who coined the term "satisficing" to account for shortcutting decisions. Cf. *Administrative Behavior: A Study of Decision-Making Processes in Administrative Organizations* (New York: Free Press, 1945).

4. H. E. Brady and P. M. Sniderman, "Attitude Attribution: A Group Basis for Political Reasoning, *American Political Science Review* 79 (1985), 1061.

5. M. Fiorina, *Retrospective Voting in American National Elections* (New Haven, Conn.: Yale University Press, 1981).

6. *Washington Post*, Sept. 21, 1990, A1.

7. Cf. W. J. McGuire, "The Effectiveness of Supportive and Refutational Defenses in Immunizing and Restoring Beliefs Against Persuasion," *Sociometry* 24 (1961), 184–97; W. J. McGuire and D. Papageorgis, "The Relative Efficacy of Various Types of Prior Belief Defense in Producing Immunity Against Persuasion," *Journal of Abnormal and Social Psychology* 62 (1961), 327–37; M. Pfau and M. Burgoon, "Inoculation in Political Campaign Communication," *Human Communication Research* 15 (1988), 91–111; Michael Pfau and Henry C. Kenski, *Attack Politics: Strategy and Defense* (New York: Praeger, 1990).

8. W. J. McGuire and D. Papageorgis, "Effectiveness in Forewarning in Developing Resistance to Persuasion," *Public Opinion Quarterly* 26 (1962), 24–34.

9. J. L. Freedman and D. O. Sears, "Warning, Distraction, and Resistance to Influence," *Journal of Personality and Social Psychology* 1 (1965), 262–66.

10. Selvini Palazzoli M.D., "Comments," *Family Process* 20 (1981), 44–45, at 45.

11. P. Watzlawick, J. H. Weakland, and R. Fisch, *Change: Principles of Problem Formation and Problem Resolution* (New York: Norton, 1974).

12. E. Jessee, G. J. Jurkovic, J. Wilkie, and M. Chiglinsky, "Positive Reframing with Children," *American Journal of Orthopsychiatry* 52 (1982), 314–22.

13. Dan Rose, "How the 1983 Mayoral Election Was Won," in *The Making of the Mayor: Chicago, 1983,* Melvin G. Holli and Paul M. Green, eds. (Grand Rapids, Mich.: W. B. Eerdmans, 1984), 119–20.

14. J. Fabry, R. Bulka, and W. Sahakian, eds. *Logotherapy in Action* (New York: Aronson, 1979).

15. Code of Professional Ethics of the American Association of Political Consultants, 1989.

Chapter 5

1. This conclusion is consistent with that of scholarship about recall of advertising and of television. Cf. D. S. Hayes and S. Pingree, "Television's Influence on Social Reality," in D. Pearl and J. Lazar, *Television and Behavior* (Washington, D.C.: U.S. Government Printing Office, 1982), 224–47; D. S. Hayes and D. W. Birnbaum, "Preschoolers' Retention of Televised Events: Is a Picture Worth a Thousand Words?" *Developmental Psychology* 16 (1980), 410–16; D. S. Hayes, B. E. Chemelaki, and D. W. Birnbaum, "Young Children's Incidental Retention of Televised Events," *Developmental Psychology* 17 (1981), 230–32; K. Pezdek and E. F. Hartman, "Children's Television Viewing: Attention and Comprehension of Auditory Versus Visual Information," *Child Development* 54 (1983), 1015–23.

The evidence does not suggest that the visual interferes with comprehension of the audio, however. Cf. D. R. Rolandelli, "Children and Television: The Visual Superiority Effect Reconsidered," *Journal of Broadcasting and Electronic Media* 33 (1989), 69–81; C. Hoffner, J. Cantor, and E. Thorson, "Children's Responses to Conflicting Auditory and Visual Features of a Televised Narrative," *Human Communication Research* 16:2, (1989), 256–78. There is evidence that the visual imagery of television changes the processing of audio. Cf. J. Beagles-Roos and I. Gat, "Specific Impact of Radio and Television on Children's Story Comprehension," *Journal of Educational Psychology* 75 (1983), 128–35.

Some have argued that Iyengar and Kinder's research calls the impact of vivid communication into question. Their summary of the existing scholarly literature states that "When vividness is defined as the contrast between personalized, case history information and abstract statistical information, the vividness hypothesis is supported every time" (p. 35). The structure of their chapter seems to suggest that they then take issue with this consensus. Yet they conclude that "Our results do not argue against vividness effects in general; they indicate only that dramatic vignettes of personal suffering do not enhance agenda setting" (p. 46). See S. Iyengar and D. Kinder, *News that Matters* (Chicago: University of Chicago Press, 1987).

Additional information on verbal/visual processing can be found in Laura M. Buchholz and Robert E. Smith, "The Role of Consumer Involvement in Determining Cognitive Response to Broadcast Advertising," *Journal of Advertising* 20:1 (1991), 4–17, and Julie Edell and Kevin Lane Keller, "The Information Processing of Coordinated Media Campaigns," *Journal of Marketing Research* 26 (May 1989), 149–63.

2. Samuel Taylor Coleridge, *Shakespeare Criticism,* Middleton Raysor, ed. (London: Dutton, 1907).

3. Cf. *The Philosophy of Literary Form,* 3rd ed. (Berkeley: University of California Press, 1973), 3 ff.

4. Robert James Bidinotto, "Getting Away With Murder," *Reader's Digest* 133 (July 1988), 57–63.

5. Susan Forrest, "How 12 Hours Shattered Two Lives," *Lawrence Eagle-Tribune,* August 16, 1987.

6. See N. S. Johnson and J. M. Mandler, "A Tale of Two Structures: Underlying and Surface Forms in Stories," *Poetics* 9 (1980), 51–86.

7. "Furloughs From Common Sense," *New York Times,* June 30, 1988, A22; Robin Toner, "Prison Furloughs in Massachusetts Threaten Dukakis Record on Crime," *New York Times,* July 5, 1988, B5.

8. "1987 Annual Statistical Report of the Furlough Program," Massachusetts Department of Correction, December 1988, 6.

9. 103CMR-157. February 2, 1990, 3.

10. Cf. Gerald Boyd, "Bush's Attack on Crime Appeals to the Emotions," *New York Times,* October 11, 1988, 12: "In addition, Mr. Bush's campaign has aired television commercials that portray the prison system in Massachusetts, where Mr. Dukakis is the Governor, as a revolving door that releases inmates on weekend passes." Gerald Boyd "Despite Vow to be 'Gentler,' Bush Stays on Attack," *New York Times,* October 29, 1988, 8: "Mr. Fuller said that although Mr. Bush hoped to end the campaign on a 'positive note,' there were no plans to remove television commercials like the one that accuses Mr. Dukakis of operating the Massachusetts prison program as a 'revolving door.' "

11. *The Media in the 1984 and 1988 Presidential Campaigns,* Guido H. Stempel III and John W. Windhauser, eds. (New York: Greenwood Press, 1991), 169. Note the tacit assumption that because the man is white, his fiancée must be white as well.

12. "Weekend Prison Passes," produced by Larry McCarthy for Americans for Bush.

13. Entman, 30.

14. *Sourcebook,* 1988, 298. Table 3.17.

15. *U.S. Dept. of Justice "Criminal Victimization in the United States, 1988."* December 1990. NCJ-122024. Table 43.

16. Edsall and Edsall, *Chain Reaction,* 236.

Chapter 6

1. *Campaign for President: The Managers Look at '88,* 142.

2. These races include the 1989 New Jersey gubernatorial, New York mayoral, and Virginia gubernatorial races, the 1990 Texas, California, and Pennsylvania gubernatorial races, and North Carolina, Massachusetts, and Illinois senatorial races.

3. *Campaign for President: The Managers Look at '88,* 136.

4. See, for example, K. Renckstorff, "Nachrichtensendungen eine empirische Studie zur Wirkung unterschiedlicher Darstellung in Fernsehnachrichten," *Me-*

dia Perspektiven (January 1977), 27–42; M. Edwardson, D. Grooms, and S. Proudlove, "Television News Information Gain from Interesting Videos and Talking Heads," *Journal of Broadcasting* 25 (1981), 15–24; C. Berry, "A Dual Effect of Pictorial Enrichment in Learning from Television News," *Journal of Educational Television* 9 (1983), 171–74.

5. CBS News/*New York Times* Poll, Released January 25, 1988, 19.

6. Interview, September 25, 1991.

7. Arnold Hamilton, "Fuming White Shifts Gears: He Changes Schedule to Answer Richards' Allegations," 33A.

8. David Elliot, "TV Tactics Leave Some Candidates Tuned Out," A1/A14.

9. R. N. Shepherd, "Recognition Memory for Words, Sentences and Pictures," *Journal of Verbal Learning and Verbal Behavior* 6 (1967), 156–63.

10. S. D. Reese, "Visual-Verbal Redundancy Effects on Television News Learning," *Journal of Broadcasting* 28 (1984), 79–87. See also E. Katz, H. Adoni, and P. Parness, "Remembering the News: What the Picture Adds to Recall," *Journalism Quarterly* 54 (1977), 231–39. E. Kozminsky, "Altering Comprehension: The Effect of Biasing Titles on Text Comprehension," *Memory and Cognition* 6 (1977), 482–90.

11. M. Dhawan and J. W. Pelligrino, "Acoustic and Semantic Interference Effects in Words and Pictures," *Memory and Cognition* 5 (1977), 340–46.

12. See Walter DeVries and V. Lance Tarrance, *The Ticket Splitter: A New Force in American Politics* (Grand Rapids, Mich.: William B. Eerdmans, 1972).

13. Ibid., 15.

14. Ibid., 119.

15. *Washington Post*, October 20, 1988, A27.

16. The survey was conducted by The Wirthlin Group and reported in the *Times-Picayune*, November 13, 1991, A-11.

17. Tyler Bridges, "Loss Isn't The End For Duke," *Times-Picayune*, November 17, 1991, A-6.

18. "Edwards Money from La." *Times-Picayune*, November 25, 1991, A-12.

19. *Times-Picayune*, November 3, 1991, A-39. I wish to thank Professors Kathleen Turner, Mary F. Hopkins, and James Mackin of Tulane University for their assistance in gathering materials on this election.

20. Dennis McGrath is co-author of *The New Democratic Politics: Paul Wellstone and the Progressive Agenda* (1992) and my source on the Minn. campaign.

21. Campaign Hotline, October 15, 1991, 13.

22. October 15, 1991, quoted in Hotline, op. cit.

23. Michael deCourcy Hinds, "Ads and Attacks Rise in Pennsylvania Senate Race," *New York Times*, November 1, 1991, A19.

Chapter 7

1. Frank E. Gannett Lecture, Washington, D.C., November 28, 1988.

2. *Grammar*, 472; *Critical Inquiry* 4 (1978), 809–38.

3. J. Crocker, S. T. Fiske, and S. E. Taylor, "Schematic Bases of Belief Change," In J. R. Eiser, ed. *Attitudinal Judgment* (New York: Springer, 1984), 197.

4. Marvin Minsky, "A Framework for Representing Knowledge," in Patrick A. Winston, ed. *The Psychology of Computer Vision* (New York: McGraw-Hill, 1975); Donald Kinder and Lynn M. Sanders, "Mimicking Political Debate with Survey

Questions: The Case of White Opinion on Affirmative Action for Blacks," *Social Cognition* 8 (1990), 73–103.

5. Robert Axelrod, "Schema Theory: An Information Processing Model of Perception and Cognition," *American Political Science Review* 67 (1973), 1248–66.

6. Roger Schank and Robert Abelson, *Scripts, Plans, Goals and Understanding: An Inquiry into Human Knowledge Structures* (Hillsdale, N.J.: Lawrence Erlbaum, 1977).

7. Ibid.

8. Donald R. Kinder, Mark D. Peters, Robert P. Abelson, and Susan T. Fiske, "Presidential Prototypes," *Political Behavior* 2 (1980), 315–37.

9. J. S. Picek, S. J. Sherman, and R. M. Shiffrin, "Cognitive Organization and Encoding of Social Structures," *Journal of Personality and Social Psychology* 31 (1975), 758–68.

10. Helen Markus, "Self-Schemata and Processing Information about the Self," *Journal of Personality and Social Psychology* 35 (1977), 63–78.

11. Helen Markus and Joseph Smith, "The Influence of Self-Schemas on the Perception of Others," in Nancy Cantor and John Kihlstrom, eds. *Personality, Cognition, and Social Interaction* (Hillsdale, N.J.: Lawrence Erlbaum, 1981).

12. See M. Fayol, "The Notion of 'Script': From General to Developmental and Social Psychology," *Cahiers de Psychologie Sociale* 8 (1988), 335–62.

13. Graber, *Mass Media and American Politics* 221.

14. *The Mass Media Election* (New York: Praeger, 1980), 105.

15. Two groups in Texas (1 in Dallas, 1 in Austin), one group in Chicago, one group in Manhattan, one group in Baltimore, one group in Minneapolis, one group in San Francisco, one group in Eugene, one group in Atlanta, one group in Salt Lake City. Each group contained ten individuals plus a non-responding moderator. Two of the six additional individuals were substitutes invited to participate when someone else could not attend. Four were "guests" brought to no more than two meetings by one of the focus group members. These six individuals have been excluded from all tracking reports.

16. Robinson and Sheehan, 148.

17. Interview by Robert Sheer, *Playboy* 23, November 1976, 66.

18. Dave Denison, "Prime-Time Politics: Why TV News Doesn't Get the Picture," *Texas Observer* (December 21, 1990), 5.

19. Frank E. Gannett Lecture, Washington, D.C., November 28, 1988.

20. Safire, 692.

21. P. Meyer, "Precision Journalism and the 1988 U.S. Election," *International Journal of Public Opinion Research* 1 (1989), 195–205. Quote is at 196.

22. Lichter, Amundson, and Noyes, 65.

23. "Public Polls and Election Participants," *Polling and Presidential Election Coverage*, Paul J. Lavrakas and Jack K. Holley, eds. (Newbury Park, Cal.: Sage, 1991), 101.

24. For an excellent discussion see F. Christopher Arterton, "Campaign Organizations Confront the Media Environment," in *Race for the Presidency: The Media and the Nominating Process*, James David Barber, ed. (Englewood Cliffs, N.J.: Prentice-Hall, 1978).

25. Sam Donaldson, "On The Dukakis Campaign Trail," *The Gannett Center Journal* (Fall 1988), 96.

26. Ibid., 100.

27. *Why Americans Hate Politics* (New York: Simon & Schuster, 1991), 332.

28. *Dallas Times Herald,* October 1, 1988. Quoted by Campaign Hotline, October 3, 1988.

29. Campaign Hotline, October 11, 1988, 8.

30. Campaign Hotline, October 17, 1988, 7.

31. *Miami Herald,* in Campaign Hotline, October 17, 1988, 7.

32. Campaign Hotline, October 17, 1988, 8.

33. For perceptive analyses of the functioning of sports, game, and war metaphors in political campaigns, see Jane Blankenship, "The Search for the 1972 Democratic Nomination: A Metaphoric Perspective," in Jane Blankenship and Hermann G. Stelzner, eds., *Rhetoric and Communication* (Urbana: University of Illinois Press, 1976); Jane Blankenship and Jong Guen Kang, "The 1964 Presidential and Vice Presidential Debates: The Printed Press and 'Construction' by Metaphor," *Presidential Studies Quarterly* 21(2), (Spring 1991), 307–18.

34. Quoted by M. Fitzgerald, "Autopsy of 1988 Campaign Reporting: Journalists and Politicians Meet in Iowa to Dissect Coverage," *Editor and Publisher* (December 8, 1988), 14–15.

35. Jerome Bruner, *Acts of Meaning* (Cambridge, Mass.: Harvard University Press, 1990), 45.

36. Dionne, 17.

37. Blumenthal, 3.

38. *The Politics of Rich and Poor: Wealth and the American Electorate in the Reagan Aftermath* (New York: Random House, 1990), ix.

Chapter 8

1. For a synthesis of the findings supporting this conclusion see Iyengar and Kinder, *News that Matters* (Chicago: University of Chicago Press, 1987), Chap. 7.

2. Shanto Iyengar, *Is Anyone Responsible: How Television Frames Political Issues* (Chicago: University of Chicago Press, 1991).

3. Ibid., 2.

4. Cf. Doris Graber, *Mass Media and American Politics* (Washington, D.C.: Congressional Quarterly Press, 1980; 1989); Doris Graber, "Press and TV as Opinion Resources in Presidential Campaigns," *Public Opinion Quarterly* 40 (1976), 285–303; Thomas Patterson and Robert McClure, *The Unseeing Eye: The Myth of Television Power in National Elections* (New York: Putnam, 1976); James Stovall, "Coverage of the 1984 Presidential Campaign," *Journalism Quarterly* 63 (1986), 443–49, 484; John M. Russonello and Frank Wolf, "Newspaper Coverage of the 1976 and 1968 Presidential Campaigns," *Journalism Quarterly* 56 (1979), 360–64, 432.

5. Bruce Buchanan, *Electing a President: The Markle Commission Research on Campaign '88* (Austin: University of Texas Press, 1991), 39.

6. Thomas Patterson, *The Mass Media Election* (New York: Praeger, 1980).

7. Larry M. Bartels, *Presidential Primaries and the Dynamics of Public Choice* (Princeton, N.J.: Princeton University Press, 1988), 42.

8. Mark Hertsgaard, *On Bended Knee* (New York: Farrar, Straus & Giroux, 1988), 267.

9. *Newsweek,* September 26, 1988, 25.

10. *Newsweek,* October 31, 1988, 27.

11. *Newsweek,* October 10, 1988, 42.

12. For a summary of the relationship between perceived goal and form of processing see Thomas K. Srull and Robert S. Wyer, "The Role of Chronic and Temporary Goals in Social Information Processing," in Richard M. Sorrentino and E. Tory Higgins, eds., *Handbook of Motivation and Cognition* (New York: Guilford Press, 1986).

13. Robert Wyer, Thomas K. Srull, Sallie E. Gordon, and Jon Hartwick, "Effects of Processing Objectives on the Recall of Prose Material," *Journal of Personality and Social Psychology* 43 (1982), 674–88.

14. John H. Lingle and Thomas M. Ostrom, "Retrieval Selectivity in Memory-Based Impression Judgments," *Journal of Personality and Social Psychology* 37 (1979), 180–94.

15. *Processing The News*, 66.

16. Susan Feeney, "Making, Breaking Promises," *Dallas Morning News*, October 27, 1991, 1/24A.

17. See *News That Matters*.

Chapter 9

1. B. I. Page, "The Theory of Political Ambiguity," *American Political Science Review* 70 (1976), 742–52; B. I. Page, *Choices and Echoes in Presidential Elections: Rational Man and Electoral Democracy* (Chicago: University of Chicago Press, 1978). See also K. A. Shepsle, "The Strategy of Ambiguity: Uncertainty and Electoral Competition," *American Political Science Review* 66 (1972), 555–68. For evidence that ambiguity can hurt a candidate, see J. Enelow and M. J. Hinich, "A New Approach to Voter Uncertainty is the Downsian Spatial Model," *American Journal of Political Science*, 25 (1981), 483–93.

2. *The Campaign for President: The Managers Look at '88*, ed. D. R. Runkel (Dover, Mass.: Auburn House, 1989).

3. *New York Times*, October 30, 1988, 30.

4. For elaboration of this claim, see *Eloquence in An Electronic Age*, Chap. 1.

5. Kiku Adatto, "Sound Bite Democracy: Network Evening News Presidential Campaign Coverage, 1968 and 1988" (Joan Shorenstein Barone Center, John F. Kennedy School of Government, Harvard University, Cambridge, Mass., June 1990); Daniel Hallin, *Sound Bite News: Television Coverage of Elections, 1968–88* (Woodrow Wilson Media Studies Project, Washington, D.C., 1990).

6. "Noonan Q and A: What She Said at the University," *New York Times*, August 5, 1990, E5.

7. See *Presidential Debates: The Challenge of Creating an Informed Electorate*.

8. The conclusion is based on an analysis of the transcripts of the debates.

9. Unless otherwise indicated, the transcripts of quoted news segments were obtained from the networks and checked for accuracy against videotapes secured from the Vanderbilt Archive.

10. "TV and the Elections," *The Cable Guide* (March 1992), 14. October 9, 1991. Clip aired on CNN.

11. Quoted by Rowland Evans, Jr., and Robert D. Novak, *Nixon in the White House: The Frustration of Power* (New York: Random House, 1971), 148.

12. *Debates and Proceedings in the Congress of the United States, 1789–1824* (Washington, D.C.: 1834–1856), (5th Congress), 3776–77.

13. Ibid., 2960–61.

14. Immanuel Kant, "Perpetual Peace," In Hans Reiss, ed., *Kant's Political Writings* (Cambridge, Mass.: Cambridge University Press, 1970), 126ff.

15. (1644) In *Complete Prose Works* (New Haven, Conn.: Yale University Press, 1959), Vol. 2, 561.

16. *The Papers of Benjamin Franklin,* ed. Leonard W. Labaree (New Haven, Conn.: Yale University Press, 1959); I, 194–95; II, 260.

17. 376 U.S. 254 (1964).

18. R. Dahl, "Procedural Democracy," pp. 104 ff.

19. Charles Arthur Willard, *A Theory of Argumentation,* (Tuscaloosa and London: University of Alabama Press, 1989), 2.

20. D. J. O'Keefe, "Two Concepts of Argument," *Journal of the American Forensic Association* 13 (1977), 121–28.

21. Stephen Toulmin, *The Uses of Argument* (Cambridge: Cambridge University Press, 1990), 97.

22. *Between Past and Future* (1968), 238.

23. S. E. Toulmin, R. Rieke, and A. Janik, *An Introduction to Reasoning* (New York: Macmillan, 1979), 158.

24. *The Essential Lippmann* (Cambridge, Mass.: Harvard University Press, 1982), 196.

25. *Packaging,* 431.

26. In the category "spot ad" I include all "paid televised programming produced by the candidate *or* by the candidate's party or by a political action committee" from ten to sixty seconds long to benefit one of the two major party candidates in the general election (any time after the first candidate's convention but before election day). This includes both nationally and regionally aired ads as well as Spanish-language ads. When only the use of Spanish distinguishes a Spanish from an English version of an ad, I have not coded it twice. When either the visual or the audio track add content not found in one of the languages, I have treated it as a separate ad. Where a sixty- and thirty-second version of the same ad exists, I have counted them as the same ad. Where a five-minute and sixty-, thirty-, fifteen-, or ten-second lift exists I have counted the five-minute as a distinct ad.

The second coding problem occurs when an ad does not air in the form that was created but does air in another context. The Pledge ad for Bush did not air in its original form at all but did air within the election eve Bush telecast in 1988. I have coded it as produced but not aired.

The third coding problem occurs in 1980 when the Reagan campaign was called on a minor error in its biographical ad. Two San Francisco newspapers merge on Sundays. The ad accurately quoted a statement in the Sunday paper but identified the quote as appearing in the other paper. The change was made. Because the ads are not substantively different as a result, I have counted that as (SP) a single time.

The fourth coding problem occurs in 1968 and 1976. In both years the Democrats aired ads inviting a comparison of the vice presidential nominees. The ads can be seen as advocacy of the positive choice of one candidate or alternatively as an implied attack on the other. Since the assumption of both ads is that the ad's claim will damage the opposing ticket, I have coded both OPP.

The final coding problem occurs in 1972. Tony Schwartz created three versions of an ad showing a woman carrying a napalmed baby. Kissinger's voice occurs in one; the question of a child in another. Because the differences between the first and second version are minor I have coded them as a single ad. I have counted the ad with the child's voice as a separate ad because that inclusion substantively alters the ad's structure and appeals.

27. In "News Media Critique Themselves: Many Reporters Unhappy with Campaign '88 Coverage," *Christian Science Monitor,* December 9, 1988, 3.

28. Michael Oreskes, "Candidates and Media at Odds Over Message," *New York Times,* October 4, 1988, 14.

29. David Broder of the *Washington Post,* Stephen Hess of the Brookings Institute, Haynes Johnson of the *Washington Post,* George Reedy, former press secretary to Lyndon Johnson and emeritus professor of Journalism at Marquette University, and Bob Shogan of the *Los Angeles Times* are among the individuals who helped me piece this together.

30. Interviews, see note 29. Thanks also to Ray Donovan and Bob Scheer.

31. See, for example, Dole, "Meet the Press," September 12, 1976.

32. "Today Show," NBC, February 7, 1972.

33. Erlichman, 327–28.

34. O'Brien, 333.

35. Cf. S. Merritt, "Negative Political Advertising: Some Empirical Findings," *Journal of Advertising* 13 (1984), 27–38; G. M. Garramone, "Effects of Negative Political Advertising: The Roles of Sponsors and Rebuttal," *Journal of Broadcasting and Electronic Media* 29 (1985), 147–59.

36. July 26, 1781, in *The Writings of Benjamin Franklin,* Albert H. Smythe, ed., Vol. 8 (New York: Macmillan, 1905–1907), 457.

37. Coyle, 337.

38. Samuel Popkin, *The Reasoning Voter* (Chicago: University of Chicago Press, 1991.

39. S. Kernell, "Presidential Popularity and Negative Voting: An Alternative Explanation of the Midterm Congressional Decline of the President's Party," *American Political Science Review* 71 (1977), 44–66.

Chapter 10

1. "Memorandum for Mr. Bundy," February 11, 1963. Reprinted in *JFK Wants to Know: Memos From the President's Desk, 1961–1963,* Edward B. Claflin, ed. (New York: William Morrow, 1991), 239.

2. Blight and Welch, 242.

3. Blight and Welch, 116.

4. *No Final Victories,* 73.

5. Burns, 159.

6. See Oral History, Joseph Rauh, Kennedy Presidential Library.

7. Cf. *New York Times,* July 5, 1960, and Parmet, *JFK,* 18 ff.

8. In Jamieson, *Packaging,* 137.

9. *New York Times,* May 23, 1955, 1.

10. See interview with Dr. Estelle Ramey in my *Packaging the Presidency,* 138.

11. Bright et al., 47.

12. Robert Kennedy, *Thirteen Days,* 46ff.

13. Interview with Dean Rusk, in *On the Brink: Americans and Soviets Reexamine the Cuban Missile Crisis,* James G. Blight and David A. Welch, eds. (New York: Farrar, Straus & Giroux, 1989; 1990), 180.

14. Roscoe Gilpatric, Kennedy Presidential Library. Oral History.

15. The statement is Kennedy's in his speech to the nation, October 22, 1962.

16. See also "White House Transcripts and Minutes of the Cuban Missile Crisis," *International Security* 10(1) (Summer 1985), 164–203; "October 27, 1962: Transcripts of the Meetings of the ExComm," *International Security* 12(3) (Winter 1987/88), 30–92.

17. Transcripts, October 27, 1962, 12ff; 51ff.

18. "Presidential Recordings. Transcripts. Cuban Missile Crisis Meetings, October 16, 1962, 27; hereafter cited as "Transcripts."

19. Sorenson, *Kennedy*, 712.

20. Telephone interview, November 20, 1991.

21. Page, 156ff.

22. FCC *Report to the Congress of the United States, March 1 1961,* Senate Committee on Interstate and Foreign Commerce, 87th Cong., 1st Sess., 115.

23. Quoted by John B. Judis, "LBJ: The First Hurrahs," *Washington Post Book World* (July 21, 1991), 7. The original citation appears in Robert Dallek's *Lone Star Rising: Lyndon Johnson and His Times 1908–1960* (New York: Oxford University Press, 1991).

24. Moyers' files, LBJ Library. Filed June 2, 1964.

25. Ibid., no pages.

26. LBJ Press Conference, September 9, 1964, in *Papers*.

27. Moyers' files, LBJ Library, Box 53 (1359). "Coordinating Washington News Briefings with Presidential Speeches out Around the Country," June 23, 1964, 1.

28. Assistant Secretary of State William P. Bundy revealed this to the Senate two years after the Resolution was passed. See Wise, 28.

29. Press conference June 2, 1964, in *Papers*.

30. Cited by Wise, 44.

31. Interview, Dec. 3, 1991.

32. Tom Wicker, *New York Times* (August 5, 1964), 1.

33. See Max Frankel, "Campaign Effect on Vietnam Policy Is Denied by Rusk," *New York Times,* October 9, 1964, 1.

34. "Washington: What Are Our War Aims in South Vietnam?" *New York Times,* October 2, 1964, 36.

35. Max Frankel, "Campaign Effect on Vietnam Policy Is Denied by Rusk," *New York Times,* October 9, 1964, 1, 2.

36. Files of Bill Moyers, LBJ Library, Box 53 (1359). "Re: Current Political Situation," July 28, 1964, 4.

37. Goldwater, *With No Apologies*, 200.

38. February 21, 1965.

39. White, 1973, 365.

40. "MacNeil/Lehrer NewsHour," November 8, 1988.

41. G. Markus, "Political Attitudes During An Election Year: A Report on the 1980 NES Panel Study," *American Political Science Review,* 76 (1982), 538–60.

42. "MacNeil/Lehrer NewsHour," November 4, 1988.

43. "MacNeil/Lehrer NewsHour," September 5, 1988.

44. George Bush, October 24, 1988, Waterbury, Connecticut.

45. These statements are contained in the "factsheet" titled "Verification for 'Tank' Ad" issued by the Bush campaign, January 14, 1988.

46. Quoted by Devlin (1989).

47. Kathleen Hall Jamieson and David Birdsell, *Presidential Debates: The Challenge of Creating an Informed Electorate* (New York: Oxford University Press, 1988).

48. On the "MacNeil/Lehrer NewsHour," excerpted on "Nightline," November 9, 1988.

49. Michael Kelly, "Perot Stresses Homey Image, But the Image Is No Accident," *New York Times* (May 16, 1992), I, A14.

Bibliography

Abramson, Paul, John Aldrich, and David Rohde. *Change and Continuity in the 1988 Elections.* Rev. ed. Washington, D.C.: Congressional Quarterly Press, 1991.

Adams, James Truslow. "Our Whispering Campaigns." *Harper's Magazine,* September 1932, 447–48.

Adams, John. Letter to Benjamin Rush, February 2, 1807. In *Dialogues of John Adams and Benjamin Rush, 1805–1813,* ed. John A. Schutz. San Marino, 1966.

Adatto, Kiku. "Sound Bite Democracy: Network Evening News Presidential Campaign Coverage, 1968 and 1988." Research paper, Shoronstein Barone Center, John F. Kennedy School of Government, Harvard University, Cambridge, Massachusetts, June 1990.

Alter, Robert. *The Pleasures of Reading in an Ideological Age.* New York: Simon & Schuster, 1989.

Ambrose, Stephen E. *Nixon: The Triumph of a Politician 1962–1972.* New York: Simon & Schuster, 1989.

Aptheker, Herbert, ed. *A Documentary History of the Negro People in the United States,* Vol. 2. New York: Carol Publishing Group, 1951.

Armstrong, G. Blake and Bradley S. Greenberg. "Background Television as an Inhibitor of Cognitive Processing." *Human Communication Research* 16 (Spring 1990): 355–86.

Arterton, F. Christopher. "Campaign Organizations Confront the Media Environment." In *Race for the Presidency: The Media and the Nominating Process,* ed. James David Barber. Englewood Cliffs, N.J.: Prentice-Hall, 1978, 3–25.

Associated Press. "Profile: David Duke." *Ruston Daily Leader,* November 15, 1991, 5.

Associated Press. "Contributions Come Pouring In." *Alexandria Town Talk,* November 16, 1991, A2.

Associated Press. "NAAWP Still Operating Out of David Duke's Office." *Alexandria Town Talk,* November 16, 1991, D10.

Atkin, Charles and Gary Heald. "Effects of Political Advertising." *Public Opinion Quarterly* 40 (Summer 1976): 216–28.

Atkin, Charles K., Lawrence Bowen, Oguz B. Nayman, and Kenneth G. Sheinkopf. "Quality versus Quantity in Televised Political Ads." *Public Opinion Quarterly* 38 (Summer 1973): 209–24.

Axelrod, Robert. "Schema Theory: An Information Processing Model of Perception and Cognition." *American Political Science Review* 67 (December 1973): 1248–66.

Axsom, Danny, Suzanne Yates, and Shelley Chaiken. "Audience Response as a Heuristic Cue in Persuasion." *Journal of Personality and Social Psychology* 53 (July 1987): 30–40.

Babad, Elisha Y., Max Birnbaum, and Kenneth D. Benne. *The Social Self: Group Influences on Personal Identity.* Beverly Hills, Calif.: Sage, 1983.

Baker, Joseph. "Duke Past Fine with Supporters." *Times-Picayune,* November 15, 1991, B9.

Bartels, Larry M. *Presidential Primaries and the Dynamics of Public Choice.* Princeton, N.J.: Princeton University Press, 1988.

Batra, R. and M. L. Ray. "Advertising Situations: Implications of Differential Involvement and Accompanying Affect Responses." In *Information Processing Research on Advertising,* ed. Richard J. Harris. Hillsdale, N.J.: Lawrence Erlbaum, 1983, 127–51.

Beagles-Roos, C. J. and I. Gat. "Specific Impact of Radio and Television on Children's Story Comprehension." *Journal of Educational Psychology* 75 (1983), 128–35.

Beers, Paul B. *Pennsylvania Politics: Today and Yesterday.* University Park: Pennsylvania State University Press, 1980.

Bell, Kevin and Chris Adams. "Time for Peace, Duke Foes Say." *Times-Picayune,* November 17, 1991, A6.

Bennett, David H. *The Party of Fear.* New York: Vintage Books, 1990.

Bennett, W. L. and M. Edelman. "Toward a New Political Narrative." *Journal of Communication* 35 (1985), 156–171.

Berelson, Bernard, Paul Lazarsfeld, and William McPhee. *Voting: A Study of Opinion Formation in a Presidential Campaign.* Chicago: University of Chicago Press, 1954.

Berry, C. "A Dual Effect of Pictorial Enrichment in Learning from Television News." *Journal of Educational Television,* 9 (1983): 171–74.

Bidinotto, Robert James. "Getting Away With Murder." *Reader's Digest* 133 (July 1988), 57–63.

Billington, Ray Allen. *The Protestant Crusade 1800–1860.* New York: Rinehart 1938; Chicago: Quadrangle Books, 1964.

Black, Christine M. and Thomas Oliphant. *All by Myself: The Unmaking of a Presidential Campaign.* Chester, Conn.: Globe Pequot Press, 1989.

Black, Earl and Merle Black. *Politics and Society in the South.* Cambridge, Mass.: Harvard University Press, 1987.

Blankenship, Jane. "The Search for the 1972 Democratic Nomination: A Metaphoric Perspective." In *Rhetoric and Communication,* eds. Jane Blankenship and Hermann G. Stelzner. Urbana: University of Illinois Press, 1976, 236–60.

Blankenship, Jane and Jong Guen Kang. "The 1964 Presidential and Vice Presidential Debates: The Printed Press and 'Construction' by Metaphor." *Presidential Studies Quarterly* 21 (Spring 1991): 307–18.

Blight, James G. and David A. Welch, eds. *On the Brink: Americans and Soviets Reexamine the Cuban Missile Crisis.* New York: Farrar, Straus & Giroux, 1989.

Bloch, Julius Marcus. *Miscegenation, Melaleukation, and Mr. Lincoln's Dog.* New York: Schaum, 1958.

Blumenthal, Sidney. *Pledging Allegiance: The Last Campaign of the Cold War.* New York: HarperCollins, 1990.

Bobo, L. and J. R. Kluegel. "Modern American Prejudice: Stereotypes, Social Distance, and Perceptions of Discrimination Toward Blacks, Hispanics and Asians." Paper presented to the American Sociological Association, Cincinnati, Ohio, August 23–27, 1991.

Boorstin, Daniel. *The Genius of American Politics.* Chicago: University of Chicago Press, 1953.

Boyd, Gerald M. "Bush's Attack on Crime Appeals to the Emotions." *New York Times,* October 11, 1988, 12.

Boyd, Gerald. "Despite Vow to Be 'Gentler,' Bush Stays on Attack." *New York Times,* October 29, 1988, 8.

Brady, H. E. and P. M. Sniderman. "Attitude Attribution: A Group Basis for Political Reasoning." *American Political Science Review* 79 (1985), 1061–78.

Bridges, Tyler. "Loss Isn't the End for Duke." *Times-Picayune,* November 17, 1991, A6.

Bruner, Jerome. *Actual Minds, Possible Worlds.* Cambridge, Mass.: Harvard University Press, 1986.

Bruner, Jerome. *Acts of Meaning.* Cambridge, Mass.: Harvard University Press, 1990.

Bryce, James. *The American Commonwealth* Vol. 2. London and New York: Macmillan, 1890.

Buchanan, Bruce. *Electing a President: The Markle Commission Research on Campaign '88.* Austin: University of Texas Press, 1991.

Buchholz, Laura M. and Robert E. Smith. "The Role of Consumer Involvement in Determining Cognitive Response to Broadcast Advertising." *Journal of Advertising* 20:1 (1991), 4–17.

Burke, Kenneth. *The Philosophy of Literary Form,* 3d ed. Berkeley: University of California Press, 1973.

Burke, Kenneth. *A Grammar of Motives.* Berkeley: University of California Press, 1945, 1969.

Burkholder, Steve. "The *Lawrence Eagle-Tribune* and the Willie Horton Story." *Washington Journalism Review* 11 (July/August 1989): 14–19.

Burns, James MacGregor. *John Kennedy: A Political Profile.* New York: Harcourt, Brace, 1959.

Camus, Albert. *Sur l'Avenir de la tragedie.* In *Theatre, recits, nouvelles.* Paris: Pleide, 1963.

Caplan, Harry. *Of Eloquence: Studies in Ancient and Medieval Rhetoric.* Ithaca, N.Y.: Cornell University Press, 1970.

Cappella, Joseph N. and Richard L. Street, Jr. "Message Effects: Theory and Research on Mental Models of Messages." In *Message Effects in Communication Studies,* ed. James J. Bradac. Newbury Park, Calif.: Sage, 1989, 24–51.

Carmines, Edward G. and James H. Kuklinski. "Incentives, Opportunities, and the Logic of Public Opinion in American Political Representation." In *Information and Democratic Processes,* eds. John A. Ferejohn and James H. Kuklinski. Urbana and Chicago: University of Illinois Press, 1990, 240–68.

Caro, Robert A. *The Years of Lyndon Johnson: Means of Ascent.* New York: Vintage Books, 1990.

Carter, Jimmy. Interview by Robert Sheer. *Playboy,* November 1976, 66.

Catledge, Turner. *My Life and Times.* New York: Harper & Row, 1971.

CBS News/New York Times Poll. Released January 25, 1988, 19.

Chaiken, Shelley. "Communicator Physical Attractiveness and Persuasion." *Journal of Personality and Social Psychology* 38 (August 1979): 1387–97.

Chaiken, Shelley. "The Heuristic Model of Persuasion." In *Social Influence: The Ontario Symposium,* Vol. 5, eds. Mark P. Zanna, J. M. Olson, and C. Peter Herman. Hillsdale, N.J.: Lawrence Erlbaum, 1987, 3–39.

Chaiken, Shelley, A. Liberman, and A. H. Eagly. "Heuristic and Systematic Information Processing Within and Beyond the Persuasion Context." In *Unintended Thought,* eds. James S. Uleman and John A. Bargh. New York: Guilford Press, 1989, 242–52.

Churchill, Allen. "The Awful Disclosures of Maria Monk." *American Mercury* 27 (January 1936): 94–98.

Cialdini, Robert B. *Influence: The New Psychology of Modern Persuasion.* New York: Quill, 1984.

Clark, Herbert H. and Eve V. Clark. *Psychology and Language.* New York: Harcourt Brace Jovanovich, 1977.

Clynes, Manfred and N. Nettheim. "The Living Quality of Music: Neurobiologic Basis of Communicating Feeling." In *Music, Mind, and Brain, The Neuropsychology of Music,* ed. Manfred Clynes. New York: Plenum Press, 1982.

Code of Professional Ethics of the American Association of Political Consultants, 1989.

Cohen, Stanley. *Rebellion Against Victorianism: The Impetus for Cultural Change in 1920s America.* New York: Oxford University Press, 1991.

Coleridge, Samuel Taylor. *Shakespeare Criticism.* Middleton Raysor, ed. London: Dutton, 1907.

Colfax, Julie George. "Time for Some Changes." *Alexandria Daily Town Talk,* November 16, 1991, A6.

Condit, C. M. "Crafting Virtue: The Rhetorical Construction of Public Morality." *Quarterly Journal of Speech* 73 (1987), 79–97.

Congressional Record, February 15, 1913.

Coyle, David Cushman. *Ordeal of the Presidency.* Washington, D.C.: Public Affairs Press, 1960.

Crocker, J., S. T. Fiske, and S. E. Taylor. "Schematic Bases of Belief Change." In *Attitudinal Judgment,* ed. J. Richard Eiser. New York: Springer-Verlag, 1984, 197–226.

Crowder, Robert G. *Principles of Learning and Memory.* Hillsdale, N.J.: Lawrence Erlbaum, 1976.

Curran, Tim. "Allen Clobbers Slaughter in Virginia Special, 62–35%." *Roll Call,* November 7, 1991, 13.

Curran, Tim. " 'Attack' Ad May Preview '92 GOP Tactics." *Roll Call,* November 4, 1991, 35.

Dahl, Robert Alan. *Modern Political Analysis,* 2nd ed. Englewood Cliffs, N.J.: Prentice-Hall, 1970.

Dahl, R. "Procedural Democracy." In James Fishkin, *Democracy and Deliberation: New Directions For Democratic Reform.* New Haven: Yale University Press, 1992.

Dallek, Robert. *Lone Star Rising: Lyndon Johnson and His Times, 1908–1960.* New York: Oxford University Press, 1991.

"Debate." *Sunday Advocate,* November 3, 1991, 4A.

Debates and Proceedings in the Congress of the United States, 1789–1824. Washington, D.C.: 1834–1856, 5th Congress.

Devlin, L. Patrick. "Contrasts in Presidential Campaign Commercials of 1988." *American Behavioral Scientist* 32(4) (March/April 1989), 389–414.

DeVries, Walter and V. Lance Tarrance. *The Ticket Splitter: A New Force in American Politics.* Grand Rapids, Mich.: Eerdmans, 1972.

Devroy, Ann and Tom Kenworthy. "GOP Aide Quits Over Foley Memo." *Washington Post,* June 8, 1989, A10.

Dewey, John. *The Public and Its Problems.* New York: Holt, 1927.

Dhawan, M. and J. W. Pelligrino. "Acoustic and Semantic Interference Effects in Words and Pictures." *Memory and Cognition* 5 (1977): 340–46.

Dionne, E. J., Jr. *Why Americans Hate Politics.* New York: Simon & Schuster, 1991.

Donald, David. "The Folklore Lincoln." In *Myth and the American Experience,* Nicholas Cords and Patrick Gerster. Beverly Hills, Cal.: Glencoe Press, 1973, 231–42.

Donaldson, Sam. "On the Dukakis Campaign Trail." *Gannett Center Journal* 2 (Fall 1988): 87–118.

Douglass, Frederick. *Narrative of the Life of Frederick Douglass, An American Slave, Written by Himself.* New York: Doubleday, 1845, 1963.

Dowd, Maureen. "Bush Portrays His Opponent as Sympathetic to Criminals." *New York Times,* October 8, 1988, 9.

Downs, Anthony. *An Economic Theory of Democracy.* New York: Harper & Row, 1957.

Drew, Dan and T. Grimes. "Audio-Visual Redundancy and TV News Recall." *Communication Research* 14 (1987): 452–61.

Drew, Dan and David Weaver. "Voter Learning in the 1988 Presidential Election: Did the Debates and the Media Matter?" *Journalism Quarterly* 68 (Spring/Summer 1991): 27–37.

"Duke Speaks at Local Rally." *Alexandria Daily Town Talk,* November 11, 1991, 1.

Dyer, Joe, Jr. "Edwards Predicts Victory." *State-Times/Morning Advocate,* November 16, 1991, 8A.

Dyer, Scott. "Crowd Cheers for Duke." *State-Times/Morning Advocate,* November 16, 1991, 8A.

Easterbrook, J. A. "The Effect of Emotion on the Utilization and the Organization of Behavior." *Psychological Review* 66 (1959): 183–201.

Edell, Julie A. and Kevin Lane Keller. "The Information Processing of Coordinated Media Campaigns." *Journal of Marketing Research* 26 (1989): 149–63.

Edelman, Murray. *Constructing the Political Spectacle*. Chicago: University of Chicago Press, 1988.

Edelman, Murray. *The Symbolic Uses of Politics*. Urbana: University of Illinois Press, 1974.

Edsall, Thomas B. "Mississippi Win Boosts GOP in South." *Washington Post*, November 7, 1991, A32.

Edsall, Thomas Byrne with Mary D. Edsall. "Race." *Atlantic Monthly* 267 (May 1991), 53–86.

Edsall, Thomas Byrne and Mary D. Edsall. *Chain Reaction: The Impact of Race, Rights, and Taxes on American Politics*. New York: Norton, 1991.

"Edwards Money from La." *Times-Picayune*, November 25, 1991, A12.

Edwardson, M., D. Grooms, and S. Proudlove. "Television News Information Gain from Interesting Videos and Talking Heads." *Journal of Broadcasting* 25 (1981): 15–24.

"Election." *Times-Picayune*, November 12, 1991, A6.

Elliot, David. "TV Tactics Leave Some Candidates Tuned Out." *Austin American-Statesman*, March 11, 1990, A1, A14.

Enelow, J. and M. J. Hinich. "A New Approach to Voter Uncertainty in the Downsian Spatial Model." *American Journal of Political Science* 25 (1981), 483–93.

English, Donald. *Political Uses of Photography in the Third French Republic, 1871–1914*. Ann Arbor: University of Michigan Research Press, 1984.

Entman, Robert M. "Modern Racism and the Images of Blacks in Local Television News." *Critical Studies in Mass Communication* 7(4), (December 1990), 332–45.

Erlichman, John. *Witness to Power: The Nixon Years*. New York: Simon & Schuster, 1982.

Fabry, J., R. Bulka, and W. Sahakian, eds. *Logotherapy in Action*. New York: Aronson, 1979.

Fayol, M. "The Notion of 'Script': From General to Developmental and Social Psychology." *Cahiers de Psychologie Sociale* 8 (1988): 335–62.

Federal Communications Commission. *Report to the Congress of the United States, March 1, 1961*. Senate Committee on Interstate and Foreign Commerce, 87th Cong. 1st Sess.

Feeney, Susan. "Making, Breaking Promises." *Dallas Morning News*, October 27, 1991, 1/24A.

Felknor, Bruce L. *Dirty Politics*. New York: Norton, 1966.

Finlay, David, Ole Holstoi, and Richard Fagen. *Enemies in Politics*. Chicago: Rand McNally, 1967.

Fiorina, M. *Retrospective Voting in American National Elections*. New Haven, Conn.: Yale University Press, 1981.

Fisher, W. R. *Human Communication as Narrative*. Columbia: University of South Carolina Press, 1987.

Fitzgerald, M. "Autopsy of 1988 Campaign Reporting: Journalists and Politicians Meet in Iowa to Dissect Coverage." *Editor and Publisher*, December 8, 1988, 14–15.

Forrest, Susan. "How 12 Hours Shattered Two Lives." *Lawrence Eagle-Tribune*, August 16, 1987.

Frankel, Max. "Campaign Effect on Vietnam Policy Is Denied by Rusk." *New York Times,* October 9, 1964, 1, 2.

Franklin, Benjamin. *The Writings of Benjamin Franklin,* Vol. 8. Edited by Albert H. Smythe. New York: Macmillan, 1905–1907.

Franklin, Benjamin. *The Papers of Benjamin Franklin.* Edited by Leonard W. Labaree. New Haven, Conn.: Yale University Press, 1959.

Franklin, John Hope and Alfred A. Moss, Jr. *From Slavery to Freedom: A History of Negro Americans.* New York: McGraw-Hill, 1988.

Frederickson, George M. *The Black Image in the White Mind.* New York: Harper Torchbooks, 1971.

Freedman, J. L. and D. O. Sears. "Warning, Distraction, and Resistance to Influence." *Journal of Personality and Social Psychology* 1 (1965), 262–66.

Fulbright, J. William. *The Price of Empire.* New York: Pantheon Books, 1989.

"Furloughs From Common Sense." *New York Times,* June 30, 1988, A22.

Garramone, G. M. "Effects of Negative Political Advertising: The Roles of Sponsors and Rebuttal." *Journal of Broadcasting and Electronic Media* 29 (1985), 147–59.

Geertz, Clifford. "Blurred Genres: The Reconfiguration of Social Thought." In *Local Knowledge.* New York: Basic Books, 1983, 19–35.

Genovese, Eugene D. *Roll Jordan Roll: The World the Slaves Made.* New York: Vintage Books, 1972.

Goldfield, David R. *Black, White, and Southern: Race Relations and Southern Culture 1940 to the Present.* Baton Rouge: Louisiana State University Press, 1990.

Goldwater, Barry M. *With No Apologies.* New York: Berkeley Books, 1979.

Graber, Doris. "Press and TV as Opinion Resources in Presidential Campaigns." *Public Opinion Quarterly* 40 (Fall 1976): 285–303.

Graber, Doris. *Mass Media and American Politics.* Washington, D.C.: Congressional Quarterly Press, 1980, 1989.

Graber, Doris. *Processing the News: How People Tame the Information Tide,* 2nd ed. New York: Longman, 1988.

Grice, H. P. "Logic and Conversation." In *Syntax and Semantics,* Volume 3: *Speech Acts,* eds. P. Cole and J. L. Morgan. New York: Seminar Press, 1975, 41–58.

Gusfield, Joseph R. *Symbolic Crusade.* Urbana: University of Illinois Press, 1963.

Hailey, Mike. "Crime Victims Condemn Dukakis." *Austin American-Statesman,* October 11, 1988, B3.

Hallin, Daniel. "Sound Bite News: Television Coverage of Elections, 1968–1988." Occasional Paper, Media Studies Project, Woodrow Wilson International Center for Scholars, Washington, D.C., 1990.

Hamilton, Arnold. "Fuming White Shifts Gears: He Changes Schedule to Answer Richards' Allegations." *Dallas Morning News,* March 10, 1990, 33A.

Harris, Richard J. and G. E. Monaco. "Psychology of Pragmatic Implication: Information Processing Between the Lines." *Journal of Experimental Psychology: General* (1978): 107, 1–27.

Hayes, D. S. and D. W. Birnbaum. "Preschoolers' Retention of Televised Events: Is a Picture Worth a Thousand Words?" *Developmental Psychology* 16 (1980), 410–16.

Hayes, D. S., B. E. Chemelaki, and D. W. Birnbaum. "Young Children's Incidental Retention of Televised Events." *Developmental Psychology* 17 (1981), 230–32.

Hayes, D. S. and S. Pingree. "Television's Influence on Social Reality." In *Television and Behavior*, eds. D. Pearl and J. Lazar. Washington, D.C.: U.S. Government Printing Office, 1982, 224–47.

Heale, M. J. *American Anticommunism: Combating the Enemy Within, 1830–1970.* Baltimore: Johns Hopkins University Press, 1990.

Hecker, S. "Music for Advertising Effect." *Psychology and Marketing* 1 (1984): 3–8.

Heinemann, Margot. *Puritanism and Theatre*. Cambridge: Cambridge University Press, 1980.

Hellman, Lillian. *Scoundrel Time*. Boston: Little, Brown, 1976.

Helms, Jesse. Letter to supporters, August 2, 1983.

Hertsgaard, Mark. *On Bended Knee*. New York: Farrar, Straus & Giroux, 1988.

Hickman, Harrison. "Public Polls and Election Participants." In *Polling and Presidential Election Coverage*, eds. Paul J. Lavrakas and Jack K. Holley. Newbury Park, Calif.: Sage, 1991, 100–33.

Higgins, E. T., J. A. Bargh, and W. Lombardi. "Nature of Priming Effects on Categorization." *Journal of Experimental Psychology: Learning, Memory, and Cognition* 11 (1985), 59–69.

Higgins, E. Tory, William S. Rholes, and Carl R. Jones. "Category Accessibility and Impression Formation." *Journal of Experimental Social Psychology* 13 (March 1977), 141–54.

Hinds, Michael deCourcy. "Ads and Attacks Rise in Pennsylvania Senate Race." *New York Times*, November 1, 1991, A19.

Hoffman, Frederick Ludwig. "Race Traits and Tendencies of the American Negro." *Publications of the American Economic Association* 11 (August 1896).

Hoffner, C., J. Cantor, and E. Thorson. "Children's Responses to Conflicting Auditory and Visual Features of a Televised Narrative." *Human Communication Research* 16:2 (1989), 256–78.

Hofstadter, Richard. *The Paranoid Style in American Politics and Other Essays*. New York: Knopf, 1965.

Hone, Philip. *The Diary of Philip Hone: 1828–1851*, ed. Allan Nevins. New York: Dodd, Mead, 1927; Reprinted New York: Kraus Reprint Co., 1969.

Horowitz, R. and S. J. Samuels. "Reading and Listening to Expository Text." *Journal of Reading Behavior* 3 (1985): 185–98.

Horsman, Reginald. *Race and Manifest Destiny*. Cambridge, Mass.: Harvard University Press, 1981.

Horwitz, M. and J. M. Rabbie. "Individuality and Membership in the Intergroup System. In *Social Identity and Intergroup Relations*, ed. Henri Tajfel. New York: Columbia University Press, 1982, 241–74.

Hudson, Hoyt Hopewell. "The Folly of Erasmus." In *The Praise of Folly*, Desiderius Erasmus, translated with an essay and commentary by Hoyt Hopewell Hudson. New York: Modern Library, 1941.

Hume, Britt. "News Media Critique Themselves: Many Reporters Unhappy with Campaign '88 Coverage." *Christian Science Monitor*, December 9, 1988, 3.

Irish, Marion. "The Southern One-Party System and National Politics." *Journal of Politics* 4 (February 1942).

Iyengar, Shanto and Donald Kinder. *News that Matters: Television and American Opinion*. Chicago: University of Chicago Press, 1987.

Iyengar, Shanto. *Is Anyone Responsible? How Television Frames Political Issues.* Chicago: University of Chicago Press, 1991.

Jackson, Andrew. *Correspondence of Andrew Jackson,* ed. John Spencer Bassett. Washington, D.C.: Carnegie Institution, 1926–1935.

Jamieson, Kathleen Hall. "For Televised Mendacity, This Year Is the Worst Ever." *Washington Post,* October 30, 1988, C1, C2.

Jamieson, Kathleen Hall. *Eloquence in an Electronic Age.* New York: Oxford University Press, 1988.

Jamieson, Kathleen Hall. *Packaging the Presidency.* New York: Oxford University Press, 1984, 1992.

Jamieson, Kathleen Hall and David S. Birdsell. *Presidential Debates: The Challenge of Creating an Informed Electorate.* New York: Oxford University Press, 1988.

Jansen, Sue Curry. *Censorship: The Knot that Binds Power and Knowledge.* New York: Oxford University Press, 1988.

Jepson, Christopher and Shelly Chaiken. "Chronic Issue-Specific Fear Inhibits Systematic Processing of Persuasive Communications." In *Communication, Cognition, and Anxiety,* ed. Melanie Booth-Butterfield. Newbury Park, Calif.: Sage, 1990, 61–84.

Jessee, E., G. J. Jurkovic, J. Wilkie, and M. Chiglinsky. "Positive Reframing with Children." *American Journal of Orthopsychiatry* 52 (1982), 314–22.

"Johnson Backers Urge Health Test." *New York Times,* July 5, 1960, 19.

Johnson, Eric J. and Amos Tversky. "Affect, Generalization, and the Perception of Risk." *Journal of Personality and Social Psychology* 45 (July 1983): 20–31.

Johnson, Lyndon B. Press Conference, June 2, 1964. In *Public Papers of the Presidents of the United States: Lyndon B. Johnson, Book I.* Washington, D.C.: U.S. Government Printing Office, 1965.

Johnson, Lyndon B. Press Conference, September 9, 1964. In *Public Papers of the President of the United States: Lyndon B. Johnson, Book II.* Washington, D.C.: U.S. Government Printing Office, 1965, 1052–57.

Johnson, Mark. *The Body in the Mind: The Bodily Basis of Meaning, Imagination, and Reason.* Chicago: University of Chicago Press, 1987.

Johnson, N. S. and J. M. Mandler. "A Tale of Two Structures: Underlying and Surface Forms in Stories." *Poetics* 9 (1980): 51–86.

Judis, John B. "LBJ: The First Hurrahs." *Washington Post Book World,* July 21, 1991.

Kagay, Michael R. "As Candidates Hunt the Big Issue, Polls Can Give Them a Few Clues." *New York Times,* October 20, 1991, 3.

Kant, Immanuel. "Perpetual Peace." In *Kant's Political Writings.* Edited by Hans Reiss. Cambridge: Cambridge University Press, 1970.

Katz, Elihu, Hanna Adoni, and Pnina Parness. "Remembering the News: What the Picture Adds to Recall." *Journalism Quarterly* 54 (Summer 1977): 231–39.

Kellermann, Kathy. "The Negativity Effect and Its Implications for Initial Interaction." *Communication Monographs* 51 (March 1984): 37–55.

Kelley, Stanely, Jr. *Professional Public Relations and Political Power.* Baltimore: Johns Hopkins University Press, 1956.

Kelso, Iris. "Fair Play and Foul Play in Campaign Television Ads." *Times-Picayune,* November 17, 1991, B11.

Kennedy, John F. "Memorandum for Mr. Bundy," February 11, 1963. In *JFK*

Wants to Know: Memos from the President's Office, 1961–1963. Edited by Edward B. Claflin. New York: Morrow, 1991.

Kennedy, Robert F. *Thirteen Days: A Memoir of the Cuban Missile Crisis*. New York: Norton, 1969.

Kernell, S. "Presidential Popularity and Negative Voting: An Alternative Explanation of the Midterm Congressional Decline of the President's Party." *American Political Science Review* 71 (1977), 44–66.

Kessner, Thomas. *Fiorello H. La Guardia*. New York: Penguin Books, 1989.

Key, V. O. *Southern Politics in State and Nation*. New York: Knopf, 1949.

Kinder, Donald R. and T. Mendelberg. "Cracks in Apartheid? Prejudice, Policy and Racial Isolation in Contemporary American Politics." Paper presented to the American Political Science Association, Washington, D.C., August 30, 1991.

Kinder, Donald and Lynn M. Sanders. "Mimicking Political Debate with Survey Questions: The Case of White Opinion on Affirmative Action for Blacks." *Social Cognition* 8 (1990): 73–103.

Kinder, Donald R., Mark D. Peters, Robert P. Abelson, and Susan T. Fiske. "Presidential Prototypes," *Political Behavior* 2 (1980): 315–37.

Kirkwood, W. G. "Storytelling and Self-Confrontation: Parables as Communication Strategies." *Quarterly Journal of Speech* 69 (1983), 58–74.

Kozminsky, E. "Altering Comprehension: The Effect of Biasing Titles on Text Comprehension." *Memory and Cognition* 5 (1977): 482–90.

Lance, David. "Narration with Words." In *Images and Understanding*, eds. Horace Barlow et al. Cambridge: Cambridge University Press, 1990, 141–53.

Lang, Annie. "Involuntary Attention and Physiological Arousal Evoked by Structural Features and Emotional Content in TV Commercials." *Communication Research* 17 (June 1990): 275–99.

Lang, P. "The Cognitive Psychophysiology of Emotion: Fear and Anxiety." In *Anxiety and the Anxiety Disorders*, eds. A. Tuma and J. Maser. Hillsdale, N.J.: Lawrence Erlbaum, 1985.

Lasswell, Harold D. *Psychopathology and Politics*. New York: Viking Press, 1960.

Lau, R. "Negativity in Political Perception." *Political Behavior* 4 (1982), 353–77.

Lau, R. "Two Explanations for Negativity Effects in Political Behavior." *American Journal of Political Science* 29 (1985), 119–38.

Lau, Richard. "Political Schema, Candidate Evaluations, and Voting Behavior." In *Political Cognition*, eds. Richard Lau and David O. Sears. Hillsdale, N.J.: Lawrence Erlbaum, 1986, 95–126.

Lawson, James D., Tioga. In "Campaign Forum." *Alexandria Town Talk*, November 11, 1991, A7.

Leuchtenburg, William. "Progressivism and Imperialism: The Progressive Movement and American Foreign Policy, 1898–1916." In *Myth and the American Experience*, Nicholas Cords and Patrick Gerster. Beverly Hills, Calif.: Glencoe Press, 1973, 339–56.

Lewis, Anthony. "Bush Campaign's Toll Remains Untallied." *Austin American-Statesman*, October 29, 1988, A14.

Lewis, Anthony. "Politics of Hate Come Calling." *Alexandria Town Talk*, November 12, 1991, opinion page.

Lewis, Anthony. Frank E. Gannett Lecture. Washington, D.C., November 28, 1988.

Lewis, W. F. "Telling America's Story: Narrative Form and the Reagan Presidency." *Quarterly Journal of Speech* 73 (1987), 280–302.

Lichter, S. Robert, Daniel Amundson, and Richard Noyes. *The Video Campaign: Network Coverage of the 1988 Primaries.* Washington, D.C.: American Enterprise Institute, 1988.

Lincoln, Abraham. *The Collected Works of Abraham Lincoln.* Edited by Roy P. Basler. New Brunswick, N.J.: Rutgers University Press, 1953.

Lingle, John H. and Thomas M. Ostrom. "Retrieval Selectivity in Memory-Based Impression Judgments." *Journal of Personality and Social Psychology* 37 (1979): 180–94.

Link, Arthur S. *Wilson: The Road to the White House.* Princeton, N.J.: Princeton University Press, 1947.

Lipset, Seymour Martin and Earl Raab. "George Wallace and the New Nativism." In *The Politics of Unreason.* New York: Harper & Row, 1970, 338–77.

Lipset, Seymour Martin and Earl Raab. *The Politics of Unreason.* New York: Harper & Row, 1970.

Lodge, Milton and Ruth Hamill. "A Partisan Schema for Political Information Processing." *American Political Science Review* 80 (1986): 505–19.

Lorando, Mark. "WDSU Reporter Flooded by Calls for Grilling Duke," *Times-Picayune,* November 8, 1991, A-8.

Loucks, Emerson H. *The Ku Klux Klan in Pennsylvania: A Study in Nativism.* New York: Telegraph Press, 1936.

Louisiana Coalition Against Racism and Nazism. "Some Change Is Only Skin Deep." Paid advertisement in the *Times-Picayune,* November 3, 1991, A39.

MacDonald, J. Fred. *Blacks and White TV.* Chicago: Nelson-Hall, 1983, 1990.

Marcus, Frances Frank. "White-Supremacist Group Fills a Corner in Duke Campaign." *New York Times,* November 14, 1991, B12.

Marcus, Gregory B. "Political Attitudes During An Election Year: A Report on the 1980 NES Panel Study." *American Political Science Review* 76 (1982), 538–60.

Margolis, John. "Edwards Bandwagon Too Full?" *Alexandria Daily Town Talk,* November 13, 1991, opinion page.

Markus, Helen. "Self-Schemata and Processing Information About the Self." *Journal of Personality and Social Psychology* 35 (February 1977): 63–78.

Markus, Helen and Joseph Smith. "The Influence of Self-Schemata on the Perception of Others." In *Personality, Cognition, and Social Interaction,* eds. Nancy Cantor and John Kihlstrom. Hillsdale, N.J.: Lawrence Erlbaum, 1981, 233–62.

Martin, D. L. "Racial Voting in 1990: Helms v. Gantt for U.S. Senator in North Carolina and Legislative Term Limitation in California." Paper presented to the American Political Science Association, Washington, D.C., August 29–September 1, 1991.

Masters, Roger D. *The Nature of Politics.* New Haven, Conn.: Yale University Press, 1989

McGee, M.C. and J. S. Nelson. "Narrative Reason in Public Argument." *Journal of Communication* 35 (1985), 139–155.

McGuire, W. J. "The Effectiveness of Supportive and Refutational Defenses in Immunizing and Restoring Beliefs Against Persuasion." *Sociometry* 24 (1961), 184–97.

McGuire, W. J. and D. Papageorgis. "The Relative Efficacy of Various Types of

Prior Belief Defense in Producing Immunity Against Persuasion. *Journal of Abnormal and Social Psychology* 26 (1961), 327–37.

McGuire, W. J. and D. Papageorgis. "Effectiveness in Forewarning in Developing Resistance to Persuasion." *Public Opinion Quarterly* 26 (1962), 24–34.

McNeely, Dave. "Bush, Dukakis Commercials Becoming Hottest Campaign Issue." *Austin American-Statesman,* October 25, 1988, B3.

Merritt, S. "Negative Political Advertising: Some Empirical Findings." *Journal of Advertising* 13 (1984), 27–38.

Meyer, P. "Precision Journalism and the 1988 U.S. Election." *International Journal of Public Opinion Research* 1 (1989): 195–205.

Miller, Suzanne M. "Monitoring and Blunting: Validation of a Questionnaire to Assess Styles of Information Seeking Under Threat." *Journal of Personality and Social Psychology* 52 (February 1987): 345–53.

Milton, John. "Areopagitica." In *Complete Works.* New Haven, Conn.: Yale University Press, 1959.

Minsky, Marvin. "A Framework for Representing Knowledge." In *The Psychology of Computer Vision,* ed. Patrick A. Winston. New York: McGraw-Hill, 1975.

Mitchell, A. "Current Perspectives and Issues Concerning the Explanation of 'Feeling' Advertising Effects." In *Nonverbal Communication in Advertising,* eds. Sid Hecker and David W. Stewart. Lexington, Mass.: Lexington Books, 1988, 127–43.

Mitchell, Andrea. Speech at the University of Pennsylvania, Philadelphia, October 22, 1990.

Morgan, Robert. "Campaign Issues Overshadowed." *Alexandria Daily Town Talk,* November 16, 1991, D-1.

Morse, Samuel F. B. *Foreign Conspiracy Against the Liberties of the United States.* New York: American Protestant Society, 1944–1946.

Morse, Samuel F. B. *Imminent Dangers to the Free Institutions of the United States.* New York: Clayton, 1953.

Moyers, Bill. "Coordinating Washington News Briefings with Presidential Speeches out Around the Country." Lyndon B. Johnson Library, Box 53 (1359), June 23, 1964.

Moyers, Bill. "Re: Current Political Situation." Lyndon B. Johnson Library, Box 53 (1359), July 28, 1964, 4.

Moyers, Bill. Files in Lyndon B. Johnson Library, June 2, 1964.

Moyers, Bill. Files in Lyndon B. Johnson Library, Box 53 (1359), September 9, 1964, 1.

Moyers, Bill. Files in Lyndon B. Johnson Library, Box 53 (1359), October 3, 1964.

Murray, Joe. "David Duke Makes It Acceptable to Hate." *Alexandria Daily Town Talk,* November 14, 1991, opinion page.

Neathamer, Richard J. "Duke Has Good Ideas." *Times-Picayune,* November 15, 1991, B9.

Nelson, T. E. and Donald R. Kinder. "Framing and Policy Debate." Paper presented to the American Psychological Association, Boston, August 10–14, 1990.

Neweth, C. J. "Differential Contributions of Majority and Minority Influence." *Psychological Review,* 93 (1986): 23–32.

Newhagen, J. and B. Reeves. "Emotion and Memory Response for Negative Political Advertising: A Study of the 1988 Presidential Campaign." Paper presented to the Association for Education in Journalism and Mass Communication, Washington, D.C. 1989.

"1987 Annual Statistical Report of the Furlough Program." Massachusetts Department of Correction, December 1988.

"1989 Annual Statistical Report of the Furlough Program." Massachusetts Department of Correction, January 1991.

"Noonan Q and A: What She Said at the University." *New York Times,* August 5, 1990, E5.

Norman, Donald A. and David E. Rumelhart, eds. *Explorations in Cognition.* San Francisco: Freeman, 1975.

O'Barr, William M. "Language and Politics in a Rural Tanzanian Council." In *Language and Politics,* eds. William M. O'Barr and Jean F. O'Barr. The Hague: Mouton, 1976, 117–133.

O'Brien, Lawrence. *No Final Victories.* New York: Ballantine Books, 1974.

"October 27, 1962: Transcripts of the Meetings of the ExComm." *International Security* 12 (Winter 1987/1988), 30–92.

Oral History, Joseph Rauh, Kennedy Presidential Library.

Oreskes, Michael. "Candidates and Media at Odds Over Message." *New York Times,* October 4, 1988, 14.

Ottati, V. C. and R. S. Wyer, Jr. "The Cognitive Mediators of Political Choice: Toward a Comprehensive Model of Political Information Processing." In *Information and Democratic Processes,* eds. J. A. Ferejohn and J. H. Kuklinski. Urbana and Chicago: University of Illinois Press, 1990, 186–216.

Pack, Robert. *Jerry Brown: The Philosopher Prince.* New York: Stein and Day, 1978.

Page, B. I. "The Theory of Political Ambiguity." *American Political Science Review* 70 (1976), 742–52.

Page, Benjamin. *Choices and Echoes in Presidential Elections: Rational Man and Electoral Democracy.* Chicago: University of Chicago Press, 1978.

Paivio, Allan. "Mental Imagery in Associative Learning and Memory." *Psychological Review* 76 (1969): 241–63.

Paivio, Allan. *Imagery and Verbal Processes.* New York: Holt, Rinehart and Winston, 1971.

Palazzoli, Selvini, M. D. "Comments." *Family Process* 20 (1981), 44–45.

Parmet, Herbert S. *JFK: The Presidency of John F. Kennedy.* New York: Dial Press, 1983.

Patterson, Thomas. *The Mass Media Election.* New York: Praeger, 1980.

Patterson, Thomas and Robert McClure. *The Unseeing Eye: The Myth of Television Power in National Elections.* New York: Putnam, 1976.

Pear, Robert. "Its Eye on Election, White House to Propose Health Care Changes." *New York Times,* November 12, 1991, A20.

Perry, Lavina, Forest Lawn. In "Campaign Forum." *Alexandria Town Talk,* November 15, 1991, A9.

Petty, Richard E. and John T. Cacioppo. "The Effects of Involvement on Responses to Argument Quantity and Quality: Central and Peripheral Routes to Persuasion." *Journal of Personality and Social Psychology* 46 (January 1984): 69–81.

Petty, Richard E., John T. Cacioppo, and D. Schumann. "Central and Peripheral Routes to Advertising Effectiveness: The Moderating Role of Involvement." *Journal of Consumer Research* 10 (1983): 135–46.

Petty, Richard E., John T. Cacioppo, and Martin Heesacker. "The Use of Rhetorical Questions in Persuasion." *Journal of Personality and Social Psychology* 40 (March 1981): 432–40.

Petty, Richard E., Thomas M. Ostrom, and Timothy C. Brock, eds. *Cognitive Responses in Persuasion*. Hillsdale, N.J.: Lawrence Erlbaum, 1981.

Petty, Richard E. and John T. Cacioppo. *Communication and Persuasion: Central and Peripheral Routes to Attitude Change*. London: Springer-Verlag, 1986.

Pezdek, K. and E. F. Hartman. "Children's Television Viewing: Attention and Comprehension of Auditory Versus Visual Information." *Child Development* 54 (1983), 1015–23.

Pfau, M. and M. Burgoon. "Innoculation in Political Campaign Communication." *Human Communication Research* 15 (1988), 91–111.

Pfau, Michael and Henry C. Kenski. *Attack Politics: Strategy and Defense*. New York: Praeger, 1990.

Phillips, Kevin. *The Politics of Rich and Poor: Wealth and the American Electorate in the Reagan Aftermath*. New York: Random House 1990.

Picek, James S., Steven J. Sherman, and Richard M. Shiffrin. "Cognitive Organization and Encoding of Social Structures." *Journal of Personality and Social Psychology* 31 (April 1975): 758–68.

Popkin, Samuel. *The Reasoning Voter*. Chicago: University of Chicago Press, 1991.

Posner, Michael I. *Chronometric Explorations of the Mind*. Hillsdale, N.J.: Lawrence Erlbaum, 1978.

Postol, Theodore A. "Lessons of the Gulf War Experience with Patriot." *International Security* 16 (1991), 119–171.

Potter, M. C. "Remembering." In *Thinking*, Vol. 3, eds. Daniel N. Osherson and Edward E. Smith. Cambridge, Mass.: MIT Press, 1990, 3–32.

Powell, Jody. *The Other Side of the Story*. New York: William Morrow, 1984.

Presidential Recordings. Transcripts. Cuban Missile Crisis Meetings, October 16, 1962.

Quindlen, Anna. "(Same Old) New Duke." *New York Times*, November 13, 1991, A25.

"Rally: Duke Says All Must Work Together." *Alexandria Town Talk*, November 11, 1991, A-2.

Reese, Stephen D. "Visual-Verbal Redundancy Effects on Television News Learning. *Journal of Broadcasting* 28 (Winter 1984): 79–87.

Reeves, Byron, Esther Thorson, and J. Schleuder. "Attention to Television: Psychological Theories and Chronometric Measures." In *Perspectives on Media Effects*, eds. Jennings Bryant and Dolf Zillmann. Hillsdale, N.J.: Lawrence Erlbaum, 1986, 251–279.

Renckstorff, K. "Nachrichtensendungen eine empirische Studie zur Wirkung unterschiedlicher Darstellung in Fernsehnachrichten." *Media Perspectiven* (January 1977): 27–42.

Reston, James. "Washington: What Are Our War Aims in South Vietnam?" *New York Times*, October 2, 1964, 36.

Revelett, David. In "Campaign Forum." *Alexandria Town Talk*, November 13, 1991, A9.

Ricoeur, Paul. *Time and Narrative*. Translated by Kathleen McLaughlin and David Pellauer. Chicago: University of Chicago Press, 1984–1986.

Robinson, John P., Dennis Davis, H. Sahin, and T. O'Toole. "Comprehension of Television News: How Alert Is the Audience?" Paper presented to the Association for Education in Journalism, Boston, 1980.

Robinson, Michael J. and Margaret A. Sheehan. *Over the Wire and on TV: CBS and UPI in Campaign '80.* New York: Russell Sage Foundation, 1983.

Rolandelli, D. R. "Children and Television: The Visual Superiority Effect Reconsidered." *Journal of Broadcasting and Electronic Media* 33 (1989), 69–81.

Roscoe, Gilpatric. Kennedy Presidential Library. Oral History.

Rose, Dan. "How the 1983 Mayoral Election Was Won." In *The Making of the Mayor: Chicago, 1983,* eds. Melvin G. Holli and Paul M. Green. Grand Rapids, Mich.: Eerdmans, 1984, 101–24.

Rothbart, M. and O. P. John. "Social Categorization and Behavioral Episodes: A Cognitive Analysis of the Effects of Intergroup Contact." *Journal of Social Issues* 41 (1985): 81–104.

Rothschild, Michael L., Esther Thorson, Byron Reeves, Judith E. Hirsch, and Robert Goldstein. "EEG Activity and the Processing of Television Commercials." *Communication Research* 13 (April 1986): 182–220.

Rowland, R. C. "On Limiting the Narrative Paradigm: Three Case Studies." *Communication Monographs* 56 (1989), 39–54.

Runkel, David R., ed. *Campaign for President: The Managers Look at '88.* Dover, Mass.: Auburn House, 1989.

Russonello, John M. and Frank Wolf. "Newspaper Coverage of the 1976 and 1968 Presidential Campaigns." *Journalism Quarterly* 56 (Summer 1979): 360–64, 432.

Safire, William. *Before the Fall: An Inside View of the Pre-Watergate White House.* New York: Belmont Tower Books, 1975.

Salomon, Gavriel. "Television Is 'Easy' and Print Is 'Tough': The Differential Investment of Mental Effort in Learning as a Function of Perceptions and Attributions." *Journal of Educational Psychology* 76 (1984): 647–58.

Sawyer, C. "Letter from Poland: Beating the Censor." *New York Times Book Review,* October 5, 1980, 7, 40.

Schank, Roger and Robert Abelson. *Scripts, Plans, Goals and Understanding: An Inquiry into Human Knowledge Structures.* Hillsdale, N.J.: Lawrence Erlbaum, 1977.

Schieffer, Bob and Gary Paul Gates. *The Acting President.* New York: Dutton, 1989.

Schleifstein, Mark and Sheila Grissett. "Religious Leaders Doubt Duke's Christianity." *Times-Picayune,* November 13, 1991, 1.

Schleuder, J., Maxwell McCombs, and Wayne Wanta. "Inside the Agenda Setting Process: How Political Advertising and TV News Prime Viewers to Think about Issues and Candidates." Paper presented to the Association for Education in Journalism and Mass Communication, Washington, D.C., 1989.

Schmitt, Eric. "Bush Is Reportedly Ready to Cut Back on Stealth Planes." *New York Times,* October 25, 1991, 1.

"Senator Kennedy Recovers and Returns to the Job." *New York Times,* May 24, 1955, 1.

Shaler, N. S. "The Negro Since the Civil War." *Popular Science Monthly* 57 (May 1990): 38–39.

Shapiro, M. A. and R. H. Rieger. "Comparing Positive and Negative Political Advertising." Paper presented to the International Communication Association, San Francisco, 1989.

Shaw, Peter. *American Patriots and the Rituals of Revolution.* Cambridge, Mass.: Harvard University Press, 1981.

Sheperd, R. N. "Recognition Memory for Words, Sentences and Pictures." *Journal of Verbal Learning and Verbal Behavior* 6 (1967): 156–63.

Shepsle, K. A. "The Strategy of Ambiguity: Uncertainty and Electoral Competition." *American Political Science Review* 66 (1972), 555–68.

Shuler, Marsha. "Past Dominates Debate." *Sunday Advocate,* November 3, 1991, 1.

Simon, H. *Administrative Behavior: A Study of Decision-Making Processes in Administrative Organizations.* New York: Free Press, 1945.

Simoneaux, Angela. "Newman Demanding Duke Stop Using His Song." *State-Times/Morning Advocate,* November 16, 1991, 9A.

Small, Bill. Interview by author. September 25, 1991.

Smith, Alfred E. *Campaign Addresses, 1928.* Washington, D.C.: Democratic National Committee, 1929.

Smith, Charles Henry. *Forum* 16 (October 1893), 176–81.

Smith, Eliot R. "Content and Process Specificity in the Effects of Prior Experiences." In *Advances in Social Cognition,* Vol. 3, eds. Thomas Srull and Robert S. Wyer, Jr. Hillsdale, N.J.: Lawrence Erlbaum, 1990, 1–60.

Snider, William D. *Helms & Hunt: The North Carolina Senate Race, 1984.* Chapel Hill: University of North Carolina Press, 1985.

Sniderman, Paul. *Personality and Democratic Politics.* Berkeley: University of California Press, 1975.

Sniderman, Paul M., M. G. Hagen, P. E. Tetlock, and H. E. Brady. "Reasoning Chains: Causal Models of Policy Reasoning in Mass Publics." *British Journal of Political Science* 16 (1986): 405–30.

Sorensen, Theodore C. *Kennedy.* New York: Harper & Row, 1965.

Sourcebook, 1988, p. 298. Table 3.17.

Srull, Thomas K. and Robert S. Wyer. "The Role of Chronic and Temporary Goals in Social Information Processing." In *Handbook of Motivation and Cognition,* eds. Richard M. Sorrentino and E. Tory Higgins. New York: Guilford Press, 1986, 503–49.

Stempel, Guido H. III and John W. Windhauser, eds. *The Media in the 1984 and 1988 Presidential Campaigns.* New York: Greenwood Press, 1991.

Stovall, James. "Coverage of the 1984 Presidential Campaign." *Journalism Quarterly* 63 (1986): 443–49, 484.

Strauss, Leo. *Persecution and the Art of Writing.* Glencoe, Ill.: Free Press, 1952.

Strong, Donald. "Alabama: Transition and Alienation." In *The Changing Politics of the South,* ed. William Harvard. Baton Rouge: Louisiana State University Press, 1972, 427–71.

Strout, Cushing. *The American Image of the Old World.* New York: Harper & Row, 1963.

Sullivan, John L., James E. Piereson, and George E. Marcus. "An Alternative Conceptualization of Political Tolerance: Illusory Increases, 1950's–1970's." *American Political Science Review* 73 (1979): 781–94.

Surlin, Stuart H. and Thomas F. Gordon. "How Values Affect Attitudes Toward Direct Reference Political Advertising." *Journalism Quarterly* 54 (Spring 1977): 89–98.

Taft, Charles P. "Campaign to Stop the Campaign Smear." *New York Times Magazine,* October 12, 1958, 11, 82–84.

Thorson, Esther, Byron Reeves, and J. Schleuder. "Message Complexity and Attention to Television." *Communication Research* 12 (1985): 427–54.

Thorson, Esther and M. Friestad. "The Effects of Emotion on Episodic Memory for Television Commercials." In *Cognitive and Affective Responses to Advertising*, eds. Patricia Cafferata and Alice M. Tybout. Lexingon, Mass.: Lexington Books, 1989, 305–25.

Times Mirror Center for the People and the Press. "The Age of Indifference: A Study of Young Americans and How They View the News," Washington, D.C., June 28, 1990.

Toner, Robin. "Prison Furloughs in Massachusetts Threaten Dukakis Record on Crime." *New York Times*, July 5, 1988, B6.

"Top Democrats Accuse Bush Campaign of Inflaming Racial Fears." *New York Times*, October 24, 1988, 10.

Turner, V. W. "Social Dramas and Stories About Them." *Critical Inquiry* 7 (1980), 141–168.

Tversky, A. and D. Kahneman. "Availability: A Heuristic for Judging Frequency and Probability." *Cognitive Psychology* 5 (1973): 207–32.

Tversky, A. and D. Kahneman. "Judgment Under Uncertainty: Heuristics and Biases." *Science* 185 (1974), 1124–31.

"TV News, Ad Images Melding." *Washington Post*, October 20, 1988, A25, A27.

U.S. Department of Justice. *Criminal Victimization in the United States, 1988*. NCJ-122024. Washington, D.C.: Bureau of Justice Statistics, December 1990.

Varney, James. "Runoff Turns to Racial Issues." *Times-Picayune*, October 24, 1991, A-9.

Verba, Sidney and Norman H. Nie. *Participation in America: Political Democracy and Social Equality*. New York: Harper & Row, 1972.

"Verification for 'Tank' Ad" "Factsheet" issued by the Bush Campaign.

Wallace, Michael. "The Uses of Violence in American History." In Nicholas Cords and Patrick Gerster, *Myth and the American Experience*. Beverly Hills, Calif.: Glencoe Press, 1973, 488–504.

Walsh, Bill and James O'Byrne. "The Voters: Who They Are and What They Think." *Times-Picayune*, November 10, 1991, 1.

Walzer, Michael. *Spheres of Justice*. New York: Basic Books, 1984.

Warnick, B. "The Narrative Paradigm: Another Story." *Quarterly Journal of Speech* 73 (1987), 172–182.

Washburn, Wilcomb E. "Campaign Banners." *American Heritage* 23(6) (October 1972), 8–13.

Washington Post, November 5, 1898.

Washington Post and Times Herald, January 9, 1957.

Washington Post, August, 5, 1987, A20.

Watzlawick, P., J. H. Weakland, and R. Fisch. *Change: Principles of Problem Formation and Problem Resolution*. New York: Norton, 1974.

Waxman, Henry. "Editorial." *The New Republic*, February 1985, 5.

Wegner, Daniel M., Richard Wenslaff, R. Michael Kerker, and Ann E. Beatie. "Incrimination Through Innuendo: Can Media Questions Become Public Answers?" *Journal of Personality and Social Psychology* 40 (May 1981): 822–32.

Weisbord, Marvin. *Campaigning for President: A New Look at the Road to the White House*. Washington, D.C.: Public Affairs Press, 1964, 164.

West Virginia State Board of Education v. Barnette, 319 U.S. 642 (1943).

White, Hayden. "The Value of Narrativity in the Representation of Reality." In *On Narrative*, ed. W. J. T. Mitchell. Chicago: University of Chicago Press, 1981, 1–23.

"White House Transcripts and Minutes of the Cuban Missile Crisis." *International Security* 10 (Summer 1985): 164–203.

White, John Kenneth. *The New Politics of Old Values*. Hanover, N.H.: University Press of New England, 1988.

White, Theodore. *The Making of the President 1972*. New York: Atheneum, 1973.

Wicker, Tom. "U.S. Planes Attack North Vietnam Base; President Orders 'Limited Retaliation After Communists' PT Boats Renew Raids, Forces Enlarged, Stevenson to Appeal for Action by U.N. on 'Open Aggression.' " *New York Times*, August 5, 1964, 1, 2.

Wimsatt, James I. *Allegory and Mirror, Tradition and Structure in Middle English Literature*. New York: Pegasus, 1970.

Wise, David. *The Politics of Lying: Government Deception, Secrecy, and Power*. New York: Random House, 1973.

Wood, G. S. "Conspiracy and Paranoid Style: Causality and Deceit in the Eighteenth Century." *William and Mary Journal* 39 (1982): 401–41.

Wright, W. A., ed. *The Advancement of Learning*. Oxford: Clarendon Press, 1900.

Wyer, Robert S. and Thomas K. Srull. "Category Accessibility: Some Theoretical and Empirical Issues Concerning the Processing of Social Stimulus Information." In *Social Cognition: The Ontario Symposium on Personality and Social Psychology*, Vol. 1, eds. E. Tory Higgens, C. Peter Herman, and Mark P. Zanna. Hillsdale, N.J.: Lawrence Erlbaum, 1981, 161–98.

Wyer, Robert, Thomas K. Srull, Sallie E. Gordon, and Jon Hartwick. "Effects of Processing Objectives on the Recall of Prose Material." *Journal of Personality and Social Psychology* 43 (October 1982): 674–88.

Zajonc, Robert B. "On the Primacy of Affect." *American Psychologist* 39 (1984): 117–23.

Zajonc, Robert B. "Social Facilitation." *Science* 149 (1965): 269–74.

Zanna, Mark P. and J. M. Olson. "Individual Differences in Attitudinal Relations." In *Consistency in Social Behavior: the Ontario Symposium*, Vol. 1, eds. E. Tory Higgins, C. Peter Herman, and Mark P. Zanna. Hillsdale, N.J.: Lawrence Erlbaum, 1981, 75–103.

Zatarain, Michael. *David Duke: Evolution of a Klansman*. Gretna, Louisiana: Pelican, 1990.

Index